The Search for Neofascism
The Use and Abuse of Social Science

The Search for Neofascism is a study of the informal logic that has governed the half-century of academic writing devoted to what has been generally identified as "neofascism," together with a careful assessment of those political movements and regimes considered the proper objects of inquiry. The intent of the study is both pedagogical and cautionary. The central thesis of the work is that terms like "fascism," "generic fascism," and "neofascism" are often used with considerable indifference, applied uniquely to political movements and regimes considered on the "right" rather than the "left," intended more often to denigrate rather than inform. The result has been confusion. Within that context some of the most important political movements of our time are considered, including the Alleanza nazionale of Italy and the Bharatiya Janata Party of India, both of which have discharged leadership roles in their respective governments. Identifying either as "neofascism" has clear implications for international relations.

A. James Gregor is Professor of Political Science at the University of California, Berkeley. He is the author of twenty-four books, including, most recently, *Mussolini's Intellectuals: Fascist Social and Political Thought*, *The Faces of Janus: Marxism and Fascism in the Twentieth Century*, and *A Place in the Sun: Marxism and Fascism in China's Long Revolution*. A previous Guggenheim Fellow, he has been awarded a Knighthood in the Order of Merit by the Italian government for his publications on the history of modern Italy.

The Search for Neofascism

The Use and Abuse of Social Science

A. JAMES GREGOR
University of California, Berkeley

CAMBRIDGE
UNIVERSITY PRESS

CAMBRIDGE UNIVERSITY PRESS
Cambridge, New York, Melbourne, Madrid, Cape Town, Singapore, São Paulo

Cambridge University Press
40 West 20th Street, New York, NY 10011-4211, USA

www.cambridge.org
Information on this title: www.cambridge.org/9780521859202

First published 2006

Printed in the United States of America

A catalog record for this publication is available from the British Library.

Library of Congress Cataloging in Publication Data

Gregor, A. James (Anthony James), 1929–
The search for neofascism : the use and abuse of social science / A. James Gregor.
p. cm.
Includes bibliographical references and index.
ISBN-13: 978-0-521-85920-2 (hardback)
ISBN-10: 0-521-85920-4 (hardback)
ISBN-13: 978-0-521-67639-7 (pbk.)
ISBN-10: 0-521-67639-8 (pbk.)
1. Fascism – Cross-cultural studies. I. Title.
JC481.G6927 2006
320.53'3–dc22   2005016879

ISBN-13   978-0-521-85920-2 hardback
ISBN-10   0-521-85920-4 hardback

ISBN-13   978-0-521-67639-7 paperback
ISBN-10   0-521-67639-8 paperback

This book is dedicated to Aage Pedersen, friend of my youth, a casualty in the invasion of Normandy, who still lives in my heart.

Contents

Preface

Throughout the last decade of the twentieth century and into the first years of the twenty-first, a curious disposition manifested itself – particularly among Anglophone thinkers. They have attempted to address the issues of political violence, racial hatred, hostility to immigrants, the invocation of "Nazi-Maoist" strategies, mayhem at soccer games, and stupidities of sundry sorts – by conceiving them all as expressions of "neofascism." Instances of "conservative," "neoconservative," "right-wing," and "radical right-wing" political behavior were all equally imagined to be similarly neofascistic. What makes that exceedingly odd is the realization that it is very unlikely that all of it might plausibly be associated with historic Fascism. It would seem that we might expect better of serious scholarship.

Somehow or other, several lifetimes after Mussolini's Fascism disappeared into history, its specter still troubles the research of some of our most industrious social scientists. They seem to find evidence of Fascism everywhere. Some find Fascism in the neofascism of the French "New Right." Some find it in the American "Radical Right," Reagan Republicans, and militia irregulars. Some find it in the neofascism of the "Stalinofascists" of Eastern Europe. Others seem to trace Fascism, as neofascism, to the "pathologically contorted idealism of religious fundamentalism."

Other than all that, we are told that contemporary Fascism, as neofascism, is to be found in the guise of racism, sexism, sadomasochism, terrorism, and anti-Semitism, as well as among aficionados of heavy metal bands and "proletarian rock." Wherever we find them, neofascists, we are told, entertain only two "absolute values": violence and war. But for those two absolutes, neofascists, heirs of Fascism, entertain no discernible ideological convictions. We are told that neofascism is "inherently protean," empty of content, always decked in "new guises." It entertains no coherent thought.

It is a prevailing belief among many academicians that no coherent thought is possible among neofascists, because only the political left and traditional liberals really concern themselves with matters ideological. We are informed that the political right (the genus, apparently, of which neo-fascism is a species) finds lucubration tedious. That is the case, we are told, because neofascism, like Fascism before it, is driven, almost exclusively, by hatred, fantasy, and occult impulse, to the exclusion of thought.

In fact, the study of neofascism, as it is presently conducted, leaves us with a ragbag of disappointments, fragments of analyses, and vague allusions to "radicalism" and "racism" as defining properties of a "right-wing extremism" that presumably provides the substance of inquiry – that frequently, and effortlessly, slips into talk of Nazism and the mass murder of innocents. All of this seems singularly unsatisfying.

The contemporary discussion of "neofascism" remains in that parlous state, providing scant satisfaction to those seeking credible information about a subject that would appear to have some immediate significance. To date, "neofascism studies" encompasses so wide a variety of topics that it is difficult, at best, to characterize its range or reference.

The work before you cannot pretend to resolve all the problems that attend so loosely jointed a study. It cannot pretend to advance a formal definition of the presumed subject matter. Neither Mussolini's Fascism nor its putative modern heirs lend themselves to such characterization.

I am convinced that to attempt formal definitions in the informal disciplines of social science and history more often than not hinders rather than furthers inquiry. Discursive disciplines do not lend themselves to the rigors of more formal inquiry. To pretend otherwise is to deceive. So we are left with informal accounts, lacking rigor, that at best are calculated to persuade – much like the judgments tendered in civil courts that turn on the preponderance of evidence, rather than those verdicts of the criminal courts that require proof beyond a reasonable doubt.

Whatever its shortcomings, this work is offered with pedagogical intent. If nothing else, it may illustrate the limitations of current efforts to discuss "neofascism" as an academic subject. In my judgment, the greater part of the contemporary work devoted to neofascism leaves a great deal to be desired. My hope is that the ensuing pages offer something that, in some fashion or other, assuages at least some of those desires.

Acknowledgments

One of the more pleasant tasks an author traditionally undertakes in the opening pages of his work is to acknowledge his debt to those who have assisted him in his task. It is a responsibility I undertake with considerable pleasure. So many persons have given of their time and their patience that I wish this book better reflected their efforts.

I would like to thank publicly the late Giorgio Almirante, leader of the neofascist *Movimento sociale italiano*, for taking the time, so many years ago, to explain to me patiently what he thought an Italian "postfascism" might be. To Oswald Mosley and A. Raven Thomson, of British Union, I owe some precious insights into what a neofascism could not be. And there were so many others, in the United States and Europe, who must remain nameless, who by speech and behavior revealed to me the tragic and dangerous lunacy of what they imagined "neofascism" might be in an advanced industrial environment. Most had learned the "neofascism" they professed from late-night television – much the same "neofascism" one can still find in some of the contemporary tracts pretending to deal with the subject.

Then there are the academicians who proved so helpful. Among them, I am particularly grateful to Professor Alessandro Campi, Professor Hervé Cavallera, and Dr. Danilo Breschi, who know so much of historic Fascism and of the remnants of Fascism that survived the Second World War. I am indebted to Professor Peter Sperlich for illuminating much of the politics of Marxism-Leninism for me, and to Dr. Chang King-yuh for insights into the history of the Kuomintang and the ideology of Maoism and post-Maoism. To students and professors at Hebrew University with whom I discussed Islamic fundamentalism, and to my black students who indulged me in exchanges concerning black nationalism, I wish to extend my sincere gratitude. Unhappily, despite all the efforts of these good people, the book before you is what it is.

Finally, without the painful pleasure of the absence of my wife, Maria Hsia Chang, and Gabriel, Christopher, and Charles, together with the rest of the brood, this book would never have been written. I owe all kinds of good things to them all.

Berkeley, California
Spring 2005

I

The Decay of an Enterprise

In the course of the closing decade of the twentieth century, a dedicated minority of journalists and academics decided that the rise of "neofascism" posed a serious threat to public decency and political integrity in the Western industrialized democracies. One consequence was that by the first years of the twenty-first century, literally hundreds of books and articles dedicated to some sort of treatment of the subject had appeared. Their intended purpose was to warn society of the insidiousness of the peril.

For these works to have accomplished their purpose, one would have expected some indication of what "neofascism" meant, followed by a serious treatment of the candidate neofascisms that constituted the menace. Unhappily, little of the former is to be found in many if not most works – and without even lexical definition, it is difficult to isolate the proper objects of concern.

It often appears that however "neofascism" is defined, its relationship to Benito Mussolini's Fascism remains, at best, obscure. Often an unspoken assumption functions as part of the sorting criteria in identifying neofascism. Most of the authors who have surfaced within the past two decades choose to fuse fascism, national socialism, and the political right together into a single subject category, usually identified as either "fascism," "neofascism," or "right-wing extremism," as though all constituted a single reference class. The consequence has been considerable confusion, with uncertainty concerning the class of political movements and/or ideologies that constitute the proper objects of scrutiny.

The issue is not simply academic. The identification, for instance, of the Silvio Berlusconi government of the Italian republic as neofascist is a matter of no small consequence.[1] That government has been an important ally of

---

[1] We are told by some, for example, that the Berlusconi government is not at all what it appears to be. We are informed that no matter the democratic pretense, the political party of Berlusconi's Vice Premier Gianfranco Fini's "AN's [Alleanza nazionale's] ideological tap-root

the United States in a variety of international circumstances. Its description as "neofascist" not only prejudices the relationship, but taints the action that is a byproduct of that relationship.

More immediately, the identification of any political movement as "neofascist" tends to limit its moral right to free expression. Any and all political movements, however eccentric, have every legal right to such expression in a representative democracy. Everyone acknowledges that the exercise of those rights is difficult for dissident movements. To insist on their "neofascism" further reduces their opportunity to gain access to a public hearing.

Other than those immediate concerns, there remain the academic responsibilities of conducting one's inquiry in accordance with generally accepted criteria of objectivity, public evidence, coherence, and consistency. Much of the subsequent discussion will trade on just those criteria.

In terms of that discussion, its explicit, initial contention is that the real or pretended study of "neofascism" is inextricably related to the study of Italian Fascism, in which the name finds its origin. That granted, the inquiry must commence with a synoptic study of a reasonably discrete, if enormously complicated, series of events that covered more than a quarter-century of European and world history during the past century. To study neofascism meaningfully would seem to necessitate that we know something substantial concerning Fascism – at least some major elements of its peculiar history and the ideology that animated its behavior. It might be further argued that a notion of a generic "fascism" would occupy conceptual space somewhere between Italian Fascism and neofascism as a transitional object of reflection in any serious cognitive enterprise. It would seem that to speak of "neofascism," one must entertain some notion of a generic fascism.

However elementary all that might appear, everything involved in the undertaking is beset by problems. Many decades after its disappearance, Mussolini's Fascism continues to remain an uncertainty in the minds of many – if not most – academics. Very few have a sure grasp of its origins, its history, or its historic impact. To this day, the literal or operational meaning of the generic term "fascism" remains sorely contested. Some, including some of the luminaries of contemporary historical research, have, in fact, denied the generic term any real referents.[2]

---

is still thrust deep into historical Fascism...retaining many Fascist core values," and that one still finds a "Fascist spirit" among those of the party, with the "ineliminable core of generic fascism still [lurking] within the AN mindset...." Roger Griffin, "The 'Post-Fascism' of the Alleanza Nazionale: A Case Study in Ideological Morphology," *Journal of Political Ideologies* 1, no. 2 (1996), pp. 138, 142.

[2] Renzo De Felice, the most prominent among them, has argued that there really was only one Fascism, and that the entire notion of a generic fascism is dubious at best. To maintain historiographic integrity, he held that any discussion of fascism as a phenomenon would have to be "rigidly limited" in time (between the two world wars) and space (Western Europe). See Renzo De Felice, *Intervista sul fascismo* (Rome: Laterza, 1975), p. 82.

Thus, while prepared to recognize some affinities between Adolf Hitler's National Socialism and Mussolini's Fascism, Renzo De Felice, one of the twentieth century's foremost scholars of Fascism, denied the reality of a generic fascism.[3] Ernst Nolte, in his major work on Fascism, while prepared to speak of a generic fascism, insisted on a studied distinction between the Fascism of Mussolini and the "radical fascism" of Hitler. National Socialism distinguished itself from Mussolini's Fascism by emphatic differences.

Irrespective of the distinctions insisted upon by the most celebrated scholars, all too often Italian Fascism is simply identified with the National Socialism of Adolf Hitler – with both conceived instances of a generic "fascism." Rarely is an argued rationale for such usage provided. It has simply become a matter more of custom and usage than historic confirmation – a practice inherited from the time of the Second World War, when the industrialized democracies found themselves embroiled in a desperate and protracted "war against fascism."

In fighting that war, to identify the enemy, without distinctions, as perfidious, racist, antihumane, and irredeemable was a major propaganda convenience. Hitler's National Socialists could easily be so characterized. Whether Mussolini's Fascists, or the imperial Japanese, could be so typified, without significant qualification, was a matter of little practical concern to the Allied powers, who were more occupied with winning the war than making fine historical distinctions. As for the intellectuals of the period, there were a sufficient number of shared properties between Nazi Germany and Fascist Italy that the identification could be advanced without excessive intellectual discomfort.[4]

Both European regimes opposed representative democracy; both insisted on ideological conformity; both were led by "charismatic" leaders; both were nationalistic; both were militaristic; both employed controlled information to create and sustain popular support; both were bellicose; both were irredentist; and both were anticommunist. That seemed to constitute a constellation

---

[3] Ibid., pp. 24, 70; see De Felice's entire discussion concerning race and anti-Semitism and the comparison between Fascism and National Socialism in De Felice, *Rosso e Nero* (Milan: Baldini and Castoldi, 1995), pp. 149–163.

[4] Prior to the war, a number of English language texts treated Fascism with considerable objectivity. None of the properties that identified Fascism with National Socialism appeared with any prominence. See, as examples, Paul Einzig, *The Economic Foundations of Fascism* (London: Macmillan and Company, 1933); G. Lowell Field, *The Syndical and Corporative Institutions of Italian Fascism* (New York: Columbia University Press, 1938); Herbert W. Schneider, *Making the Fascist State* (New York: Oxford University Press, 1928); William G. Welk, *Fascist Economic Policy: An Analysis of Italy's Economic Experiment* (Cambridge, MA: Harvard University Press, 1938). There were, of course, "committed" scholars, mostly Marxists and Marxist-Leninists, who saw Fascism only as "reactionary" and "antihumane" because it was anti-Marxist. With the advent of the war, it was eminently simple to identify Fascism with National Socialism. In the propaganda efforts strenuously pursued during the war, there even was an attempt to identify the Japanese wartime leadership as "fascist."

of traits sufficient to license the use of the generic "fascist" to cover both Hitler's National Socialism and Mussolini's Fascism.

Given all that, in the context of a war for survival, the facile identification of Fascism and National Socialism was only to be expected. What that identification did not address, of course, were the clear and cognitively significant distinctions between the regimes.

De Felice suggested some of the consequences. Appalled by the singularly horrific consequences of Hitler's racism and anti-Semitism and the ready identification of Fascism with National Socialism, both were characterized by the same moral disabilities. That tended to support an interpretation that saw both, Italian Fascism as well as Hitler's National Socialism, as instances of a "collapse of Western moral values." Generic fascism was understood to be the result of a lapsed moral conscience on the part of Central and Southern Europeans. Even immediately prior to the Second World War, more emphatically during that war, and for a not inconsiderable time thereafter, the fascists, as "enemies of Western civilization," were in effect demonized, identified as peoples who had forsworn Christianity and who suffered grievous psychoanalytic and psychiatric morbidities. They were little more than embodiments of unmitigated evil.[5] For both academics and lay persons, generic fascism tended to represent evil incarnate.

For a long time after the conclusion of the Second World War, a substantial minority of lay persons and academics were ill disposed to abandon such an apodictic moral interpretation of what had transpired. The mass murders associated with National Socialism in the context of a dictatorial system decked in all the trappings of violence and war were sufficient to convince many that the moral characterizations were true of all "fascisms." The many so convinced were to serve as teachers for postwar generations. They transmitted to their intellectual heirs a conviction that saw generic fascism as the monstrous product of a kind of moral madness. The judgments were so effectively transmitted from the wartime generation to subsequent ones that, in general and until today, generic fascism is still depicted in much the same terms.

Together with the host of moralizers who collected around the interpretation of fascism as the product of moral decay were the Marxists and sometimes Marxists who, before, during, and after the war, argued that generic fascism was the predictable product of a universal "class struggle" of "proletarians" against oppressive capitalism. Fascism, in whatever form, was understood to be an excrescence of industrial and/or finance capitalism, a weapon in capitalism's reactionary struggle against the advent of a liberating proletarian revolution. Based on the theoretical Marxism of the

---

[5] See A. James Gregor, *Interpretations of Fascism* (New Brunswick, NJ: Transaction, 2000), chaps. 2 and 3.

nineteenth century, committed scholarship left little room for any alternative interpretation.

The role of Fascism was understood to be the domestication of workers' organizations in the service of monopoly capitalism. Since capitalism, to sustain its profitability, must restrict its labor costs and increase prices, the most propitious environment would be one in which the nation is at war. Price controls restrict the movement of wages, and the escalating demand for products inflates prices. Since the wartime demand for products is critical to the nation's very survival, "Big Business" receives whatever it demands from the government for its output.[6]

In such circumstances, Fascism, in the service of its masters, is required to keep the nation either in conflict or on a war footing. The unrelenting drive to involve Italy in war had to be understood as an irrepressible and inextricable feature of Mussolini's rule. Fascism's military adventures in Ethiopia, Spain, and the Balkans, concluding with Italy's catastrophic involvement in the Second World War, were simply the necessary consequence of Mussolini's subservience to his masters' interests.[7]

While distinctive in its own right, the Marxist interpretation, which rapidly became an interpretation of generic fascism, enjoyed an easy compatibility with the moral assessment that colored prevailing judgments. Capitalists were oppressors and exploiters – and fascists were their janissaries. The proletariat was the savior of freedom and fulfillment – and fascists were their sworn adversaries. Fascists represented the immoral and reactionary "right," while the "left" embodied all the virtues of the European Enlightenment.

Fascists, of whatever provenance, were of the right because they were the hewers of wood and the drawers of water for "finance capitalists."[8] Since industrial capitalism could no longer sustain itself, given the "laws" of capitalism outlined in the work of Karl Marx, the leaders of industry were compelled to seek recourse outside the traditional liberal democratic system in which they had found their origin and in which they had originally prospered. The Fascists were funded, organized, and elevated to power in order to create the conditions for economic survival in circumstances of declining rates of profit – made inevitable, according to Marx, by the very conditions of advanced industrialization.

The interpretation, which quickly became identified with Joseph Stalin, became standard for Marxist-Leninists in general, and adherents of the Third

---

[6] See the discussion in Paul A. Baran and Paul M. Sweezy, *Monopoly Capital: An Essay on the American Economic and Social Order* (New York: Monthly Review Press, 1966), pp. 156–7.

[7] The most direct expression of these theses is to be found in Rajani Palme Dutt, *Fascism and Social Revolution* (New York: International Books, 1934).

[8] See Georgi Dimitroff's report to the Seventh World Congress of the Communist International, 1935, reprinted in *The United Front Against War and Fascism* (New York: Gamma, 1974), p. 7.

International in particular. It made all and any "fascism" a "right-wing extremism," defined as any movement or regime committed to the defense of capitalism – at the price of interminable involvement in bloodshed and organized violence.

Those Marxists independent of the Third International very early took exception to the "standard version." They argued that Italian Fascism gave every indication of being an autonomous, mass-mobilizing movement that arose in social and economic circumstances in which the established elites found it impossible to rule effectively. Whatever else Fascism did, it arrogated to itself political power, and if capitalists, finance or industrial, profited as a consequence, it was largely because their profit served the political interests of Mussolini and his entourage.[9]

Some independent Marxists went further. Fascism's "task" was seen as the "further development of the productive forces" of the peninsula. Fascism was seen as having "systematically spurred" development in heavy industry, in its chemical, automotive, aircraft, and maritime branches. Otto Bauer, Franz Borkenau, Arthur Rosenberg, and August Thalheimer, as independent Marxists, were prepared to acknowledge the developmental intentions of Fascism. However much capitalists may have benefited, Fascism's purposes were "progressive."[10] Fascism was hardly the creature of finance or industrial capitalism; whatever benefits Italian capitalism may have enjoyed were purchased by submission to the totalitarian rule of Mussolini.

The opening of Italian archives after the war revealed no evidence of a conspiracy between the "magnates of industry" and Mussolini's Fascism. In fact, there is ample evidence of a mounting resistance to Fascist rule by the leaders of industry throughout the twenty years of its tenure. Fascism had gradually assumed control over fundamental aspects of the overall Italian economy. By the mid-1930s, most of the critically important functions of enterprise had been surrendered to Fascist control. The availability of credit was largely determined by members of the Fascist elite. The peculiar development of domestic manufacturing was largely controlled by the Fascist government through the corporative agencies fabricated by those around Mussolini.[11]

After the termination of the Second World War, Italian economists affirmed that "after 1936 the Fascist government controlled proportionately a larger share of Italy's industrial base than any other nation in Europe other than the Soviet Union."[12] Equally clear is the fact that the Italian

[9] See the discussion in August Thalheimer, "Über den Faschismus," in W. Abendroth (ed.), *Faschismus und Kapitalismus* (Berlin: Europäische Verlagsanstalt, 1967), pp. 19–38.

[10] See the discussion in Renzo De Felice, *Interpretations of Fascism* (Cambridge, MA: Harvard University Press, 1977), pp. 31–54; Gregor, *Interpretations of Fascism*, chap. 5.

[11] See the discussion in Rosario Romeo, *Breve storia della grande industria in Italia* (Rocca San Casciano: Casa Editrice Licinio Capelli, 1967, third edition), pp. 134–201.

[12] Ibid., p. 173.

business community, in general, welcomed the disappearance of Fascism. Fascism never served the interests of Italian business. As will be argued, Fascism had made its revolution with the rapid expansion and technological development of Italian industry as one of its programmatic goals. As a consequence, the Italian entrepreneurial class did benefit – but at the cost of its independence.

Curiously enough, beginning in the decade of the 1960s, particularly outside of the intellectual environment of the advanced industrial democracies, the interpretation of fascism as a tool of "capitalism," in general, or "finance capitalism" in particular, gradually receded. In the Soviet Union, the formal Stalinist interpretation of the interwar years gradually gave way to a much more nuanced account that saw Italian Fascism, as distinct from Hitler's National Socialism, a multiclass response to late industrial development. While still a "class phenomenon," Italian Fascism was beginning to be understood as a far more complex and functional response to a set of socioeconomic conditions than Marxist-Leninists had ever previously considered.[13] By that time, it had become increasingly difficult to understand why Fascism represented a "right-wing" political response to issues. It was certainly not the White Guard of capitalism. In the late 1920s, Fascism had declared private property rights and private initiative to be contingent on their service to the state.[14] By the mid-1930s, foreign observers could maintain that "the [Fascist corporative] system has been and is likely to continue to be ... not an agency for the economic self-government of the Italian people but an instrument of economic control used by the totalitarian Fascist state for the achievement of its ultimate economic and political ends."[15]

Why any of that made Fascism "right-wing" is difficult to understand. That it was not a democracy seems clear, but not all antidemocratic polities are right-wing. Furthermore, there is no credible evidence that Fascism controlled the nation's economy for the benefit of the "possessing classes."

All the evidence notwithstanding, for decades after the end of the Second World War, Fascism continued to be identified with the interests of capitalism and private enterprise at the expense of the "common man." Many academics in the West were convinced that only "left-wing" arrangements could provide succorance to the needy and oppressed.

---

[13] I have outlined the process in A. James Gregor, *The Faces of Janus: Marxism and Fascism in the Twentieth Century* (New Haven, CT: Yale University Press, 2000), chaps. 3–5.

[14] "All labor, under all its managerial and executive, intellectual, technical, and manual forms, is a social duty.... The corporative state considers private initiative in the arena of production as the most efficient instrument in the service of the nation.... Should private initiative prove to be inadequate, or when the political interests of the state are in play, the state will intervene in the form of direct control, encouragement and direct development." *La carta del lavoro* (Rome: Edizioni del "Diritto del lavoro," 1928), paras. 2, 7, 9, pp. 115, 117–18.

[15] William G. Welk, *Fascist Economic Policy: An Analysis of Italy's Economic Experiment* (Cambridge, MA: Harvard University Press, 1938), p. 250.

For a time, scholars in the Soviet Union were standard-bearers of just that sort of interpretation of the domestic and international political and economic order. Marxism-Leninism was left-wing, and Fascism in all its variants was right-wing. Many academics in the West simply accepted such a construal of the then-contemporary world.

For years after the war, many in the West imagined Joseph Stalin to be the moral guide for a left-wing, liberating revolution of workers and peasants. Not until after Stalin's death and the revelation of massive violation of citizens' rights, the abuse of minority groups, and the mass murder of innocents in the Soviet Union did many of those Western intellectuals who identified human liberation with the Soviet Union think better of their position. The Soviet Union under Stalin had begun to look remarkably like Germany under the ministrations of Hitler. The right-wing/left-wing distinction began to become undone.

For many Western intellectuals, one of the consequences of the revelations concerning the Great Terror, the death of millions, and the anti-Semitism of Stalinism was the abandonment not of the right-wing/left-wing distinction, but of Soviet Marxism as the normative guide to liberation. Stalinism was forsaken and some of those self-same intellectuals simply transferred their loyalties to the Marxism-Leninism of Mao Zedong. For a not inconsiderable number, Mao's China assumed the role of a leftist vanguard of human liberation. Given the circumstances, even after the abandonment of Stalinism, the interpretation of fascism as an immoral, right-wing anticommunist tool of reaction continued to maintain a semblance of plausibility.

In that intellectual environment, any anticommunist effort on the part of individuals, groups, governments, or confederations was interpreted by some to be a sure sign of "right-wing fascism." Greek colonels, Chilean generals, and any anticommunist authoritarianism, anywhere in North or South America, Asia, Africa, or the Middle East, were immediately perceived as "fascist." The study of fascism and the "new postwar fascism" – "neofascism" – was embarrassed by riches. So many candidate neofascisms were available for scrutiny that their characterization had, of necessity, to be very general. They were all "reactionary" and "right-wing," which seemed to mean anticommunist or, alternatively, that they were allied to a power or powers that were anticommunist. That sort of notion was supplemented by the conviction that such right-wing fascisms were devoted to the oppression of the dispossessed and vulnerable. Thus, it was argued that while the left-wing Maoist government on the mainland of China was unshackling workers and peasants, the right-wing Kuomintang government on the island of Taiwan was subjecting its population to fascist reaction. As these interpretations continued, developments took place in the Western academic community that were to address the facile identification of the "right" with neofascism, while the generic "left" was conceived a liberating force in the service of the wretched of the earth. In the 1950s, the concept "totalitarianism"

gradually made its appearance, to offer an interpretive classification prepared to subsume fascism and the Marxist-Leninist dictatorships, as species
or subspecies, under one inclusive antidemocratic political genus.[16]

Conceived as better representing the reality of a bipolar world of democratic and antidemocratic political polities, the concept "totalitarianism"
was pressed into service to better understand the evolving Cold War. While
a subsidiary distinction between the left and the right persisted, it no longer
carried the weight of moral contrast.

Fascism and National Socialism remained kindred, but their kinship
became more abstract, generous enough to reveal their affinities with
Marxist-Leninist systems. The international politics of the period accom-
modated, fostered, and sustained the interpretation. There was clear political advantage in identifying the enemies of democracy with the National
Socialism of Adolf Hitler and the Fascism of Benito Mussolini – and there
were entirely plausible institutional similarities supporting the notion of a
totalitarian kinship between them all.[17]

In the course of these developments, a group of scholars emerged who
were to influence the interpretation of fascism in ways that were to transform
the character of "fascism studies." Of those scholars, Ernst Nolte and Renzo
De Felice were among the most important. Together they were to give shape
to a subdiscipline that had become increasingly amorphous over the years
since the termination of the Second World War.

Their respective efforts, while different in a variety of fashions, shared
several common features: There was a clear conviction that however odious
their crimes, National Socialism and Fascism were historical phenomena that
required the same systematic objectivity in their study as any complex historical event.[18] Moreover, both treated the ideas that animated fascism with measured consideration. Rather than dismissing fascism's political convictions
as simply "right-wing," "irrational," "immoral," and "contradictory" – as
had generally been the wont – they accorded them the same seriousness as
others did the ideology of Marxism-Leninism in all its many variants.

While both De Felice and Nolte used the concept "totalitarianism" only
with considerable reservation and abundant caution, they both accepted
it in principle. Within the context of a kind of inclusive totalitarianism,
both sought to restrict their study to those interwar and wartime systems

---

[16] The major works included Hannah Arendt, *The Origins of Totalitarianism* (New York:
Harcourt, Brace, 1951); Carl Friedrich and Zbigniew K. Brzezinski, *Totalitarian Dictatorship
and Autocracy* (New York: Praeger, 1956).

[17] See the discussion in A. James Gregor, "'Totalitarianism' Revisited," in Ernest A. Menze
(ed.), *Totalitarianism Reconsidered* (London: Kennikat Press, 1981), pp. 130–45.

[18] See the discussion in De Felice, *Interpretations of Fascism*, chap. 1; Ernst Nolte, "Author's
Preface to the English Translation," in *Three Faces of Fascism: Action Française Italian
Fascism National Socialism* (New York: Holt, Rinehart and Winston, 1966), pp. ix–xi,
chap. 3.

they identified as fascist. They both were exceedingly skeptical about any fascisms that were extraeuropean or that survived the Second World War. It seemed evident that outside of Europe and after the end of the Second World War, there were no candidates that might really pass as both fascist and totalitarian. For De Felice and Nolte, fascism was intimately and inextricably connected with Europe and the social, political, and economic consequences of the First World War.[19] Even those fascisms that emerged in Southern and Eastern Europe in the years following the First World War were held to be largely mimetic and a peculiar product of time-conditioned strategic and political circumstances. De Felice, more demanding than Nolte, dismissed most interwar and wartime "fascisms" as not fascisms at all. Other than National Socialism and Italian Fascism, there were no authentic fascisms – and even National Socialism and Fascism distinguished themselves from each other by very fundamental ideological and behavioral differences.[20] For De Felice, Fascism meant essentially Italian Fascism. His employment of the term "right-wing" was restricted to mean "anticommunist" or "anti-Marxist," without the baggage that frequently accompanied its use. Moreover, while prepared to grant that Fascism shared some minimal affinities with National Socialism, he insisted on the "enormous differences between Italian Fascism and German National Socialism." For De Felice, Mussolini's Fascism and Hitler's National Socialism arose out of "two worlds, two traditions, two histories so different that it is extremely difficult to address them both within a single discussion."[21]

Like Nolte, De Felice dismissed the possibility of a fascism outside the historic parameters of the interwar and war years and the geographic confines of Western Europe.[22] As a consequence, any talk of a "neofascism," the heir of the fascism of the interwar and wartime years, was dismissed. Like De Felice, Nolte did not pretend that it was their right-wing properties that linked Fascism and National Socialism. Right-wing properties played no significant role in the identification of generic fascism. In general, the term

[19] See De Felice, *Interpretations of Fascism*, chap. 1; Ernst Nolte, *Die faschistischen Bewegungen: Die Krise des liberalen Systems und die Entwicklung der Faschismen* (Munich: Deutscher Taschenbuch Verlag, 1966), chap. 1.

[20] Hitler's racial ideology, and the attendant mass murder of innocents, was one of the major distinctions between National Socialism and Fascism – but that was predicated on deep historic, cultural, and social differences that distinguished the two systems. See the discussions in De Felice's introduction to the new edition of *Storia degli ebrei italiani sotto il fascismo* (Turin: Einaudi, 1993), pp. vii–xix. See his discussion concerning Fascist anti-Semitism at its most vile, during the last years of the Fascist Social Republic, 1943–5, *ibid.*, pp. 446–86.

[21] De Felice, *Intervista sul fascismo*, p. 24.

[22] De Felice dismisses those social science generalizations that "greatly diffuse the geographical and chronological scope of the Fascist phenomenon.... [and which overlook] one of the fundamental characteristics of Fascism: its intrinsic relation to the moral, economic, social and political crisis of European society in the aftermath of World War I." De Felice, *Interpretations of Fascism*, p. 77.

referred to fascism's anticommunist orientation. As a consequence, Nolte was ill disposed to use "right-wing" as an omnibus notion that might cover all "fascisms," providing grounds for the discovery of "neofascisms" after the termination of the Second World War.

As far as he was concerned, De Felice saw very little affinity between the political radicalism that surfaced in Europe after the Second World War and the Fascism that he understood so well. The characterization "right-wing" hardly made the requisite connection.

Nolte, for his part, dismissed the possibility of a fascism that might survive the Second World War. In his studied judgment, fascism had disappeared with the close of its "epoch." Whatever antidemocratic radicalisms might manifest themselves in the postwar years would be something very different from the fascism that had been the object of his research.

During the 1980s, the study of fascism was supplemented by the work of another major analyst, Zeev Sternhell. Beginning with the ideologies of the French nationalists of the nineteenth century,[23] Sternhell systematically formulated an account of the development of Fascist thought in early-twentieth-century Italy.[24]

Like Nolte, Sternhell saw the elements of fascism in the thought of nineteenth-century French nationalism. What distinguished his work from many of his contemporaries in the field was his particular readiness to acknowledge the existence of a reasonably coherent and intellectually defensible Fascist ideology – neither of the political right nor the political left – that performed the same functions for Fascists as their respective ideologies did for liberals and Marxists.

Perhaps for the first time since the end of the Second World War, a major figure in the study of Italian Fascism was prepared to argue that Fascism was animated by a well-formulated body of thought. In his judgment:

... the philosophy of fascism was ... fully elaborated even before the movement came to power. ... In [that] respect, Mussolini's political actions no more represented a coarse pragmatism or a vulgar opportunism than did those of Lenin. ... Indeed, the realities of the Italian regime of the interwar period were a faithful reflection of the principles that Mussolini and his associates professed at the moment when they were the first people in the twentieth century to terminate a liberal democratic regime.[25]

Together with that assessment, Sternhell continued the arguments advanced by both Nolte and De Felice that sharply distinguished Fascism from National Socialism. Sternhell held that "Fascism can in no way be

---

[23] Zeev Sternhell, *La droite révolutionnaire 1885–1914: Les origines Françaises du Fascisme* (Paris: Editions du Seuil, 1978).

[24] Zeev Sternhell, *Ni droite ni gauche: L'Ideologie fasciste en France* (Paris: Editions du Seuil, 1983); Zeev Sternhell with Mario Sznajder and Maia Asheri, *The Birth of Fascist Ideology* (Princeton, NJ: Princeton University Press, 1994).

[25] Ibid., p. 229.

identified with Nazism."[26] Whatever common features they shared were of relatively minor historical significance compared to their differences. Hitler's racism and anti-Semitism sharply distinguished National Socialism from Mussolini's Fascism. It had taken more than a generation of scholarship, in fact, to make the case for what were for De Felice, Nolte, and Sternhell obvious differences. Why that had been the case was not difficult to appreciate.

The fact that so many participants in the discussion concerning fascism and neofascism had bound themselves to the fancied distinction between the political right and political left had obscured the fundamental differences between Hitler's National Socialism and Mussolini's Fascism – just as it had obscured the clear affinities between Fascism and the Marxist-Leninist systems in Albania, Cuba, and, Yugoslavia.

Whatever the argued distinctions between the right and the left, the term "fascist," regardless of its reference, has remained, in ordinary language, a general term of disapprobation, having emotive impact but scant cognitive content. In contemporary discourse, when one speaks of "fascists," one almost invariably means "nazis." Like some other terms in contemporary political use, the term "fascist," as used in ordinary speech, is almost entirely without substantive meaning or specific reference.[27]

The fact is that there is very little excuse for such profligate employment. We know a great deal about Italian Fascism – certainly enough to distinguish it from National Socialism. We know a good deal about its origins in time, the principal components of its belief system, those population elements that made up a substantial part of its membership, the contingent circumstances that created the revolutionary environment in which it thrived, and the influences that shaped the course of its trajectory over time. Identifying it as "right-wing" adds nothing to comprehension.

Someone wisely proposed that in order to understand Fascism, one must write its history. While sage, such advice perhaps conceals as much as it reveals. Before one can write a comprehensible history, one must have some initial notions of what that history is about. History is composed of too much to allow anyone to formulate a simple rendering without any guide whatsoever. Without at least some counsel regarding relevance, anyone attempting to write a complete and comprehensive history of any time sequence would find himself or herself overwhelmed by minutiae. There would be no way to decide what should and what should not be included.

[26] Ibid., p. 4.

[27] The term has become so devoid of substantive meaning that in some academic discussions, "fascism" has been somehow associated with "Ronald Reagan Republicans." See the comments by Leonard Weinberg, "Conclusions," in Peter H. Merkl and Leonard Weinberg (eds), *The Revival of Right-Wing Extremism in the Nineties* (London: Frank Cass, 1997), p. 279.

Thus, not only are much of history's traces lost with the passage of time, but often what remains is so abundant that it requires thoughtful winnowing before it can take on comprehensible form. We cannot and generally do not attempt to report on everything that survives the ravages of time, much less everything that transpired in time. To write a history of anything cannot be to write a history of everything. We must decide what is important enough to be recorded. There must be selective criteria available that govern our choices and ultimately mold our account.

It is evident that the rendering of the Fascist period by a convinced Marxist would be, and historically has been, fundamentally different from that of a non-Marxist[28] – and that of a dedicated democrat far different from that of a nondemocrat. All of this suggests that the writing of history is, whatever public criteria guide the enterprise, at best less than entirely "objective." It is in no fashion simply a catalog of events "as they really happened." Embedded in the processes involved in the writing of history are irrepressible subjective elements that, in the least, shape its form and color its expression. A signal of the presence of bias is the use of terms like "right-wing" without the pretense of definition and the provision of evidence to support the naming.

Acknowledging all that, what is equally evident is that historic evidence, in the final analysis, must be made available to affirm or disconfirm any given account – be it the product of whatever enthusiasm or whatever perspective. An interpretation largely survives or fails in terms of the historic evidence marshaled in its support or as its counter. As a case in point and as has been suggested, very few academics today imagine that Mussolini was a simple tool of "high finance" in a conspiratorial struggle to defeat the "universal proletarian revolution,"[29] a thesis that Marxist scholars widely broadcast, with absolute conviction, during the interwar years that separated the First from the Second World War.

In effect, there is a complex interrelationship among the conceptual sorting devices, the political "perspectives" employed to "make sense" of complex temporal sequences, and the empirical, and specifically documentary,

---

[28] The contention that each historian shapes his or her account of Fascism in accordance with his or her respective political persuasion appears to be the central notion in R. J. B. Bosworth, *The Italian Dictatorship: Problems and Perspectives in the Interpretation of Mussolini and Fascism* (London: Arnold, 1998).

[29] The orthodox interpretation of the Third International provided by Dimitroff in *The United Front Against War and Fascism* was provided a more exhaustive delivery in the contemporary work of Palme Dutt, *Fascism and Social Revolution*. A similar effort was undertaken by other Marxists, including that of anti-Stalinists. The "Trotskyist" version was very similar. See Daniel Guerin, *Fascism and Big Business* (New York: Monad Press, 1939). De Felice, who had exhaustively reviewed the documentary evidence simply dismissed the thesis. See, for example, De Felice, *Fascism: An Informal Introduction to Its Theory and Practice* (New Brunswick, NJ: Transaction, 1976), pp. 62–63; Gregor, *Interpretations of Fascism*, chap. 5.

evidence that historical research provides.[30] There is no simple way of writing history, nor is there one "true" account. The best we can attempt is to put together a maximally plausible version of what we believe to have transpired over an enormously complicated sequence, however brief in time, bringing surviving evidence to bear upon specific empirical claims and assessing the merits of those generalizations employed to provide form to the confirmed empirical substance.[31]

Italian Fascism has been particularly susceptible to the influence of prejudgment in any accounting. In the long struggle by the industrially advanced nations against both the Fascism of Mussolini as well as the "generic fascisms"[32] that collected around it, the passions of all antifascists, including academics, were mobilized to the cause. Together with the "committed scholarship" of Marxists, the result was a caricature assessment of Fascism that saw it as a "right-wing" dictatorship indistinguishable from Hitlerism. The identification made both equally possessed of an irreducible irrationality, inhumanity, violence, and genocidal intent. By the end of the 1980s, through the works of De Felice, Nolte, and Sternhell, all that had changed in substantial measure.

To produce a reasonably balanced narrative concerning Mussolini's Fascism had literally required generations of scholarship. Only by the commencement of the last decade of the twentieth century had so significant a body of information been collected and reported that one could begin to speak of a history of Fascism that provided a reasonably accurate recitation of its intricate and vanished reality.[33]

Among Anglophones, Stanley Payne has provided the academic community with an eminently defensible *History of Fascism*, affording an

---

[30] The literature on historiographic methods is abundant. See Arthur Danto, *Analytic Philosophy of History* (New York: Cambridge University Press, 1965); A. James Gregor *Metascience and Politics: An Inquiry into the Conceptual Language of Political Science* (New Brunswick, NJ: Transaction, 2003), chaps. 5–8; G. H. Nadel (ed.), *Studies in the Philosophy of History* (New York: Harper, 1965).

[31] See A. James Gregor, *Storiografia e relatività della storia* (Rome: Fondazione Gioacchino Volpe, 1976).

[32] It has become the convention among Anglophone scholars to employ the capitalized term "Fascism" to refer to Italian Fascism, and the lower-case "fascism" to have an ill-defined range of political thinkers, movements, and regimes as its generic referent.

[33] Central to the historical account of Mussolini's Fascism is the work of Renzo De Felice, *Mussolini il rivoluzionario 1883–1920* (Turin: Giulio Einaudi editore, 1963); *Mussolini il fascista: La conquista del potere 1921–1925* (Turin: Giulio Einaudi editore, 1966); *Mussolini il fascista: L'organizzazione dello Stato fascista 1925–1929* (Turin: Giulio Einaudi editore, 1968); *Mussolini il duce: Gli anni del consenso 1929–1936* (Turin: Giulio Einaudi editore, 1974); *Mussolini il duce: Lo Stato totalitario 1936–1940* (Turin: Giulio Einaudi editore, 1981); *Mussolini l'alleato: I. L'Italia in guerra 1940–1943. 1. Dalla guerra 'breve' alla guerra lunga* (Turin: Giulio Einaudi editore, 1986); *Mussolini l'alleato: I. L'Italia in guerra 1940–1943. 2. Crisi e agonia del regime* (Turin: Giulio Einaudi editore, 1991); *Mussolini l'alleato: II. La guerra civile 1943–1945* (Turin: Giulio Einaudi editore, 1997).

interpretive story of its epoch, 1914 through 1945.[34] Together with Renzo De Felice's magisterial biography of Mussolini and the work of Ernst Nolte, a competent and comprehensive account of Fascism was made available to the scholarship of the new century. However true that account might have been, parallel to that realization another development was proceeding apace that was to color the intellectual environment of the twenty-first century. Alongside the interpretation of Fascism per se, the specialized study of "neo-fascism" began to occupy more and more time among a growing number of scholars.

The study of neofascism has revealed itself to be a distinctive enterprise having, at times, only tenuous relationship to Fascism as a historic phenomenon. While one can speak with a degree of confidence concerning historic Fascism, the traits that serve to define the object of inquiry for students of neofascism remain not only ill defined but often internally inconsistent. To compound the difficulties, those inconsistencies are often simply attributed to the phenomena under scrutiny without the least reflection or persuasive warrant.

The influences that shape those responses are fairly commonplace. Researchers will frequently choose the objects of their inquiry based on some privative or too expansive notions of what "fascism" might mean. Thus, during the 1980s, as a case in point, there was increasing political discomfort in Western Europe with the rise of instances of "xenophobia" and anti-Semitism, together with violence against immigrants by, among others, gangs of indigenous "skinheads." All of these instances were identified as evidence of the growing influence of "right-wing extremist groups." Almost without reflection, the characterization "right-wing" was more and more frequently employed as a synonym for "fascism."

In 1989, the European Parliament commissioned a committee of inquiry to study "racism and xenophobia" in the European Union. The results of that study were subsequently published in a volume titled *Fascist Europe*.[35] Racism and xenophobia, together with any and all "right-wing groups," were identified as "fascist," as though neither racism nor xenophobia were to be found anywhere other than in right-wing and/or fascist environs. The suggestion seemed to be that all instances of racial prejudice, ethnic murder, tribal genocide, and brutality against foreigners were, by definition, both "right-wing" and/or "fascist." All the distinctions carefully developed by scholarship for about four decades were all but entirely abandoned. Wherever there was any instance of graveyard vandalism, cross burning, acts of terror against immigrants, "hate speech," journalistic accounts of

---

[34] Stanley G. Payne, *A History of Fascism 1914–1945* (Madison, WI: University of Wisconsin Press, 1995).

[35] Glyn Ford (ed.), *Fascist Europe: The Rise of Racism and Xenophobia* (London: Pluto Press, 1992).

the abuse of a social security system by "foreigners," or "hooliganism" directed against non-Christians, "fascism" or "neofascism" was identified as its source.

How this became possible is difficult to document. What seems evident is that almost from the time of the close of the Second World War, the idea was advanced that fascism might reappear, to bring, once again, brutality, destruction, and death to a world that had only just survived the most tragic period of wholesale violence in its history.

Initially the concern largely of journalists and sensationalists, very soon the issue of the reappearance of Fascism as neofascism engaged the interest of more serious scholars. They faced the same problems encountered by all those who propose to study novel subject matter: how to circumscribe their specific range of interest and render it intelligible to a reasonably well-informed public.

Scholars in informal disciplines such as intellectual history, comparative ideologies, history, or political science employ a variety of strategies to demarcate the proper range of their subject matter. They sometimes provide their audience a lexical definition, declaring an obscure term or concept synonymous with others more familiar. Thus the unfamiliar or obscure term "fascism" might be defined as "the open terroristic dictatorship of the most reactionary, most chauvinistic and most imperialistic elements of finance capital"[36] – lay concepts that are presumably more familiar.

Such a definition is generally unpacked into a fairly complex notion of a relationship between "big business" and "fascist" political agents doing their bidding.[37] The lexical definition is often a "carrier" for a fairly intricate "theory" of socioeconomic and political dynamics. Without considering the problems that attend any such theories, it is obvious that even the simplest of such definitions involves considerable reworking. Critical terms like "big business," familiar in ordinary speech, require precision if they are to be employed in serious inquiry. What distinguishes a "big business" from any other kind of business? What can "chauvinism" be taken to mean – in order that it can be observed with certainty? What is the observable reference for "finance capitalism"? Without even addressing the question of how one might confirm the claim that finance capitalists promote, foster, and sustain

[36] The definition supplied by the Thirteenth Plenary Meeting of the Executive Committee of the Communist International in December 1933, as repeated in the editorial of the *World Marxist Review*, April 1962, and published as *The New Fascist Danger* (New York: New Century Publishers, 1962), p. 7.

[37] Thus Mike Newberry speaks without qualification of the "upper echelons of the big businessmen" who subventionize and direct those political organizations calculated to defend their "monopoly capitalist" interests. Those organizations represent a "fascist revival" after fascism's defeat in the Second World War. Mike Newberry, *The Fascist Revival: The Inside Story of the John Birch Society; Who Is It? Who Is Behind It? Who Directs and Finances It?* (New York: New Century, 1961), pp. 6–7, 38–9, 42.

fascism, it is clear that lexical definitions are actually very complex cognitive undertakings.

In effect, lexical definitions often require considerable explication before they become serviceable for historical or social science research. The familiarity of terms employed does not, in and of itself, ensure their utility in empirical, quantitative research, particularly when the entire exercise rests on social science conjectures about complex empirical relations.

At times historians and researchers offer criterial definitions, identifying their subject matter by providing a reasonably discrete catalog of observable properties that identify members of the class under scrutiny. Thus, the members of the committees of inquiry of the European Parliament chose to identify those groups that they deemed anti-Semitic and/or xenophobic to be "fascist."

Criterial definitions share some fundamental traits with those lexical in character. Although the defining properties used in criterial definitions are directly observable in principle, "xenophobic" or "anti-Semitic" behavior has to be operationally defined. Anti-Semitic or xenophobic behavior is not always patently obvious. Two observers might well disagree as to whether or not what they both observed was an anti-Semitic or xenophobic act. The advantage criterial definitions enjoy turns on the fact that such definitions do not necessarily rest upon any particular theoretical foundation. Such definitions only require that the criterial properties that serve to identify members of a class be, in principle, empirically observable and ideally quantifiable.

The most singular feature of the evolving study of neofascism has been the lack of any consistency in defining the subject of inquiry. For decades after the war, European Marxists were disposed to identify any anticommunist political movement of whatever ideological persuasion as "neofascist." Because they were anticommunist, such political manifestations were, by definition, "reactionary." That was because Marxists entertained the "scientific" conviction that the workers' revolution was ineluctible – and that whenever and wherever "a social revolution is pending, and, for whatever reason, is not accomplished, reaction is the alternative."[38]

Since the advocates of "progressive" communism were of the political "left," neofascism, as reactionary and anticommunist, must, of necessity, be of the "right." Such characterizations, however anachronistic, had been made familiar by the Marxist literature of the prewar and wartime period, and soon became standard in accounts devoted to neofascism.

Soon the term "neofascism" came to refer to any organization that hosted conservatives, free-market enthusiasts, fundamentalist Christians, and almost anyone of whatever political persuasion as long as they were

---

[38] Daniel De Leon as cited by Eric Hass, *The Reactionary Right: Incipient Fascism* (New York: New York Labor News, 1966), p. 5.

anticommunist, that is, right-wing. Frequently that came to mean that any individual or organization that was anticommunist was neofascist.[39]

By the end of the 1960s, before more serious work would undermine their notions, many researchers had settled on a slightly more sophisticated Marxist interpretation of Fascism in general and neofascism in particular. There were those who argued that while Fascism may have been the consequence of the intervention into the political by the "economic ruling class" of post–World War I Italy, seeking to "survive and strengthen its own position," they were equally prepared to grant that it was "absurd" to pretend that Mussolini was "merely the material executor of orders issued by the Italian industrialists" – the rule of "big business" was rather more subtle and "dialectical."[40] For all that, the Marxist notion persisted that Fascism and neofascism remained servants of moribund capitalism and as such were "rightist" and "reactionary."

The quasimarxist net was cast so wide that not only did General Francisco Franco qualify as a fascist, but so did General Charles De Gaulle – as did the Ku Klux Klan, the John Birch Society, and "near Fascists" such as Barry Goldwater. We were told, at the time, that Goldwater's "ambition was to restore the America of the 1920s . . . or perhaps even the America of 1898, before the days of Theodore Roosevelt." In a textbook case of circular reasoning, we were told that Goldwater must have been a neofascist since he was supported by neofascists everywhere.[41] Thus, while specialists like Renzo De Felice and Ernst Nolte were putting together an account of Fascism that served to disqualify the variety of Marxist interpretations then prominent in the intellectual environment of the West, some of those who were searching out neofascism lapsed back into some of the least persuasive of the wartime renderings of what Fascism, and by implication what neofascism, was supposed to be.

At about the same time that some authors were reconfirming that Fascism was simply a tool of industrialists and financiers, there was developing in the Soviet Union a modified interpretation of Fascism. Fascism was no longer to be understood as a simple instrument of the possessing classes. Fascism might also be a weapon in the arsenal of "pseudosocialist," "petty bourgeois" governments that controlled, even if they pretended not to own, property. In effect, by the mid-1970s, Soviet thinkers had discovered that Chinese Maoism, for all its pretended left-wing convictions, was actually of the

---

[39] Thus by the end of the 1960s, any anticommunist was, by definition, a neofascist. It was an interpretation that was to become fairly standard among some academics and journalists. Thus, some were to argue that Barry Goldwater, an American conservative, threatened to be the "man on horseback" who would help create fascism in the United States. See Angelo Del Boca and Mario Giovanna, *Fascism Today: A World Survey* (New York: Pantheon, 1969), chap. 15.

[40] Ibid., pp. 7, 9.

[41] Ibid., pp. 331, 337.

"right," a variant of European fascism.[42] For Soviet theoreticians, Maoists were, in fact, neofascists. They were irrational, nationalistic, aggressive, militaristic, and ruled by a "Chairman" who pretended to transrational wisdom – whose every word was conceived true – and who was to be obeyed whether citizens understood his orders or not.[43]

It was in that parlous state that the burgeoning study of neofascism continued through much of the 1970s. Toward the end of the decade, Alexander Yanov called the academic community's attention to the fact that "rightists" were making their appearance in the leadership circles of the Soviet Union. They were those who were unmitigated nationalists, etatists, and authoritarians, who sought the "Russification" of the entire population of the Union. They spoke of will as a major determinant of human performance, of the role of ethnicity in the affairs of civilization, and of hierarchy as part of the natural order of things. For Yanov, they were, in effect, Russian neofascists.[44] Suddenly there were right-wing extremists – that is, neofascists – at the highest levels not only of the Chinese Communist Party but of the Communist Party of the Soviet Union as well.[45] Members of what the Western academic community had long characterized as the "revolutionary left" had transformed themselves into right-wing neofascists.[46]

By the beginning of the 1980s, neofascism was apparently to be found almost everywhere in the world – on the right and on the left. One or another author found neofascism pullulating in the United States among right-wing extremists, fundamentalist Christians, and Republicans; in Angola, where Marxist revolutionaries faced "neofascist mercenaries"; in Bolivia, where peasants were oppressed by the "fascist" Ugo Banzer; in Brazil, where the "fascist regime" sought to murder the members of the Vanguard of the Popular Revolution; in Chile, where General Augusto Pinochet led his "fascist" forces against democratic Chileans; in Fidel Castro's Cuba, which was a "typical case of a fascio-communism or nationalcommunism"; and in India, where the government was attempting to impose a "fascist dictatorship" on the people. Scholars plying their trade in the subdiscipline of fascist studies were doing land-office business.[47] The 1980s saw the beginnings of a

---

[42] See the entire discussion in Gregor, *The Faces of Janus*, chap. 4.

[43] See the discussion in A. James Gregor, "Fascism, Marxism and Some Considerations Concerning Classification," *Totalitarian Movements and Political Religions* 1, no. 2 (Autumn 2002), pp. 61–82.

[44] Alexander Yanov, *The Russian New Right: Right-Wing Ideologies in the Contemporary USSR* (Berkeley, CA: Institute of International Studies, 1978).

[45] See Gregor, *The Faces of Janus*, pp. 77–82.

[46] In this context, see A. James Gregor, *A Place in the Sun: Marxism and Fascism in China's Long Revolution* (Boulder, CO: Westview Press, 2000).

[47] Claudio Quarantotto has conveniently cataloged all the "fascist" and "neofascist" leaders, activities, movements, and regimes as they were to be found by various authors by the mid-1970s. Claudio Quarantotto, *Tutti fascisti!* (Rome: Il Borghese, 1976).

transformation that would fundamentally modify the intellectual environment. Mikhail Gorbachev would attempt to reform the lumbering institutions of what the Soviet Union had become. Among those reforms was an
effort at *glasnost'*, "openness," permission for the public discussion of political issues. By the mid-1980s, Soviet academicians were attempting to analyze
the origins, nature, and scope of the Soviet tragedy, and Marxism-Leninism's
complete failure to realize any of the revolutionary goals advertised by
Bolshevism in 1917. There was an attempt to understand both the mass murder of innocents by the "proletarian dictatorship" as well as the existence of
a monstrous archipelago of camps in which so many workers and peasants
lost part or all of their lives. Soviet social scientists lamented the emergence of
an "administered society" in the Soviet Union, lacking democratic opportunities and burdened by a "leadership principle" that reduced all decisions to
executive fiat. They spoke of the complete abandonment of "socialist principles" by a Stalin who had lapsed into complete "irrationality" – a man who
employed "violence as an indispensable component of unlimited power."
For Stalin, "violence" had served "as a universal tool."[48] Such a leader was
not only cruel, but gave every evidence of being a "neofascist" as well.

Given their evident disillusion, Soviet historians came to acknowledge the
pervasive similarities that constituted the empirical basis for the use of the
term "totalitarianism" to cover Italian Fascism, German National Socialism,
and Stalinism.[49] In effect, the right/left distinction so labored by Western
historians and social scientists for so long a period no longer appeared as
persuasive as it once did.

Under the evolving circumstances, it became increasingly difficult to
identify the "progressive" features that had made the Soviet Union "left-
wing" for so long a period, while Fascism, far less totalitarian,[50] was to be

---

[48] *The Stalin Phenomenon* (edited by a collective of scholars) (Moscow: Novosti Press Agency
Publishing House, 1988). For the quotations, see Dmitry Volkogonov, "The Stalin Phenomenon," ibid., pp. 43, 48, 49.

[49] See the discussion in Walter Laqueur, *The Dream That Failed: Reflections on the Soviet
Union* (New York: Oxford University Press, 1994), chap. 4.

[50] See Stanislaw Andreski, *Max Weber's Insights and Errors* (London: Oxford University Press,
1984), p. 44. The first Fascists recognized the vast uncertainties that surrounded the notion
of a "left" and a "right" in contemporary politics. Mussolini himself regularly mocked the
"right/left," "reactionary/progressive" distinction insisted upon by intellectuals. He pointed
out that by the early 1920s, the Bolsheviks had abandoned every leftist programmatic commitment they had made in the years before their seizure of power. He pointed out that not only
did the Bolsheviks kill more peasants and workers than had the "reactionaries" who preceded
them, but that the Bolsheviks were in the process of constructing one of the most authoritarian and oppressive states in history, using violence and terror to sustain their control.
They were not only guilty of failing to achieve their domestic leftist ends, but then proceeded
to send their armies to invade their neighbors. He argued if all that was what "leftism"
and "progressivism" entailed, Fascists would be true to their revolutionary and progressive commitments and consign themselves to being called "reactionaries" and "rightists."
See, for example, Benito Mussolini, "Noi 'reazionari'," "Un 'reazionario': Rinaldo Rigola,"

identified as a "reactionary," "right-wing" aberrancy. Some of the informal logic of the study of neofascism had been seriously compromised. There was very little that could be charged to Mussolini's Fascism that was not more convincingly true of the Soviet Union. The Soviet Union was as nationalistic, as irredentist, as militaristic, as etatist, as oppressive, as violative of human and political rights as ever was Fascist Italy.[51] It rapidly became reasonably clear that the lines of distinction between left- and right-wing "extremists" were neither easy to draw nor defend. There were very few "who could deny in good conscience that important features were common to fascist and communist rule."[52] The consequence was that it became increasingly difficult to provide a working definition of "neofascism" that might serve the purposes of historiographic and social science research. It had become evident that the properties customarily assigned neofascism were properties shared with Marxist systems on the left.

By the beginning of the 1990s, it became increasingly the case that researchers and journalists found more and more neofascist features among the institutions and political practices of those nations long imagined to represent the revolutionary left.[53] More and more authors spoke of some sort of "Stalinofascism" that the Marxist-Leninist nations of Eastern Europe had long harbored. It was discovered, for example, that the leftist, communist government of Nicolae Ceausescu had actually always been a sort of fascism. The legitimating ideology of the regime had been a kind of neofascist "syncretic mixture of decayed Marxist tenets, self-aggrandizing ethnocentric myths, and the unabashed celebration of Ceausescu himself. Xenophobia, autarchy, isolationism, anti-Occidentalism, and anti-intellectualism were the main motifs underlying this ideological construct."[54]

These were among the properties that had been used to identify neofascism for almost half a century. It was discovered that "quasifascism," "protofascism," and "incipient fascism" were to be discovered almost everywhere in Eastern Europe and the Balkans. It would seem that latent neofascism had

---

"La fine di una illusione: 'Il Bolscevismo e incapace di realizzare l'opera di costruzione sociale' dice Kropotkin," "Finis Poloniae?" "Nel paradiso Bolscevico," *Opera omnia* (Florence: La fenice, 1954–64), 14, pp. 191–3; 15, pp. 44–6, 97–9, 148–9; 18, pp. 397–8.

[51] See the discussion of all these features in the political history of the Soviet Union in Mikhail Agursky, *The Third Rome: National Bolshevism in the USSR* (Boulder, CO: Westview Press, 1987), and *Contemporary Russian Nationalism: History Revised* (Jerusalem: Soviet and East European Research Centre, January 1982).

[52] Laqueur, *The Dream That Failed*, p. 80.

[53] Semyon Reznik's *The Nazification of Russia: Antisemitism in the Post-Soviet Era* (Washington, DC: Challenge Publications, 1996) is a discussion devoted largely to anti-Semitism in the Soviet and post-Soviet period. It traces many "neofascist" (one might rather say "neonazi") elements throughout the history of the Soviet Union.

[54] Vladimir Tismaneanu and Dan Pavel, "Romania's Mystical Revolutionaries: The Generation of Angst and Adventure Revisited," *Eastern European Politics and Societies* 8, no. 3 (Fall 1994), p. 402.

been everywhere for decades – particularly in the former Soviet Union.[55] In Yugoslavia, egregious acts of "ethnic cleansing" – which many saw as fascist – were undertaken by some of the socialist leadership.[56]

By the early 1990s, it was very clear that the study of neofascism had become increasingly uncertain concerning its subject matter. The Marxist interpretation, which had provided the substance of a great deal of the neofascist accounts for decades, had been largely abandoned by Marxist theoreticians in the Soviet Union and Communist China. Over the course of time, some of the specialists in Marxist-Leninist Eastern Europe had not only rejected the traditional Marxist-Leninist interpretation of fascism and neofascism, but they argued that Italian Fascism had been the only "progressive" solution to the social and economic crisis that had beset Italy after the First World War.[57] It was no longer obvious that Fascism, fascism, or neofascism were unequivocally of the retrograde, antimodern "right."

By the early 1990s, it was clear to specialists that the distinction between Fascism, National Socialism, and the varieties of Marxism-Leninism was not at all obvious. By that time, scholars simply acknowledged that observable reality had "undermined the established concepts of right and left in politics." It seemed evident that rather than a linear relationship between the left and right, the antidemocratic right and left were actually related in curvilinear fashion, with "the extremes on the right and left" meeting to produce the evident similarities shared by fascism and Marxism-Leninism.[58] Notable specialists made the point. There were fundamental affinities between the various forms of Marxist-Leninist rule and the varieties of fascism.[59]

The situation had become very awkward for academics who sought to standardize the study of neofascism. It was uncertain what they were to study. By the last years of the past century, it had become evident that the meaning of what neofascism was taken to be would have to be recast. By the

55 See, for example, the accounts in John B. Dunlop, *The Rise of Russia and the Fall of the Soviet Empire* (Princeton, NJ: Princeton University Press, 1993); Jeremy Lester, *Modern Tsars and Princes: The Struggle for Hegemony in Russia* (London: Verson, 1995), pp. 149–68; Jonathan Steele, *Eternal Russia: Yeltsin, Gorbachev, and the Mirage of Democracy* (Cambridge, MA: Harvard University Press, 1994), chap. 13. In this regard, Alexander Yanov is particularly strident. See Alexander Yanov, *Weimar Russia and What We Can Do About It* (New York: Slovo-word, 1995).

56 See, for example, the account given in Lenard J. Cohen, *Serpent in the Bosom: The Rise and Fall of Slobodan Milosevic* (Boulder, CO: Westview Press, 2001).

57 See Mihaly Vajda, *Fascisme et mouvement de masse* (Paris: Le sycomore, 1979), and the discussion in Gregor, *Interpretations of Fascism*, pp. 166–170.

58 Jaroslav Krejci, "Introduction: Concepts of Right and Left," in Luciano Cheles, Ronnie Ferguson, and Michalina Vaughan (eds.), *Neo-fascism in Europe* (London: Longman, 1991), pp. 1, 3.

59 See the discussion in Ian Kershaw and Moshe Lewin, *Stalinism and Nazism: Dictatorship in Comparison* (New York: Cambridge University Press, 1997); Richard Pipes, *Russia Under the Bolshevik Regime* (New York: Vintage, 1995), chap. 5.

mid-1990s, some Marxist scholars sought to retrench after the collapse of the Soviet Union and the economic transformation of post-Maoist China. Stalinism and Maoism, we were told, were not and had never really been Marxist regimes. Many who sought to salvage Marxism fell back to pre-Stalinist or non-Stalinist authors – Antonio Gramsci, Angelo Tasca, and Leon Trotsky – in order to reinterpret Fascism and neofascism. It was Trotsky, after all, who had pointed out the "fateful similarities" shared by Stalinism and Fascism.[60] However many leftists might have considered the Soviet Union to have been the Marxist "vanguard of communism," it was perfectly clear that such had never been the case.[61] Marx's epigones were constrained to begin at the beginning. By the end of the 1990s, the wiser among them attempted a reformulation. Very little attention was devoted to the histories of flawed Marxist regimes. The theoretical retrenchment proceeded as though the statism, the "cult of personality," the hegemonic single party, the ideological conformity, the concentration camps, the mass murders, the economic exploitation, and the countless economic failures that filled the history of Marxist-Leninist China or the Soviet Union were completely irrelevant to the contemporary search for neofascism.

Fascism was once again identified as the all-but-exclusive source of genocidal violence, irrationality, and reaction. Some authors wrote as though the sad histories of mass murder in the Soviet Union, China, or Kampuchea had never taken place. If the twentieth century was the history of war, mass murder, and irrationality, fascism was its sole source. It was fascism – committed to but two absolute principles, violence and war – that inspired the mayhem of the entire century. Marxist-Leninist regimes seem to have had precious little to do with any of it. More than that, fascism, itself, was the inevitable byproduct of capitalism. We are told, with absolute confidence, that "fascism is first and foremost an ideology generated by modern industrial capitalism." We are informed, at the cusp of the twenty-first century, that fascism comes to power through the connivance of the "establishment" and proceeds to increase the profits of capitalism through the "exploitation of ordinary workers." The existence of "private property" under the conditions of monopoly capitalism generates "alienation and exploitation." Fascist rule exacerbates that alienation and exploitation and produces the "social contradictions" that only violence or revolution can resolve.[62] We find ourselves once again in the infancy of fascist studies.

---

[60] Leon Trotsky, *The Revolution Betrayed* (New York: Doubleday, 1937), p. 278.
[61] Mark Neocleous, *Fascism* (Minneapolis, MN: University of Michigan Press, 1997), p. 90.
[62] Ibid., pp. xi, 17. Dave Renton, with equal confidence, informs us that "fascist ideology has acted in the clear interests of capital," and that both Mussolini and Hitler came to power with the "support" of the establishment in order to "increase . . . capitalist profits . . . through the increased exploitation of ordinary workers." Dave Renton, *Fascism: Theory and Practice* (London: Pluto Press, 1999), p. 106.

It is not at all clear how such notions provide any insight into what neo-fascism might be or how any of this explains the elements of neofascism clearly evident in the former "socialist" nations of Eastern Europe and Asia, where private property no longer existed by law. The fact that the numbers involved in the mass murders in the Soviet Union, China, and Kampuchea exceeded those under fascism is neither explained nor addressed at all. The entire issue is dismissed as unworthy of discussion.[63]

Whatever the disposition of postcommunist Marxists not to speak to the question of violence, murder, and irrationality in Marxist regimes, the many difficulties that collect around the study of neofascism cry out for some kind of resolution. If capitalism is the taproot of fascism, and it is only fascism that causes war and commits genocide and mass murder, how can one explain wars between socialist countries and the mass murder of incalculable numbers of innocents in Marxist systems?

In effect, it is very difficult to put together arguments that are very com-pelling concerning the relationship between capitalism and fascism that answer the question of how one might identify neofascist movements and regimes in the twenty-first century. If there is a relationship between the two, it is a very complex one, and it is counterintuitive to imagine that capital-ists dominated Mussolini – still less Hitler – to produce the enormities we tend to identify with either or both. We can say that with some confidence, since noncapitalist systems like Stalinist Russia and Maoist China produced enormities of greater magnitude.

What emerges from all this is the realization that the 1990s were criti-cal years for the study of neofascism. While the study of historic Fascism had matured to the point at which one might speak of an abiding con-sensus of opinion among specialists, the study of neofascism proceeded to unravel. Neomarxists attempted to reattach fascism to capitalism, indus-trial capitalism, or finance capitalism, according to their respective fancies, but the enterprise did not prosper. Nonetheless, almost everyone who was devoting time to the search for neofascism appeared comfortable with the identification of his or her subject matter with individuals, groupuscules, movements, and even governments that might be somehow characterized as "reactionary" and "right-wing." Very few chose to attempt compara-tive studies of historic Marxist-Leninist and fascist regimes as a preamble to their primary undertaking. No one chose to compare left-wing Marxist regimes with the so-called right-wing Fascism of Mussolini in terms of their respective antidemocratic orientation, "charismatic" leadership, single-party

---

[63] "I would . . . suggest that Stalinist Russia, despite the gulags, was not fascist. . . ." Ibid., p. 109. Neocleous mentions the "Soviet extermination of the kulaks" only in passing, offering abso-lutely no explanation of mass murder in a society in which capitalism no longer existed. Neocleous, *Fascism*, p. 93.

dominance, putative irrationality, and disposition to employ violence, countenance genocide, and seek political resolution through war.

The 1990s created very special problems for the study of neofascism. Most European scholars were content to deal with the issue with the commonplace distinctions with which they had grown comfortable. They had been students of professors who never hesitated to speak of Fascism, fascism, and neofascism as reactionary, right-wing, and devoid of even the suggestion of serious political and social thought. They had learned well. For them, Fascism would forever remain devoid of thought, reactionary, racist, and fratricidal. For over half a century, students had learned little else. By the 1990s, remarkably few chose to speak to the issue of how Marxism-Leninism, or Maoism, or Polpotism – which appeared to share so much with neofascism – might figure in comparative reflections. Many authors chose to deal exclusively with those "right-wing" political expressions one found in Central and Eastern Europe in particular – but only after 1989, essentially after the disappearance of Marxism-Leninism.[64] Under those circumstances, one was not expected to deal with the problems of a "left-wing" fascism. Given all that, a great many persons appeared comfortable with the readiness with which references to the "radical right" dilated into a discussion about "neofascism" as though both shared some intrinsic, if fugitive, meaning. The increasingly urgent search for contemporary neofascism began to take on singular features.

Before the century came to a close, quite independent of the neomarxist revival, the study of neofascism was destined to undergo yet further transformation. Initially, the new candidate interpretations gave the appearance of being more sophisticated and objective than most of their predecessors. We were told, for example, that the term "extreme right" failed to "pick up the fact that fascism's intellectual pedigree has not been uniquely right-wing," and that behind the movement and regime "lay a coherent body of thought" that could not be "dismissed as necessarily irrational." Moreover, an attempt was made to distinguish the neofascism of the post–World War II period from conservative dictatorships and military authoritarianism. At the same time, diminishing effort was employed to acknowledge the differences between Fascism and National Socialism.

What had become a fairly standard distinction between Hitler's National Socialism and Mussolini's Fascism by the early 1980s was no longer allowed. That National Socialism was fundamentally racist and distinct from the doctrinal nationalism of Fascism was no longer accepted as credible. Homicidal anti-Semitism no longer ideologically distinguished Hitlerism from Fascism. Anti-Semites, and those who denied that the massacre of Jews took place under the ministrations of Hitler's forces, were all uniformly spoken of as

---

[64] See, for example, Sabrina P. Ramet (ed.), *The Radical Right in Central and Eastern Europe Since 1989* (University Park, PA: Pennsylvania State University Press, 1999).

"neofascist." Irrespective of how carefully the best of the historians of Italian Fascism had been in drawing the radical differences between the anti-Semitism and racism that one might have found in the last years of Mussolini's rule and the anti-Semitism and racism of Hitler,[65] every feature of the anti-Semitism and racism of National Socialism was attributed – without argument – to Fascism. Anti-Semitism and genocidal racism became defining properties of an ill-considered, all-inclusive neofascism.[66]

While specialists in the study of historic Fascism had been clear that there were major and unbridgeable differences between Mussolini's regime and that of Adolf Hitler, by the 1990s the students of neofascism seemed prepared, for whatever reason, to revert to the wartime identification of the two. No matter the apparent sophistication of the discussion, the students of neofascism in the 1990s were prepared to merge, literally without remainder, Italian Fascism with German National Socialism,[67] thereby making any intimation of anti-Semitism grounds for one's identification as neofascist. Any suggestion that the massacre of Jews had not taken place under Nazi auspices during the Second World War was considered sufficient to identify one as neofascist.

By the mid-1990s, the entry criteria for admission into the class of neofascists had become increasingly slack. Any opposition to free immigration from anywhere and under any circumstances afforded immediate entry – as a "racist" – into the class of neofascists.

Little in the way of an explanation can be offered for the intensity with which the search for neofascism has proceeded since the middle of the 1990s. There has been constant talk of the "rise" of neofascism throughout Europe – and yet those groups that might be credibly identified as neofascist achieved little electoral success. Those that have been successful – like the Italian *Alleanza nazionale* – display, as will be argued, very few features that might objectively be identified as neofascist.[68]

For all that, those dedicated to the pursuit of neofascism have continued with their task. Distinct from those who have once again taken up the notion that Fascism and neofascism can only be understood as tools of industrial

---

[65] See, for example and particularly, the discussion in De Felice, "Introduction to the New Pocket Edition," pp. vii–xxii.

[66] Roger Eatwell, *Fascism: A History* (New York: Penguin, 1995), pp. xix, xx, xxiv, xxv.

[67] Eatwell was prepared to identify those neofascisms that "look back to Hitler's regime for inspiration" as neonazi. Eatwell, *Fascism*, p. xxv. Few students of neofascism have been that responsible.

[68] Some of those who insist on the neofascism of the Alleanza nazionale seem prepared to grant that it is antitotalitarian and antiracist, unequivocally committing itself to the defense of the liberal political institutions of Italy's "Second Republic." For all that, there is the insistence that the Alleanza still represents a "democratic fascism" – which is really neofascism. See Roger Griffin, "The 'Post-Fascism' of the Alleanza Nazionale: A Case Study in Ideological Morphology," *Journal of Political Ideologies* 1, no. 2 (1996), pp. 123–45. The discussion will proceed in greater detail in Chapter 3.

capital, the nonmarxists have sought to sustain their efforts by providing a somewhat novel rationale. While eclectic in terms of its substance – picking through those interpretations of Fascism considered and largely dismissed by their predecessors – some of the spokespersons for the new orientation have chosen to return to the convictions entertained by those who fought the Second World War. We are told that if we wish to comprehend how so much violence and bloodshed marred the history of the twentieth century, we must first appreciate that Hitler's National Socialism and Mussolini's Fascism were essentially one and the same, and that together they were afflicted with a special pathology that "lies behind the hatred and destructiveness." Fascism, in some real sense or another, was the source of the mass murder, barbarism, and inhumanity that martyred humanity throughout the past century.[69]

While there was a recognition that the political violence and brutality of Fascist Italy "paled into insignificance"[70] when compared with that of National Socialist Germany or Stalin's Soviet Union, the term "neofascism" was reserved for the regimes of Hitler and Mussolini, with scant attention devoted to the mass murder regimes of Stalin, Mao, or Pol Pot.

We are told that Hitler was narcissistic and megalomaniacal in the effort to explain his homicidal destructiveness – but little along these lines are said of Stalin, or Mao, or Pol Pot, as though genocidal impulses were the affliction of fascists alone. Only those movements and regimes animated by "a political ideology based on paligenetic ultra-nationalism" were deemed capable of the kind of inhumanity that had fueled the massacre of millions.[71]

It seems obvious that if such were the case, then all the Marxist-Leninist regimes of the twentieth century must have been regimes predicated on "palingenetic ultra-nationalism," for none of them were less destructive of human life than was National Socialist Germany.[72] There seems to be very little other than a choice between identifying all Marxist-Leninist political systems as palingenetic ultra nationalisms or that palingenetic ultra nationalism is not the sole source of barbarism, inhumanity, and mass murder. The latter seems more plausible, but we are never quite sure where this kind of analysis might lead one. Now that we know that Joseph Stalin was an

---

[69] Roger Griffin, *The Nature of Fascism* (London: Routledge, 1991), pp. xi, xii, 225–35, and the comments on the book jacket.

[70] Ibid., p. 225.

[71] Ibid., pp. 229, 234. Griffin clearly acknowledges that the Cambodian Khmer Rouge and Stalin were guilty of murder on a scale that perhaps exceeded that of Hitler (for example, ibid., pp. 177–8), yet he spends a considerable amount of time discussing the "uniqueness" of the murderousness of National Socialism.

[72] See the documented catalog of murder that is now available in Stephane Courtois, Nicolas Werth, Jean-Louis Panne, Andrzej Paczkowski, Karel Bartosek, and Jean-Louis Margolin, *The Black Book of Communism: Crimes Terror Repression* (Cambridge, MA: Harvard University Press, 1999).

anti-Semite and a nationalist,[73] we are left with the suspicion that Soviet Marxism might really have been a variant of Hitler's National Socialism.

The worst was yet to come. The search for neofascism had entered into crisis. Efforts were undertaken to negotiate the difficulties. Some made recourse to "postmodern" insights, and to attendant hermeneutic strategies apparently invoked to "demystify" the conceptual confusions that had collected around the subdiscipline. Metaphors, trope, "idealized abstractions," and analogies were all pressed into service as "heuristic devices" intended to illuminate the undertaking. To study neofascism effectively, we were counseled to consider it to be something like "slime mold," brainless and amorphic, enjoying a capacity to undertake "remarkable" metamorphoses. Neofascism, previously just difficult to define, was spoken of as possessed of a "protean quality to generate myriad permutation." Over time, apparently in no particular sequence, neofascism not only adopts and adapts a "radically changed . . . ideological content," its ideology and structure are equally subject to "major mutation in the way it can manifest itself outwardly as an antisystemic political force." It can everywhere and at any time assume "new guises." As a consequence, it can assume postures that distinguish it from both historic Fascism and National Socialism – to present us with what can only be an insoluble conundrum.[74]

We are left with the counsel that we can expect neofascism to appear in any and all forms, without the semblance of ideological continuity with its historical antecedents, in totally unpredictable manifestations. All of this really leaves us with little to guide our efforts. Neofascism apparently can assume any guise, any institutional form, or any ideological content. Given all that, it is difficult to imagine what the term "neofascist" might mean. There seems, for example, to be little pretense that one might expect to find any particular Fascist content in the ideology of any presumptive contemporary neofascism. But without any identifiable content, neofascism could manifest itself as anything. Thus, fundamentalist Christians, libertarians, and economic conservatives can all be held to be neofascists – no matter what their beliefs and however much they insist that their doctrines preclude any such association. For the postmodernist search for neofascism, almost anything, including the "proletarian racism" to be found among punk rock and heavy metal bands, constitutes a "current of fascism."[75] It is as though all the work undertaken by specialists to provide us some coherent

---

[73] See the discussions in Jonathan Brent and Vladimir P. Naumov, *Stalin's Last Crime: The Plot Against the Jewish Doctors 1948–1953* (New York: Perennial, 2003); Gennadi Kostyrchenko, *Out of the Red Shadows: Anti-Semitism in Stalin's Russia* (Amherst, NY: Prometheus, 1995); Arkady Vaksberg, *Stalin Against the Jews* (New York: Knopf, 1994).

[74] Roger Griffin, "Fascism's New Faces (and New Facelessness) in the 'Post-Fascist' Epoch," *Erwägen Wissen Ethik* 15, no. 3 (2004), pp. 287–300; see also James Gregor, "Response," ibid. 15, no. 4 (2004), p. 595, n. 5.

[75] Griffin, "Fascism's New Faces," p. 295.

understanding of Italian Fascism is of no relevance to the contemporary study of neofascism. To accept postmodernist guidance in the pursuit of neofascism is to leave us without direction and bereft of any hope of real success.

By the beginning of the twenty-first century, the frenetic search for neofascism had fallen on evil times. It was acknowledged by some that "the term 'Fascism' fits everything." Thus, even if we were to "add the cult of Celtic mythology and the mysticism of the Grail" to some set of beliefs or another, admittedly "completely extraneous to official Fascism," we could still identify that set of beliefs as a neofascist variant of Fascism – so accommodating do the postmodernist standards of evidence appear to be. One of the apparent consequences of all this is simply to have us acknowledge the existence of an "Ur-Fascism," an "eternal Fascism," that will forever be with us – like the burden of Original Sin.[76]

In effect, it appears that the contemporary search for neofascism has not been particularly productive of cognitively reliable results. We are left with an incredibly confused picture of the past, implausible strategies for understanding the present, and a hopelessly baffling outlook on the future. It is not clear that the study of neofascism, as it has matured over the past half-century, justifies the expenditure in time and treasure that has accompanied it. It is not evident that anything that can be done in the near future to change those realities very much. So many of our academics, trained by a committed generation of scholars and their immediate heirs, seem inextricably wedded to a left/right dichotomy that narrows the intellectual vision, blurs comparative perspective, and confounds objective judgment. Perhaps going over the field once again may offer the occasion of reviewing what we do know about paradigmatic Fascism in a fashion that might suggest, implicitly or by indirection, something that influences others to refocus attention and recalibrate judgment.

---

[76] Umberto Eco, *Five Moral Pieces* (New York: Harcourt, 1997), p. 77.

2

Fascism

Almost every scholar who pretends to a study of neofascism offers a summary account of Fascism – and almost all accounts differ in substantial fashion. Attempting to encapsule a quarter of a century of intense political activity in the relatively brief compass of an expository outline is difficult at best. There is always the exercise of judgment and the influence of bias in the winnowing of the enormous abundance of the historic record. Nonetheless, the work of some of the major historians of the twentieth century permits a stenographic rendering of the entire Fascist sequence that is plausible and in large part unobjectionable.[1] We can now be reasonably confident that we know at least some of the essentials of Italian Fascism.

We know that Fascism arose in a new nation, politically reunited after almost one thousand years of dismemberment, strife, political occupation, poverty, and internecine warfare. We know that the fractured Italic peninsula was also host to almost a thousand years of creativity, episodic ebullience, and commercial expansion. For the purposes of discussion, nonetheless, it is important to recognize that the several hundred years before Italy's reunification were particularly marked by recurrent expressions of individual and collective humiliation to be found in the lamentations of many of the nation's foremost spokespeople.

As early as the beginning of the sixteenth century, Niccolo Machiavelli exhorted the people of the peninsula to make the effort to unite against the depredations of foreigners. He held Italy to be subject to a form of servitude more unendurable than that of the ancient Hebrews. Italians, he insisted, are "greater slaves than the Israelites, more oppressed than the Persians,

---

[1] Obviously the work of Renzo De Felice enjoys pride of place in any exposition of Italian Fascism. The following account owes much of its substance to the De Felice's detailed treatment of Benito Mussolini's life in the context of Italian Fascism. While I am solely responsible for the account, De Felice's history provides its historical foundation.

and still more dispersed than the Athenians.... In a word," he maintained, Italians were "without chiefs, pillaged, torn to pieces, and enslaved by foreign powers."[2]

These were themes that appeared with metronomic regularity in the work of some of the most prominent of Italian literary figures. Italy was disunited and ungovernable – afflicted by the impostures of foreigners and torn between local, provincial, and regional demands. Toward the end of Machiavelli's century, it was said, "Venice endures, but does not live; Florence lives, but does not create; Rome governs, but does not reign; Naples reigns, but does not govern; Turin both reigns and governs, but only obscurely."[3]

At the turn of the next century, Alessandro Tassoni could complain that Italians allowed themselves to be "downtrodden by the arrogance and conceit of foreign peoples."[4] These jeremiads continued throughout the century until at the commencement of the next, Giambattista Vico sought to marshal Italians by a clarion call of renewal. He inspired them with the anticipation of a nation freed from foreign intervention, "master of itself, great among the great nations of Europe,... conscious of its dignity, proud of its glory,... capable of the most splendid arts and original science."[5]

For all that, at the end of the eighteenth century, Vittorio Alfieri could still speak of a disunited Italy as that "August Matron" who had for so long been the "principal seat of all human wisdom and values," and who, nonetheless, found herself "disarmed, divided, despised [and] enslaved."[6] Whatever the admonitions of Vico and Alfieri, the Italians of the nineteenth century found themselves continuing to lament the "pitiful condition" of the nation, divested of its former glory, "sad and abandoned," still so disheartened that she was compelled, in Giacomo Leopardi's judgment, to "conceal her face" from the world.[7]

All of this articulated the primal elements of *reactive nationalism*, a form of generic ingroup sentiment exacerbated by a real or fancied sense of protracted humiliation on the part of a political and/or ethnic community that is, or imagines itself to be, the object of abuse at the hands of others.

---

[2] Niccolo Machiavelli, *The History of Florence and the Prince* (London: George Bell and Sons, 1891), p. 484 (chap. 26 of *The Prince*).

[3] As cited in Alfredo Oriani, *La lotta politica in Italia: Origini della lotta attuale 476/1887* (Rocca San Casciano: Cappelli, 1956), p. 106.

[4] Alessandro Tassoni, "Filippiche contro gli spagnuoli," *Prose politiche e morali* (Bari: Laterza, 1930), pp. 341–2.

[5] See Giovanni Gentile, *Giambattista Vico* (Florence: Sansoni, 1936), p. 5; *Studi Vichiani* (Florence: Felice le Monnier, 1927).

[6] As cited in Ronaldo S. Cunsolo, *Italian Nationalism* (Malabar, FL: Robert E. Krieger, 1990), p. 184.

[7] Giacomo Leopardi, *Opere* (Milan: Communità, 1937) 1, pp. 137–8.

Reactive nationalism is a particular and exaggerated expression of ingroup amity and outgroup enmity.[8] Throughout history, such reactive patterns have been observed in conflict situations involving organized communities, whether they were or are, among others, tribes, moieties, clans, confederations, city-states, or nations.[9] The entities involved are not as important, for our purposes, as the group sentiments that are fostered by the particular circumstances.

In the nineteenth century, the sentiments that typify reactive nationalism found expression in an Italy only recently reunited, and still economically, politically and militarily handicapped. Nineteenth-century Italy was alive with the sentiments of aggrieved nationalism. In the mid-nineteenth century, Vincenzo Gioberti sought to inspire Italians with an appeal to ingroup sentiment. He pretended to their intrinsic superiority in almost every human endeavor. His volume on the moral and civil primacy of Italians[10] was calculated to give his conationals heart. He gave voice to the desire among the intellectual leaders of the peninsula that Italy, once again, accede to its former glory.

Throughout the century, in both history and romance, Italians regularly reinvoked the glories of ancient Rome. There was an insistent appeal to the grandeur of the past, as a counterpoint to the debasement and servility of the Italy of the then present.

In Europe, the entire nineteenth century was alive with the sentiments of injured nationalism. The French Revolution and the Napoleonic expansion into the continental heartland had unleashed reactive forces among the national fragments of what was to become Germany, Italy, and the sometimes nations of Southeastern Europe and the Balkans. Everywhere there

---

[8] In social science, these features of group life are generally discussed under the rubric "ethnocentrism." Fascist intellectuals were familiar with the early discussions concerning the "laws of association" governing life lived in common, and gave political expression to the phenomena. An interesting exposition of these notions is found in A. O. Olivetti, *Il sindacalismo come filosofia e come politica: Lineamenti di sintesi universale* (Milan: Alpes, 1924). At the end of the Fascist period, Italians were still addressing the issue of ethnocentrism and some of its implications for then-contemporary politics. See, for example, Mario Canella, *Principi di psicologia razziale* (Florence: Sansoni, 1941), particularly chap. 2.

[9] The issues involved here are very complex. For the purposes of the present discussion, the intellectuals who gathered around Fascism were familiar with the forms of ethnocentrism discussed by early social science theorists such as Ludwig Gumplowicz, in his *Der Rassenkampf: Sociologische Untersuchungen* (Innsbruck: Verlag der Wagner'schen Univ.-Buchhandlung, 1883), and *Outlines of Sociology* (New York: Paine-Whitman, 1963), which originally appeared in German in 1885. Many Fascist intellectuals were familiar with the work of Gumplowicz and referred to it regularly in their work. See A. James Gregor, *Mussolini's Intellectuals: Fascist Economic, Social and Political Thought* (Princeton, NJ: Princeton University Press, 2004), chap. 4.

[10] Vincenzo Gioberti, *Prolegomeri del primato morale e civile degli italiani* (Capolago: Casa Editrice Principato, 1846), first published in 1843, ran into many editions.

was a cry of wounded sensibilities, and the demand for political nationhood, reunification, and renewal.

Italy's *Risorgimento*, its own effort at reunification and rebirth, saw Giuseppe Mazzini as its standard-bearer. Mazzini spoke of a reunited and redeemed Italy that would once again rekindle the flame that had been Rome. He spoke of a "Third Rome," intending thereby to link his advocacy to the memories of a long-ago empire and a universal church. He spoke of the "great memories" of the past with which he sought to fuel the energies of the "new mission" the times required. The new-old nation was once again to be inspired by a "vast ambition . . . , intoxicated by its independence of the foreigner, [and] founded by its own strength."[11]

Mazzini's was a call to commitment, dedication, and remembered grandeur. He spoke of the nation as "something more than an aggregation of individuals born to produce and consume corn." He spoke of a "fraternity of faith," predicated on a "consciousness of a common *ideal.*" He spoke of "*duty.* . . . and self-sacrifice [as] . . . the sole standard of life and the only pure virtues, holy and mighty in power, the noblest jewels that crown and hallow the human soul."[12] Mazzini's call was one of redemption, for the renewal of Italian greatness.

By the end of the nineteenth century, industrially backward and economically retrograde Italy had embarked upon a rate of material growth that distinguished it among the nations of Eastern Europe and the Mediterranean. Italy's textile industries commenced to compete with those of France. Commercial traffic began to stimulate demands for the expansion of railroads that would lace together the reaches of the peninsula from Sicily to the Alps.

Throughout Europe, the tempo of industrial and economic development accelerated apace. The continent was alive with energy. British, French, and Belgian imperialism swept over Africa and Asia, until by the beginning of the First World War, those nations controlled about 80 percent of the world's surface – while Italy found itself bottled within the confines of the Mediterranean. Great Britain dominated Gibraltar and the canal at Suez, while France, from Corsica and North Africa, largely controlled the internal sealines of communication in the Mediterranean. Italy, with one of the longest coastlines in Europe, had only limited access to an inland sea.

Without natural resources, Italy was compelled to depend on mercantile traffic to supply its industrial needs, and to earn the foreign exchange that would pay for them. Its geographic circumstances left the emerging nation severely disadvantaged in a competitive world arena dominated by the advanced industrial powers.

---

[11] Giuseppe Mazzini, "To the Italians: The Program of the 'Roma del Popolo,' (1871)," in *The Duties of Man and Other Essays* (New York: E. P. Dutton, 1907), pp. 222, 228.

[12] Ibid., pp. 231–4, 238.

By the beginning of the twentieth century, a vocal minority of Italians produced a series of publications such as *Lacerba, La Voce, Leonardo,* and *Il Regno,* in which one finds a demanding restlessness, a recognition of the nation's deficiencies, and an invocation to adventure, power, and self-expression. In their pages, one also finds an insistence that Italian subservience to foreign powers end, and that the affronts of tourists who rummage through the debris of Italy's past cease. One finds a call for an end to the somnolence of *"dolce far niente"* – and a rejection of political democracy, seen as an artifice of foreign manufacture, intended to keep Italy ill organized and politically vulnerable.

By the first decade of the new century, there was a concerted outcry for a national "reawakening." There was a call to muster all Italians to the pursuit of "a grand common purpose," a "mission" that would foster enterprise, sharpen the will, and focus the skills of a people who once again heard the flutter of Roman eagles – a people all infilled with a "sentiment of rebirth and of pride."[13]

It was within that fragment of time that Gabriele D'Annunzio spoke of "placing not only [his] thought but [his] actions in the service of [his] ideal homeland ... ," acknowledging the "sacred ties" that bound him to his native Italy. He made sibyline allusions to the intellectual luminaries of the nation's past, identifying them with the community's life and energy. He spoke of the Italian peasants – "strong, tenacious, sober and healthy" – as bringing the "scythe and pitchfork into the dignity of communal life."[14] All of Italy – its entrepreneurs, its workers, and its peasants were to be renewed with the energies and symbols of the past.

In 1912, Giovanni Papini published his *Un uomo finito,* an autobiography that captured much of the restless temper of the times. Two years later, together with Giuseppe Prezzolini, he published *Vecchio e nuovo nazionalismo,* in which one finds all the constituent elements that would surface in the revolution that overwhelmed Italy at the end of the First World War.

In their work, Papini and Prezzolini anticipated the advent of a revolutionary Italy, its bourgeoisie, proletariat, and peasantry reborn out of its ancient grandeur in the form of a disciplined, obedient, dignified, precise, responsible, punctual, clean, and sober people, pragmatic and industrializing, led by an exiguous elite, and given more to action than chatter. It would be a new nation that would have to overcome all the infirmities of late development: lack of natural resources, exhaustion of the support capacity of the soil,

---

[13] See the modern introduction of Piero Buscaroli to Giovanni Papini and Giuseppe Prezzolini, *Vecchio e nuovo nazionalismo* (Rome: Volpe, 1967, reprint of the 1914 edition), pp. 3–5, and the "Preface" by Prezzolini, written in April 1914, ibid., p. i.

[14] As cited in Anthony Rhodes, *D'Annunzio: The Poet as Superman* (New York: McDowell, Oblensky, 1959), pp. 81, 89.

overpopulation, illiteracy, lack of technical skills, absence of adequate investment capital, together with the psychology of defeat that typified the Italian of the early twentieth century.[15]

By the advent of the First World War, all the peninsula's dissidents gave voice to a recurrent set of political themes. The revolutionary nationalists of Enrico Corradini, the syndicalists of A. O. Olivetti and Filippo Corridoni, together with the Futurists of F. T. Marinetti, all sought to articulate, in one way or another, a call to greatness that might resonate among Italians.[16]

The coming of the First World War succeeded in aggravating the conditions that prompted systemic dislocations. Troop levies siphoned millions of young men from familiar environments and traditional support structures and thrust them into a maelstrom of brutality, violence, and death. Six hundred thousand young Italians were sacrificed in the slaughterhouse that was the First World War. The restlessness and disquiet of those who survived were only made worse. The young intellectuals who had filled the leadership ranks of the nationalists, the anarchists, the syndicalists, and the Futurists came out of the war trained in the art of mayhem, accustomed to conflict, and athirst for armed victory. They perceived themselves members of a warrior elite, having purchased the right to decide the future of their nation by virtue of their sacrifice and that of their fallen comrades.[17]

They had seen antebellum Italy undertake its first steps at modernization, the expansion of its narrow industrial base, the increasing urbanization of its rural population, its first successful test of arms in the North African war in Tripoli, and the extension of suffrage to increasing numbers of common citizens. They had witnessed the first signs of awakening; Italy, "the Great Proletariat," was astir.

Italy's dissident intellectuals saw the nation in the same terms that Karl Marx had conceived the proletariat – as oppressed and worthy – as an agent of world history. With resolve steeled by war, and change seen as the product of organized violence, the veterans of the First World War came home to an Italy alive with a sense of change.

The historic circumstances were classic harbingers of systemic revolutionary transformation. The war had displaced masses of young men, the traditional instruments of radical social change. They had been trained in violence and obedience, fashioned into potential foot soldiers of a mass-mobilizing, revolutionary movement. Shorn of their conventional constraints, convinced of their moral superiority, they would be the agents of transformative change.

---

[15] See Papini and Prezzolini, *Vecchio e nuovo nazionalismo*, pp. viii, xi, 4–5, 13–15, 24–7, 31–3.

[16] See the discussion in Gregor, *Mussolini's Intellectuals*, chap. 2, and *The Ideology of Fascism: The Rationale of Totalitarianism* (New York: Free Press, 1969), chap. 2.

[17] Camillo Pellizzi, *Una rivoluzione mancata* (Milan: Longanesi., 1949), has left us a brief but illustrative account of the role of the survivors of the trenches in the revolution that immediately followed the termination of the First World War. See ibid., Part 1, pp. 15–29.

As combat veterans, demobilized soldiers returned to an Italy that both respected and feared them. The nation's security forces identified with them. Inservice military and the constabulary clearly favored them. Encouraged by that collateral support, organized as Fascist *squadristi*, the returning combat veterans brought violence to all those who resisted their vision of a Greater Italy.

The parliamentary socialists who had resisted the "capitalists' war," who had defamed those who fought, who defended deserters from the military, and who rejected patriotism as a snare employed by the possessing class became the object of sometimes spontaneous and sometimes carefully calculated violence. The violence was designed to destroy the socialist communications and command infrastructure, as well as the antinationalist support base in the cities and countryside. Ultimately, all of Italy stood in the shadow of Fascist revolutionaries.

Those armed men, wearing the black shirts of the *Arditi*, the special operations forces who had distinguished themselves in combat, counted some of Italy's most articulate intellectuals among their number. They were the alienated intellectuals whose thought so often constitutes the rationale of modern revolution. Such intellectuals are the dissident learned who, in every modern revolution, supply the iconoclastic systems of belief for which revolutionaries are prepared to kill and be killed. In their ranks, in both war and the subsequent fragile peace, were radicals such as Benito Mussolini, the former leader of Italy's revolutionary socialists. To the guidons of the first Fascism, he drew together a collection of notable intellectuals, including nationalists, Futurists, and revolutionary syndicalists of the caliber of Sergio Panunzio and A. O. Olivetti.[18]

That synthesis of ideas and armed men was thrown into an environment in which important elements of society were in unstable combination. The localized industrial development that took place during the two decades that preceded the First World War prompted a crisis of expectations among those caught up in the rapid economic changes. The financial and economic dislocations that followed the end of the conflict in Europe, together with the threats to property mounted by doctrinaire socialists in both town and country, worked to the advantage of Fascist squads. All those discomfitted and threatened turned to the Fascist *squadristi*, who promised a restoration of order and a rekindling of economic growth. Funding from just such sources supplied the weapons and made possible the mobility of those squads that became increasing efficient in destroying not only socialist forces, but any political opposition that by that time many saw as corrupt and inefficient – as well as essentially antinational and antidevelopmental in inspiration.

---

[18] For an account of the belief system and the intellectuals responsible for its articulation during the first period of pre-Fascist and Fascist mobilization, see A. James Gregor, *Young Mussolini and the Intellectual Origins of Fascism* (Los Angeles: University of California Press, 1979).

All those proprietors of small landholdings, who for the first time had acquired land in the wartime boom, finding themselves threatened by the socialist demand for land redistribution, were quick to provide material and moral support to the Fascists. The struggle against the socialist leagues in the agrarian countryside of northern Italy expanded and drew still more support for Fascist activity.

The socialist and communist seizure of the factories in the urban sector in the years immediately following the war mobilized opposition from almost all segments of the population. The seizure of workplaces by radical organizations left whole regions without an effective economy. Those who had seized the factories could not maintain production, ship products, nor market them effectively. Ultimately, the effort at "revolutionary expropriation" disintegrated, leaving behind only a cynical population ready to accept the intervention of any political force that held forth the promise of order and stability.

By the time Fascism decided to make its effort to seize power on the peninsula, it had collected around itself support that actively or passively included almost all population categories. In their ranks, the Fascist syndicates included hundreds of thousands of urban and agrarian workers, and its armed squads enlisted tens of thousands of combat veterans and students. In forays against the urban centers, Fascist squads seized administrations and occupied whole cities. Throughout critical regions of the country, they systematically destroyed socialist and communist communications and control facilities and dispersed party members.

By 1922, with Fascism's rural organizations controlling the northern countryside – favored, and often aided and abetted, by the nation's security forces – there no longer was any opposition that might thwart Mussolini's purpose. In October of that year, Mussolini assumed the responsibilities as head of government on the invitation of the king, Vittorio Emanuele III.

Mussolini brought with him a clutch of ideas – formulated in the years before his accession to power – that clearly shared an intrinsic logic. He had woven together the threads of a belief system that had its origins in the thought of intellectuals who had long preceded him. Like them, he saw the people of the peninsula suffering depredations that had endured for countless years.

One of the themes iterated and reiterated during and immediately after the end of the First World War was the fact that Italy and Italians had been "humiliated for centuries" – dismissed as of little historic moment. Italians were "mandolin players," the ineffectual denizens of an insignificant country that provided little more than a vacation playground for dynamic North Europeans.[19] The "plutocrats" of the north acknowledged

---

[19] Benito Mussolini, "Scoperte...." *Opera omnia* (Milan: La Fenice, 1952–63. [hereafter cited as *Oo*.]), 11, p. 288.

Italy only insofar as they found it an interesting place where they might turn over ancient rocks and visit equally ancient ruins in their leisure time.[20]

Mussolini was emphatic in his insistence that the valor and sacrifice of troops along the Carso and the Piave had redeemed Italian manhood forever.[21] The troops, who had paid with their lives and limbs for the victory, had established that manhood for themselves and the emerging nation.

When the veterans organized themselves in the Fascist squads that were to win the political victories that brought Mussolini to power, they insisted on wearing their uniforms, adorned with their medals of valor, in what has been spoken of as "masculine protest" – the reaction of a people long demeaned as inferiors by those from the more industrially advanced nations. They, themselves, chose to retain military bearing, and sought to impose it on the nation.

Those postures reflected the psychology of a people whom Mussolini insisted had long suffered abuse at the hands of foreigners. Italy was to take its place beside those who had earned recognition for themselves in the military history of the world. He held that from the eighteenth through the nineteenth centuries, the long-suffering nation had found itself a beast of burden in yoke to advanced industrial powers. If Italy was to be "reborn" as a new race of warrior-producers,[22] even against the disposition of those Italians who had habituated themselves to the abuse of foreigners,[23] it would require the development of an independent economic base – accelerated economic growth as well as industrial and technological proficiency – predicated on a foundation of accessible raw materials, capital resources, and the acquisition of skills.[24] The redemption of the nation required intensified production if it were to meet the challenges of international economic, and future military, competition.[25]

---

[20] One of the most revealing instances of this is Mussolini's angry characterization of the judgment by "plutocrats" of "Italietta" – the "little Italy" of their stereotype. Mussolini, "Torino," *Oo*, 14, p. 424. See his acid reference to the sacrifice of "mandolin playing" Italians in the defeat of the Central Powers. Mussolini, "Epilogo," *Oo*, 11, p. 456.

[21] See, for example, Mussolini, "Restituire Caporetto," *Oo*, 11, pp. 436–8; "La vittoria è nostra!" *Oo*, 11, 452–3; "Epilogo," *Oo*, 11, p. 454; "L'ora della gioia," *Oo*, 11, 455–7.

[22] See Mussolini, "Intermezzo velivolare," *Oo*, 11, p. 171.

[23] Mussolini spoke candidly of the fact that the re-creation of Italians had been conducted, since the time of Risorgimento, against the resistance of Italians themselves. Mussolini, "La data," *Oo*, 11, p. 370.

[24] These were recurrent themes throughout the entire Fascist period. They are highlighted here to establish their early iteration by Mussolini himself.

[25] Mussolini, "La vittorio fatale," *Oo*, 11, pp. 79–87, particularly pp. 86–7; "Nell'attesa," *Oo*, 10, p. 21; "Il nostro dovere è quello di liberarci dal giogo della plutocrazia internazionale," *Oo*, 14, pp. 222–4; "Per rinascere e progredire: Politica orientale," *Oo*, 14, 225–7; "Sindacalismo francese: Una dichiarazione programma," *Oo*, 14, pp. 246–7; "Variazioni su vecchio motivo: Il fucile e la vanga," *Oo*, 11, pp. 34–5.

By 1918, Mussolini identified the survivors of the trenches not only as warriors, but as "producers," as those prepared to labor, in discipline and sacrifice, in the service of national redemption.[26] They would serve the nation as a "new aristocracy" – a hierarchically deployed aristocracy of will and determination. Having suffered, they would be prepared to suffer further for the nation.[27] It was they who represented the "new Italy." The old Italy of itinerant balladeers and tour guides was to disappear in the thunder of machines, the clammer of construction, and the rumble of blasting powder. "The essential," Mussolini told his followers in 1918, "is to produce. That," he went on, "is to be the beginning." In the course of that process, revolutionary workers and combat veterans would discharge "an historic function."[28] If Italy once more was to be great, it would have to sustain that greatness with its potentially "marvelous industrial power."[29]

By that time, Mussolini had already rejected orthodox Marxism with all its "demogogic" convictions concerning the "final crisis of capitalism." He argued that not only was capitalism not suffering its terminal crisis, but the resurgent nation, emeshed in a web of foreign constraints, required the further extension and accelerated deepening of market-based enterprise. He identified the Fascist revolution with a "productive socialism," a socialism that rejected the anarchronism of class warfare in the service of the common interest. He cited the strategy of the French syndicalists, who did not reject industrial capitalism but chose to "insert themselves within its processes, to stimulate, perfect, energize and further its growth."[30] Mussolini identified the system of which he spoke as a synthesis of socialism and nationalism.[31]

Mussolini argued that the Marxism the world had witnessed with the Russian Revolution could only be a signal failure. Whatever had transpired in the Russian Revolution could hardly qualify, in his judgment, as "Marxist" in

---

[26] Mussolini accordingly changed the title of his daily newspaper, *Il popolo d'Italia*, to a "Journal of Veterans and Producers." See Mussolini, "Novità...." *Oo*, 11, p. 241. He spoke of the necessities of hierarchies and discipline in the development of production. See Mussolini, "Variazioni su vecchio motivo: Il fucile e la vanga," *Oo*, 11, p. 35. Mussolini reminded his audience that even Lenin had finally had to call for "discipline" among the workers of the "proletarian state." Discipline, Mussolini argued, was an essential part of rapid industrial development. See Mussolini, "Un appello alla solidarietà per gli scioperanti metallurgici aderenti all'U.S.M." *Oo*, 13, p. 348; "Crepuscoli: I templi e gli idoli," *Oo*, 14, p. 339.

[27] See Mussolini, "La vittoria fatale," *Oo*, 11, p. 87; "L'Ora presente," *Oo*, 11, p. 143. Mussolini regularly argued that those who had led Italy into the war, and served in its defense, were to be its leaders. See Mussolini, "L'Italia e immortale," *Oo*, 10, pp. 344–5, 348–9.

[28] Mussolini, "Orientamenti e problemi," *Oo*, 11, pp. 282–4; "L'adunata di Roma," *Oo*, 10, 433–5.

[29] See Mussolini, "Patria e terra," *Oo*, 10, pp. 55–6.

[30] Mussolini, "Nel mondo sindacale italiano: Rettifiche di tiro," *Oo*, 12, pp. 249–52; "Logica e demagogia," *Oo*, 14, pp. 85–7; "Sindacalismo francese: Una dichiarazione-programma," *Oo*, 14, p. 247.

[31] Mussolini, "Amilcare Cipriani è morto," *Oo*, 11, p. 37.

any responsible theoreticial sense. Karl Marx and Friedrich Engels had both insisted that the "proletarian revolution" could transpire and be successful only in the most highly industrialized nations, with their concentrations of capital, urbanization, and mobilization and training of workers. Those workers, easily massed and organized in cities, suffering "emiseration" – persistent and increasing underemployment and endemic poverty – would "ineluctably" be driven to revolution. Then the workers, already trained in its maintenance, would succeed in overtaking the productive system, distributing its goods, eliminating exploitation, and sustaining equity.

Instead of all that, the pretended followers of Marx made revolutions in the most backward parts of Europe: in the East and in Czarist Russia. In making their revolutions in those regions, Mussolini argued that Marxists had demonstrated their failure to understand their own theoretical convictions. They sought to make "proletarian revolution" in places where there were no proletarians, in retrograde economic conditions where even the best-intentioned revolutionaries could find only poverty, ignorance, and barbarism. They made revolutions that promised a redistribution of wealth where – because there was scant material production – there was little wealth to redistribute after the first redistributionist episodes.[32]

Mussolini argued that having failed to appreciate their own doctrinal commitments, the revolutionary Marxists of Russia could only damage their own economic base.[33] They exhausted resources and alienated both entrepreneurs and workers alike, making Russia singularly unattractive to foreign investors, and a threat to foreign governments.

What all that meant for Italians was that Marxism, in whatever form, would be damaging to the dream of the nation's rebirth. Rebirth required an enhancement of Italy's economic potential, an increase in agricultural production, together with a deepening and expansion of its industries. Every scintilla of evidence, Mussolini argued, confirmed that any attempt to impose a Leninist Marxism on the nation could only be disastrous to any efforts at economic growth and industrial expansion. A Marxist revolution on the peninsula would leave stillborn the nation's rebirth.

As it was, the rapid growth, extension and sophistication of the Italian economy would tax the nation's determination and human resources. It would require collaboration of all the elements of production, together with a measure of discipline and self-sacrifice that was martial in character. There was no place for "class warfare" in such circumstances.

---

[32] Mussolini, "Divagazioni pel centenario," *Oo*, 11, pp. 44–7; "Divagazione," *Oo*, 11, pp. 341–4; "Posizioni e obiettivi," *Oo*, 13, pp. 14–16; "Crepuscolo," *Oo*, 14, pp. 67–9; "Illusioni e mistificazioni: Il paradiso leninista," *Oo*, 14, pp. 117–18. See the discussion in Mussolini, "In Russia: Ritorno al capitalismo!" *Oo*, 14, pp. 366–8.

[33] See Mussolini, "Posizioni," *Oo*, 13, pp. 28–30; "La politica nazionale: Primo squillo," *Oo*, 12, pp. 222–3.

If it were to pursue greatness, Italy required the collaboration of all its citizens, as well as the acquisition and ready supply of almost every basic essential of industrial production. The Italian peninsula was bereft of coal and iron ore. Moreover, it required grain for a population that exceeded the carrying capacity of the soil.[34] It was a community that lacked investment capital. As one of the first consequences of its shortcomings, Italy was a nation that was compelled to concern itself with maritime trade and the freedom of the seas, because to achieve its rebirth as a major power, Italy required accelerated industrial development. That necessary condition required, in turn, steady increases in both import and export traffic.

Italy, to become an international competitor of the developed industrial powers, would not only have to import raw materials and foodstuffs, but export in sufficient abundance to pay for them. Mussolini was convinced that Italy, if it were to be successful, was compelled to assume, once again, its historic role as a major maritime power.[35] That would place it in direct competition with some of the advanced industrial nations. It would be a risk, Mussolini was to insist, that could not be avoided if Italy were to realize its ambitions.[36]

All of this makes very clear the central imperative upon which Mussolini's belief system turned: that Italy become, once again, and as rapidly as possible, a force with which the world would have to reckon.[37] No longer would the nation be subservient to that coalition of "plutocracies" – the advanced industrial powers – that had arbitrarily partitioned the world into their own colonies and spheres of influence. In Mussolini's judgment, those powers, sated and powerful, sought to maintain, in perpetuity, Italy's subservient role as a "proletarian" resource of cheap labor and a market supplement to absorb advanced capitalism's surplus products.[38]

By the time Fascism had established itself as a revolutionary force on the Italian peninsula, it had settled on its decisive doctrinal imperatives. Mussolini insisted that there was but one directive that guided his activities: to pursue whatever efforts might contribute to the restored grandeur of the

---

[34] See the discussion in Mussolini, "La politica estera di domani: L'Italia e l'Oriente," *Oo*, 14, pp. 217–20.

[35] Mussolini, "Per rinascere e progredire: Italia marinara, avanti!" *Oo*, 14, pp. 203–6.

[36] See the relevant discussion in Robert Mallett, *The Italian Navy and Fascist Expansionism 1935–1940* (London: Frank Cass, 1998), particularly chap. 1.

[37] See Mussolini, "Discorso di Piazza Belgioioso," *Oo*, 14, p. 124.

[38] See Mussolini, "Gesto di rivolta," *Oo*, 14, p. 5; "Governo vile!" *Oo*, 14, pp. 8–9; "Il Bavaglio," *Oo*, 14, pp. 12–13; "Decidersi o perire!" *Oo*, 14, pp. 28–9; "Il discorso," *Oo*, 14, pp. 30–1; "Per rinascere e progredire: Politica orientale," *Oo*, 14, p. 227. Mussolini spoke of Italy as a "proletarian nation" surrounded by those that were sated and "bourgeois." See Mussolini, "Ideali e affari," *Oo*, 13, p. 72; "Un altro passo," *Oo*, 13, pp. 228–30. At the founding meeting of the Fasci di combattimento, in March 1919, Mussolini spoke of the "rich nations" seeking to keep those nations that were "proletarian" in perpetual bondage. Mussolini, "Atto di nascita del fascismo," *Oo*, 13, p. 323.

Italian people. For Fascists, the governing enjoinment of that effort was: "the nation before and above all else."[39]

To serve the nation's rebirth, Mussolini held that the "commanding imperative" – governing all the efforts to serve the nation's majesty – was "production." Whatever system ultimately prevailed on the peninsula, it would have to foster, sustain, and enhance the material productivity of the nation.[40]

It is, within that context, that Mussolini's tactics during the initial period of Fascist mobilization are to be understood. He spoke, without restraint, of extraordinary taxes to be imposed on the "excess profits" made by some capitalists during the war – as one form of "primitive capital accumulation" so necessary for development.[41] He also spoke of imposing discipline on those proletarians whose work stoppages impaired the productivity of the nation.[42] And he spoke of compelling all human factors of production to assume their daunting historic responsibilities.

Mussolini could take such positions, threatening to alienate almost every active category of the nation's citizenry, because he was convinced that his revolution tapped the sentiment and interests of at least that significant minority necessary for the provision of support and sustenance for his movement.[43] He argued that there was really very little substance in what Marxists chose to identify as "class interests." Mussolini held that the notion of "class" was, in significant measure, at best, obscure.[44] Human beings were informed by more general interests than those of class or simple economic category. Historic and cultural entities, such as the nation, invoked in human beings a readiness to discipline and sacrifice largely misunderstood by those who had not gone through the school of nineteenth- and early-twentieth-century Italian social science.[45]

---

39 Mussolini, "La prima adunata fascista," *Oo*, 14, p. 44.

40 Mussolini, "Per l'intesa e per l'azione fra gli interventisti di sinistra," *Oo*, 13, p. 252. See also Mussolini, "Chi possiede, paghi!" *Oo*, 13, p. 224. In general, Mussolini argued that production was central to the political concerns of Italians. See Mussolini, "Cifre da meditare," *Oo*, 13, pp. 282–4. It is clear that it was not only a preoccupation with well-being, but with international political and ultimately military power. See, for example, Mussolini, "Dopo quattro anni," *Oo*, 11, pp. 54–6; "La vittoria fatale," *Oo*, 11, pp. 79–87.

41 See Mussolini's allusions in "L'Ordine regna...," *Oo*, 11, pp. 191–2.

42 See Mussolini's discussion in "Consensi," *Oo*, 11, p. 349, where he informs workers' organization that Fascists will defend their rights as long as those "rights" do not threaten production and thereby compromise the nation's future.

43 Years later, in his interview with Emil Ludwig, Mussolini identified the levers of political mobilization as both sentiment and interest. See his account in Emil Ludwig, *Colloqui con Mussolini* (Verona: Arnoldo Mondadori Editore, 1932), pp. 119–20.

44 Mussolini, "XIV Luglio," *Oo*, 11, p. 204.

45 See Mussolini's discussion in "Terza, ma forse non ultima divagazione: 'Tu quoque' Jouhaux?" *Oo*, 11, pp. 356–60. See the discussion of Mussolini's background in Gregor, *Young Mussolini and the Intellectual Origins of Fascism*, chaps. 3–7.

Mussolini argued, moreover, that the entire notion of class and class interests was largely irrelevant in the situation in which the Fascists found themselves. That was because most families in Italy had, during the long years of war, either lost a loved one or had some member who had served in the defense of the nation. The result was the "sanctification," through their blood and sacrifice, of the Fatherland.[46] That sentiment overrode any presumptive class interest. The explicit program of rapid and extensive economic development would muster everyone to the cause, whether because the war had made the nation an object of irrepressible sentimental reverence, or because everyone – peasants, workers, landholders, manual laborers, entrepreneurs, and managers – could anticipate real and material benefit from the economic growth and industrial development that would result.[47]

Given such a collection of convictions, it is not difficult to understand which beliefs were strategic and which were tactical for Mussolini. Taxing the propertied classes, expropriating Church possessions, or maintaining a system of low wages, could all serve as tactical devices for generating investment capital. All, together and/or individually, served the ultimate purpose of accelerating production and contributing to the international competitiveness of the Fatherland. Which tactic was chosen at any given juncture was largely a function of circumstances and the advice that Mussolini, and his entourage, chose to consider.

For at least a significant period, several years after the assumption of power, for example, Mussolini was clearly influenced by the free-market liberalism of Vilfredo Pareto and Maffeo Pantaleoni. They both favored economic liberalism and argued for the reduction of state involvement in specifically economic matters.[48]

Pantaleoni made very clear his adherence to Fascism, precisely for the reasons Mussolini had early expressed: Italy required rapid economic development; Bolshevism had demonstrated that its efforts to control the stabilization and expansion of the economy through state agencies were a monumental failure; and history afforded ample evidence that market-governed economies are those most capable of dynamic growth and technological

---

[46] Mussolini, "L'Italia e immortale," *Oo*, 10, pp. 348–9. Mussolini regularly spoke of the "unity" that the sacrifices of the war had wrought in Italy. See "Ancora un discorso," *Oo*, 11, p. 277.

[47] See Mussolini, "Sui fatti del 15 Aprile 1919," *Oo*, 13, pp. 73–4. See Mussolini's discussion of the "social content" of the war in "Patria e terra," *Oo*, 10, pp. 55–7; "Produrre per vincere," *Oo*, 10, 99–101; "Fra il segreto e il pubblico," *Oo*, 10, pp. 137–9; "Trincerocrazia," *Oo*, 10, pp. 140–2; "Il prestito della riscossa: Milano darà un miliardo?" *Oo*, 10, pp. 258–60.

[48] See the reflection of their judgments in Mussolini's discussion of the "Manchestrian state" as appropriate for Italy. Mussolini, "Divagazione: L'ora e gli orologi," *Oo*, 14, pp. 396–8. Some of these notions found their way into some of Fascism's earliest doctrinal statements.

articulation.[49] As long as Mussolini found such arguments persuasive, he conformed Fascist tactics to their requirements. The goals remained constant, the tactics might alter.

Fascist tactics did alter over time and in response to circumstance. But there was something more in the change of tactics than simply opportunism. It was clear that Mussolini entertained an entire collection of notions concerning governance that provided the argued basis of his overall political behavior. Behavior would be a function of holding certain convictions as constants, deriving recommended behaviors from them by introducing some contingent factors as qualifiers. One might plausibly explain a good deal of the behavior of the Fascist regime by drawing inferences from some set of premises that support that behavior once the constants, and impinging contingencies upon which the inference depends, are identified.

What is being suggested is that a kind of primitive calculus can be reconstructed that reveals something of the implicit reasoning that serves as a preamble to the conduct. Positing the central primacy of the nation, and holding some empirical premises as true, one can begin to explain some of the decisions made by the Fascist leadership.

Holding the primacy of the nation, its redemption and restoration, as a constant, Fascist policies can be credibly assessed as a function of entertaining that fixed premise in conjunction with some other, empirical and time-specific premises. Thus, Mussolini always believed that a people, any people, considered collectively, provided leaders with the raw material out of which almost anything might be fashioned. If a people, as raw material, were to serve as a factor in the re-creation of a nation, certain conditions would have to obtain. Mussolini was convinced that human beings, particularly when they found themselves facing special difficulties, would instinctively respond to confident leadership, authority, and hierarchical control – in an arrangement that might best be depicted as *military*.

Fascist experience had come together to fuse the masculine protest of combat veterans with the management and motivational requirements of rapid economic growth and industrial development. Italy was to proceed, in uniform, with its program of accelerated expansion. Uniforms proliferated, and workers, students, and children were organized in paramilitary legions and cohorts. Italy was to make itself a "Great Nation," marching in martial cadence. Mussolini was convinced that such arrangements, accompanied by dramatic ceremony and quasireligious liturgy, were essential to the achievement of purpose when a people is called to sacrifice and protracted effort. It is all necessary for the success of a people

---

[49] See the discussion in Maffeo Pantaleoni, *Bolcevismo italiano* (Bari: Gius, Laterza & Figli, 1922). Pantaleoni makes his Fascist sympathies emphatic throughout the text. There is ample evidence that Mussolini found the thought of Pareto and Pantaleoni important in terms of the initial Fascist programs.

that finds itself in a Darwinian world of threat, high moral tension, and stress.[50]

Under such circumstances, Mussolini argued, conjointly with the recommended arrangements, only that information should be supplied that would generate, sustain, and enhance a unanimity of opinion and commitment essential to secure success in enterprise. That, together with the carefully choreographed ritual and ceremony, was understood to be essential to the furtherance of active consensus. Mussolini argued that just that kind of political system was calculated to deliver leadership the highest probability of success.[51]

Mussolini made it clear, before his accession to power, that he believed such population management techniques were more critical to political leadership and its success than material advantages. He held that such techniques should simply be part of the management inventory employed by serious revolutionary leaders. The orchestration of opinion, the function of political theater, and the creation of a moral consensus governing the behavior of masses, were matters of the most "elementary collective psychology."[52]

If one holds constant Mussolini's political imperatives, together with the management techniques to which he was committed as early as 1917, one easily anticipates the central features of the regime he would create in the 1930s. Questions of economic liberalism and patterns of taxation were, at the very best, transitory concerns of his rule. The central properties of the regime turned on certain Fascist postulates operative in the historic, economic, social, and political circumstances of the two decades between 1922 and 1945. In effect, once his political perspective is understood, Mussolini's rule was no more "contradictory," "venal," or "opportunistic" than that of almost any other political system, authoritarian or democratic. Its "pragmatism" was governed largely by judgments that result from calculations based on holding some few principles constant within a given set of variable conditions.

The political regime crafted by Mussolini was a product of holding certain imperatives constant in changing contexts. Those constants are fairly obvious. For the most part, they have been captured by the descriptive accounts

---

[50] In this context, see Mussolini's very candid comments concerning population mobilization in his discussion with Ludwig, *Colloqui con Mussolini*, pp. 119–30.

[51] Mussolini, "I nostri postulati: Disciplina di guerra," *Oo*, 10, pp. 36–8; "I nostri postulati: Per la storia di una settimana," *Oo*, 10, p. 87; "Tutto ai nostri soldati," *Oo*, 10, pp. 299–301; "Un po' di verità nel paradosso: I giornali sono necessari?" *Oo*, 10, pp. 316–19; "Il 'morale'," *Oo*, 11, pp. 132–4.

[52] Mussolini, "Tutto ai nostri soldati," p. 300. Years later, Mussolini elaborated on these principles of population management to Emil Ludwig. He spoke of masses requiring leadership and societies necessitating leadership. He spoke of the role of gestures, rituals, and political liturgies, all in the service of molding those who are governed. Lugwig, *Colloqui con Mussolini*, pp. 121–5.

that have come down to us. We can say, with considerable confidence, that the Fascist movement and the regime that was its subsequent embodiment were supremely *nationalistic*. The legitimating charter *myth* of the system was the nation.[53]

In the operations of Fascism as a political system, the concept of political myth served a central purpose. For Mussolini, a "myth" was neither an irrationality nor a fiction. It was a figure of speech that gave expression to an "ideal representation of a possible future." It was calculated to "reinforce the will, and consolidate the faith."[54] To secure the grandeur of the nation, as a case in point, would entail efforts that would tax the loyalty and obedience of a people, as well as extract a measure of sacrifice rarely demanded of subjects. To sustain such efforts, inspiration was required – and only myth might so serve. For Fascists, the charter myth behind its simple and complex political strategies was the restoration of the lost grandeur of the Fatherland.

Fascists believed that to achieve the greatness of the nation in the contemporary world, the satisfaction of at least one necessary condition was essential: rapid economic growth and industrial expansion. To accomplish that effectively, the nation must undertake a total mobilization of human and material resources organized in economic categories that, together, made up the corporative arrangements through which the state would exercise directive, if collaborative, control.[55] The demand for sustained effort and commitment in unity necessitated, in turn, the suppression of any dissidence that threatened to dissipate energy.

The effort to preclude the occurrence of any such dissidence recommended the systematic control over all the sources of information, ranging from general and specific education to news production and distribution. The effective channeling of collective energies suggested nothing less to Mussolini and his followers.

What immediately suggests itself is that *any institution* that would attend and sustain such a system would be *one in which* there could only be, in all probability, one dominant, hegemonic party led by a political elite convinced of its moral right to rule: an epistemocracy. Such a system is predicated on the conviction that those who made successful revolution were certified by that success as being not only possessed of moral authority and associated virtues, but sagacity as well.

---

[53] See the discussion in Gregor, *The Ideology of Fascism*, pp. 191–3.

[54] Mussolini, "Resistere per vincere!" *Oo*, 10, p. 195.

[55] As early as 1920, Mussolini spoke of "committees of competence," and of the formation of "national technical councils of labor, industry, transportation, communication and social services, composed of elected professionals," who would engage rights and responsibilities in a ministry of their own. This anticipated the principal features of the subsequent "Fascist Corporative State." See Mussolini, "Dopo un anno: Il fascismo," *Oo*, 14, p. 380. For a more extensive account, see Gregor, *Mussolini's Intellectuals*.

The control structure of the system was the analog of military command. With the nation in uniform, one could easily anticipate that, in time, the system's survival might recommend that both authority and wisdom be embodied in a single leader rather than a vanguard party composed of potentially fractious constituents. As in any military command, responsibility must ultimately devolve upon one person. As is the case with military leadership, such a leader would not only become the linchpin of the system, but would provide those subject to his command the suggestion of infallible guidance that would see them through the long and arduous periods of challenge and contest. Such a belief in the infallibility of leadership might well be required by those suffering an indefinite postponement of personal goals and individual comforts.

All this is easily understood, given the environment in which it takes place. The "unfailing leader" would provide the emotional sustenance for a people required to potentially risk personal losses and collective devastation, in the struggle and sacrifice that was almost inevitable if the Fatherland were to secure its place in the sun in any encounters with the advanced industrial powers.

The system, even as it was developing, described itself as totalitarian. What was sought was a seamless union of people and political leadership, committed to national renewal, the creation of a new civilization, and to the making of new citizens to be its stalwarts. "Totalitarianism" was a term that seemed to capture such features.

The new citizens who were expected to be the products of totalitarianism, as a political system, would be unique human beings. They were expected to be indefatigable, heroic, and selfless warrior-producers, who saw in death for the Fatherland their ultimate moral fulfillment.[56] They were to be the "new men" anticipated in the very first doctrinal statements of Fascism as a movement.

Out of such recognition, one can distill a credible criterial list of prominent traits that one might pretend to employ not only to identify Mussolini's Fascism, but any of its possible variants. Fascism was an antidemocratic, intensely nationalistic system, infilled by a formal ideology, employed to justify totalitarian rule, which, coupled with the repression of opposition and the employment of ceremony and ritual to evoke and sustain an ethic of sacrifice and obedience, was designed to achieve national redemption. That redemption was clearly predicated on several instrumentalities – accelerated economic growth and industrial expansion – necessary as a support base for military development and the required production of sophisticated weapons

---

[56] All of this can be found in Mussolini, "La dottrina del Fascismo," *Oo*, 34, pp. 117–38. The first portion of the *dottrina* was written by Giovanni Gentile, who supplied Fascism its essentially philosophic and normative content. See A. James Gregor, *Giovanni Gentile: Philosopher of Fascism* (New Brunswick, NJ: Transaction, 2001).

platforms. Such a system suggests potentialities that do not augur well for the peaceful resolution of international problems. One would expect such a system to be reactive, assertive, and irredentist – in general, more given to violence than debate. And such seemed to be the case.

Mussolini chose to bring Italy into a war against powers possessed of potential industrial and military capabilities that would tax the response capacities of a country that had barely emerged from an essentially agrarian economy. Conflict in Ethiopia and the military adventure in Spain had all but exhausted the material and psychological resources of Fascist Italy. The Second World War demonstrated its military inferiority.

The Fascist experiment was overwhelmed by the catastrophic losses that attended Italy's participation in the war. Allied wartime propaganda succeeded in identifying the domestic regime with that of Adolf Hitler, and Fascism was evermore to remain indistinguishable from Nazism for many Western scholars.

As a result, Fascism was depicted as a reactionary, homicidal militarism committed to little more than deluding Italians into thinking that Italy might become a major international power. As a characterizaion of Fascism, it resulted only in mischief. Any movement or regime held to be brutal or militaristic was immediately identified as fascist or neofascist. The terms became simple terms of derogation. The identification of Fascism with National Socialism has served very little purpose.

That is not to say that the criterial definition that sees Fascism to have been an intensely nationalistic, antidemocratic, totalitarian, single-party–dominant, developmental system, animated by a mass-mobilizing formal ideology, irredentist in character, and essentially militaristic, promises success in the study of neofascisms.

Such a criterial account perhaps serves didactic purpose, but its utility as a heuristic device requires considerable honing. The properties attributed to Fascism in any such a summary catalog are not provided any sort of "operational definition." How, for example, might "intense nationalism" be measured, in order to distinguish it from less-than-intense nationalism? When the leaders of the former Soviet Union spoke of "Soviet patriotism," was that an exemplar of "intense nationalism"? If not, why not?

What of the "formality" of an ideology? How is the "formality" of a collection of convictions measured? Does "formality" require logical integrity? If so, in what measure?

One might so proceed throughout the entire criterial list. The fact is that such a list best serves not as a heuristic guide for research, but as a mnemonic aid, providing cues for recalling to mind a long and complicated history. Only after one had learned a great deal about the history of Mussolini's Fascism might it be summarized, to some cognitive purpose, in terms of such a criterial list of traits. Unless the list succeeds in conjuring up the substance of which it is an abstraction, the list, in and of itself, is anything but helpful in identifying "fascisms."

Problems arise when one does not use such a criterial list as a recall device, but attempts to employ it as a sorting device to isolate, out of the prodigal abundance of the actual world of political movements and regimes, those movements and regimes one would call "fascist" – and worse yet, "neofascist," "protofascist," "parafascist," or "cryptofascist." The reason for that is fairly obvious.

The proposed list does not offer any specificity concerning the required measure of each property a movement or regime must display to qualify, nor does it indicate how many of the traits, out of the total number, a movement or regime must evidence to satisfy the entry criteria for admission into the class of "fascisms," "neofascisms," or whatever. One is left with the necessity of making intuitive choices. The result can only be arbitrary decisions, often counterintuitive to those who appreciate the responsibilities that accompany classification in the social sciences.

Consider the following as cases in point: In reviewing the criterial list, does it unequivocally identify Mussolini's Fascism as "rightist"? Does such a list necessarily exclude "Marxist" movements and regimes? Are Marxist movements and regimes excluded a priori – even when such movements and regimes display one or more of the criterial properties? If they are so excluded under such circumstances, is it because those traits are somehow measurably different from those of fascist movements and regimes? The fact is that many authors simply decide, quite arbitrarily, that one or another movement or regime qualifies as "fascist," "rightist," or "reactionary," and others do not. For example, some authors include the interwar Romanian Legion of the Archangel Michael as fascist. Others include the Hungarian Arrow Cross as well. At the same time, others, equally informed, refuse to identify either as fascist, instead speaking of both as "false fascisms."[57]

How might one describe the regime of Fidel Castro? It seems reasonably evident that it displays at least some of the criterial properties of "fascism."[58] How, then, does one decide that it does *not* qualify as either "neofascism," "protofascism," or a titillating "cryptofascism"? And what of

---

[57] Compare Mariano Ambri, *I falsi fascismi: Ungheria, Jugoslavia, Romania 1919–1945* (Rome: Jouvence, 1980), and Nicholas M. Nagly-Talavera, *The Green Shirts and the Others: A History of Fascism in Hungary and Rumania* (Stanford, CA: Hoover Institution Press, 1970).

[58] Maurice Bardeche, who is one of the few authors of the post–World War II period who identified himself as a "fascist," argued that Castro's regime displayed many of the traits of Mussolini's Fascism. The question is, how many of the criterial traits cataloged must a movement or regime display before it qualifies as a "fascism"? Ultimately, Bardeche decided Castroism was not a fascism, but see the discussion in Maurice Bardeche, *Qu'est-ce que le Fascisme?* (Paris: Les Sept Couleurs, 1961), Part 2, chap. 3.

the contemporary People's Republic of China? Does it feature such traits?[59] If so, is contemporary "Marxist" China perhaps "quasifascist"?

Social scientists have long recognized these classificatory problems. They are behind the controversial, long-ago decision to consider all radical, antidemocratic, mass-mobilizing, single-party–dominant, ideocratic movements and regimes, led by "charismatics," to be members of a family of movements and regimes categorized as "totalitarian."[60] Whatever distinguished Marxist from "fascist" movements or regimes were considered *subspecific* differences within a species. For years, social scientists of all levels of competence have debated these issues. All of this serves as testimony to the difficulties that surround "experimental naming" in empirical social science.

What seems perfectly clear in all of this is that Mussolini, and the best of Fascist theoreticians, recognized the evident similarities between Fascism and Marxist-Leninist regimes.[61] They acknowledged the shared properties and anticipated that ultimately all single-party regimes would approximate each other in terms of institutional features that were understood to be the result of functional requirements.

Understanding that, it is not difficult to appreciate why the comparative study of nondemocratic, epistemarchic, single-party, and totalitarian movements and regimes taxes the ingenuity of academics. What properties, for example, made Mussolini's Fascism uniquely "rightist"? Should it be the "protection" of private property afforded by the system? Should that be the case, why should post-Maoist China be considered "leftist" now that it not only shares features with Mussolini's Fascism, but provides institutional protection for property?

As will be indicated, many Marxists have lamented that post-Maoist China had transformed itself into a "socialism with fascist characteristics."[62] Similar complaints were lodged against the Soviet Union some considerable time before its disappearance. Undone in all of that was the distinction

---

[59] I have undertaken a discussion of just such a possibility in A. James Gregor, *A Place in the Sun: Marxism and Fascism in China's Long Revolution* (Boulder, CO: Westview Press, 2000).

[60] See the discussion in Ernest A. Menze (ed.), *Totalitarianism Reconsidered* (London: Kennikat Press, 1981). Any number of volumes have been devoted to this issue. For some time, the term "totalitarianism" has referred to an acknowledged category in social science lexicons. See, for example, Leonard Schapiro, *Totalitarianism* (New York: Praeger, 1972).

[61] See Mussolini's comments in Ludwig, *Colloqui con Mussolini*, pp. 92, 129, 148. Particularly instructive is the analysis of Sergio Panunzio, one of Fascism's major theoreticians, in Sergio Panunzio, *Teoria general dello stato fascista* (Padua: CEDAM, 1939), particularly pp. 3–14, 458–73. There were any number of comparative studies of single-party governance and totalitarianism among theoreticians during the Fascist and National Socialist period in Europe. See, for example, Mihail Manoilescu, *Die einzige Partei* (Berlin: Stollberg, 1941).

[62] See, for example, the comments of Charles Bettleheim, in Charles Bettelheim and Neil Burton, *China Since Mao* (New York: Monthly Review Press, 1978), pp. 78, 112. See the entire discussion in Chen Erjin, *China: Crossroads Socialism* (London: Verso, 1984).

between the "revolutionary left" and the "reactionary right" traditionally entertained by academic comparativists.[63]

It has been within these fundamental complexities that social science has proceeded to attempt the study of that collection of post–World War II movements and regimes that some have sought to classify as neofascisms. At the beginning of the effort, it seemed that the enterprise might enjoy some success. In the period immediately following the end of the Second World War, most social scientists were prepared to entertain an intuitive distinction between "left-wing" revolutionary movements and regimes and those that were characterized as "right-wing." It was said, at the time, that the left-wing regimes served the interests of the working classes while those on the right served the interests of the possessing classes. Very few still continue to entertain that thought. That the Soviet or Maoist "proletarian dictatorship" was committed to the interests of workers has long since shown itself to be as idle as the notion that Mussolini's "State of Labor" truly concerned itself exclusively with the interests of the workers.

Some hung the left/right distinction on the conviction that the right-wing regimes of then-recent memory – Mussolini's Fascism and Hitler's National Socialism – favored private property and capitalism, in general, while the regimes on the left opposed both. That seemed to be sufficient to support the intuitive distinction. None of that seems decisive any longer.

Other than that, it was held at the time that while the right was guilty of mass murder, the left was not. The world had suffered through the gruesome revelations that followed the conquest of National Socialist Germany. Everyone had been exposed to the evidence of carnage in the death camps. Only when it became evident that the left-wing regimes were as guilty of mass murder as those of the right were reservations introduced. The disposition to commit mass murder could no longer serve as a uniquely distinguishing species trait of right-wing "reactionary" movements or regimes. The evidence reveals that the "revolutionary" left-wing regimes of Stalin, Mao, and Pol Pot have left us a history of human bestiality and homocidal violence that easily matches that of National Socialist Germany.

It was precisely within that context that Hannah Arendt, one of the most prominent social science thinkers of the immediate postwar period, made a point of the relative benignity of Mussolini's Fascism in terms of political repression and mass murder when compared to the homicidal regimes of some of those on the left.[64] However unwelcome the fact was to their left-wing supporters in the industrial democracies, some left-wing revolutionary

---

[63] I have attempted to deal with these issues in more detail in A. James Gregor, *The Faces of Janus: Marxism and Fascism in the Twentieth Century* (New Haven, CT: Yale University Press, 2000), and *A Place in the Sun*.

[64] See Hannah Arendt, *The Origins of Totalitarianism* (New York: Harcourt, Brace, 1951), particularly pp. 303–4, p. 303, n. 8.

movements and regimes were more oppressive and murderous than some of the "reactionary" movements and regimes on the right.

Over the years immediately following the end of the Second World War, it became increasingly evident that the hard distinctions, entertained by some commentators, between the left and right with respect to the interwar dictatorships could no longer be defended without qualification. Even the distinctions with respect to property and class, defended with such intransigency by their protagonists, began to dissipate as Marxist regimes began to experiment with market adjuncts to their respective command economies – until finally China's Communist Party not only allowed private property to flourish, and market modalities to govern large segments of the national economy, but to invite capitalists themselves to join the party and in effect enter into the control apparatus of the state.[65]

For a time after the termination of the Second World War, the study of neofascism could proceed without such considerations. Often, neofascism could be identified because of the biological continuity between the "old" Fascists and the "new" neofascists. The leadership of the neofascist groups often consisted of persons who had survived the apocalyptic destruction of the ruling Fascist party at the conclusion of the military conflict.

Even though many of those movements expressed only few of the doctrinal commitments of interwar Fascism, the presence in the ranks, or among their leadership, of members of the old party was enough to license their identification as "neofascist."[66] With the passing of those age cohorts, there was less and less that might legitimize the identification of such groups as members of the class of postwar fascisms.

Coupled with the revelations concerning oppression, incarceration, racism, and mass murder in so-called left-wing revolutionary systems, the academic pursuit of neofascism as "right-wing" and "reactionary" produced results that became more and more unconvincing. However one chooses to characterize right-wing movements, as distinct from those of the left, it is not at all clear that "right-wing extremism" can be equated, with any confidence, with historic Fascism. The entire enterprise becomes still further fraught with problems when individuals, movements, or regimes are identified vaguely as "parafascist," "protofascist," or "cryptofascist." At some point, tax protesters, soccer thugs, graveyard vandals, money cranks, religious fanatics, sexual deviants, racists, and footpads are all mustered into the

---

[65] See Bruce J. Dickson, *Red Capitalists in China: The Party, Private Entrepreneurs, and Prospects for Political Change* (New York: Cambridge University Press, 2003); compare Gregor, *A Place in the Sun*, particularly chaps. 6–7.

[66] I have argued elsewhere that even the Movimento sociale italiano (MSI), the survivor movement of Italian Fascism, was not really Fascist in any doctrinal sense. Built on a basis of nostalgia and loyalties to defunct leaders, the MSI displayed less of the presumed features of Fascism than did some of the Marxist parties. See A. James Gregor, *Phoenix: Fascism in Our Time* (New Brunswick, NJ: Transaction, 1999), chap. 1.

subject ranks of presumptive neofascism, and it is no longer at all certain just what is being studied.

This is the unhappy state in which the study of neofascism is currently found. A great deal of activity has collected itself around the undertaking, but it is not at all clear what has been or is being accomplished.

What seems to recommend itself is a reasonably careful review of what those who would study neofascism have attempted: What have they considered to be its properties? How have they assessed some of the candidates who have been advanced as being representative of "neofascism" as a class? Reflection might also be directed to those political organizations and movements on the left that have *not* been considered members of the class but which, nonetheless, seem to display some of the prominent properties of paradigmatic Fascism. The results might well be helpful in trying to understand something about the complex and threatening world of the twenty-first century.

3

Neofascism

Some Presumptive Candidates

As has been suggested, in the years immediately following the end of the Second World War, lay persons, journalists, and academics began to speak of "neofascism" to identify those small groups of individuals, formerly National Socialists or Fascists, who had survived the carnage of the conflict and who continued to identify, in some sense or other, with their past loyalties. Given the propaganda conveniences afforded by the practice, we have seen that it had become standard, in the course of the Second World War, simply to refer to both National Socialist Germany and Fascist Italy as "fascist."[1] The manifest differences between the two movements and regimes notwithstanding, the practice continued after the war. As a result, in the years immediately following the Second World War, any individuals and their political activities that could be directly or indirectly associated with either Hitler's Germany or Mussolini's Italy were spoken of as representing a generic "neofascism" – a characterization that generally meant little more than that the individuals and/or groups involved showed some real or presumed sympathy for the Nazism and/or Fascism of their respective nation's past. In general, the term was applied to such individuals and the disjointed, fragmentary and transient associations in which they collected themselves.[2] Little concern was devoted to the coherence, integrity, or fascist quality of their individual or collective belief systems. They were all simply neofascists, indelibly identified by their individual histories and connected by the most casual of associations.

In the years immediately following the termination of the war, there were any number of such small groups, usually composed of survivors of the Nazi

---

[1] See the discussion in Renzo De Felice, *Rosso e Nero* (Milano: Baldini & Castoldi, 1995), pp. 157–9.

[2] One of the better accounts of all the "neofascists" discovered by connecting them through the most transient of connections is that of Kevin Coogan, *Dreamer of the Day: Francis Parker Yockey and the Postwar Fascist International* (Brooklyn, NY: Automedia, 1999).

and Fascist armed forces and/or political formations. In Italy, for example, there was the Proletarian Union of Giuseppe Albano, which organized some of the youthful legionnaires of Mussolini's Social Republic of Salò who remained after the bloodletting that marked the end of the war in northern Italy.

Literally dozens of such minuscule groups arose in Italy during the first years after the end of the war. There was LUPA, the Patriotic Unifying League of Anti-Communists, for instance, and the National Fusionist Party, which carried the well-remembered initials PNF – Partito nazionale fascista. There was SAM, the Squadre di azione Mussolini – the Action Squads of Mussolini. Thousands of survivors of the Fascist period sought, among themselves, community and expression. Around them, all the small organizations proliferated.[3]

Such groups were almost uniformly identified as "neofascist." Their membership was composed largely of persons who shared a history of association with Fascist organizations during the war. Their fascist bona fides, by and large, were established by their biographies. Their individual histories were directly associated with historic Fascism. They had been members of the Fascist party or had served the Fascist government. Should there have been others that did not so qualify, they almost invariably were the children of those who had been members or who had so served.

There was not an overwhelming number of such persons. The war had been so catastrophically lost, and the costs so astronomically high, that most Italians sought to distance themselves from Fascism and all its memories. The general response was to attempt to reconstruct the semblance of a life amid the mountains of ruins that every day reminded Italians of the material and spiritual costs of the Fascist adventure.

In that environment, there were other groups, dissident in some significant sense or other, that did not identify themselves with either the victors or Mussolini's Fascism, and that, in fact, may have denied any such affiliation – and yet were still to be spoken of as "neofascist." One such group, as an illustrative case, was Guglielmo Giannini's Uomo Qualunque, a political association intended to provide sanctuary for "the common man" – to protect him from the exploitation of professional politicians who, the *qualunquisti* claimed, used every and any opportunity to wring taxes and compliance from the subject masses.

In the story of the search for neofascism, the Giannini case is interesting for a number of reasons. In the first place, Giannini had antifascist credentials. He had been an antifascist before the fall of the regime. Moreover, he was dispositionally antipolitical. He was disdainful of professional politicians and his principal political thrust was to "free" the "little man"

---

[3] See the discussion in Mario Giovana, *Le nuove camicie nere* (Turin: Edizioni dell'Albero, 1966), chap. 3.

from the tax burdens and collectivistic exactions that he felt typified all
and every government. Among the disordered collection of ideas he entertained, there was an irreducible surd of anarchism and individualism that
had absolutely nothing to do with Fascism in any sense of the term. Giannini, in fact, was an advocate of the "minimalist state" of traditional liberalism. For the *qualunquisti*, the state was the enemy, and it was the desire
of the followers of Giannini that the state make its presence felt as little as
possible.[4]

This was so evident at the time that Giannini had no reticence in making public overtures to Benedetto Croce to assume a leadership role in the
party.[5] Croce had been a spokesperson for antifascist intellectuals since the
mid-1920s. Giannini fully expected Croce to participate in his movement
since, by the time the movement had become a political force, it was unmistakable that the *qualunquisti* identified themselves with ninteenth-century
liberal economic and political thought.[6] They were conservatives of the old
school.

The fact is that Giannini was an "afascist," a nonfascist who conceived the appeal to "antifascism" of postwar politicians – who had themselves been Fascists for two decades – as little other than a strategem for
extorting benefits from their inert constituencies. Giannini ridiculed those
who had discovered their antifascism only after Fascism's defeat – and he
deplored those who used the charge of "fascist sympathies" to abuse their
fellows.

At the time there were many, both former Fascists and nonfascists alike,
who felt that Giannini accurately characterized the prevailing circumstances
in Italy immediately following the end of the Second World War. Some former Fascists did join his association, – but far more joined the Communist
Party and still more joined the Christian Democrats.[7] Moreover, while some
industrialists who had formerly been Fascist[8] contributed funds to Giannini's

---

4 One can find nothing specifically "Fascist" about Giannini's political opinions. Even in the
   summary accounts made available in the discussions of "neofascism," one finds nothing. See,
   for example, Roberto Chiarini, "The 'Movimento Sociale Italiano': A Historical Profile," in
   Luciano Cheles, Ronnie Ferguson, and Michalina Vaughan (eds.), *Neo-fascism in Europe*
   (New York: Longman, 1991), pp. 23–6. See the brief discussion in A. James Gregor, *Phoenix:
   Fascism in Our Time* (New Brunswick, NJ: Transaction, 1999), pp. 12–13.
5 Angelo Del Boca and Mario Giovana, *Fascism Today: A World Survey* (New York: Pantheon,
   1969), p. 129.
6 See Mario Tedeschi, *Fascisti dopo Mussolini* (Rome: L'Arnia, 1950), pp. 150–1.
7 Many books are available listing the names of many Fascists, often prominent during the years
   of the regime, who joined either the Communist Party or the Christian Democrats immediately after the end of the Second World War. See, for example, the book written anonymously,
   Camerata dove sei? (Rome: B&C, 1976); see G. Silvano Spinetti, *Venti'anni dopo: Ricomin-
   ciare da zero* (Rome: Edizioni di "Solidarismo," 1964), chap. 6.
8 One must ask oneself how many industrialists of any importance had *not* been Fascists during
   the Fascist *ventennio*?

efforts, many more wealthy individuals, with an equal history of affiliation with Mussolini's regime, contributed to all the other parties, including the Communists. One is at a loss as to what all that might mean in terms of identifying "neofascists."

Very little of Giannini's political program was Fascist in any determinate sense. He called Italians to labor in their own self-interest – to restore the nation's ruined economy. In defense of a market-governed economy, he advocated that tax benefits be extended to attract foreign capital investment and technology transfers. He made an emphatic defense of profit incentives and market influences and rejected state interference in the general economy.

That was sufficient for most commentators to identify him as a "rightist." In the conceptual language of postwar Italy, with the liberation from Fascism identified in large measure with communist partisans, to be "rightist" was to be Fascist. Although Fascism had consistently violated the rights of private property, divested industrialists of control over their own institutions, and sought to dominate all Italians through totalitarian controls,[9] the tendency to identify anyone who pretends to defend private property as a generic fascist surfaced immediately after the termination of the Second World War and, lamentably, was never again to be entirely abandoned.

One need only reflect on just some of the consequences of such an intellectual disposition. Any individual, group, or political party that chose to defend private property or a market-governed economy would be, ipso facto, fascist. Almost every political party in the Western world, other than those composed entirely of doctrinaire antiproperty and antimarket Marxists, would immediately become a candidate "neofascism." Other than that, all that was really necessary to qualify for just such status was to behave in what was spoken of as "typically Fascist style"[10] – whatever that was taken to mean.

In fact, Mussolini's Fascism was never "rightist" in the sense of having offered an unqualified defense of private property. The extension of protection to private property and the employment of market modalities in their developmental programs were always contingent on Fascist purpose – and continued only so long as such employments satisfied those purposes. There was never any *intrinsic* relationship between Fascism and the defense of property or the commitment to the commodity market. To imagine that Mussolini was a defender of capitalism, and somehow a "tool" of industrial barons, may well have been a constant feature of Marxist conviction, but, as has been indicated, is a claim for which there is no persuasive evidence. To

[9] See the discussion in A. James Gregor, *Mussolini's Intellectuals: Fascist Social and Political Thought* (Princeton, NJ: Princeton University Press, 2005), and *Italian Fascism and Developmental Dictatorship* (Princeton, NJ: Princeton University Press, 1979), chaps. 5, 6.
[10] Del Boca and Giovana, *Fascism Today*, p. 130.

this day, some Marxists have continued to pretend that such was the case, but few knowledgeable social analysts still entertain the notion.[11]

The cognitive and classificatory issue of whether Fascism was the White Guard of capitalism or a "right-wing extremism" did not really arise in the earliest reflections on the rise of neofascism in the immediate postwar years. It really was not necessary. Identifying neofascists did not require the availability of a suitable social science definition. Former Fascists simply organized themselves in political associations that were clearly philofascist: The Movimento sociale italiano, the MSI – the Italian Social Movement – was principal among them.

The founders and the original members of the MSI were almost all survivors of the Fascist Italian Social Republic (RSI). The Social Republic was the product of that unfortunate political effort undertaken by Mussolini – after the collapse of his regime in July 1943, and his rescue by German special operations forces in September – to continue in what was by that time clearly a lost cause. Those Italians who collected around the RSI were not all Fascists by conviction. Many had responded because they were convinced that the nation's honor was at stake. Italy, having committed itself to the Axis powers, had obliged itself not to sue for a separate peace. Many including some nonfascists, felt that Italians were honor-bound to respect the commitment.[12] Those nonfascist participants in the RSI were essentially apolitical and sought little more than to defend the nation's honor. Other than the afascists, there were socialists of a variety of persuasions who became involved in the RSI, and saw in its ideological postures the potential realization of their economic, social, and political convictions. Among the nonfascists were also traditional political liberals such as Vittorio Rolandi Ricci.[13] None of them identified with Fascism as an ideological or institutional system.

Fascism had a distinctive ideological and political profile, some of the principal features of which were captured in the Program Manifesto of Verona, the provisional constitution of the Social Republic.[14] The Program Manifesto did not stand alone. It was the culmination of more than two decades of doctrinal elaboration by some of Fascism's finest intellects.[15] Not all the

---

[11] See the interesting comments by François Furet, *The Passing of an Illusion: The Idea of Communism in the Twentieth Century* (Chicago: University of Chicago Press, 1999), pp. 177–81.

[12] See the account of the personalities involved in the RSI in Fabio Andriola (ed.), *Uomini e scelte della RSI: I protagonisti della Repubblica di Mussolini* (Foggia: Bastogi, 2000).

[13] See, for example, the case of the socialist Carlo Silvestri, in Gloria Gabrielli, "Carlo Silvestri," in ibid., pp. 115–28, and the case of the liberal Vittorio Rolandi Ricci, ibid., pp. 209–15.

[14] See "The Program Manifesto of the Fascist Republican Party," in A. James Gregor, *The Ideology of Fascism: The Rationale of Totalitarianism* (New York: Free Press, 1969), Appendix B, pp. 387–91.

[15] See the account in Gregor, *Mussolini's Intellectuals*, particularly chap. 10.

participants, nor all the survivors of the Social Republic of Salò, knew or understood any of that.

With the defeat of Fascism, those followers who survived, both those who had been prominent during the history of the regime as well as those of lesser rank, were turned out into a world dominated by antifascist partisans – communist and liberal. During the first days of "liberation," thousands upon thousands of disarmed Fascists were massacred in a paroxysm of vengeance – the product of a civil war that had seen unspeakable brutality exercised by participants on all sides.

Immediately following the end of the war, many survivors of the RSI were forced into hiding in the effort to escape the postwar violence and the threat of prison. Finally, after the amnesty of 1946, some began to draw together, to provide each other comradeship and afford succourance. Many were very young men, barely in their twenties. Few had any comprehension of what had, and what was, transpiring. They knew only that they had fought, some for years, for the grandeur of an Italy to which they had returned to find in ruins. Many of them had little if any comprehension of what Fascism had been as an ideology. Most had only known a wartime Fascism that, in alliance with Nazi Germany, had taken on emphatically alien features.

Most of those who had served the Fascist regime in the military simply accepted defeat and returned home to take up their private lives as best they could. Only a small number of survivors sought to react, to punish those who, in their judgment, had "betrayed" the Motherland, who had conspired with the enemy, and who, in the course of a sanguinary civil war, were responsible for the death of their friends and comrades.

They were the individuals who made up the membership of the plethora of small groups that sprang up in the years immediately following the end of the war. Some of those groups were composed of fanatics prepared to employ senseless violence against anyone or anything they associated with antifascism. Some groups were animated by the distracted conviction that all that was necessary to restore the defunct Fascist regime was street violence that would destabilize Italian democracy and attract the masses who had never really abandoned Mussolini.

Almost all these groupuscules made only transient appearance in the years following the war. Only the MSI was to prove itself a durable contender for political power in the Italy that emerged after 1945. As a political association composed of those who harkened back to the Fascism of Mussolini, the MSI was, by definition, neofascist.

It was neofascist precisely because it provided an institutional home for those Italians nostalgic for the days of Fascist rule. In the Italy of the years after the Second World War, there were not many of them. In the decades following the conclusion of the war, the MSI, using a variety of lures, never succeeded in garnering more than 4 to 6 percent of the total votes cast in national elections.[16] The MSI, as a neofascist organization, was always essentially a marginalized and marginal political party.

The MSI was founded on December 26, 1946, by those who had survived the civil war that brought antifascists into armed conflict with those, Fascist and nonfascist alike, who had collected around Mussolini's Republic of Salò. Antifascism had triumphed and made its antifascism an inextricable component of the nation's creed. Antifascism became an integral, legal constituent of Italy's postfascist government.

As a consequence, the MSI was compelled to organize itself in an environment in which any effort at the "reconstitution of the Fascist party" was an actionable criminal offense. A proscriptive law was first promulgated by the provisional government of Italy immediately following the conclusion of the war. A similar proscription, article number 17, was introduced into the peace treaty with the Allies, and further reaffirmed by a law (number 1546) enacted by the postfascist Constituent Assembly. Finally, the postwar Italian constitution itself included, as a "transitional proscription," the ban on attempting the reconstitution of Fascism.[17]

The war and its devastation had exhausted the nation. Italians gave every evidence of wishing only to be allowed to reconstruct their lives as best they could. For antifascists, it simply was not possible to allow life to return to "normality." For almost a quarter-century, the normality of life included Fascism. After the war, the antifascist victors wished to assure themselves and the nation that such a "normality" would never resurface. That the antifascists chose to exclude and isolate Fascists from political life in the immediate postwar years is perfectly comprehensible. Together with the Italy that antifascism aspired to leave to its heirs, it was impossible to dissipate the rancor and bitterness that the civil war had begotten. Both Fascists and antifascists lived in a poisoned atmosphere of tension and distrust.

As a result, the MSI was everywhere confined by law. Within such constraints, it was never really free to articulate its ideology. We will never be quite sure what that ideology might have been had the Movement not been so confined. One cannot deal persuasively with counterfactuals. We do not know what the ideology of the Movimento might have been had its leadership, and its members, been free to articulate it as they saw fit. Moreover, and perhaps more important than any other consideration, the Movement's neofascism evolved in an Italy that had been transformed, sharing remarkably little with the Italy of the post–World War I period. For contemporary purposes, the only thing that can be responsibly considered is what the ideology of the MSI, in fact, became in the peculiar environment of post–World War II Italy.

---

[16] See the figures in Chiarini, "The 'Movimento Sociale Italiano,'" p. 19.
[17] See the discussion in Giuseppe Maggiore, "Il delitto di 'Ricostituzione del disciolto Partito fascista,'" *Rivista penale*, fasc. 7 (July 1950), pp. 3–21.

Whatever its specific doctrinal content, it was clear from its first trappings and liturgy that its sympathies were with prewar Fascism, but its public doctrine was never really Fascist. The first programmatic statements of the party did contain an appeal to the trinity of basic Fascist concerns: the nation, the state, and the social revolution. This appeal translated itself into an explicit concern for the loss of territories that Italy and claimed and "restored" following the First World War and during the Fascist period. The talk of the state turned on its sovereign independence and its function as a guardian of public order. The allusion to social revolution invoked the recent memory of the corporative state and worker participation in the management of industry.

All of that might well count as Fascist. But alongside the commonplace components of historic Fascism, there was also an appeal to the right of citizens to "choose their own rulers" and the right to be judged by an "independent judiciary" when charged with criminal offense. There was also a call for a defense of the freedoms of speech, press, and association – hardly features one might easily identify as particularly Fascist.[18]

The political environment of the time made the logic of such a position perfectly obvious. If the neofascists hoped to survive in a postwar environment in which almost every man was either their enemy or indifferent to their doctrinal blandishments, they would have to have constitutional protections available.

There was more than that. At the very foundation of the party, it was clear that it would be composed of persons of very disparate political orientations. There were those who were more temporate, and those who conceived themselves more radical. Whatever the case, from the very foundation of the MSI, it was uncertain what the ideology of "neofascism" might be. All the members of the Movement, of course, were prepared to identify themselves with historic Fascism. They would hardly have been there otherwise. What was uncertain was to what doctrinal directives they were prepared to commit themselves in the postwar environment. What was clear to everyone involved in the MSI was that postwar Italy was not the Italy of 1920, or 1930, or 1940. Postwar Italy faced problems entirely unanticipated by paradigmatic Fascism, the Fascism of Mussolini. By the mid-1970s, Giorgio Almirante, one of the few persons who might best typify postwar Italian neofascism, drew out all the implications of such political realities.

The leadership of the Movement attempted a variety of political strategies, none particularly successful. By the mid-1970s, Italy had transformed

---

[18] See the account in Giorgio Almirante, *Autobiografia di un "Fucilatore"* (Milan: Edizioni del Borghese, 1974), pp. 44–5; the references in Leonard B. Weinberg, *After Mussolini: Italian Neo-Fascism and the Nature of Fascism* (Washington, DC. University Press of America, 1979), p. 17.

itself. It was enjoying its own peculiar economic miracle and had begun to take on the features of a postindustrial society – with all the virtues and disabilities.

What had become eminently clear to Almirante, in the course of those systemic changes, was that the MSI could no longer look to the Fascist past for political direction. Neofascism in Italy was no longer to be simply nostalgic. He allowed that the members of the MSI were to be nostalgics only insofar as being nostalgic did not impair their ability to deal with contemporary problems and anticipate those of the future. The leaders and members of the Movement were to respect their Fascist antecedents and the Fascist history of the nation, but they were to focus on the problems of the present and the future.

By that time, the features of Italian neofascism had stabilized around a number of convictions. It was understood that, a quarter-century after the passing of institutional Fascism, Italy had been transformed by history and economic development. If Fascism were to be relevant to Italians, it would have to offer them solutions for their current problems. While *Missini* (members of the MSI) were to respect their historic past, and the sacrifice of a generation, Almirante reminded them that it would be "grotesque" and "anarchronistic" to attempt to impose yesterday's answers on today's problems.[19]

In that sense, the MSI was neofascistic. Its animating sentiment was Fascist. Its ardor was nationalistic. Its concern was for the sovereign independence of the state. And its dispositions were anticommunistic. All of that found expression in a general sense of pride in the Fascist history of Italy, in an abiding passion for Italians, as an ideal community, and in the advocacy of a strong executive for the nation. Other than displaying pictures of Mussolini in their homes, or carrying Fascist talismen on their persons, or taking personal pride in the history of their parents or relatives who had served Il Duce, there was very little, by that time, that distinguished the neofascists of the MSI from other Italians. That had become eminently clear to Almirante, who proceeded to lead the way.[20]

By the 1970s, it was abundantly clear that the MSI sought full legitimation within the Italian party system. Party leaders saw the party as a contender in a broadly democratic context. Almirante made perfectly clear the elements and the structure of the supporting argument.

It was transparent in everything Almirante said and wrote that he understood perfectly well that the Italy of his time was not the Italy of 1920. There could be no armed rebellion by *squadristi*. There could be no revolutionary coup d'etat. Unlike the time of Fascism's advent, when all the evidence

---

[19] See Almirante's speech, *Il secolo d'Italia*, 7 April 1970, p. 3.
[20] See Almirante's account of the role of "nostalgia" in the party's program in *Autobiografia di un "Fucilatore,"* pp. 43–4.

indicates that the vast majority of Italians tolerated Fascist violence as part of the defense against the threat of "Bolshevik" revolution, the vast majority of Italians, during the immediate decades after the Second World War, had found a satisfactory place among the Christian Democrats, the traditional Socialists, or the Communists. With the continued political and military support of the Americans, Italians had every reason to feel confident that there would be no violent communist revolution.

In those circumstances, Almirante argued that the small groups of intransigent neofascists, disposed to individual acts of violence against nameless persons or property, were not only ineffectual, but criminal.[21] Such acts were cowardly, and no invocation of slogans from the past could make them anything else. More important, perhaps, was the fact that such criminal acts alienated the vast majority of Italians, whatever their political persuasion.[22] Almirante asked the youth of the party to cultivate "a serenity that was almost superhuman," and to maintain that serenity even before the bodies of their fallen heroes and comrades. He admonished them that "One does not struggle for civilization employing the arms used by barbarism to defeat it."[23]

By the mid-1970s, it was clear that street violence hardly served the political purposes of the MSI. The evidence of almost three decades of postwar Italian life confirmed that it was counterproductive. That recognition, together with some measure of sophistication, shaped the doctrinal evolution of the MSI.

Whatever else he was, Almirante was not foolish. He fully appreciated the fact that, over the years, the term "Fascist" had taken on the depreciatory meaning assigned to it by the opposition. In his judgment, the neofascists had lost "the war of words." To be identified as a "Fascist" or a "neofascist" was to be identified as a criminal, devoid of humanity, and committed to tyranny and totalitarianism as well as violence for its own sake.[24]

In response, Almirante sought to guide the party to an abandonment of "infantile nostalgia." He recommended that the MSI identify itself as

---

[21] However frequently the claim is repeated, it is not true that Fascist violence was simply violence for its own sake, or that it was terroristic in character and intent. Stanley Payne correctly affirms that "ordinary terrorism...was rare in historic fascism." Stanley Payne, *A History of Fascism 1914–1945* (Madison, WI: University of Wisconsin Press, 1995), p. 498. Sergio Panunzio, who was to become one of the principal ideologues of Fascism, and who was directly connected to Italo Balbo, one of the major leaders of the *squadristi*, wrote an entire treatise on the use of violence, in which he separated revolutionary violence from counterproductive terrorism. See Sergio Panunzio, *Diritto, forza e violenza: Lineamenti di una teoria della violenza* (Bologna: Licinio Cappelli, 1921).

[22] While critics have consistently maintained that Almirante either tolerated or secretly supported neofascist violence, the Italian courts never convicted him of any such offense.

[23] Almirante, *Autobiografia di un "Fucilatore,"* pp. 155, 181, 185, 241.

[24] Ibid., pp. 225–8.

of the "Right," rather than "Fascist."[25] The Italian historic Right had a perfectly respectable tradition and carried none of the baggage with which the term "Fascist" was freighted. He went on to advocate the abandonment of those features of the Fascist past inappropriate for the then present. He spoke, for example, of a rejection of dictatorship and totalitarianism, of a rejection of any advocacy of press censorship or the suppression of freedom of expression. He spoke of the defense of both and the need for civil political discourse to address effectively the problems that beset the nation.[26]

More than that, Almirante spoke of the Jewish friends who had lent him succour while he was a hunted fugitive immediately following the end of the war. He spoke with gratitude of their unqualified assistance and of his debt to them. He spoke of the immorality of the racial laws that marred the history of Italian Fascism, and deplored the indignities, pain, and violence inflicted on the innocent that was their consequence.[27]

What had become clear by the 1970s was the realization that there was no prospect that anything like the Fascism of recent history could be restored to the peninsula – with or without violence. Almirante insisted that "we have no intention of restoring Fascism," but went on to add, "nor will we surrender before the negative logic of antifascism. We would be the architects of a postfascism, that is to say of an era that will belong, finally, to all Italians of good will."[28]

In substance, what that meant was that Almirante was prepared to leave the ultimate assessment of the meaning of Fascism to history. While the MSI would continue to explore themes that had shaped political life in the Fascist era,[29] it chose to identify itself explicitly thereafter with the broader "national Right," aligning itself with individuals and groups with which it found itself compatible. At least one critical tenet bound all such groups together: the

---

[25] This was something Fascists, in their time, were reluctant to do. See Payne, *A History of Fascism*, p. 497.

[26] Almirante, *Autobiografia di un "Fucilatore,"* pp. 30, 55, 57, 149–50.

[27] Ibid., pp. 133–6. This was particularly important since Almirante, as a young journalist, had served as a minor functionary for the scurrilous publication *Difesa della razza*, published by Fascists after 1938, in which the most indefensible anti-Semitic material was printed. Whatever evidence we have indicates that as a functionary in the Social Republic, Almirante sought to mitigate the anti-Semitism insisted upon by the Nazi authorities. See ibid., p. 123.

[28] Ibid., p. 34.

[29] See, for example, the work of the Institute of Corporative Studies, which published the journal *Rivista di studi corporativi* in a series of volumes, including Gaetano Rasi, *La società corporativa: Partecipazione Programmazione* (Rome: Istituto di studi corporativi, 1973), in which one found technical study of the institutional arrangement of a corporative state. The journal regularly referenced literature and authors of the Fascist period and addressed the question of differences that would obtain between the corporative structure of the Fascist state and the anticipated state of the future.

commitment to a consistent policy of anticommunism.[30] That decision was in large part based on the conviction that not only was communism, in general, "oppressive," but Marxism, as it was practiced in postwar Italy, had shown itself destructive of the nation's economic productivity.[31]

In the quarter-century that followed (Almirante died in 1988), his protégé, Gianfranco Fini, acceded to party leadership. Fini's political orienation followed the lines laid down by Almirante. By the mid-1990s, various members of the MSI were surprisingly successful in their respective bids for public office. Mussolini's granddaughter, Alessandra, almost won the mayoral race in Naples, and Fini attracted 47 percent of the vote in his campaign for mayor of Rome.

In an Italy awash in political scandal, Gianfranco Fini emerged as an attractive candidate. Free of the suggestion of corruption, he came to the attention of Silvio Berlusconi, one of Italy's wealthiest entrepreneurs, a master of the media in Italy's advertising and electronic information age. As a consequence, the young Fini enjoyed more, and more favorable, public attention than had previous leaders of the MSI. In 1994, trafficking on his popularity with Italian voters, Fini, following Almirante's suggestions of a quarter of a century earlier, chose a new name for his "postfascist" party: the Alleanza nazionale – the National Alliance.

At about the same time, the leadership of the Alleanza prepared a fairly elaborate statement of its doctrinal commitments in its *Pensiamo l'Italia: Il domani c'è già* (Thinking About Italy: The Future is Now).[32] Not at all surprising in terms of its content, the *Pensiamo l'Italia* simply reiterated the central convictions that Almirante had advanced two decades before. The document clearly rejected any antidemocratic Fascist alternative. It advocated the reform of what it held to be a flawed representative system – but always within the limits of "freedom and liberty as unimpeachable values."

The document explicitly rejected totalitarianism and "any form of dictatorship." It rejected any form of racism and anti-Semitism, even that form of anti-Semitism that had become increasingly popular in Italy and Europe – however concealed it might have been as "anti-Zionist or anti-Israeli polemic."[33]

At the same time, the document did not dismiss, nor denigrate, the Fascist history of the nation. As was the case with Almirante, there was no rejection of those, however mistaken in their policies, who had sought to bring grandeur to the nation. The Alleanza maintained its sentimental

---

[30] Almirante, *Autobiografia di un "Fucilatore,"* p. 233.

[31] See, for example, the discussion in *Libro bianco sulla politica economica del MSI-DN* (Rome: Settore Sociale ed Economico, 1977), particularly Almirante's comments on pp. 88–91.

[32] *Pensiamo l'Italia: Il domani c'è già. Valori, idee e progetti per l'Alleanza Nazionale. Tesi politiche approvate dal congresso di Fiuggi* (Rome: Alleanza nazionale, 1995).

[33] Ibid., pp. 4, 10.

attachment to the leaders and followers who had fallen in the service of Fascism.

The National Alliance pursued political postures that had long characterized the MSI: the advocacy of a strong executive for the Italian system as well as the employment of populist instrumentalities to involve Italians more effectively in public service and public participation. There was an emphasis on the traditional values of the family and the sovereign territorial integrity of the nation.

In June 1994, the Alleanza nazionale won eleven seats in the European Parliament. In the party congress of January 1995, Fini advocated that the National Alliance formally announce its specific commitment to "Freedom, Justice, and Democracy." With only one dissenting vote, the party rejected "all forms of racism and totalitarianism." The party distanced itself from all forms of anti-Semitism as morally reprehensible, specifically denouncing those anti-Semitic and racist groupuscules, more Nazi than Fascist, that still gravitated around the party.[34]

After the elections in 2001, with Berlusconi Italy's prime minister, Fini assumed the responsibilities of vice premier. While Berlusconi provoked a storm of criticism by making statements that could be interpreted as less than critical of Mussolini, Fini has been explicit in his rejection "of the shameful chapters in the history of Italy" that included "disgraceful Fascist race laws."[35]

In fact, both Berlusconi and Fini have been among the most committed allies of Israel in Europe. That some have sought to uncover "Fascism" and/or "neofascism" in all of that is at least curious. Some have insisted that there is a "cryptofascism" hidden beneath all these doctrinal statements and public behaviors. Others have insisted that a "democratic fascism" was empirically "untenable." It would simply have to dissolve inevitably into its constituent components.[36]

Others have been content to tender the suggestion that somehow or other, a principled anticommunism, a support for United States policies in the Middle East, and a somewhat qualified defense of market-governed economic strategies must be "neofascist."[37] The Alleanza must forever remain neofascist, cryptofascist, protofascist, or quasifascist – irrespective of what it says and whatever it does.

There is very little in the political position of Gianfranco Fini that is not to be found in the political postures of Giorgio Almirante more than a quarter

---

[34] See the account in Roger Eatwell, *Fascism: A History* (New York: Penquin, 1997), pp. 266–71.

[35] See "Mussolini Not a Killer, Says Italian Leader," *San Francisco Chronicle*, 12 September 2003, p. A14; "Italian Official Reaches Out to Israelis," ibid., 25 November 2003, p. A10.

[36] See the discussion in Roger Griffin, "The 'Post-Fascism' of the Alleanza Nazionale: A Case Study in Ideological Morphology," *Journal of Political Ideologies* 1, no. 2 (1996), pp. 142–5.

[37] See, for example, Jane Kramer, "All He Surveys: Silvio Berlusconi Liked Italy So Much He Bought the Country," *New Yorker*, 10 November 2003, pp. 95–105.

of a century before. What had become clear to anyone not irremediably biased was the fact that the neofascism of the MSI resided in the Fascist sentiments of its members. Much of the reasoning upon which its policies were based, on the other hand, had very little to do with Mussolini's Fascism. Granted the increased retirement of Fascist trappings and Fascist liturgy, many of Almirante's ideas survive in the Alleanza nazionale. The Alliance has become more economically conservative, and the commitment to representative democracy more entrenched, but the lines of its continuity with the MSI are unmistakable. How much Fascism remains to be found in the Alleanza of the twenty-first century, of course, remains a matter of judgment. But with the passing of the last of its members who retain conscious recollection of historic Fascism, one can anticipate that ultimately the Alleanza nazionale will be indistinguishable from almost any other conservative party in Europe.

The Alleanza nazionale is the Italian neofascism of the twenty-first century. It is the lineal descendent of the Movimento sociale Italiano, originally composed of the Fascist survivors of the Second World War. What it has become seems hardly threatening to European democracy.

If outside of that, of course, there remain those small, politically insignificant groups that still succeed in scandalizing public sensibilities with Fascist salutes, Black Shirts, and anti-Semitic graffiti, they could only represent the "infantile nostalgics," who with their "subversive and vaguely revolutionary" posturing, were dismissed by Almirante in the 1970s as psychologically disturbed.[38] That the social science practitioners who have charged themselves with the responsibility of assessing the neofascism of our time seem reluctant to acknowledge what has transpired is not a recommendation.

If we accept the Alleanza, together with all the neonazi and exalted occult groupuscules that torment the peace of the Italian peninsula as all equally neofascist, we have a classificatory typology that clearly lacks all discrimination. What can one possibly make of such neofascisms? The European neofascism that appears most successful hardly seems Fascist at all, and the groupuscule neofascisms that appear to some social science analysts as most Fascist appear as little more than grotesque caricatures of the historic system. For whatever reason, there has been a desperate attempt to lump all these disparate "neofascisms" together. Almirante, and Fini, it is still argued, whatever they may have publicly advocated, really supported terrorism and totalitarianism. They are, after all, *really* Fascists.[39]

---

[38] See Almirante's discussion of "ridiculous nostalgics," in *Autobiografia di un "Fucilatore,"* pp. 149, 181.

[39] Luciano Cheles provides a fairly elaborate argument that the MSI sought to address two different audiences in its propaganda: those who were intransigent Fascists, and those of the general public. The MSI, and presumably the Alleanza by entailment, apparently remained "cryptofascist," harboring a secret Fascist agenda. See the account in L. Cheles, "'Nostalgia dell'Avvenire'. The New Propaganda of the MSI Between Tradition and Innovation," in Cheles, Ferguson, and Vaughan (eds.), *Neofascism in Europe*, pp. 43–65.

The notion of a "cryptofascism" found its source in just such circular reasoning. The entire notion of identifying "neofascism" in the contemporary world has collapsed into an uncertain strategy of subjective judgment that defies empirical confirmation or disconfirmation. Whatever a group says or does, it remains "neofascist." One of the major disabilities of this cognitive strategy is simply to identify the "neofascism" of the Alleanza nazionale with other "neofascisms" active in the Italian political environment.

Since a number of criminal groups identify themselves, or are identified, in some sense, as "neofascist" and/or of the "extreme right," this permits the transfer of their traits to the Alleanza. Since the decision has been made that all these groups are neofascist, and we know that neofascists are criminals, therefore Alleanza must be criminal.

Only by inextricably linking the Alleanza with those driven by criminal ferocity and a lunatic conviction that Hitlerian racism is the only solution to decay in the Western world might one speak of a unitary neofascism calculated to outrage public morality. The price one pays for using such a strategy is to impair our ability to isolate those properties that might actually permit us to identify neofascism either inside or outside the Italian context.

Somehow, we all pretend to be able to identify Marxist movements and regimes on the basis of the simplest inspection. However different Fidel Castro might be when compared to Mao Zedong or Joseph Stalin, we all somehow seem to know that he is a "Marxist" – as were they not all. Thus, the homicidal Khmer Rouge was as Marxist as was the stone age dictatorship of Enver Hoxha.

Few serious contemporary analysts fail to recognize how futile all that is and was. All those political regimes were very briefly allied, and the major Western powers found it tactically useful to conceive them as a single monolithic conspiracy opposed to democracy and decency – until there was a major falling out among them. Among themselves, they castigated each other as "turncoats," "counterrevolutionaries," "reactionaries," and "fascists." Very few social scientists in the Western world knew what to make of that. Nonetheless, they all continued to be categorized as "Marxist" or "Marxist-Leninist" in the literature – until almost all collapsed – and now we are not at all sure what to call them. To this day, no one seems to know if a transmogrified China, a "Communist China," dominated by an export-driven, market-based economy, sustained by direct and indirect foreign investment and private property, is still Marxist or not.

This indifferent search for names with which to parse out the complexity of our world does not really contribute much to our understanding of our own time. Dealing with the issue of identifying instances of neofascism in the contemporary world is, in some fundamental sense, not very different.

The principal difference lies in the fact that Marxists have always taken pride in so identifying themselves, however much they may have differed from other Marxists. Unlike Marxists, many political associations in the world that social scientists identify as "neofascist" refuse the title. Very few contemporary political organizations in the world today are anxious to identify themselves as "fascist" or "neofascist." Their neofascism is generally attributed to them by others, who, when they find themselves facing any classificatory or cognitive difficulties in assigning the title, often proceed to speak of their subjects not as neofascists, but as "parafascists," "quasifascists," or "cryptofascists." Labeling associations in this way may or may not afford an expository convenience, but it hardly recommends itself as an intellectual resolution of what is a major problem in experimental naming.

One need only review the descriptive properties that characterized historic Fascism to realize the distance that separates it from the neofascism we pretend to discover at the commencement of the twenty-first century. Making recourse to Mussolini's description of the institutions of the Fascist state is instructive. In 1933, he spoke of the essentials of the Fascist state. It was a revolutionary state that was fundamentally antiliberal, that increasingly regulated the productive processes of the nation. Its economy neither exemplified traditional capitalism, nor was it an embodiment of Marxist-Leninist socialism. Fascist corporativism necessarily involved a "regulated" and "controlled economy" that "superceded socialism and superceded [economic] liberalism, to establish a new synthesis ... that inherited everything that was vital in each of them."

The system, Mussolini continued, required "three conditions" for its full realization. The first was a commitment to a single, hegemonic party in order to maintain the political and economic discipline essential to unity of purpose. The second was the institutionalization of the totalitarian state, which employed the single party to "absorb the energy, interests and aspirations of the people in order that they might be transformed and uplifted." And finally, essential to accomplishing those goals was the studied maintenance of a domestic state of "high moral tension."[40]

Nor was any of this an afterthought. The major elements of just such a doctrine are found in the earliest literature of the Fascist movement. Fascism was a synthesis of radical nationalism, revolutionary syndicalism, and neo-Hegelian idealism, and the single party, the regulated economy, and the totalitarian state were the natural byproduct.

The Italian neofascism identified by commentators after the end of the Second World War shares few defining features with the paradigmatic Fascism of Mussolini. That presents us with a curiosity of some cognitive significance.

Of all the postwar movements scrutinized for their Fascist credentials, one would have expected those of the Movimento sociale italiano to have

[40] Benito Mussolini, "Discorso per lo stato corporativo," *Opera omnia* (Florence: La fenice, 1958), 26, pp. 93–6.

been most in order. The leadership and the membership of the movement were composed of those who had been Fascist party members and had served, and had fought for, the Fascist regime. One might have expected the political association to display unmistakable Fascist features. And yet, for whatever reasons, from the moment of its founding, the MSI displayed anomalous traits. Over time, but for expressions of Fascist sympathies, the movement evinced little that could pass, without significant qualification, as Fascist substance.

The MSI and subsequently the Alleanza nazionale hardly represents any credible form of Fascism. Neither ever really sought the destruction of the representative system that tolerated and tolerates them. They sought changes in the existing system that would accommodate their historic sympathies, protect the territorial integrity of the nation, and allow for the professional corporate representation that was a feature of Fascism. With the turn of the new century, even those political goals have been modified until the National Alliance emerged as a form of modern conservatism having nothing substantive to do with the fundamentally anticonservative, antidemocratic, and totalitarian Fascism of Mussolini.[41]

For that reason alone, we can understand why contemporary commentators on neofascism make ready recourse to locutions such as "parafascist" and "cryptofascist" with such tedious regularity. The facile use of such expressions, while convenient, invariably produces cognitively unsatisfactory products. Its emotive function is evident. The term "fascist" in all its uses serves as a pejorative. It evokes images of violence, brutality, mass murder, and cataclysmic warfare.

The dilation of the term "Fascist" to "neofascism" often involves the abandonment of analytic and descriptive rigor. The latter term has sometimes become coextensive with "ultranationalism," "conservativism," "right-wing," "radical," or "extreme right" orientation, and sometimes includes those who are anti-Marxist, antiliberal, or anticommunist, who oppose a variety of "politically correct" postures ranging from gun control to liberalized immigration. Sometimes those who are little more than tax protesters are classified as "neofascists." On the fringes, there are soccer thugs, skinheads, and graveyard vandals who overturn Jewish headstones. All, at one time or another, by one or another analyst, have been identified as neofascist.

Only with this feckless employment of terms might General Charles de Gaulle be identified as a fascist. Not only had Jean-Paul Sartre so

---

[41] "Mussolini's Fascism was based on the idea of a charismatic leader, on corporativism, on the utopia of the 'fateful destiny of Rome,' on the imperialistic will to conquer new lands, on inflammatory notions, on the ideal of an entirely regimented nation of Blackshirts, on the rejection of parliamentary democracy.... I admit that Alleanza Nazionale, which sprang from the Movimento Sociale Italiano, is certainly a right-wing party, but it has little to do with the old Fascism." Umberto Eco, *Five Moral Pieces* (New York: Harcourt, 1997), p. 69.

identified him, but serious analysts repeated the characterization. He was "nationalistic," "authoritarian," and "conservative" – indisputably "Fascist tendencies" in the judgment of such authors. More than that, the anticommunism of De Gaulle's *Rassemblement du peuple Français* reminded those same commentators of "the Fascist 'action squads' of the 1920s," revealing, once again, the "Fascist tendencies" that informed the general's nationalism and his conservatism.[42] That the Italian MSI found French Gaullism attractive was seen as confirming their judgment – although more judicious commentators did concede that Gaullism "was not truly fascist."[43] It may have been "prefascist," or perhaps it had "gone beyond Fascism in order to conform with the demands and ways of modern industrial society."[44]

We were told that Charles de Gaulle was really most comfortable with "the representatives of big capital and the largest French banks," and that he "instinctively served the interests of his own class." And then, one must not forget that the godfather of his son was Marshal Philippe Petain of ill-fame – the leader of Vichy France.[45] All of that, coupled with the fact that De Gaulle "officially revived the cult of nationalism and . . . restored to France the notion of her *grandeur*,"[46] could only make of him a Fascist or a neofascist in the eyes of some. Nor did the apparent march of neofascism in France end with Gaullism.

In the mid-1950s, a shopkeeper named Pierre Poujade organized a union for the "Defense of Shopkeepers and Artisans." Its purpose was to insulate the proprietors of small businesses in France from the exactions of the tax collector. In effect, "Poujadism," however idiosyncratic, was a form of anti-tax populism, opposed to the income tax exactions typical of representative democracy, and vaguely attracted by the notion that professional rather than geographic representation in the nation's legislative body would improve its overall performance.[47] That any of that should qualify as fascism or neofascism is testimony of how unhinged an academic inquiry can become.

Poujadism may not be necessarily interesting in itself, but it does provide a link to a more contemporary issue. One of the Poujadist members of the French parliament was Jean-Marie Le Pen, who was to go on to organize his Front National (FN) in 1972, animated, we are told, by "fascist views."[48] A decade later, it could command the votes of 10 percent of the electorate in local elections. In 1986, the FN collected 2.7 million votes in the elections

---

[42] See Del Boc and Giovana, *Fascism Today*, pp. 182–5.

[43] Roger Eatwell, *Fascism: A History* (New York: Penguin, 1996), p. 303.

[44] Del Boca and Giovana, *Fascism Today*, p. 203.

[45] We are told by others, in the form of an aside, that "Vichy was far from fascist in its inspiration." Roger Griffin, *The Nature of Fascism* (New York: Routledge, 1991), p. 135.

[46] Del Boca and Giovana, *Fascism Today*, pp. 204–5.

[47] See the discussion in S. Hofman, *Le mouvement Poujade* (Paris: Colin, 1956).

[48] Glyn Ford, "Introduction," in Glyn Ford (ed.), *Fascist Europe: The Rise of Racism and Xenophobia* (London: Pluto Press, 1992), p. xiii.

for the National Assembly and secured thirty-five seats. In the June 1989 elections to the European Parliament, the FN won ten seats.

Lepenism seems to qualify as neofascist because it is nationalistic in inspiration, supportive of family values, opposes abortion on demand, is procapitalist, and correspondingly anticommunist. It has opposed itself to liberal immigration policies and the "Islamization of France" that it identifies as the consequence. Lepenism penetrated the historic heartland of the French Communist Party in Seine–St. Denis in the working-class districts around Paris, winning votes from those who are supposed to be the natural constituents of the "proletarian parties." Some see this phenomenon as the consequence of a typical fascist deception – pretending to be anticapitalist – when, it seems to be suggested, it is universally known that fascists are, by definition, procapitalist[49] – an unremarkable piece of circular reasoning. Moreover, the FN has entered into informal pacts with traditional conservatives in contesting elections – clearly a fascist trait.[50]

Some have argued that fascism is to be found at the "core" of Le Pen's ideological convictions. His ideal is an integral, "holistic community" threatened by unassimilable immigrants neither sharing French culture nor prepared to adapt to it. He has maintained that unfettered market-governed economic activity can well impair the life circumstances of many, and advocates some state control as a "balance." Some have even identified a "corporatist" strand in some of his speeches in the 1990s – surely a sign of neofascism. But then again, we are told that Le Pen is a "master of disguises," and that one can hardly have any confidence in anything he says.[51] He is perhaps a "cryptofascist."

The problem with all this is perhaps highlighted by the social science assessments of the Nouvelle Droite, the French New Right, an intellectual current that has accompanied all the developments of putative neofascism in France since the late 1960s.

After the political turmoil that attended the Algerian revolt and domestic student rebellion, a group of French intellectuals emerged who sought to bring together those desiring to restore France's integrity in the ongoing conflict with what they held to be the "forces of national disintegration."

Principal among those forces they identified communism, both domestic and international. For some, Christianity, with its egalitarianism, pacifism, and humility, was a prescription for decline and an invitation to communist domination.

---

[49] See the discussion in ibid., pp. 21–2.
[50] Roger Griffin is more constrained. He rejects the notion that Le Pen's National Front is fascist. It is not "revolutionary" enough – satisfied as it is with reforming the system. Griffin, *The Nature of Fascism*, p. 161.
[51] Eatwell, *Fascism*, pp. 324–5.

At the same time, a number of centers for cultural and political studies grew up around the intellectual leaders of the New Right. Among the most important was the Groupement de Recherche et d'Etudes pour la Civilisation Européenne (GRECE). The theoretical journal *Nouvelle Ecole* and the periodical *Elements* were among the publications associated with GRECE. Alain de Benoist, perhaps the best-known representative of what was to be identified as the French New Right, typified the eclectic character of the political persuasion.

Unlike the traditional right in French politics, the New Right is neither fundamentalist Roman Catholic nor an advocate of free-market economics. It has, for example, attacked social conservatism and the dominant values of the middle class. It has specifically rejected biological racism and, in general, conceives culture an artifact of society.[52] Its reflections on race have very little to do with biological determinism, but turn on the well-researched phenomenon of ethnocentrism – the natural disposition of members of a cohesive community, sharing a common culture, to identify with similars and show diffidence toward outgroup members.

Perhaps among the most consequential ideas articulated by the New Right in France, these reflections on ethnocentrism became part of the intellectual armarium of Lepenism in its political struggle against continued immigration into the French metropole. In its simplest form, the argument proceeded in something like the following fashion: Every vital community, including each historic culture, has a right to maintain itself – the French no less than any other. To refuse to accept immigration if it can be anticipated that such influx would undermine a prevailing culture and generate unmanageable social tension is a right that cannot be denied the nation.[53]

De Benoist has taken the time to reject such an application of his ideas concerning the right of cultural integrity. Originally formulated to defend the cultures of the less-developed world from the impostures of American "cultural globalization," De Benoist has maintained that the concept was never intended for use against immigrants.[54] Employing a dialectic familiar to critical theory and phenomenology, De Benoist has argued that immigrants, with their natural differences, provide a dialogue against which one defines one's identity. Differences are necessary for the articulation of self. He has deplored the uniformity, homogenization, and totalitarianism that would extinguish differentiation and individuality.

---

[52] See the extensive quotes from GRECE, reproduced in Coogan, *Dreamer of the Day*, p. 539, n. 24.

[53] See Jean-Marie Le Pen, *Les Français d'abord* (Paris: Carrere, 1984), see also the discussion in J. Y. Le Gallou, *La Preference Nationale: Responce a l'immigration* (Paris: Albin Michel, 1985).

[54] See Alain de Benoist, *Europe, tiers monde, meme combat* (Paris: Robert Laffont, 1986).

For De Benoist, France's identity was being swamped not by immigration or miscegenation, but by American "cultural imperialism." France's problem was essentially one of resisting the malevolent influence of the United States rather than curtailing immigration.[55] It was not immigration that was threatening France's future. It was North American economic hegemony.

As early as 1979, De Benoist expressed his impatience with the standard right/left distinction that commonly structured political and cultural discussion throughout the Western world. Since then, he has lamented the fact that he is regularly charged by the right with defending left-wing ideas, and by the left for being an "extreme rightist." In 1993, in response to critics on the Left who advised vigilance against the threats from the New Right, he admitted that it was "not easy trying to choose between the stupidity of the right and the dishonesty of the left."[56]

Over the years, De Benoist and the entire New Right in France have been associated with chauvinism and a "new racism." They have been charged with having broadcast attacks on egalitarianism, supported those who deny the massacre of Jews in Hitler's Europe, and bruited antidemocratic sentiments. It has been suggested that, in the final analysis, all the lucubrations of the New Right are nothing but "a camouflaged and coded postwar version of prewar Fascism." Even though some of the critical colleagues of De Benoist and leaders of GRECE have consistently denied traditional right-wing affiliations,[57] Raymond Aron, one of France's most accomplished intellectuals, nonetheless continued to suggest that De Benoist's "manner of thinking and reasoning" was not only akin to that of the traditional right-wing, but "was often similar to that of the National-Socialists and the Fascists"[58] – whatever that might be taken to mean.

Whatever else it was, it was a manner of reasoning that brought De Benoist an invitation to Moscow in April 1992, to meet with Aleksandr Prokhanov, one of the advisers of the Communist Party of the Russian Federation. In that same year, De Benoist spoke before the French Communist Party's Institut de Recherches Marxistes. All of this provoked a kind of intrapsychic tension among analysts that has produced some remarkable assessments.

It is very difficult to understand how neofascists have come to interact with communists and Marxists with such fraternal affability. It seems clear

55 De Benoist, as cited in Coogan, *Dreamer of the Day*, pp. 534–5.

56 As cited, Frank H. Adler, "Razzismo, differenza e destra in Francia," in Alessandro Campi and Ambrogio Santambrogio (eds.), *Destra/sinistra: Storia e fenomenologia di una dicotomia politica* (Rome: Antonio Pellicani Editore, 1997), p. 294, n. 7; "Left Vigilance in France," *Telos*, 98–9 (Winter–Spring 1993–4), pp. 23–33.

57 In 1979, Pierre Vial, secretary general of GRECE, spoke of elaborating "a new culture" that might be described as of the Right, but which was, in fact, closer to the "New Left" than the traditional Right. See the interview in *Le Monde*, 24 August 1979, p. 2.

58 Douglas Johnson, "The New Right in France," in Cheles, Ferguson, and Vaughan, *Neo-Fascism in Europe*, p. 239.

that the issue demanded some resolution. How might neofascists and leftists find common ideological ground?

One of those who has addressed the issue directly is Piero Ignazi. He has written extensively on the subject of the "extreme right" in Europe and reveals something of the difficulty that attends contemporary discussion. Ignazi tells us that most authors who deal with neofascism approach their subject with considerable indifference. They treat their material "impressionistically." There is, we are informed, a "virtual absence of any effort at definition" of what it means to be of the extreme, or radical, right. Which political movements or regimes might the expression encompass? Commentators have long lamented that there is no consensus among academic researchers as to what might count as a common denominator for the family of fascist parties, much less those that are conservative or those spoken of as of the extreme right.

Ignazi argues that by employing a somewhat generous "connotative" approach, one can maintain that "the extreme right's ideology is provided by fascism." Speaking connotatively, it can be argued that the ideology of generic fascism might be synoptically captured in "the idea of resurgence from a dark period, the emphasis on the nation as a collective, organic body, the projection into a glorious and beaming future, [with] mass mobilization mainly through the leader's charismatic appeal." Given such an insight, we can proceed to the stipulation that "by extreme right we mean that political/ideological space where fascism is the key reference"[59] – and that should be sufficient for research purpose.

All of this can only strike one as rather curious. With so "connotative" a definition, so loosely contrived, it really would not be difficult to accommodate not only some of the East European communist parties under the neofascist rubric, but Stalinism, Maoism, and Castroism as well.[60] Ignazi is sufficiently astute to recognize that the "post-industrial extreme right parties" are, in fact, "alien to the fascist tradition" – whatever he may have said about them being in that tradition. Ignazi insists that the contemporary right-wing extremists "are not old, disguised neo-fascist parties." Their success – and the French Front National is a prototypical contemporary extreme right party – is "not based on the revival of the fascist tradition." All the extreme right parties "fiercely deny any linkage to fascism." The denial is most emphatic among the German "neofascist" parties.[61]

To confound us still further, we are told that unlike the "traditional" fascist parties, the modern extreme right parties, however critical they may be,

---

[59] Piero Ignazi, "The Extreme Right in Europe: A Survey," in Peter H. Merkl and Leonard Weinberg, *The Revival of Right-Wing Extremism in the Nineties* (London: Frank Cass, 1997), pp. 47–9.

[60] See, for example, Gregor, *Phoenix*: chap. 7.

[61] Ibid., pp. 57–58.

seem prepared, in general, to accommodate themselves to the prevailing representative system, and rather than rejecting the capitalist productive system, they advocate its defense. They do show a preference for "law and order," and appear to be more comfortable in a system of authoritarian rule.[62] That seems to satisfy the "connotative" definition. One can only wonder if such parties can meaningfully be spoken of as "neofascist"?

Recent history has demonstrated the ideological mutability of communist parties. The Communist Party of the Russian Federation has shown itself, however "revolutionary," prepared to operate within the prevailing "bourgeois" political system. It is prepared, as is the Communist Party of China, to foster market-governed economic modalities in the face of the evident failure of command alternatives. The Chinese Communists have not only provided for the reintroduction of capitalism, but have written private property protection into their newly revised constitution. Law and order are critical, central concerns for both the Russian and Chinese communist parties, as is nationalism and the secure continuation of authoritarian rule.[63] Are such systems "connotatively" neofascist?

Broad, connotative definitions of political systems are really never particularly helpful in serious investigation. The connotative meaning of "neofascism," as it is presently entertained in some social science literature, allows almost any set of convictions to qualify. There is often easy transit from "neofascism" to "neonazism," to "right-wing extremism" with "right-wing extremism ... associated with attitudes of racism, xenophobia and religious bigotry, anti-Semitism especially." With so wide a net, one is inevitably embarrassed by riches. Skinheads are caught up in its trammels, and there are times when evangelical Protestants barely escape. We are reminded, with a meaningful nod, that Roman Catholics had no small part in the "fascism" of the Franco regime in Spain and in fostering and sustaining the Romanian Legion of the Archangel Michael.[64]

Entirely forgotten in all of this is the fact that the only confirmable "postfascist" party in Europe, that of Almirante and Fini, has consistently opposed racism and anti-Semitism, and never given itself over to religious bigotry. That it has supported some free-market economic modalities is more evidence of its nonfascist, rather than fascist, political propensities.

In all of this, it is evident that there are some contemporary groupuscules in Europe and North America that might licitly be spoken of as

---

[62] See ibid., pp. 48–60.

[63] See the more ample discussion in A. James Gregor, *The Faces of Janus: Marxism and Fascism in the Twentieth Century* (New Haven, CT: Yale University Press, 2000), chaps. 5–8, and *A Place in the Sun: Marxism and Fascism in China's Long Revolution* (Boulder, CO: Westview Press, 2000), chaps. 5–8.

[64] See the account in Leonard Weinberg, "The American Radical Right in Comparative Perspective," Merkl and Weinberg, *The Revival of Right-Wing Extremism in the Nineties*, pp. 231–53, with cited material on pp. 233, 235–9.

"neonazi" – political associations that are prepared to defend National Socialist racial notions, celebrate Hitler's birthday, turn over grave stones in Jewish cemetaries, and make common cause with fundamentalist Muslims whose anti-Semitism is irremediable.[65] Such entities are clearly inspired by the National Socialism of Adolf Hitler. They hardly qualify as "neofascists."

Such marginal groups are very small. Estimates of their numbers confirm their fringe character. In Great Britain, where political democracy allows them to undertake political activity almost without constraint, such grouplets are both explicit and emphatic concerning their racism and anti-Semitism. They variously identify themselves as members of the "World Union of National Socialists," or as members of Colin Jordan's one time National Socialist Movement, so that there can be little confusion concerning their ideological convictions. Other conservative, extreme right, or neofascist individuals or associations in most of continental Europe are hardly as easy to categorize. We are left, once again, with the difficulty of coming to grips with what the term "neofascism" might mean in our own time.

Through the end of the twentieth century, some academics have made efforts at responsible definition. Relevant to the conceptualization of neofascism, for example, Stanley Payne has offered a tripartite classification of the *authoritarian nationalisms* of the interwar years. We find, there, a "working definition" that distinguishes between "Fascism," the "Radical Right." and the "Conservative Right," all sufficiently different to allow their respective identification.[66] The distinctions allow more plausible characterizations than those omnibus "connotative" definitions that seem to find neofascism everywhere.

For Payne, the MSI was hardly neofascist by almost any standard. It was a "movement of the parliamentary authoritarian or semiauthoritarian right" that gradually evolved into the Alleanza nazionale, a "moderately rightist," nationalist, parliamentary party.[67] Whatever the personal history of its members or its leadership, it would be difficult to speak plausibly of the Alleanza nazionale as neofascist.

Similar distinctions reduce the number of neofascist groups in either Europe or North America to a remarkably small number – and it is clear that any typology that does not distinguish neofascism from neonazism requires considerable overhaul. More than that, most contemporary social scientists, in their search for neofascists, focus their attention on the Western democracies, hardly fertile ground for the development of serious fascist movements.

---

[65] Coogan, *Dreamer of the Day*, provides a surfeit of individuals and groupuscules that would so qualify.

[66] Payne, "Introduction," *A History of Fascism*; *Fascism: Comparison and Definition* (Madison, WI: University of Wisconsin Press, 1980), chap. 1.

[67] Ibid., pp. 504, 508.

One finds so little serious neofascist political activity in the industrially advanced West simply because the prerequisites for the emergence of fascism no longer obtain. Almost every historian and social scientist has acknowledged as much. Most dismiss the prospects for any form of neofascism in the industrialized West. Unless one chooses to lump together tax protesters, rural militiamen,[68] adolescent skinheads, soccer thugs, and graveyard vandals, very few neofascists are to be found in Europe or North America. Social scientists have scoured the "right" and have discovered only political caricatures. Hardly anyone has sought neofascism among the movements or spokespersons of the left. At best, the search for neofascism in the West has become something of a kind of harmless busy-work for academics.

By the early 1990s, that had become fairly evident to many. Nonetheless, there were those who remained wedded to the "connotative" renderings of what neofascism might be taken to mean. Neofascism covered a loosely defined collection of instances that included everything from General Augusto Pinochet's coup in Chile to the feckless violence of the skinheads of Rostock, East London, and New York. Everyone from Jean-Marie Le Pen to Timothy McVeigh enters the lists. Neofascism collapsed into the "radical or extreme right," and Ronald Reagan becomes its guiding star.[69] Gianfranco Fini's Alleanza nazionale resurfaces not only as neofascist, but as "the first identifiable fascist party to join the governing coalition of a major European country since 1945."[70] What still remains painfully obscure is how, other than by making reference to the biological history of some of its members, the Alleanza nazionale, or any others groups on the "right," whatever their history, might credibly be identified as "neofascist."

By the end of the twentieth century, it was evident to anyone who surveyed the literature with any application that the study of neofascism had all but lapsed into irrelevance. There were no discernible criteria by virtue of which one might distinguish neofascism from the communist parties of Russia and/or China, the new nationalisms in the Balkans with their "ethnic cleansing," or the Conservative Party of the United Kingdom.

As has already been suggested, in the last years of the twentieth century, one final, desperate effort was made to rest the characterization of neofascism on a theoretic base. Rather than loosely formulated connotations, Marxist theory was, once again, mustered to the purpose of identifying the defining features of neofascism.

The reappearance of the "Marxist" interpretation of Fascism at the end of the twentieth century signals the desperation produced by the inability

---

[68] See the discussion in Richard Abanes, *American Militias: Rebellion, Racism and Religion* (Downers Grove, IL: InterVarsity Press, 1996).

[69] Leonard Weinberg, "Conclusions," in Merkl and Weinberg, *The Revival of Right-Wing Extremism in the Nineties*, p. 279.

[70] See Dave Renton, *Fascism: Theory and Practice* (London: Pluto Press, 1999), chap. 1, with the quotation to be found on pp. 7–8.

of academics to identify credibly the defining properties of Fascism or, as a consequence, those of neofascism. Unable to identify instances of neofascism, scholars have fallen back to a position long since abandoned. The "Marxist" interpretation of Fascism is one with which almost everyone is familiar.

We are told, once again, that Fascism was, and is, "an ideology generated by modern industrial capitalism" – an ideology featuring "counterrevolutionary aims [and].... reactionary political goals.," employing some sort of "reactionary modernism" that "denounced rational argument and glorified the nonrational."[71] Fascism, we are told, "is returning" in the guise of neofascism. And once again, we are told that it is returning in the politics of Margaret Thatcher and any defense of the "capitalist social order" together with a "reaction against working-class revolutionary potential."[72]

That kind of characterization allows us to identify not only the Alleanza nazionale as neofascist, with a "fascist core and leader," but any number of other European political candidates as well. Not only is the British National Front neofascist, but Britain's Conservative Party is as well, since both pursue the politics of "reaction" and never really succeed in becoming "truly rational."[73] That having been said, one is left with the immediate and irrepressible sense of déjà vu and the realization that none of the discussion is, in any measure, credible.[74]

Actually, there really is little justification for allowing the study of neofascism to lapse into such circumstances. We do have a criterial list of properties that surface after a systematic review of the history of Mussolini's Fascism. Fascism did, in fact, have observable properties that typified it throughout its history, to be found in embryonic form in its first appearance, and to achieve manifest expression and persist throughout the life of the regime. If the term "neofascism" is to mean anything, one could reasonably argue that it should display at least some of the major features of paradigmatic Fascism – the Fascism of Mussolini.

As has been argued, driven by an abiding feeling of collective humiliation, a conviction that the "plutocratic" nations had consigned them to inferior

---

[71] Mark Neocleous, *Fascism* (Minneapolis, MN: University of Minnesota Press, 1997), pp. x–xi.

[72] Ibid., pp. 43, 56, 89.

[73] Ibid., pp. 90–1, 94.

[74] Roger Eatwell has addressed himself to the overall implausibility of the majority of efforts to identify Fascism and neofascism. He dismisses the identification of conservative nationalists and the advocates of the free market as "neofascists," and rejects the identification of Fascism with irrationalism and the simple advocacy of violence. He speaks of Fascism's "serious intellectual basis" and the fact that Italian Fascism was not intrinsically anti-Semitic. See Roger Eatwell, "On Defining the 'Fascist Minimum': The Centrality of Ideology," *Journal of Political Ideologies* 1, no. 3 (1996), pp. 303–19. Unhappily, these qualifications do not appear to have influenced Eatwell's discussion of neofascism in his volume *Fascism: A History*. There, he still speaks, for example, of Gianfranco Fini and the Alleanza nazionale as neofascist, although he is prepared to grant that the party appears as only moderately right-wing. Ibid., p. 269.

status in the contemporary world, Fascists demanded a "place in the sun," one commensurate with the history of the peninsula that once hosted the Roman Empire. To once again restore the grandeur of the nation, it would be necessary to create a suitable industrial base, a base that would provide the weapon systems that would allow the nation to defend itself against the pretensions of the advanced industrial powers as well as project power to the surrounding environment.

To marshal the human and material resources necessary to accomplish that, a single, dominant political party would be required. The revolutionary party would retain control over all the means of communication, education, and the flow of information. That party would assume quasimilitary command over a population, with a leader, credited with infallible sagacity, exercising authoritarian governance.

Under such a leader, and through the instrumentalities of his party, an entire population was to be integrated into a totalitarian system of political involvement, with real or potential control extending throughout the institutional infrastructure. Characterized by "masculine protest," uniforms were all but universal among those in the population, and the common language was the language of struggle, battle, and conflict. The animating ethic was selfless sacrifice, obedience, and dedication. Manhood restored implied aggressive response to real or fancied slight, a search for the occasion for heroism, a conviction in the justness of one's cause, and a fevered sense of mission.

The twentieth century was filled with revolutionary movements and regimes that shared at least some of these features. It was a time of leaders – whether they be a Duce, a Führer, a Voshd, a Lider Massismo, a Conducator, an Osagyefo, or a Chairman. It was a time of elites and hegemonic "unitary parties." It was a world of uniforms and weapons platforms, of aggressive assertiveness, and the clash of arms. It does not appear that the twenty-first century will be much different.

For our purposes, sorting through all that to identify the neofascisms of our own time is no small task. The academicians who have undertaken the responsibility to date have not succeeded very well. Most of their search for neofascisms has been restricted to real or fancied "right-wing" movements and regimes in Europe and North America, when everything suggests that such movements hardly pose a real threat to the security of our new century.

What many academicians have done is to identify implicitly fascism of whatever sort with the political right, excluding, by definition, anything on the political left. Somehow or other, Italian Fascism, generic fascism, and neofascism can be found only on the right. To assure that outcome, many commentators have proceeded to identify the political right with potential pathological irrationality, the violation of human rights, an irrepressible urge to violence, and a virulent racism that must necessarily lead to mass murder and genocidal outrage.

Every schoolchild is familiar with just such a checklist of "fascist traits." The term "fascist" has entered our common language as a general term of disapprobation, and the tendency is to use it for emotive rather than cognitive purpose. How unhelpful all that is has become abundantly clear.

Any number of left-wing movements and regimes have been irrational, violative of human rights, violent, racist, and given to mass murder – and yet have not been identified as fascist.[75] Why that should be the case remains uncertain. Such movements and polities have featured charismatic leaders and single-party regimes that controlled information, education, and communication. They have embarked on aggressive wars and dressed their citizens, both adult and and those not adult, in uniform, and have proceeded to massacre innocents without number. And yet they have not been identified as fascist or neofascist.

Why this remains the case even after the revelations that followed the fall of the Soviet and Eastern European Marxist regimes is obscure. Part of the answer lies in the fact that for the larger part of the twentieth century, the obligatory distinction between the left and the right in revolutionary politics has remained steadfast.[76]

At the same time, only the political right has been metronomically assigned the most repugnant features of Hitler's National Socialism. The terms "fascism" and "neofascism" are now exclusively employed to refer to the putative class of right-wing movements and regimes that are irrational and homicidal[77] – precisely at the time when the right/left distinction in radical politics has shown itself to be increasingly problematic.

For all that, some academics still insist on the distinction, and persist in identifying irrationality and violence exclusively with movements and regimes they consider right- rather than left-wing. The collection of traits has been projected over all those political movements or regimes that one wishes, for one reason or another, to deplore. Thus "fascist systems" are all racist, even though the concept of race played a relatively negligible role in Mussolini's Italy – certainly no more malevolent than the role that racism played in Stalin's Soviet Russia.[78]

If only "fascist systems" are irrational and homicidal, how is one to explain the ideology or the practices of Pol Pot or the system that survives

---

[75] See the accounts in Stephane Courtois, Nicolas Werth, Jean-Louis Panne, Andrzej Paczkowski, Karel Bartosek, and Jean-Leouis Margolin, *The Black Book of Communism: Crimes, Terror, Repression* (Cambridge, MA.: Harvard University Press, 1999).

[76] In this context, see the discussion in Campi and Santambrogio, *Destra/sinistra*.

[77] Neocleous, *Fascism*, chap. 1.

[78] There is now ample literature dealing with Fascist and comparative racism. See *Giovanni Gentile: Philosopher of Fascism* (New Brunswick, NJ: Transaction, 2001), chap. 8; Gregor, *The Faces of Janus*, chap. 8, *The Ideology of Fascism*, chap. 6,. For Soviet anti-Semitism, see Arkady Vaksberg, *Stalin Against the Jews* (New York: Knopf), Gennadi Kostyrchenko, *Out of the Red Shadows: Anti-Semitsim in Stalin's Russia* (Amherst, NY: Prometheus, 1995); Arkady Vaksberg, Stalin Against the Jews (New York: Knopf, 1994).

in Kim Jong-Il's North Korea? If only "fascist systems" are genocidal, how
does one explain the mass murders in Stalin's Soviet Union, Mao's China, or
Pol Pot's Kampuchea?

The one-party states that exist or have existed in various parts of Africa
evidence features that might be classified either as right- or left-wing. The
Ghanese one-party state of Kwame Nkrumah might just as easily be identified
as right-wing as left-wing, and neofascist as well. Racial discrimination is
pandemic throughout much of sub-Saharan Africa. Is all this left- or right-
wing? Is any of it neofascist?[79]

In effect, it is very hard to divine the logic of much of the present system of right- and left-wing classificatory distinctions – not to address the
further question of how "neofascism" is supposed to be identified within
those supposed parameters. Given the state of the discipline, one can only be
puzzled why it is the case that some Marxist systems, past and present, are
not identified as fascist or neofascist. It is even more difficult to understand
why some non-Marxist political movements or regimes are not immediately
so classified.

What shall be attempted here is a review of some lesser-known candidates
for identification as neofascisms, in part to illustrate how unconvincing the
contemporary classificatory schemata are in fact, and in part to suggest alternative classificatory criteria. It will be an exercise in experimental naming,
didactic in intent, and perhaps therapeutic in effect.

The first effort will address issues that directly engage those seriously
interested in intellectual history. The account should also be instructive to all
who reflect on how one classifies revolutionary thinkers and the movements
they presumably inspire. The treatment deals with the work of Julius Evola,
identified by many, with great assurance, as the inspiration for contemporary
neofascists and the political movements that serve them as host. One author
has gone so far as to identify Evola not only as providing the ideological
inspiration for universal neofascism, but as "one of the most respected gurus
of Fascism."[80] Such a judgment, it will be argued, tell us very little about
neofascism, but a great deal about the character and quality of neofascism
studies.

---

[79] See Krejci, "Introduction: Concepts of Right and Left," in Cheles, Ferguson, and Vaughan
(eds.), *Neofascism* in Europe, p. 15.
[80] Eco, *Five Moral Pieces*, p. 77. See a similar judgment cited in Eatwell, *Fascism*, p. 254.

4

Julius Evola, Fascism, and Neofascism

One of the more curious features of the search for neofascism after the termination of the Second World War is the insistence, on the part of some of the most widely known researchers, that Julius Cesare Andrae Evola, born in Rome on the 19 May 1898, scion of an ancient aristocratic family, provided the neofascism of post–World War II Europe its ideology. Evola has been seen as the source of neofascism's ideological rationale. It was his ideas that lent neofascism its substance. Umberto Eco, who identifies "traditionalism" as essential to the "Ur Fascism" that he argues serves as the core of generic neofascism, cites no one other than Evola as its critical exponent.[1]

Others have identified Evola's thought as quintessentially fascist, as "creative" and "original."[2] For still others, he is spoken of as a "post-war fascist," insisting that, after the passing of historic Fascism, his thought provided the inspiration for a resuscitated European neofascism.[3] Together with that, we are confidently told that Evola became a source of neofascist ideological thought because Mussolini's "Fascism had few true believers who could...write articles and books."[4] Because so few Fascists of the time of the *Ventennio* were capable of writing articles or books, Evola, as one of the few, provided the texts that became one of "the most important" sources for the neofascism that arose out of the ruins of the Second World War.[5] Even one of the theoreticians of Italian neofascism chose to identify Evola as

---

[1] Umberto Eco, "Pointing a Finger at the Fascists," *Guardian*, 19 August 1995, p. 27. See Eco's comments in *Five Moral Pieces* (New York: Harcourt, 1997), pp. 77–9.

[2] Roger Eatwell, *Fascism: A History* (New York: Penguin, 1997), p. 254. Capitalized "Fascism," throughout, will refer to Mussolini's Fascism; a lower-case "fascism" will refer to generic fascism.

[3] Roger Griffin, in Griffin (ed.), *Fascism* (New York: Oxford University Press, 1995), p. 111.

[4] Walter Laqueur, *Fascism: Past, Present, Future* (New York: Oxford University Press, 1996), p. 97.

[5] Roger Griffin, *The Nature of Fascism* (London: Routledge, 1991), p. 169.

"the most authoritative theorist of the most vital currents of neofascism."[6] What all that is supposed to mean remains more than obscure to this very day.

The fact is that Evola's relationship to Fascism over almost a quarter-century of its history – and his relationship to the neofascism that followed – was always, and throughout, highly problematic. All things considered, it is difficult to see Julius Evola as any kind of fascist at all. Nothing in his youth and young manhood marked him as one of those few who could and would write the articles and books of Fascist apologetics.

Evola, as a nineteen-year-old, served in the Italian armed forces in the First World War. But unlike those who advocated Italian intervention in that war and would enter Fascist ranks in the years that were to follow immediately, he objected to his nation's alliance with the industrial democracies. Rather, he favored alliance with the more "traditional" Wilhelminian Germany and monarchial Austria-Hungary. As a scant seventeen-year-old, Evola already sought to foster the "traditionalism" he identified in the beliefs and politics of the Central Powers.

In the course of the First World War, while Fascism was little more than an aspiration, Evola reported enjoying "supersensible" experiences in the mountains of northern Italy. He spoke of undertaking occult practices while not being fully occupied as an artillery officer. It was in those mountains, and at that time, that Evola succeeded in "separating himself from his body," to come into contact with "invisible presences." He enjoyed experiences he identified as "transfigurations" – as "ecstasy, a joyful expansion of consciousness." Before he was twenty, Evola had already embarked on his mystic journey as an initiate, seeking transcendent "liberation" and personal "power" through "magic."[7]

Unlike those who would enter Fascist ranks after 1919, Evola, with the termination of the war, gave himself over to abstract art, mysticism, and occult studies. He became an advocate and a protagonist of Tristan Tzara's avant-garde Dadaism, in which he discovered some sort of affinities with Rudolf Steiner's Anthroposophical "science of the invisible."[8] In making the connection, Evola explicitly rejected the alternative art movement prominent in his immediate environment – Futurism – the singular creation of F. T. Marinetti.

Evola found Futurism objectionable because Marinetti used the movement to advocate the rapid industrial and technological development of Italy.

---

[6] Marco Tarchi, "Introduction," in Julius Evola, *Diorama filosofico* (Rome: Edizioni Europa, 1974), p. lxxviii.

[7] Iagla (Evola), "Experiences: The Law of Beings," in Micheal Moynihan (ed.), *Introduction to Magic: Rituals and Practical Techniques for the Magus* (Rochester, VT: Inner Traditions, 2001), pp. 167–72.

[8] See A. P. Shepherd, *Rudolf Steiner: Scientist of the Invisible* (Rochester, VT: Inner Traditions, 1954).

The advocacy was infused with an intense nationalism – all of which Evola found objectionable.[9] Furthermore, nationalistic Futurism, which early identified itself with Mussolini's Fasci di combattimento, advertised itself as a modernizing movement. Like Fascism, in general, the Futurists were advocates of industrial and technological growth and development for Italy, with all its attendant factories, machine production, motoring, and mechanical flight.[10]

Evola denounced all of that. He held that industrial and technological development was manifest evidence of the fundamental failure of the modern world to live beyond the confines of gross materialism. It was a materialism that "killed the spirit." There was nothing *spiritual* to be found in technology and machine production. All the vaunted power of what Evola called "profane science" – that constituted the knowledge base of such material accomplishments – could only provide mechanical substitutes for what traditionally had been the power of "a few superior beings" who had the ability to effect results, not through the employment of machines and technology, but by invoking the cosmic forces of the spiritual world behind the world of ordinary things.

For Evola, "true power" was that power that infilled only those unique individuals who had made the tortuous ascent to the "heights" of otherwordly "Being" through the agencies of initiatic ritual and ascetic discipline. What Evola sought was not the material power that he was convinced "desacralized" existence – the power that everyone, and anyone, might "democratically" acquire by learning to conform to "natural, physical laws." Rather, Evola sought a "higher power," the product of both *noetic* and *metaphysical* knowledge, accessed through "special faculties" that could only be the result of long and demanding occult training.[11]

That Evola rejected Futurism signaled, in fact, his essentially anti-Fascist disposition. Evola's esotericism was predicated on a radical individualism that found expression in epistemological solipsism,[12] in political antinomianism, coupled with a set of abiding reactionary social and economic convictions.

---

[9] Years later, Evola reiterated his objections. See Julius Evola, *Il cammino del cinabro* (Milan: All'Insegna del Pesce d'Oro, 1963), pp. 18–19. Evola reported that Marinetti had confided to him at the time that "your [Evola's] ideas are as remote from mine as those of an eskimo." Ibid., p. 19.

[10] See Evola, *Saggi sull'Idealismo Magico* (Rome: Alkaest, n.d., but originally published in 1925), p. 191, n. 2.

[11] Evola, *The Yoga of Power: Tantra, Shakti, and the Secret Way* (Rochester, VT: Inner Traditions, 1992), chap. 2, originally published in Italian as *L'uomo come Potenza* (Rome: Atanor, Todi, 1925), then revised and republished in the early 1940s as *The Yoga of Power*.

[12] Years later, Evola admitted to his epistemological solipsism, although he took exception to the word (which he found "inadequate"). "The world," for Evola, "could only be 'my' world." See Evola, *Il cammino del cinabro*, pp. 41–2.

As a consequence, Evola's first political writings were explicitly anti-Fascist. In 1925, three years after the March on Rome brought Mussolini to power, and upon the invitation of one of his occultist colleagues, Evola wrote his first political article for the journal *Lo stato democratico*: an attack on Fascism.[13]

Evola spoke of Fascism as a "caricature" and "parody" of a real revolution. For Evola, Fascism was simply based on material strength; it possessed neither cultural nor spiritual roots. In his article, Evola rejected any form of nationalism as simple foolishness, predicated on empty sentiment. Manipulating "chauvinistic" sentiments, Fascist "pseudorevolutionaries" had stage-managed a "laughable revolution" – all this at the time when it was perfectly clear to everyone that nationalism was the central, mobilizing "myth" of Fascism.[14] Three years after Mussolini assumed power in Italy, Evola insisted that to be "truly human," one would have to "overcome brotherly contamination"; one must "purge oneself" of the feeling that one is united with others "because of blood, affections, country or human destiny."[15] Such ingroup sentiment, the core of Fascist nationalism,[16] had no place in Evola's inventory of "Traditional" virtues. Evola was, and remained, an emphatic antinationalist throughout his life.[17]

Beyond that, Evola objected to any revolution that took on "plebeian" properties – any revolution originating among the "lowly" rather than those informed from "on high." Much to Evola's discomfort, the *squadristi* who collected around the guidons of Mussolini's Fascism – to fight its battles – were largely undistinguished veterans of the war, the ordinary unemployed, and impoverished students, all joined together with less-than-lettered delinquents.[18]

Evola found it exceedingly unfortunate that Mussolini had been a socialist prior to the war, and had involved himself with equally questionable elements: the revolutionary syndicalists as well as the Futurists of F. T. Marinetti. All were known to concern themselves with rapid industrial development and radical social and economic reform. They spoke of the

---

[13] Evola, "Stato, Potenza e Libertà," *Lo Stato Democratico*, 1, no. 7 (May 1925); pp. 98–112; see Evola, *Il cammino del cinabro*, pp. 82–3.

[14] On 24 October 1922, Mussolini said, "We have created our myth. The myth is a faith, a passion.... Our myth is the nation." Mussolini, "Il discorso di Napoli," *Opera omnia* (Florence: La Fenice, 1955–63 [hereafter cited as Oo]), 18, p. 457.

[15] See Evola's comments in Ea (Evola), "On the Magical View of Life," in Moynihan (ed.), *Introduction to Magic*, p. 158, written at almost the same time.

[16] See the discussion in A. James Gregor, *The Ideology of Fascism: The Rationale of Totalitarianism* (New York: Free Press, 1969), pp. 72–92, 252–60, and *Phoenix: Fascism in Our Time* (New Brunswick, NJ: Transaction, 1999), pp. 74–81.

[17] See Julius Evola, *Il fascismo: Saggio di una analisi critica dal punto di vista della Destra* (Rome: Volpe, 1964), pp. 20–1, and passim.

[18] See Guido Fracastoro di Fornello, *Noi squadristi* (Verona: Casa editrice S. A. Albarelli-Marchesetti, 1939).

"corporative" restructuring of industry. And there was talk of demographic policies to increase the birthrate and reduce infant mortality – to provide the citizens to sustain it all. Evola found all such policies deplorable.[19]

Worse still, Mussolini had shown himself to be tendentially secular, and antimonarchial as well. Unhappily, Mussolini's secularism was not the kind that would render him unreservedly anti-Catholic,[20] and his attitude toward the monarchy was entirely pragmatic, having nothing whatever to do with the mystic feelings that Evola attached to the institution. In effect, Evola found nothing attractive in the first Fascism. Nor did that change with the passage of time.[21]

The fact is that Evola never was any kind of Fascist. He was neither a "cryptofascist," a "parafascist," a "superfascist," nor a "neofascist." He was and always remained an occultist, a pagan "magus," a devotee of "initi-atic science" – the lifetime advocate of a "science" predicated on "different criteria of truth and knowledge from those predominant in modern culture and thought."[22]

As a consequence, he identified the fundamental problem of philosophy as epistemological – the articulation and defense of the criteria employed to establish the truth status of empirical, normative, or philosophical claims.[23] Epistemologically, Evola was a solipsist, a radical individualist. The world in which he lived could only be *his* world.[24] His most elaborate treat-ment of epistemological issues, written during the mid-1920s, was contained in his *Theory of the Absolute Individual* and his *Phenomenology of the Absolute Individual*, both of which were essentially solipistic – governed by the premise that epistemological, ontological, and deontological truth claims must be measured by, and against, the "power and freedom of the real individual."[25]

By the time of the appearance of his two major philosophic works, Evola was an aggressive anti-Gentilean at a time when Giovanni Gentile was rig-orously defending Fascism against its foreign and domestic critics.[26] Evola dismissed Gentile's "Actualism" as a sterile enterprise, holding forth the

[19] Evola never abandoned those objections. Toward the end of his life, he repeated precisely the same objections to Fascism. See Evola, *Il fascismo*, pp. 36, 68–9, 71–80.

[20] See Marco Rossi, "'Lo stato democratico' (1925) e l'antifascismo antidemocratico di Julius Evola," *Storia contemporanea* 20, no. 1 (February 1989).

[21] See Evola, *Il cammino del cinabro*, pp. 107–16.

[22] Ea (Evola), "The Nature of Initiatic Knowledge," in Moynitian (ed.), *Introduction to Magic*, p. 29.

[23] Evola, *Saggi sull'Idealismo Magico* (Rome: Alkaest, n.d., originally published in 1925), pp. 5–6, and Ea (Evola), "The Nature of Initiatic Knowledge," in Moynitian (ed.), *Intro-duction to Magic*, p. 27.

[24] See Evola, *Il cammino del cinabro*, p. 42.

[25] Evola, *Fenomenologia dell'Individuo assoluto* (Turin: Bocca, 1930), pp. xii, 1.

[26] See A. James Gregor, *Giovanni Gentile: Philosopher of Fascism* (New Brunswick, NJ: Transaction, 2001).

promise of the individual occupying the center of life's experience, and then surrendering to intellectual abstraction, fearful of facing the prospect of the individual actually shaping the world. Evola insisted that academic philosophers such as Gentile were typically afraid to acknowledge the real power of thought – a power that the gnostic wisdom of Tradition had always assigned it. Evola chose to conceive the notion of a "transcendental ego" quite literally. He argued that only in "mysticism" would the basic epistemological and ontological problems of philosophy be successfully resolved. Academic philosophers feared the occult and consequently had little, if anything, to offer the world in crisis. Only mysticism offered contemporary humans true freedom and real power.[27] Thereafter, Evola had only distain for Gentile's Actualism, the philosophical perspective Mussolini had made the foundation of the official doctrine of Fascism.[28]

Evola consistently maintained that the true power and freedom of the individual could be truly understood only in the occult tradition of East and South Asia and the ancient cultures of the Eastern Mediterranean, Greece, and Rome. Given that peculiar orientation, Evola was not only an essentially apolitical individualist, but an antinomian whose behaviors were governed exclusively by "principles" only he could divine. Evola was essentially a mysteriosophist – a fact that hardly recommended him for membership in the Partito nazionale fascista. In fact, Evola never ever became a member of the Fascist Party.[29]

Evola was never a member of the Fascist Party because he never met the minimum criteria for membership. Evola was a mystic in search of his own peculiar, rather than Fascist, "truths." In that pursuit, he advocated a "suprarational" or "sacred," as distinct from a "profane," science. Unlike standard science, Evola's sacred science was "universal" and "infallible."[30] It was a science that rejected the notion of an "ordinary world," a world in which phenomena were the transient sensory effects of the impact on the individual of a finite, contingent, and "accidental" atomic and subatomic reality. For sacred science, the world was an interplay of etheric beings, of supersensible forces pursuing mystic purpose in accordance with unalterable, transcendent "principle." For Evola, we ordinary humans only occasionally

---

[27] Evola, *Phenomenologia dell'individuo assoluto*, pp. 2, 187–97.
[28] Mussolini had assigned to Gentile the responsibility of writing the philosophical portion of the official *Dottrina del fascismo*. See Gregor, *Giovanni Gentile*, pp. 63–5.
[29] See Evola's *Autodifesa*, his "self-defense" against the postwar criminal charge of having "glorified Fascism," as an appendix to Evola, *Men Among the Ruins: Post-War Reflections of a Radical Traditionalist* (Rochester, VT: Inner Traditions, 2002), p. 292. Evola was never a member of the Fascist Party – during the first period because he chose not to petition for membership, and during the last period of Fascist rule, because his application was rejected for political reasons. See H. T. Hansen, "Introduction: Julius Evola's Political Endeavors," in ibid., p. 46.
[30] Evola, *Saggi sull'Idealismo Magico*, pp. 66–7.

glimpse the sacred world behind the world – through paranormal experience, psychokinesis, precognition, time travel, and astral projection.[31]

In the journals *UR*[32] and *Krur*, which he edited during this period, Evola articulated all this with the absolute assurance of a sleepwalker. Like Rudolf Steiner, the Anthroposophist – who exercised major influence on his development – Evola could "perceive" realities denied ordinary mortals.[33] Because of his special gifts, possessed of his infallible truths, Evola objected both to the Catholic Church as well as Mussolini's "pedagogical" and "ethical" state. He raised his objections in the mid-1920s and persisted in them until his death.[34]

Toward the end of the 1920s, Evola prepared himself to pursue his ideas more fully in the political arena. He had learned that he could not simply reject the Fascism he deplored. Rather, he would seek to influence the political system from within. His first tactic in pursuit of that strategy was to appeal to Giuseppe Bottai, a major figure of the regime, with whom he had served in the military.

Bottai gave Evola access to *Critica Fascista*, one of the more important journals of the period, in which Evola immediately proceeded to publish two articles, largely a restatement and an elaboration of the intellectual and political postures already assumed.[35] This was followed in 1928 by the publication of Evola's first major, specifically political manuscript, *Pagan Imperialism*.[36]

Imperialismo pagano was a frank statement of Evola's views. The exercise commenced with Evola's judgment concerning Fascism's therapeutic

---

[31] *Ibid.*, pp. 67–73, and Ea (Evola), "Freedom, Precognition, and the Relativity of Time," in Moynitian (ed.), *Introduction to Magic*, pp. 304–14.

[32] Some of the articles from *UR* are available in English, in the collection edited by Michael Moynihan, *Introduction to Magic*.

[33] See the account in Shepherd, *Rudolf Steiner*, pp. 20–6. Evola made no secret of his qualified connection with Theosophists, Anthroposophists, and occultists of all sorts. His relationship with Steiner was complex. He frequently qualified his approval of Steiner (as he did with all "spiritualists"), but it is clear that Evola associated positive features of his own occult views with him. See, for example, the appendix to Evola, *Saggi sull'Idealismo Magico*, p. 191, n. 2. Evola even used pictures of Steiner to illustrate the racial types that showed the peculiar "power of spiritual penetration." Evola, *Sintesi di dottrina della razza* (Milan: Hoepli, 1941), pp. 275–6, photographs nos. 2 and 3. During the last years of the 1920s, Evola was deeply involved with Theosophists and Anthroposophists.

[34] In this context, see Evola, *Il fascismo*, pp. 35–6; Evola, *Imperialismo pagano: Il fascismo dinnanzi al pericolo Euro-Cristiano* (Roma: Atanor, 1928), passim. See also the discussions in Evola, *Men Among the Ruins*, passim.

[35] See Evola, "Idee su uno stato come potenza," *Critica Fascista* 3, no. 21 (1 September 1926), and "Il Fascismo quale volontà di impero e il Cristianesimo," ibid. 3, no. 12 (15 June 1927). Another article by Evola, "Fascismo antifilosofico e tradizione mediterraneo," ibid. 5, no. 12 (15 June 1929), also appeared as well. In all, Evola was to publish seven articles in the pages of *Critica Fascista* over the next two decades.

[36] Evola, *Imperialismo pagano*.

potential, given what he perceived to be the advanced state of Europe's systemic illness. After six years of Fascist rule, and a full two or three years of
dictatorship, Evola decided that if Fascism were to have any salutary effect
at all, it would have to develop a "soul." Evola proceeded to advise the followers of Mussolini that only if Fascism became something it was not – by
becoming the agent of the hermetic "Wisdom" of antiquity, abandoning all
the "empty" social, economic, and military programs it had made its own –
might it become the harbinger of a *true* revolution.

Fascism, Evola argued, was the counterfeit of revolution. "It arose from
below, from confused conditions, and the brute forces unleashed by the Great
War. Fascism prevailed through compromise and rhetoric, fed by the petty
ambitions of petty persons.... Fascism has taken shape, but it remains a
form without a soul."[37]

To provide Fascism its soul would necessitate the full adoption of what
Evola, at that time, called the "Mediterranean and Pythagorean Tradition" –
that was, for all the world, identical to the esoteric Wisdom of the Orient.
This meant, by implication, that Fascism would have to follow the "Sacred
Science" of the *Upanishad*, the *Bhagavad gita*, the *Samkhya*, and the *Tantra*
if it were to be anything other than a failed effort at revolution.[38]

The first consequence of such a transformation, Evola insisted, would
be Fascism's abandonment of everything associated with "modern social,
economic and industrial institutions," and "the restoration of the caste
system and the aristocracy" of antiquity. "Wisdom would replace positive
science and initiation would take the place of religion and morality. Magic,"
Evola continued, "would take the place of technology."[39] That would begin
to make Fascism a "true" revolution. Without that transformation, Fascism
would remain unredeemed. The only thing that would salvage the failed
revolution would be a return to pagan Tradition.[40]

More important, perhaps, than anything else, Fascism would have to commit itself to the kind of radical individualism to which Evola subscribed,[41]
abandoning all the collectivism implied in nationalism, statism, and corporativism. All the latter – the "economic, industrial, military, and administrative" elements of Fascism as it had, until that time, defined itself – were,
according to Evola, completely irrelevant.[42] They were simply *material*.
What Fascism required was *spirit*, and that could be found only in the sacred
science that animated the world long before the coming of Christ.

[37] Ibid., p. 11.
[38] Ibid., p. 31.
[39] Ibid., p. 94; see pp. 27, 66–7, 71, 74–6, 79, 131.
[40] Ibid., p. 25.
[41] Ibid., p. 49.
[42] Ibid., p. 18.

What is entirely transparent in all of this is that the "anti-Fascist" Evola of the 1925, author of the article written for *Lo Stato Democratico*, was the same Evola who only barely concealed his contempt for Fascism in his *Imperialismo pagano* of 1928. What was involved, as has been suggested, was a change in tactics. There was no change in the substance of his ideas. If Evola was an anti-Fascist in 1925, he remained an anti-Fascist in 1928.

With the publication of *Imperialismo pagano*, there was a flurry of activity by Fascist intellectuals. More than its simple anti-Fascism, the abrasive anti-Christian polemic of the work scandalized them.

Imperialismo pagano appeared precisely during the period in which Mussolini was involved in the negotiations calculated to produce a political resolution of the long-standing dispute between the Roman Catholic Church and the post-Risorgimento Italian state. Evola's volume was a long diatribe – purportedly in the name of Fascism – against the Roman Catholic Church.

For its part, almost the entire Fascist hierarchy of the period hoped that the negotiations with the Church would be successful, with the regime crowned with a spectacular political victory. To many if not all Fascists, *Imperialismo pagano* constituted a threat to that eventuality.

The reality was that Mussolini welcomed Evola's intervention. He wanted the fulminations of what he identified as a "hysterical anti-cleric" in order to bait the representatives of the Vatican. Mussolini imagined that the papal delegates would be more manageable if they found themselves threatened by the possibility of an implacable "anti-clerical Fascism" taking the place of the "moderate" head of government in the course of their deliberations.[43]

Mussolini's stratagem worked eminently well. The result was an agreement that allowed Mussolini to insist that he had obtained essentially what he wanted from the Lateran Accords.[44] He had pressed Evola into temporary service to manipulate the representatives of the Church. He had been successful. Evola had served his purposes.

Following that, Evola was dismissed from consciousness. The major Fascist periodicals spoke of his work as "formless and unsophisticated" – works in which "every line concealed a coarse error." Evola's publications, it was said, were not serious, deserving little more than "to be put aside and thought no more about."[45]

---

[43] See the account in Richard Drake, "Julius Evola, Radical Fascism, and the Lateran Accords," *Catholic Historical Review*, no. 74 (1988), p. 411.

[44] Mussolini, "Relazione alla camera dei deputati sugli Accordi del Laterano," *Oo*, 24, p. 44.

[45] Ugo d'Andrea, "Imperialismo pagano," *Critica Fascista*, 6 (15 August 1928), pp. 319–20; Luigi Volpicelli, "Imperialismo fascista," *Educazione fascista*, 6 (September 1928), p. 561.

Undaunted, Evola continued his attempt to fill, with his esoteric Wisdom, what he held to be the empty vessel that was Fascism. In the beginning of the 1930s, he commenced the publication of a new, essentially political journal, *La Torre*, which would serve as a staging area from which the knights of sacred Tradition might sally forth to give battle.[46]

The publication attracted a number of relatively well-known figures, mostly from the occult initiatic community. Some of the same Theosophists and esotericists who contributed to *UR* and *Krur* in the 1920s reappeared to lend support to the new venture. Prominent among them was René Guénon, whose views had initially helped to shape those of Evola.[47]

Guénon was an "orientalist," whose rejection of the modern world found fulsome expression in Evola's Traditionalism.[48] It was, at least in part, from Guénon that Evola learned that all of modern learning was to be rejected – that permanent and unalterable "Truth" was to be found only in the "transcendent realism" of the Sacred Science of the *Vedanta* and the Sanskrit musings of South Asia – more "objective than anything to be found in whatever profane science."[49]

Guénon's position on the nature of science was perfectly clear. For Guénon, "science" had very little to do with empirical observation, hypothesis formation, and testing. "True" science was Sacred Science, a "pure metaphysics," the result of the "intuitive intelligence" of "initiates." The "higher science" that so revealed itself was predicated on infallible and universal "principles" from which all subsidiary truths of the empirical and the "transempirical" world could be deduced (apparently like some sort of sacred Euclidean geometry).[50]

Guénon supported Evola's dismissal of profane science as uncertain and impermanent, because of its reliance on sensory observation, logical deduction, time- and circumstance-specific prediction, together with constant empirical review and revision. Whatever the differences between Guénon and Evola – for example, in terms of the definition of "self" and "ego," among others – were differences common among occultists, Theosophists, Anthroposophists, and hermetic metaphysicians. What they all agreed on was the recognition that all of modern science was to be rejected as having killed the "spirit" of humanity.

Like Evola, Guénon saw truth, not in standard science, but in myth, metaphor, and analogy. Both rejected "discursive" thought. Evola was fond of repeating the epigram of Laotze: "Those who know the truth do not

---

[46] See Evola, *Il cammino del cinabro*, pp. 107–16.

[47] See Evola's comments in ibid., p. 13.

[48] See René Guénon, *La crisi del mondo moderno* (translated by Julius Evola. Milan: Editore Ulrico Hoepli, 1937). The original French volume was published in the early 1920s.

[49] Evola, "Introduction" to ibid., pp. 1–14. Citations are from p. 5.

[50] Guénon, ibid., chap. 4; cf. René Guénon, *Man and His Becoming According to the Vedanta* (New York: Noonday Press, 1958), Preface and chap. 1.

discuss it; those who discuss it, do not know it." What is evident in almost everything that Evola wrote was that his ideas had been fixed in his early manhood and never substantially changed over the next half-century. Similarly, Evola's tactics, like his views, changed remarkably little over the years, except superficially. He always insisted that only if Fascism would transform itself into the system that he advertised would it be truly worthy. That would mean that Fascism, to be truly revolutionary in Evola's judgment, would have to abandon everything to which it had committed itself in terms of its philosophical, political, social, economic, strategic, and religious convictions. Should that be accepted as a serious proposal, it would be hard to imagine that whatever emerged from the transfiguration would qualify, by any measure, as Fascism.

Once that is acknowledged, it is not difficult to identify the themes that were to appear in the pages of his magazine, *La Torre*. In the first issue, with perfect candor, Evola made his intentions clear:

> Our magazine was not created to "whisper" and "insinuate" something to Fascism or to . . . Mussolini, because neither . . . would know what to do with that. Our magazine was created rather to defend *principles* that for us are always and absolutely the same, independently of whether we are under a communist, anarchist, or democratic regime. . . . Up to the point, that Fascism follows and defends those principles, up to that point we can consider ourselves Fascists. And that is all.[51]

By the time the fifth issue of the journal appeared, Evola felt compelled to write, "We are neither 'Fascists' nor 'anti-Fascists.' 'Anti-Fascism' is nothing. But for those of us . . . who are irreducibly opposed to any plebeian politics and every 'nationalistic' ideology . . . *Fascism is not enough*." When Evola was reminded that Mussolini did not entertain any of the ideas broadcast in the pages of *La Torre*, he responded, "So much the worse for Mussolini."[52]

What is perfectly transparent is that there was very little that could pass as "Fascism" in Evola's belief system. By 1930, he had offended almost all of the members of the Fascist hierarchy – not to speak of the majority of Fascist intellectuals. Evola opposed literally every feature of Fascism. In that year, Ugo Spirito, a major Fascist ideologue, wrote a devastating review of some of Evola's work.

Evola, Spirito wrote, was a person with a "mania for originality at any cost, a vain taste for novel constructions and an ill-concealed insufferance for the demanding moral discipline that is central to a well understood idealism." Spirito dismissed as confusion and self-delusion Evola's singular convictions concerning the secret science that would allow human beings to transform themselves into transcendent entities. Evola's notion of a superior being, the "concrete individual" he saw as "creator of the world" – possessed of

---

51 Evola, "Carta d'identità," *La Torre*, no. 1 (1 February 1930), p. 43.
52 See the discussion in Hansen, "Introduction" to Evola, *Men Among the Ruins*, pp. 40–3.

"absolute power... in perfect and complete possession of himself" – Spirito dismissed as the consequence of Evola's intoxication with an exotic "Westernized Orientalism."[53]

By the time the first issues of *La Torre* appeared, Fascists, in general, were thoroughly alienated. Their objections to Evola, and his ideas, came in the form of systematic criticism. Bottai, who had provided a platform for Evola a few years before, characterized his work as "an arbitrary coupling of a mass of ill-digested notions."[54]

Together with the intellectual criticisms came threats of physical violence – and for a time Evola moved about Rome with a bodyguard. More damaging was the pressure from authorities. It became more and more difficult for Evola to publish his journal. With the appearance of the tenth issue, on 15 June 1930, *La Torre* ceased publication.

By that time, Evola realized that if he intended to survive as a voice for Tradition, he would have to abandon his efforts at absolute independence. He needed allies. Pursuant to that "more mature" strategy, Evola sought alliance with Giovanni Preziosi and, through him, with Roberto Farinacci, a former secretary general of the Fascist Party. Neither Preziosi or Farinacci had ever been, or ever expected to be, "orthodox" Fascists.[55]

Preziosi was violently anticlerical. A defrocked priest, he was to become one of the very few true anti-Semites in Fascist Italy. As early as 1920, his journal, *La vita italiana*, was a conduit for the most violent anti-Semitism. As an anti-Semite, Preziosi had few followers in Fascist Italy. During the years under review, Mussolini himself gave little evidence of personal or political anti-Semitism. Some of his closest collaborators were Jews, ranging from his friend and political collaborator A. O. Olivetti, to his workmate and mistress, Margherita Sarfatti.[56]

In effect, during the years under consideration, Preziosi was a marginal, and largely inconsequential, figure. The case with Farinacci was somewhat different. Farinacci was a prominent leader of the original *squadristi* that provided the armed militia of the original Fascism. On the basis of his early importance, Farinacci, thereafter, always presented himself as a political force with whom to reckon. He was often at odds with Mussolini and a frequent opponent of his policies. During the years under review, he served briefly as party secretary and then retreated to his provincial base, from which he continued to operate with considerable autonomy. What we find is

---

53 The volumes reviewed included Evola's *Saggi sull'Idealismo Magico* and *L'uomo come potenza*, published in 1925 and 1926 respectively. Ugo Spirito, "L'Idealismo magico," in Spirito, *L'Idealismo italiano e i suoi critici* (Florence: Felice le Monnier, 1930), pp. 192, 197, 200.

54 As cited, Mario Giovana, *Le nuove camicie nere* (Turin: Edizione dell'Albero, 1966), p. 7.

55 See Evola's comments in *La cammino del cinabro*, pp. 111–12.

56 See the account in Renzo De Felice, *Gli ebrei italiani sotto il fascismo* (Turin: Giulio Einaudi editore, 1962), pp. 75–81.

that Evola sought succorance in the company of allies who were anti-Semitic, and tendentially pro-German – that is to say, National Socialist.[57] Neither, it very quickly became evident, were "Mussoliniani." Both, as was the case with Evola, sought an alternative "Fascism."

It was with the support of such persons that Evola survived in what was, without question, an increasingly hostile environment. Evola escaped into the essentially private publications of Preziosi and Farinacci, where – although charged by the "orthodox" as being anti-Fascist – he sought to further the cause of what he called the "authentic Right."[58]

By the early 1930s, Evola was fully aware that his ideas had struck no lasting resonance in Fascist Italy. The small collection of esotericists who had collected around him remained what they had always been: political eccentrics and marginal persons. That translated into a grudging acknowledgment that Fascism would not serve as a vehicle for his sacred science.

At almost the same time, there were several interesting developments that were to influence the character and content of Evola's subsequent work. First, the translation of his *Imperialismo pagano* into German provided the occasion for Evola to develop contacts in Germany at a time when both the German right – largely conservative and composed of members of the lesser nobility – and Hitler's National Socialists were increasingly active. Evola began to devote his time to cultivating German contacts.

In the German translation of *Imperialismo pagano*, Evola was careful to marginalize Fascism in the course of his exposition.[59] More than that, the text, which appeared as *Heidnischer Imperialismus*,[60] is a document that strongly suggests that Evola was no more National Socialist than he was a Fascist.

The text largely reiterates the familiar catalog of Evola's mysteriosophic notions. Once again, it repeats the critique of Mussolini's Fascism. Once again, we are told of how Fascism came to pass, peopled by the most plebeian elements of Italian society. Once again, we are told of the syndicalists and corporativists who seek to succor the "inferiors" – looking to Bolshevism as

---

[57] These characterizations must be understood for what they are. In the early 1930s, anti-Semitism had not taken on all the connotations that inevitably follow the characterization after the mass murder of Jews by National Socialists. Preziosi's anti-Semitism was extremely ugly, and he did support the National Socialists throughout the Second World War. How responsible he was for the death of innocents is very difficult to determine. He committed suicide at the conclusion of the war.

Farinacci's affinities with the National Socialists can be traced at least as early as 1940, when Hitler specifically asked that Farinacci be made the Italian representative to Berlin. Thereafter, Farinacci was a loyal spokesperson for German interests in Italy. How opposed he was to Mussolini is evidenced by the fact that Hitler once soundly rebuked Farinacci for speaking ill of the Duce to him in a private conference.

[58] Evola, *Il cammino del cinabro*, pp. 112–14.

[59] Evola specifically confirms as much in his intellectual biography. See ibid., p. 149.

[60] Evola, *Heidnischer Imperialismus* (Leipzig: Armanen Verlag, 1933).

their normative model. Once again, we are told of the fictive hierarchy jerry-built by Fascists, composed of moral defectives and poseurs. Once again, we are told that Fascism did not understand the role of monarchy, allowing the King of Italy to vegetate on the margins of the political system. Once again we are told of machine industry and technological concerns that succeed in "killing the spirit." Once again, the existence of a mass party is deplored, together with the totalitarian ethic that denies the individual the liberty and fulfillment that is at the center of Tradition.

In the German text, we are explicitly informed if anti-Bolshevik and antidemocratic dictatorship is to have any historic meaning whatever, it must be nothing other than a transitional regime that would ultimately resolve itself in the reconstruction of Traditional society, institutionally informed by castes, discipline, and aristocracy – directed, ultimately, by "transcendent invisible forces."[61] Anyone reading *Heidnischer Imperialismus* could hardly fail to realize that both Fascism and National Socialism, in Evola's cosmic view of history, failed all the historic tests proposed. In Evola's clear judgment, both National Socialism and Fascism were, at best, place holders for an "authentic right."

But there was something more to be found in the text of *Heidnischer Imperialismus*. In a brief, closing account of Evola's intellectual itinerary, the editors of Armanen Verlag, reminded their readers that "in Italy, Evola is virtually the only representative of the Nordic-Aryan and anti-Semitic idea"[62] – a depiction that was only partially true and intrinsically misleading. The "Nordic-Aryan" and "anti-Semitic" ideas Evola entertained were very singular, and only part of a complicated, tortured, and bizarre ideological belief system.

Since his young manhood, Evola was convinced that more elements of a truly Traditional society survived in Germany than almost anywhere else in Europe. Throughout his active political life, Evola addressed himself to those persons and groups of persons who represented those elements – essentially members of the land-based, military, and public official Junker class who were supposed to embody Prussian virtues. He found his "natural environment" among the members of the Herrenklub of Berlin, an association of "conservatives," members of the German nobility who had survived the First World War.[63]

As was the case with Fascism, Evola was prepared to work through Hitler's National Socialists, recognizing among them all the deficiencies he had identified among Mussolini's Fascists. That notwithstanding, he imagined he found among the National Socialists certain occult features: the invocation of pagan ritual and runes, tentative organizations that took on

---

[61] See the account in ibid., pp. 95–101.
[62] Ibid., p. 112.
[63] See Evola, *Il cammino del cinabro*, pp. 148–50.

some features of the premodern knightly orders, as well as some semblance of the reconstruction of castes based on the deterministic distinctions presumably drawn between "creators," "bearers," and those who could only destroy culture. It was more than he had found in Mussolini's Fascism.

What Evola proceeded to do was to address his efforts toward Germans. As Hitler rose to power, Evola completed what was to remain his major work, *Revolt Against the Modern World*.[64] As might well have been anticipated, the publication went entirely unnoticed in Fascist Italy. In the "new Germany" of Adolf Hitler, on the other hand, it attracted some considerable attention.[65]

There seem to be several reasons for that. Evola appears to have tailored the text to a German, tendentially National Socialist, audience. As was the case with the German translation of his *Imperialismo pagano*, the revolution he advocated for Germany no longer sought to restore a "Mediterranean, Pythagorean Tradition." *Rivolta contro il mondo moderno* made its appeal to a tradition more familiar to Germans and National Socialists: that which was "Nordic-Aryan."

More than that, the entire issue of race became a central concern of Evola's work in *Rivolta contro il mondo moderno*. Hardly mentioned at all in the 1928 version of *Imperialismo pagano*, it was recurrent in the later text. Equally emphatic was anti-Semitism, as a critical feature of the discussions concerning race.

Although anti-Semitism is present in *Imperialismo pagano*, it was a minor issue.[66] In *Rivolta contro il mondo moderno*, on the other hand, it is one of the more central concerns. Semites and Jews are portrayed as millennial opponents of sacred science and Traditional society. We are told that they constitute "a ferment of decomposition" among the peoples of the ancient world. Many of the anti-Traditional defects of the Christian churches, such as their humanistic sentimentality and much of the "collectivism" subversive of Nordic-Aryan individualism – all of which fed into the cult of equality, Marxism, capitalism, revolutionary communism, and Bolshevism itself, and all or which were inimical to Tradition – were all traced to the influence of generic "Semites."[67]

---

[64] Evola, *Rivolta contro il mondo moderno* (Milan: Editore Ulrico Hoepli, 1934). A considerably modified English translation is available as *Revolt Against the Modern World* (Rochester, VT: Inner Traditions, 1995).

[65] Evola, *Il cammino del cinabro*, pp. 148–50.

[66] See Evola's depreciatory references to Jews and "Semites" in *Imperialismo pagano*, pp. 16, 29–33. In the text of *Heidnischer Imperialismus*, we are told that anti-Semitism must be part of the solution to the political and social problems of the modern world. There is a constant reference to the destructive influence of Semites and Jews; see pp. 8–9, 11–12, 16, 19, 21, and passim.

[67] Evola, *Rivolta contro il mondo moderno*, p. 314. See Evola's comments in which the "southern, Semitic spirit" is portrayed as the antipode of the "solar and Aryan spirit." Ibid., p. 365; see, in this context, pp. 312–13, 421, n. 9, 428, n. 1a, 436–7, n. 12.

Whatever "Mediterranean" features there were associated with Tradition in *Imperialismo pagan* are spoken of in *Rivolta contro il mondo moderno* as the product of "Ur-Aryan" origins, the result of primordial Nordic-Aryan migrations from Hyperborea, Thule, Atlantis, and Lemuria. In the course of the discussion, Evola was not above citing Alfred Rosenberg's *Mythus des XX. Jahrhunderts* in support of some of his conjectures.

There can be little doubt that, in 1933 and 1934, Evola wrote *Rivolta contro il mondo moderno* with a German audience in mind. He had no influence whatsoever among Italian Fascists. German National Socialism, on the other hand, seemed to offer him more fertile possibilities. Granted that it cannot be taken to mean that Evola adapted his views to his audience, in a venal search for advantage, at the expense of his most fundamental convictions. Beneath the overt and in part cosmetic changes in his delivery, the fundamental core of his Traditional beliefs remained unaltered. Nor did he conceal that fact from his chosen audiences. He warned them that the modern world had become so steeped in crass materialism that every effort to reintroduce the sacral idea of virility, of action, of personhood, and of independence would probably result in their immediate transformation into their secular counterparts as material success in mechanical invention, financial success in sport, and simple conquest in warfare. He proceeded to warn his audiences that the simple fact that Fascism and National Socialism had invoked the symbols of primordial Nordicity and ancient Rome meant nothing. Both could very easily decay into political ideologies, lacking all transcendent, supermondane, and transrational Traditional substance.[68]

Evola's conviction was that by somehow mixing his sacred science with the surface features of Fascism and National Socialism, he might somehow increase its survival potential in the toxic modern world. Thus, he spoke of his spiritual "solar Hyperborean race" as "Nordic" and "Aryan." He emphasized the negative historic role of Semites and Jews. He spoke of his Nordic-Aryans as a physical race of virile, heroic, and culture-creating blonds. He spoke sepulchrally of racial miscegenation and enthused about the virtues of the German tribes and the Holy Roman Empire. He seemed to be articulating a form of biological racism that the world recognizes as that found in Hitler's *Mein Kampf*. Actually, as we shall argue, very little of what Evola wrote was "racist" in that easily understood sense. What he said, in fact, had precious little to do with National Socialist ideology and still less to do with Fascism. His association with both was founded on the hope that he might use either or both as carriers for his Traditionalism.

In the years that were immediately to follow the appearance of the *Rivolta contro il mondo moderno*, Evola was to publish an inordinate

---

[68] Ibid., p. 475. These notions remain, with some changes, in the English text; see *Revolt Against the Modern World*, p. 362.

amount of material on racial questions – and thereby contributed to the monumental intellectual confusion that surrounds his political ideas to this day. There is every indication that Evola materially and consciously contributed to that confusion. In effect, the confusion that resulted was intentional. By 1934, Evola had clearly decided to attempt to influence the political hierarchy of National Socialist Germany by couching his recommendations in familiar terms. Just as the terms "hierarchy," "heroism," "mysticism," "anti-intellectualism," "leadership," "antiparliamentarianism," "discipline," "asceticism," "struggle," and "imperialism" meant something in the lexicon of Fascism, Evola took those terms and conscripted them to his own service – providing them entirely different meaning. Similarly, all the terms made familiar by National Socialist "race science" made their appearance in Evola's subsequent publications. As we shall see, their meaning, in almost every case, was entirely transformed.

Evola's first major publication devoted entirely to the race issue, *The Myth of Blood*,[69] appeared in 1937. The full statement of his initiatic views appeared four years later, in *Synthesis of the Doctrine of Race*,[70] in the course of the war that would destroy both Fascism and National Socialism.

Il mito del sangue was unique in the sense that it is perhaps the only work in which Evola did not make his position eminently clear throughout. His intention was to provide a kind of encyclopedia of racist thought as it evolved since Johann Gottlieb Fichte, Johann Gottfried Herder, and Franz Bopp through Adolf Hitler.[71] His exposition covered the general thoughts of the various authors, separating out of that thought the major themes: Nordic superiority, anti-Semitism, the genetic transmission of physical and psychic traits, problems of typology and classification, as well as the "racist" conception of history, law, and responsive legislation.

Although Evola does not really contest any of the specific claims made by the various racist theoreticians with whom he deals, he does maintain an evident degree of detachment. Even in the case of very prominent National Socialist theoreticians such as Alfred Rosenberg, Evola raised critical reflections. In one place, he seems to suggest that Rosenberg involved himself in a vicious circularity, insisting that Nordics are the sole culture creators and then defining "culture" as that which Nordics create.[72]

Moreover, there is a decided undercurrent of objection, on Evola's part, to the use of the term "spirit" when it is applied to a biological community identified as a "race." This becomes particularly apparent when he discusses

[69] Evola, *Il mito del sangue* (Milan: Editore Ulrico Hoepli, 1937).

[70] Evola, *Sintesi di dottrina della razza* (Milan: Editore Ulrico Hoepli, 1941).

[71] See the comments by Enrico Nistri in his review of *Il mito del sangue* in *Diorama letterario*, no. 15 (November 1978).

[72] Evola, *Il mito del sangue*, p. 174.

the ideology of Hitler. "Spirit" appears to have had a special, if ill defined, meaning for Evola.

The entire chapter devoted to Hitler's ideas emphasizes the Führer's preoccupation with the somatotype of Germans. Hitler's express concern with the overt anthropological traits of Germans was clearly predicated on the conviction that the preferred "spiritual" properties that presumably typified Nordics were necessarily associated with Nordic physical traits. In his discussion, Evola made evident that he refused to make any such association. He refused to countenance any suggestion that "true spirituality" could be predicated on a person's physical properties alone. It is apparent that however cautious of expression Evola remained in the course of his exposition, his reservations concerning Hitler's biological "materialism" surfaced with insistent regularity.

In fact, Evola's objections were emphatic. In the chapter devoted to Hitler's ideas, Evola remarked that, in general, "prevailing" racist thought has succeeded in demeaning itself by "exaggeration, confusion, over generalization, and through the employment of politically charged terms" – all of which discredited the entire enterprise.[73] In substance, Evola cannot credibly be characterized as simply an apologist for Hitler's racism. He was not at that time, nor was he in later years. Evola's racism was neither Fascist nor National Socialist.

In the years that were to follow the publication of *Il mito del sangue*, Evola fully developed his own conceptions on what was at the time identified as the "race issue." After 1938, his ruminations concerning what he called "totalitarian race theory"[74] appeared with some regularity in the semiofficial Italian publication, *Difesa della razza* – the *Defense of the Race* – that appeared almost immediately after the official publication of the statement on Fascist race doctrine on 15 July 1938. The document contained ten brief paragraphs that provided an account of the official Fascist position on the "race question."[75]

Between the appearance of *Il mito del sangue* in 1937 and the publication of his *Sintesi di dottrina della razza* in 1941, Evola devoted the majority of his efforts to producing what he considered a comprehensive, initiatic theory of

---

[73] Ibid., pp. 241, 255–8.
[74] Evola, "Supremi valori della razza ariana," *Difesa della razza* 3, no. 7 (5 February 1940), p. 15.
[75] An English translation is available in Gregor, *The Ideology of Fascism*, Appendix A, pp. 383–6. The Italian text is available in Aldo Capasso, *Idee chiare sul razzismo* (Rome: Edizioni Augustea, 1942), pp. 5–6. While we are given 15 July 1938 as the official date of the appearance of the document, in the first issue of the *Difesa della razza*, we are informed that minister of popular culture authorized the statement not on the fifteen, but 26 July 1938. See "Il partito e il razzismo italiano," *Difesa della razza* 1, no. 1 (5 August 1938), p. 2. Whatever the case, the first issue of *Difesa della razza* appeared almost immediately.

race, derivative of the principles of Tradition. Throughout the period under review, he published a flurry of articles in *Difesa della razza* – a journal that attracted very few, if any, major Fascist theoreticians.

In one of those published articles, Evola outlined the unique features of his methodology, in which he dismissed the "myopic and empty . . . positivistic" methods of "academic philology and archaeology" – to advocate recourse to the intuitive interpretation of myths and symbols. Evola held that myths and symbols afford "vehicles most adequate to give expressions of spiritual significance" that provide, to the esotericist, admittance to an otherwise inaccessible "metaphysical . . . suprarational world."[76]

For Evola, the intuitive interpretation of myth and symbol would provide more credible information about the past and the present – as well as the "transrational" and "supermondane" – than any form of systematic collection and "profane" assessment of historical, or physical anthropological and archaeological, traces. Clearly, such a conviction was part of Evola's entire repertoire of occult beliefs. Similar statements are found throughout his writings, and were clearly expressed in his *Rivolta contro il mondo moderno*.

In his introduction to that work, he expressed his distain for the "historical sciences" or the "modern 'knowledge'" they advertise. He simply dismisses the materials that profane science credits with having the greatest scientific value. Instead, Evola identifies those "mythical, legendary, and epic elements denied historical truth and demonstrative value" by standard science as the invaluable "superindividual and nonhuman" source of "real and certain knowledge."[77]

Upon that foundation, Evola constructed his theory of race. Commencing with the beginning of 1939, Evola gave full expression to his "totalitarian" notion of how "race" is to be understood.

Each race, according to Evola, can be approached at three distinct levels: the physical or anthropological, the characterological, and, finally, the "spiritual," level. Evola spoke of the first as "biological" or "material," and the second as a function of "soul." The nature of the third, the "spiritual," was never clearly defined. It is clear that "spirit" refers to something that is "transcendent" and "suprabiological," but such notions defy any kind of operational definition.[78] In one place, Evola defines "spirituality" as "actually what has been successfully actualized and translated into a sense of superiority which is experienced inside by the soul, and a noble demeanor,

---

[76] Evola, "La dottrina romana della vittoria," *Difesa della razza* 3, no. 6 (20 January 1940), p. 38; see "Simboli eroici della tradizione Ario-Romana: L'ascia," ibid. 4, no. 1 (5 November 1940), p. 34.

[77] Evola, *Rivolta contro il mondo moderno*, pp. 7–8.

[78] See the discussion in Evola, "I tre gradi del problema della razza," *Difesa della razza* 2, no. 5 (5 January 1939), pp. 11–13.

which is expressed in the body."[79] None of this seems to be particularly illuminating.[80]

It seems that "spirituality," for Evola, refers to some extrasensory, transcendent power that dynamically influences human beings, to generate in them a sense of superiority and power that manifests itself in distinctive, empirically overt behaviors. The behaviors include "heroic" and "sacral" demonstrations of "faith," "loyalty," "discipline," and "asceticism." For Evola, such manifest behavioral traits are not simply the consequence of the possession of a "soul." They are the product of "spirit" – something "supernatural" that somehow acts on the soul.[81] Since Evola dismisses the notion of any lawlike regularities governing phenomena as one of the delusions of "profane" science, the relationship between character (as "soul") and "spirit" is not at all transparent.

What *is* clear is that Evola was convinced that all of this is the deductive result of holding some Traditional premises as unalterably true.[82] According to Evola, if one holds some collection of "suprarational" premises as impeccably true, one can deduce from a single rite, a set of symbols, or a tissue of myths the complex life circumstances of entire historic peoples in terms of their biological race, and the very essence of their civilization.[83] On the basis of these sorts of mysteriosophic conjectures, Evola produced his *Sintesi di dottrina della razza*.

In his work, Evola tells the story of a "mysterious, primordial olympian and solar Hyperborean race," possessed of "non-human spirituality," that apparently had no evolutionary history.[84] That "supernatural" race was suddenly simply there, the product of "invisible and intangible forces that are its metaphysical source and true life."[85] At some time in the hoary past, a shift in the earth's axis brought ice and darkness to Hyperborea – that fabulous land of sunshine and abundance – and drove its population south and east, to mystic Atlantis, legendary Thule, and fabulous Mu.

---

[79] Evola, "The Mountain and Spirituality," in *Meditations on the Peaks* (Rochester, VT: Inner Traditions, 1998), p. 4. The specific date of this article is not provided, but it probably was written toward the end of the 1930s.

[80] In another place, Evola offered an equally unenlightening definition of "spirit" as what "the wellborn have always said were the marks of *race*: namely, straightforwardness, inner unity, character, courage, virtue, immediate and instant sensitivity for all values, which are present in every great human being and which, since they stand well beyond all chance-subjected reality, they also dominate." Evola, *Vita italiana*, 30 (September 1942).

[81] Evola, "La razza e la guerra: Due eroismi," *Difesa della razza* 3, no. 2 (20 November 1939), p. 18.

[82] See Evola, "Panorama razziale dell'Italia preromana," *Difesa della razza* 4, no. 16 (20 June 1941), p. 9.

[83] See the discussion in Evola, "Roma aria: Le origini," *Difesa della razza* 4, no. 17 (5 July 1941), p. 22.

[84] See Evola, *Rivolta contro il mondo moderno*, p. 244.

[85] See ibid., p. 15.

As the Hyperboreans traversed the globe, they established civilization and culture everywhere: in North, Central, and South America; in East and South Asia; in the eastern Mediterranean and the Mediterranean littoral; and finally in Europe. The Hyperboreans were generic Aryans, who in their travels, and through miscegenation with lesser peoples, gave rise to the variety of Aryans who now people the globe.[86] The Germanic Nordics and the Mediterranean Aryans are the historic remnants of the Hyperborean "super race." As racial intermixture increased with the migrations of the primordial Hyperboreans, their creative talents diminished. The heirs of the Hyperboreans are now found in diverse regions of the world, some of whom are still latently, or "subconsciously," possessed of the spiritual qualities of their forebears.[87]

The migration of Hyperboreans and their Aryan heirs distributed over the globe those solar, cyclopean civilizations that remain the pride of humanity. Those civilizations sought to preserve the talents of their founders by establishing a complex array of hereditary caste arrangements that blocked the infusion of inferior blood into that of the culture creators. The caste systems of ancient China, India, Sparta, and Egypt reflect that universal attempt. The increasing relaxation of caste restrictions – as humanity proceeded from the Golden Age to modernity – gave rise to intercaste fraternization that resulted in the impaired descendants who could no longer preserve and sustain the cultures they had inherited.

The inferior races with which the Aryans interbred were the residues of previous "race cycles" – human debris. Other than the "obscure" races found in sub-Saharan Africa, that debris included all those fossil races, and their descendants, discovered by paleontologists and cultural anthropologists, and imagined to be the "missing links" required by what Evola dismissed as Darwinian evolutionary fantasies.

Evola argued that all those skeletal remains were not our forebears, but the remains of previous race cycles. Living "primitives" – sub-Saharan blacks, the pre-Dravidian indigenous populations of South Asia and the Indonesian archipelago – were all considered "inferior" by Evola. Beyond that, and subject to particular opprobrium, were Jews. They were the bearers of a spirit that made them the "germ of decomposition" within Aryan cultures – "dionysiac" and "telluric" in disposition, sensualistic, abstractly intellectualistic, materialistic, and collectivistic. They were fundamentally destructive, the "precious instrument for the secret front of global subversion."[88]

Evola's antipathy toward the Jews had its origin in his early manhood. One finds traces in *Imperialismo pagano*, where he speaks of "Semitic

---

[86] Evola, "Simboli eroici della tradizione Ario-Romana: L'ascia," *Difesa della razza* 4, no. 1 (5 November 1940), pp. 34–5; see Evola, *Rivolta contro il mondo moderno*, part 2, chap. 3, *Sintesi di dottrina della razza*, pp. 66–77.

[87] Evola, *Sintesi di dottrina della razza*, p. 86.

[88] Ibid., pp. 172–3.

contamination" of the Mediterranean tradition.[89] His anti-Semitism becomes increasingly shrill in *Rivolta contra il mondo moderno*, to become venomous and all-pervasive in *Sintesi di dottrina della razza*.

That was the racial doctrine that Evola urged on Fascism. It was a doctrine – as Evola insisted – that was derivative of esoteric gnostic and initiatic wisdom. It was a doctrine that he was convinced would provide a spiritually empty Fascism its missing substance.[90] It was a doctrine discovered by Evola through intuition, the interpretation of myth, the scrutiny of symbols, and the reading of the primary literature of remote antiquity. That together with the writings of nineteenth- and early-twentieth-century racists seems to have exhausted Evola's reading. There is very little evidence of his having read anything of the literature of standard anthropology, genetics, philology, or history.

As singular as his speculations were, some of his individual notions were more singular still. Evola believed, for example, that genetic mutations, "idiovariations," were caused by "suprabiological" influences of the "supranatural" world behind the world. These "inexplicable" changes in genetic structure, that shape races in mysterious ways, originate from "on high," from a "nonterrestrial" source.

Human beings may constructively contribute to the process of racial change, initiated from on high, by consciously creating an environment that might stimulate and foster those heroic and sacral virtues of the primordial Hyperboreans, thereby harmonizing the individual will with that which is superhuman.[91] Together with the restoration of some form of caste arrangement to proscribe miscegenation between the "higher" and "lower" races, such efforts might begin to reconstitute the lost virtues of the primordial Hyperboreans.

When one disinters the details of Evola's views, the picture becomes increasingly odd. Everywhere in his discussions, after the production of *Rivolta contro il mondo moderno*, Evola speaks of the "organic harmony" of the three components of each human being. In the true human, the ideal member of a "pure" race, the *soma*, the physical body, is fully compatible with the soul, which, in turn, is fully compatible with the spirit. However desirable, it is not at once clear how one might certify anyone's organic harmony.

Evola discusses the problem with some solemnity. On one instructive occasion, he undertook a review of the work of a then-contemporary German psychologist, Ludwig Klages.

Evola found the work of Klages objectionable. He claimed that it failed to comprehend the subtleties of true racism and consequently had a deleterious

---

[89] Evola, *Imperialismo pagano*, pp. 16, 30–1, 33.
[90] Ibid., p. 159.
[91] Evola, *Sintesi di dottrina della razza*, pp. 79, 136, 139.

influence on racial thinking in National Socialist Germany. Evola used the case to warn those he would influence that it was not enough to identify a subject as "Aryan" – simply because the appropriate documentary evidence of racial descent could be produced, or because he displayed all the preferred physical traits of Aryan Nordicity.

Evola argued that Klages was not a Nordic-Aryan because his published work clearly showed affinities to the work produced by Jews – by Sigmund Freud, Henri Bergson, and Alfred Adler. Klages apparently possessed a "Jewish spirit," or had been "Jewified." He no longer "connected" with his "blood" or with the "great olympic and transcendent forces of Hyperborean origin."[92] Somehow or other – irrespective of all the physical and documentary evidence – Klages was a Jew.

The implications of this kind of argument are evident. Evola's racism was not concerned with the social visibility or evidentiary bases of racial identity. Whatever rehearsals he undertook cataloging Aryan physical traits were, in the last analysis, of only secondary importance, if important at all. It really was not at all telling how persons appeared. What was primary and determinate for Evola was their manifest behavior.

That critical distinction is confirmed by Evola's own history. His intellectual development was influenced, to a significant degree, by at least two Jews: Carlo Michelstaedter and Otto Weininger.[93] Their respective behaviors were apparently sufficiently heroic, ascetic, and sacral to qualify somehow as those of "residual" Hyperboreans or, at least, seeming Aryans.

Given just such considerations, it is perfectly clear that Evola's anti-Semitism could not be consistently maintained.[94] While he spoke at great length, and almost everywhere, of Semitic influences undermining the Aryan world, it was almost invariably about their behavior and not their biology. In the last analysis, Evola's notions concerning race were really only an elaborate afterthought – largely precipitated by contingencies – jerry built on the foundation of his magic idealism.

Most serious Fascist thinkers recognized as much. In 1941, serious physical scientists in Fascist Italy dismissed Evola as given to "bizarre,... metaphysical and anti-scientific... theses, in part fantasies, sustained by... occultists who imagine they have unique access to... divine truths."

---

[92] Evola, "La razza e la filosofia della vita," *Difesa della razza* 4, no. 3 (5 December 1940), pp. 27–9.

[93] See Philippe Baillet, *Julius Evola e l'affermazione assoluta* (Padua: Editzioni di Ar, 1978), p. 12.

[94] Guido Landra, one of the more insistent racists in Fascist Italy, pointed out that Evola held that "an Aryan can have the soul of a Jew or vice-versa. And that therefore unfair measures could be taken against a Jew, because he was a Jew, even though he might possess the soul of an Aryan – this seems to us theoretically untenable. The practical acceptance of such a principle would have terrible consequences for racism." *Vita italiana*, no. 31 (February 1943), p. 151.

The fact that Evola, "adept of magic science and esoteric traditions," rejected, as foolish, the Darwinian notion of human evolution, was simply dismissed as arrant nonsense.[95]

In 1942, in the course of the Second World War, Fascist intellectuals published excoriating criticism of Evola's racism. There were reviews of *Sintesi di dottrina della razza* that entirely dismantled the complex structure of Evola's exposition. The argument was made that if the *spirit* of humankind were Evola's concern, and there were Jews, or perhaps blacks, who displayed the heroic and sublime properties of the Hyperboreans, what difference did it make if that spirit were housed in "non-Aryan bodies"? Of what conceivable importance were physical properties when the real concern is with spirituality? In one of Fascism's most important theoretical journals, Evola's critic pointed out that many Nordic-Aryans, not to speak of Mediterranean Aryans, fail to demonstrate any Hyperborean properties. Instead, they make obvious their materialism, their sensuality, their indifference to loyalty and sacrifice, together with their consuming greed. How do they differ from "inferior" races, and why should anyone wish, in any way, to favor them?

The criticism continued. Evola, it was pointed out, rejected almost every feature of Fascism: its nationalism, its unitary party, its social and economic policies, its corporativism, its appeal to the Italy of the Renaissance with its profane science, and the Italy of the Risorgimento, the Italy of Mazzini, and so on.[96] It was recalled to the attention of all that Evola, on more than one occasion, had publicly announced that "he was not a Fascist and rejected, as an aristocrat, plebeian politics, nationalist ideology of any sort, political party intrigues, as well as any form of socialism, whatever its trappings...."[97]

At almost the same time, Michele Sciacca published the last volume of his history of Italian philosophy in the twentieth century, in which the "magic idealism" of Evola was allotted a few pages. Sciacca, in large part, dismissed Evola's peculiar esotericism with its singular ontological idealism that almost immediately decayed into a form of absolute solipsism – that, in turn, provided the grounds for the deification of the individual through some sort of arcane process. The remainder of Evola's occult system was largely dismissed as an undisciplined idiosyncrasy.[98]

All the evidence suggests that Fascist intellectuals never took Julius Evola seriously as a thinker, much less a "Fascist" thinker – and, in fact, Evola

---

[95] See Mario F. Canella, *Principi di psicologia razziale* (Florence: G. C. Sansoni, 1941), pp. 59, 61, n. 1, 203, n. 2.

[96] Ugoberto Alfassio Grimaldi di Bellino, "Recensioni," and "Note e discussioni: Ai margini di una polemica sulla validità di un esoterismo razzista," *Civiltà fascista* 9, no. 4 (February 1942), and 9, no. 10 (August 1942), pp. 647–52.

[97] Riccardo Carbonelli, *Roma fascista*, no. 23 (9 April 1942), p. 3.

[98] Michele Federico Sciacca, *Storia della filosofia italiana: Il secolo XX* (Milan: Bocca, 1942), pp. 529–32.

himself never pretended to be a Fascist. The few Fascists who allowed Evola to use their facilities to broadcast his conjectures were, for all intents and purposes, marginal political figures. Almost every major Fascist thinker publicly rejected Evola's Traditionalism.

By the advent of the Second World War, there were practically no Fascists and precious few National Socialists who counted Evola among those cataloged as "Fascist thinkers." More than that, National Socialists perhaps thought less of Evola than did Italian Fascists.[99]

Soon after Evola began his courtship of Hitler's Germany, Heinrich Himmler's personal staff reported that, in their judgment, Evola represented nothing more than curious "utopian" and "pseudoscientific" views that had as their inspiration a body of thought calculated to fuel "an insurrection of the old aristocracy against the modern world." The report indicated that Evola was, at best, only "tolerated and hardly supported by Fascism," and concluded with the recommendation that "there is not even a tactical need to assist him."[100] And the National Socialists were as good as their word.[101]

With Fascism's cataclysmic collapse in 1943, and the German effort at politically reestablishing Mussolini in the north of Italy under National Socialist auspices, Evola refused to commit himself to either Fascism or Mussolini.[102] The reasons were not far to seek. They were the same that had made him reticent to join the Fascist Party for two decades. Instead, he remained in Rome, as he recounted later, to prepare the foundations for a future movement that would represent the "authentic right" as he conceived it.[103]

In 1951, after he had begun his attempt to found such a movement, he was indicted by the post-Fascist government of Italy for the crime of "glorifying Fascism" and attempting its "reconstitution." Evola replied directly and, in large measure, truthfully to the charges. He held that he never was either a Fascist or a National Socialist. All their respective "theories" were wrong, and he repeated, once again, the same affirmation he made at the time that the Fascist dictatorship had only just begun its historic parabola. He insisted

---

[99] Evola admitted that almost all prominent figures in Fascist Italy objected to his ideas. When he proposed that Mussolini underwrite a journal to be published in both Italy and Germany that would expand on the ideas found in *Sistesi di dottrina della razza*, Fascists from every part of the party and government raised objections. See Evola, *Il cammino del cinabro*, pp. 170–2.

[100] As cited by H. T. Hansen, "A Short Introduction to Julius Evola," in Evola, *Revolt Against the Modern World*, p. xviii.

[101] For a period toward the end of the Second World War, Evola worked for one or another National Socialist agency on a research project dealing with "secret societies." Nothing seems to have come of the effort.

[102] See the discussion in Gianfrano de Turris, "Julius Evola," in Fabio Andriola (ed.), *Uomini e scelte della RSI: I protagonisti della Repubblica di Mussolini* (Foggia: Bastogi, 2000), pp. 179–97.

[103] See Evola, *Il cammino del cinabro*, pp. 175–6.

that he was only a Fascist insofar as and in the measure that Fascism supported some ideas that "were superior and anterior to Fascism." To make his point, he went on to recite the entire roster of his objections to Mussolini's Fascism, objections he had very early made known. He opposed Fascism because of its "socialism," its totalitarianism, its corporativism, its commitment to industrialization and economic development, its infatuation with the philosophical ideas of Giovanni Gentile, its single-party structure, its lack of "spirituality,"[104] its materialism, its antimonarchial tactics, and its "collectivism" – to identify only his most evident objections.[105] If he seemed to support Fascism, it was only because some of its ideas, in some sense, mimicked "truths" to be found in the *Bhagavad-gita* or among the gnostics of antiquity.

The Court of Assizes in Rome duly found Evola innocent of all charges. Evola was not then, and never had been, an apologist for Fascism.

In the years that were to follow, Evola repeated the same ideas he had put together in his young manhood. Whomever he influenced, he influenced them with doctrines that could only be characterized as "Traditional" – certainly not Fascist. To speak of Evola's ideas as the "quintessential fascist blend of rationality and myth"[106] is to commit a number of errors. Evola was not a Fascist thinker, so it would be hard to imagine that his ideas might be "quintessentially" Fascist. More than that, Evola's notions of "rationality" and "myth" were idiosyncratic, to say the least, and certainly not Fascist. His ideas could only be quintessentially Evola.

It seems that Anglo-American commentators choose to identify any body of thought that is, in any sense, antidemocratic, racist, anticommunist, or antifeminist as "neofascist." This appears to be more emphatically so if something "mystic," "occult," or "mythical" can be found somewhere among its doctrines. As has been suggested, unless such terms as "mystical" and "anti-intellectual" are defined with some precision, they can be deceptive and employed to serve only prejudicial purpose.

For example, Fascism did have its "School of Fascist Mysticism," and some have seized upon the fact as evidence that Fascism was intrinsically and pejoratively "irrational." In fact, the "mysticism" of the School of Fascist Mysticism defined "mysticism" as the kind of "spiritualism" to be found in the first, philosophical portion of the official *Dottrina del fascismo* – written by Giovanni Gentile – which served as the ideological rationale for the regime. Fascist "mysticism" is defined in the "Fundamental Ideas" of

---

[104] Evola insisted that Mussolini simply did not have the sense of "spirituality" necessary to understand the insights he was being offered. See ibid., p. 97.

[105] See "Evola's *Autodifesa* (Self-Defense Statement)," in Evola, *Men Among the Ruins*, Appendix, pp. 287–97. In 1950, Evola had outlined all his objections to Fascism. They were exhaustive. Not surprisingly, Evola approved of very little. See Evola, *Orientamenti* (Rome: "Imperium," 1950), particularly pp. 11–17.

[106] Eatwell, *Fascism: A History*, p. 254.

the *Dottrina* – that is, in terms of preeminently rational (not rationalist) Gentilean philosophy.[107] There was nothing of the "transrational magic idealism" of Evola to be found in the School of Fascist Mysticism.[108]

The fact is that because fascism is considered so reprehensible, Anglo-American academics do not feel themselves obliged to treat the subject with any professional detachment. Cavalier and irresponsible claims can and have been made. Thus, not only is Evola identified as a Fascist, his mysteriosophic notions and his bizarre views concerning science and race are made part of the defining traits of historic Fascism.[109]

Since Fascism is almost universally held to be an unmitigated evil, no one really expects to be held accountable for their treatment of its ideas. The results are apparent. Very few academics would tolerate similar treatment of Marxist, or Marxist-Leninist, ideas.

The consequence is that, more often than not, we are treated to a caricature of Fascist thought. Few academics bother to read the primary literature. That is held to be an unconscionable waste of time, since everyone knows, intuitively, that Fascists never entertained any real ideas. It is a common

---

[107] Mussolini, "Idee fondamentali," of "La dottrina del fascismo," *Oo*, 34, pp. 117–21. The Fascist "spiritual" conception of life was characterized in the exposition of Giovanni Gentile in the first portion of the *Dottrina del fascismo*. The "life of the spirit" manifested itself as "God, as Fatherland, as Nation, and as civilization." Its mysticism found expression in the selfless readiness to sacrifice for God and country – to sacrifice for something superior to the individual. Fascist mysticism distinguished itself from Christian mysticism in that it sought to serve the world as well as God. As a consequence, it rejected as vain all those lamentations about the "decline of the West." Fascism emphasized faith in renewal. See Ettore Martinoli, *Funzione della mistica nella rivoluzione fascista* (Udine: Casa editrice C. U. Trani, 1940), pp. 13–14, 25, 36–7, 40–5.

[108] See the treatment in G. S. Spinetti, *Mistica fascista nel pensiero di Arnaldo Mussolini* (Milan: Editore Ulrico Hoepli, 1936). It is also interesting to see what Fascist racists meant by "mysticism." See Enzo Leoni, *Mistica del razzismo fascista* (Milan: La Tipograficavarese, 1941), a monograph of *Dottrina fascista*, January 1941.

[109] See the references to Evola in Roger Griffin (ed.), *Fascism* (New York: Oxford University Press, 1995). He is referred to as "for a time Mussolini's favorite theorist of Fascism's version of Aryan racism." Griffin, *The Nature of Fascism*, p. 169. I have dealt with such claims in considerable detail in A. James Gregor, *Mussolini's Intellectuals: Fascist Social and Political Thought* (Princeton, NJ: Princeton University Press), chap. 9, particularly pp. 217–19. As was the case during the negotiations with the Vatican concerning the Lateran Accords, Mussolini used Evola's quaint ideas to serve Fascism's tactical purposes. As he had in the late 1920s, Mussolini apparently allowed the dissemination of Evola's ideas on race in the early 1940s for tactical purposes – to insist on Fascism's theoretical independence from National Socialist race theory. Mussolini rejected biological determinism. Evola clearly made the case. More important, however, was the official Fascist position with respect to racial differences. The official *Manifesto of Fascist Racism* rejected, in principle, the notion of categorical racial "superiority" and "inferiority." That Mussolini accepted any of the arguments advanced by Evola is most improbable. In this context, see the more exhaustive discussion of Fascist racism in Gregor, *The Ideology of Fascism*, chap. 6, and the English translation of "The Manifesto of Fascist Racism," in ibid., pp. 383–6.

judgment among many that Marx, Lenin, Mao Zedong, and Fidel Castro had real ideas, but Fascists never did.

As a result, we have no idea what to expect of the thought of "neofascists." As we have suggested, some see "neofascism" in the political thought of Reagan Republicans, tax protesters, soccer thugs, skinheads, graveyard vandals, militia members, antisocialists, anti-egalitarians, and anyone who refuses to conform to the strictures of "political correctness." The results have been intellectually embarrassing.

The nonfascist thought of an occultist such as Evola is conceived fascist, while ideas having unmistakable fascist properties often fail to be so considered. This is nowhere more evident than in the treatment of patterns of thought that are somehow insulated from criticism.

In the United States, an abundance of revolutionary political thought is just so insulated. Black protest thought is hardly ever considered in a comparative context. More often than not, it is treated as though it were *sui generis*, a unique product reflecting incomparable experience. Actually, more fascism is to be found in black protest literature than in all the works of Julius Evola – and yet, one is at a loss to find any of it, or any mention of it, in the anthologies of neofascist reflection. It is to an analysis of some black protest literature to which we can profitably turn our attention.

5

Black Nationalism and Neofascism

Marcus Garvey and the Universal Negro Improvement Association

Julius Evola was always an improbable Fascist. He insisted that the ideas he defended were not Fascist; they were "superior and anterior to Fascism."[1] The journalists who early sought out "neofascists" after the Second World War should certainly have been aware that Evola was never considered to have been a Fascist during the years of Mussolini's regime. It was known that Giuseppe Bottai, a prominent Fascist gerarch, had dismissed Evola's ideas as a "mass of ill-digested and arbitrarily coupled notions."[2] Bottai's distain was not unique. Almost every major Fascist intellectual rejected Evola's strange ideas. Evola, in fact, consistently denied he was ever a Fascist. All that notwithstanding, journalists and scholars seeking neofascists and neofascism have consistently argued that Evola was the major source of neofascist ideas in post–World War II Europe. His name still appears regularly in almost every contemporary volume devoted to neofascism.

Conversely, scholars have long been aware that during the interwar years Marcus Garvey, the leader of the Universal Negro Improvement Association (UNIA), insisted that he and his organization "were the first Fascists," and went on to claim that "when we had 100,000 disciplined men, and were training children, Mussolini was still unknown. Mussolini copied our fascism."[3]

Knowing that, there has been literally no discussion of the "fascism" of Marcus Garvey.[4] Evola, who never claimed to be a Fascist, and whose work was uniformly dismissed by Fascist intellectuals during the years of Mussolini's rule, has been pressed into service as the source of contemporary

---

[1] Julius Evola, "Autodifesa," in *Men Among the Ruins: Post-War Reflections of a Radical Traditionalist* (Rochester, VI: Inner Traditions, 2002), p. 293.

[2] As quoted in Mario Giovana, *Le nuove camicie nere* (Turin: Edizioni dell'Albero, 1966), p. 7.

[3] As quoted in Robert A. Hill and Barbara Bair (eds.), *Marcus Garvey: Life and Lessons* (Berkeley, CA: University of California Press, 1987), p. lviii.

[4] I addressed the issue in A. James Gregor, *The Fascist Persuasion in Radical Politics* (Princeton, NJ: Princeton University Press, 1974), pp. 360–75, but I am unaware of any further discussion.

neofascism for half a century. It is hard to explain the difference in treatment. It is particularly hard to understand since the contemporary custom is to identify "fascism" – however defined – with "racism" – however defined.[5]

If one reviews the relevant literature with any care, one finds that the term "racism" is generally used with considerable abandon. Not only are important distinctions neglected, but "racism" obscures anything else that might be said about one or another ideology. Thus, because some form of racism was attributed to Mussolini's regime, Fascism was conceived indistinguishable from Hitler's National Socialism – even though Nazi racism was of an entirely different order.[6] The distinction between Fascism and National Socialism having been vacated, the generic term "fascism" came to serve as a universal term, having National Socialism, Fascism, Falangism, Vichy traditionalism, Portugese syndicalism, the Hungarian Arrow Cross, and the Romanian Legion of the Archangel Michael, among others, as its referents. They were all fascists because all were somehow conceived racists of one sort or another. It did not matter what kind of racists they might be – and it turned out that some could hardly be spoken of as racists at all.[7]

Racism became the defining trait of fascism, and if it were not found, it was inferred. Thus, if a belief system or a political organization, having absolutely nothing to do with historic Fascism, articulated any form of racism, it was immediately identified as a "cryptofascism" or a "parafascism." Conversely, if a belief system or a political organization was fascist – because of some historic association, however obscure – it was, by implication, racist. Regardless of how one chooses to deal with that circularity, the difficulties it inspires are evident.

However scholars manage all that, it is curious that there are some ideologies and some political movements that are *not* identified as fascist or neofascist, even though they are clearly *predicated* on racism, and clearly share features with the movement founded by Mussolini. This is particularly puzzling because racism has figured so prominently in the analyses of social scientists. For half a century after the Second World War,

---

[5] Fascist racism was markedly different from National Socialist racism, both from the nature of its sociobiological rationale and the treatment of its victims. For years prior to and during the Second World War, Fascist Italy assisted Jews in escaping Hitler's National Socialists. Fascists became complicit in Hitler's murder of the Jews only when they no longer controlled their environment and only to the extent that Italian Jews were forced into camps from which they were transported by German troops – an eventuality that was tantamount to their execution. See the discussion in A. James Gregor, *Giovanni Gentile: Philosopher of Fascism* (New Brunswick, NJ: Transaction, 2001), chap. 8.

[6] See the entire discussion in Renzo De Felice, "Introduction to the New Pocket Edition," in *Storia degli ebrei italiani sotto il fascismo* (Turin: Einaudi, 1993), pp. vii–xxii, and chap. 8.

[7] See, for example, António Costa Pinto, *The Blue Shirts: Portuguese Fascists and the New State* (New York: Columbia University Press, 2000). Racism played little if any part in the evolution of "Portuguese fascism."

academicians were perfectly comfortable speaking of any form of anti-Semitism or racism as "fascist inspired,"[8] as though either or both must be necessarily and exclusively fascist in origin.

And yet, throughout the entire period from the end of the First World War to the turn of the twenty-first century, movements such as Marcus Garvey's UNIA and Elijah Muhammad's Lost-Found Nation of Islam – at the center of which were black racism and more than a suggestion of anti-Semitism – were very rarely, if ever, spoken of as fascist or neofascist.

Why that should be the case is difficult to comprehend, particularly since some post–World War II political movements apparently cannot escape being neofascist and racist, because of some historic connection with wartime Fascism – even though they have publicly abjured both Fascism and racism.[9] Black protest movements in the United States, on the other hand, no matter their racism and their evident fascist propensities, never seem to qualify as either racist or neofascist.

Movements, interest groups, or academics who oppose one or another immigration policy of their respective communities are almost invariably identified as racist – hence neofascist.[10] Some marginal political groups that are, in any sense, anti-Semitic, are immediately stigmatized as either fascist or nazi.[11] And yet, it will be argued that there are groups, clearly racist and arguably anti-Semitic, that are rarely, if ever, identified as either fascist, neofascist, or nazi. The terms are apparently to be used selectively, with selectivity based on some set of idiosyncratic criteria.

What seems evident is that the terms "fascist" and "nazi" are often employed to do little more than signal disapproval. But it is not their employment as terms of disapprobation that is the current concern. It is the inconsistency, and sometimes vacuity, of their use.

The inconsistency is nowhere more apparent than in the treatment of the thought and political practice of Marcus Garvey, the founder of the UNIA, and Elijah Muhammad, long-time leader of the Nation of Islam. Both committed themselves, and their organizations, to overt racism and some form of anti-Semitism – and yet, they or their organizations are rarely identified as neofascist.[12] Irrespective of the fact that Garvey identified himself and

---

[8] Glyn Ford (ed.), "Introduction," *Fascist Europe: The Rise of Racism and Xenophobia* (London: Pluto Press, 1992), p. x.

[9] See the discussion in A. James Gregor, *Phoenix: Fascism in Our Time* (New Brunswick, NJ: Transaction, 1999), pp. 10–14.

[10] See, for example, the accounts of neofascism found in texts like Roger Eatwell, *Fascism: A History* (New York: Penguin, 1995), part III.

[11] See, for example, Semyon Reznik, *The Nazification of Russia: Antisemitism in the Post-Soviet Era* (Washington, DC: Challenge, 1996); Alexander Yanov, *Weimar Russia and What We Can Do About It* (New York: Slovo-Word, 1995).

[12] This must be qualified by the recognition that Hill and Bair refer to Garvey's apparent affinities with Mussolini's Fascism and anti-Semitism – but the analysis does not proceed much further. See Hill and Bair, *Marcus Garvey: Life and Lessons*, pp. lvi–lx.

the UNIA with Mussolini's Fascism, Garvey and his uniformed legions are rarely, if ever, associated with generic fascism.

How that is to be interpreted is part of the story of one of the most fascinating revolutionaries of the twentieth century – a man who was ultimately to become leader of the largest mass organization of blacks in American history. He was Marcus Mosiah Garvey, the grandchild of black slaves, who was born on 17 August 1887 in the small village of Saint Ann's Bay on Jamaica's north coast.[13]

By his early twenties, Garvey had committed himself to the struggle for the economic, social, political, and psychological rescue of blacks. Like all contemporary blacks, he suffered the abiding sense of humiliation that afflicted them all, whether they found themselves strewn throughout the Caribbean or Central, South, or North America in the Western Hemisphere or in continental Africa. Denied political or social equality, blacks everywhere were burdened by a prevailing sense of inefficacy and inferiority.

By 1914, Garvey undertook the organization of the blacks of Jamaica in an association that sought their uplift. Limited to an area and a population that could hardly serve his ultimate vision, Garvey migrated to the United States in 1916, where he found a society in turmoil.

After the Civil War, there had been massive migration of blacks from the South in the effort to find security and opportunity in the North. Uprooted from familiar circumstances, confused and threatened by the very newness of their environment, blacks were available for mobilization. Increasingly exposed to urban violence and languishing in general poverty, even the prospect of improvement proved daunting.

Blacks thus found themselves in a revolutionary situation similar to that found elsewhere in the modern world: geographic displacement, the absence of traditional constraints, the alienation of their own elites, and exposure to rapid social, economic, and political change. They gave voice to increasingly assertive demands for systemic social change. By the end of 1917, Garvey's Universal Negro Improvement Association was prepared to thrust itself into that situation and sought to satisfy those exigencies.

By the time the UNIA lost its impetus in the late 1920s, it had gathered into membership hundred of thousands, if not millions, of blacks throughout

---

[13] There are a number of political biographies of Garvey available. See John Hendrick Clarke, *Garvey and the Vision of Africa* (New York: Random House, 1974); David Cronon, *Black Moses: The Story of Marcus Garvey and the Universal Negro Improvement Association* (Madison, WI: University of Wisconsin Press, 1969); Elton C. Fax, *Garvey: The Story of a Pioneer Black Nationalist* (New York: Dodd Mead, 1972); Tony Martin, *Marcus Garvey, Hero: A First Biography* (Dover, MA: Majority Press, 1983), and *Races First: The Ideological and Organizational Struggles of Marcus Garvey and the Universal Negro Improvement Association* (Dover, MA: Majority Press, 1976); Lenford S. Nembhard, *Trials and Triumphs of Marcus Garvey* (Millwood, NY: Kraus Reprint, 1978).

the United States, the Western Hemisphere, and, in smaller measure, in continental Africa. Throughout its first years of existence, it organized thousands of urban blacks in the paramilitary formations of the African Legion. Ancillary to them, were the disciplined black women of the Black Cross auxiliaries. Children were mobilized by the UNIA and immersed in its ideology. Like almost all the revolutionaries of the twentieth century, Garvey fully understood the psychological function of military discipline, uniforms, and the readiness to sacrifice.

To a defeated and humbled people, the wearing of a uniform provides the pretense of success. Marching together, the individual is multiplied, and is often possessed of a sense of invincibility. Men, women, and children are organized and disciplined. In uniform, those who hungered for prestige sample it for perhaps the very first time. Mussolini's Fascists were among the first to understand that spontaneously. Garvey had preceded them by several years.

Other than affording North American blacks the occasion of donning uniforms, the UNIA also founded small businesses, gave employment to thousands of blacks, and sought involvement in international politics, commerce, and trade. The Association underwrote the establishment of retail service industries in black communities. Blacks were employed in millinery shops, laundries, restaurants, and clothing stores. Through its agencies, the UNIA acquired seagoing vessels, manned essentially by blacks, calculated not only to unite all the scattered elements of the race, but to stimulate a sense of accomplishment among them all.

In retrospect, it appears certain that the United States government, already fearful of the "red menace" of revolutionary Bolshevism, saw in Garveyism the potential source of racial strife and revolutionary dislocation. In the space of a few short years, the UNIA had managed to attract the support of hundreds of thousands, if not millions, of American blacks. That, together with the fact that thousands of disciplined blacks were marching in seried ranks throughout Harlem, could only trouble authorities. It was not long before pretexts were found to charge Garvey with a variety of felonies, including stock fraud and using the federal mail for his criminal purpose. Convicted, Garvey served his sentence in federal prison and was subsequently deported.

Garvey and his most loyal followers attempted to hold the UNIA together, but it soon began to disintegrate. Garvey continued his efforts from Jamaica and finally from London, but his organization fragmented and its membership dissipated, to find solace in a number of essentially religious organizations that offered blacks the promise of succorance. Marcus Garvey died in London on 10 June 1940, in the course of the Second World War – a war he had anticipated – on the date that Fascist Italy declared war on Great Britain and France.

Garvey passed into history as a "black revolutionary," the inspiration for the anticolonialist, pan-Africanist movement that changed the history

of Africa at the conclusion of the Second World War. He is spoken of as
providing some of the doctrinal elements that contributed to the strategies
of the Black Power movement in the United States. So conceived, he is rarely
considered in the broader context of the non-black ideologies that shaped
revolutionary impulse in the twentieth century. He is seen almost exclusively
as a *black* revolutionary.

This seems to produce the indisposition among social theorists to consider Garvey in the comparative context of the major ideological contests
of the last century – as though such comparison is somehow improper. The
possible conscious or unconscious motives for that are difficult to determine
with any confidence. What it does is to isolate Garvey's thought as pecu-
liarly black – as though black intellectuals occupy a segregated niche among
political thinkers.

Whatever its motives, there has been a decided disinclination to associate
the UNIA with fascism – irrespective of the fact that Garvey himself had
so conceived it. There has even been an effort to insist that the palpable
racism of the UNIA is not racism at all. It is sometimes argued that racism
is not racism when it is "defensive" or "reactive." We are further told that
neither American nor international blacks have the power to implement their
racism – therefore, it really should not be considered racism. None of that
seems relevant to the cognitive issue of social science classification.

If a movement, an interest group, an individual or a political community
is to be identified as fascist or neofascist because it is "racist," in any sense
whatever, are black racists not fascists or neofascists? It hardly seems relevant to dismiss their racism because it is either reactive or cannot be fully
implemented. If that were the case, then Adolf Hitler, who conceived himself "reacting" to "Jewish oppressors," was not a racist until he came to
power.

It is clear that such distinctions are counterintuitive. They are largely
irrelevant to any serious cognitive assessment of revolutionary thought in
the twentieth or its successor century. They do not speak to the central issues
of the present enterprise.

What is beyond cavil is the fact that the belief system of Garvey's UNIA
included an unmistakable form of overt and emphatic racism. Once again,
if that is the case, why should not both he and his movement be classified as
a form of neofascism?

The issues involved are both cognitive and perlocutionary – or normative,
if one prefers. In everyday discourse, a word like "racism" is used not primarily to serve cognitive purpose, but in order to *influence* opinion through
sentiment or feeling. It is employed to mold the behavior of persons, not to
educate them.

Whatever its cognitive uses, the term "racism" has undisputed negative
affect. Apparently for that reason, some academicians refuse to refer to
either Garvey or the UNIA as being, or as having been, racist. Because most

non-black intellectuals tend, for whatever reason, to favor black political protest, they refuse to associate that protest negatively with either racism or neofascism.

A number of concerns remain associated with the history of domestic American, and international, black protest that address the entire issue of the social scientific study of neofascism. Some of those concerns illuminate a number of cognitive problems that have always surrounded responsible inquiry into Fascism, generic fascism, and neofascism.

A treatment of black movements that considers the entire issue of black racism is one way to deal systematically, if selectively, with those concerns. As a consequence, Garvey's UNIA recommends itself to our attention. It manifests features that are basic to our general analysis.

First of all, there is more to the notion of a black neofascism than the issue of racism. To explore the broader dimensions of a black neofascism has much to recommend it. Such a discussion allows a more intensive treatment of the complex entirety of what a true neofascism might be. What will become increasingly evident is that it cannot be racism alone, or primarily, that defines the concept. In fact, it will be argued that racism is neither neofascism's central nor most significant attribute.

Clearly, any discussion of modern neofascism must necessarily involve some treatment of the historic circumstances in which such movements emerged, developed, and sustained themselves. This is particularly true about any black neofascism, emerging in very unique circumstances in either the Western Hemisphere or Africa. That is to say, black political responses can only be considered in their appropriate context.

In the course of the history of the United States, blacks were taken by force from their homeland and sold to individuals as chattel – a unique modern experience. If one is to speak persuasively of a black neofascism, one is required to pursue the discussion in just that setting.

After emancipation in the United States, blacks constituted a minority within a hostile majority population that denied them civil and political rights, as well as the opportunities necessary to alleviate their distress and improve their status. As a community characterized by high social visibility, individual blacks could not escape abuse as persons, and violence as members of a racist society. Everything contributed to their sense of abiding threat, unrelieved humiliation, and tragic inferiority.

If one of the factors fueling the generation of fascist thought, fascist political protest, and fascist assertiveness is a sense of humiliation and imposed inferiority, then certainly domestic American blacks met that first requirement. One need only have the faintest appreciation of black history to appreciate that fully.[14]

---

[14] See the summary account in Theodore G. Vincent, *Black Power and the Garvey Movement* (Berkeley, CA: Ramparts Press, n.d.), chap. 2.

That understood, one can begin an analysis of the sustained similarities shared by the first Fascists and the leaders and members of the black protest movement in the United States. One can only be impressed by the features, easily identified, that are common to both.

As a case in point, if one recognizes that Mussolini's Fascists sought the industrial and economic development of Italy in order to accomplish the peninsula's "redemption," its "palingenesis" (as Fascists were fond of saying), then one has no difficulty anticipating the character and intentions of the economic program of Garvey's UNIA.

Fascists sought the accelerated industrialization and economic development of retrograde Italy, at the turn of the twentieth century, in order to ensure the peninsula its "place in the sun" – and assuage the sense of inferiority from which Italians had suffered at least since the time of Machiavelli. For much the same reasons, Marcus Garvey regularly spoke of Negroes[15] demanding and deserving their "place in the sun."[16] And he understood, as did the original Fascists, what attaining that place involved. As often as he spoke of the black man's place in the sun, he consistently identified what would be required to "advance" people "in the respect and appreciation" of others: "industrial and commercial progress."[17]

With elementary analysis, the logic becomes apparent. Like the first Fascists, Garvey maintained that without the possession of power and authority, neither individuals nor communities could expect to be accorded respect nor could they expect to enjoy security. That judgment followed from the argument, similar to that advanced by the first Fascists, that humankind could not be expected to be spontaneously virtuous. Rather, one could only expect human beings to respect each other when denizens of a well-ordered community in which law was sustained by force. In the last analysis, only force assured justice. Garvey went on – once again like the first Fascists – to emphasize that "the only protection against injustice in man is power." He counseled his followers that "the powers opposed to Negro progress will not be influenced in the slightest by mere verbal protests. . . . In the last analysis, whatever influence is brought to bear against [them] . . . must contain the element of force in order to accomplish its purpose. . . . Power," he continued, "is the only argument that satisfies man."

He drew out the implications of his position. Any community that sought that kind of power would have to create for itself a "solid industrial

---

[15] I will employ "Negro," "black," or "African American" where it seems appropriate. Garvey always employed the term "Negro" to identify his race.

[16] Garvey spoke candidly of a "racial empire upon which 'the sun shall never set.'" Garvey, "African Fundamentalism," in Hill and Bair, *Marcus Garvey: Life and Lessons*, p. 5. He spoke of the "awakened Negro" crying out for "a place in the sun." Marcus Garvey, *Philosophy and Opinions* (edited by Amy J. Garvey. New York: Atheneum, 1969), 2, p. 6.

[17] Amy Jacques Garvey, *Garvey and Garveyism* (Kingston, Jamaica: Amy Jacques Garvey, 1963), pp. 22, 64.

foundation" for its generation and maintenance. Only that would allow the black man to "blast a way through the industrial monopoly of races and nations" and achieve his rightful place – armed with the power and authority that would be his certain protection against injustice and degradation.[18]

One must, of course, recognize that Garvey was addressing himself primarily to American blacks, who constituted a relatively small minority of the total population in which they found themselves. The original Fascists, on the other hand, were concerned with an economically and industrially less-developed but established *nation*. Their purpose was international power and international recognition within the context of a world system in which Italy already had a national presence. Garvey's immediate purpose was to palliate the circumstances of black Americans, confined as they were within a system of overarching control.[19] Creating an industrial and commercial base for American blacks would not afford them particular political leverage within a system that had already consigned them to "their place"; it would only provide blacks, as individuals and as a group, with employment opportunities and some measure of economic security in an eminently insecure environment.

Thus, the UNIA's Negro Factory Corporation was calculated to provide those opportunities and that security through the acquisition of factories and small retail outlets where blacks might obtain employment. All of that seems perfectly obvious. Beyond those obvious qualifications governing the immediate implementation of his program, however, it is evident that Garvey accepted the more general logic of the original Fascist analysis.[20] It is eminently clear that Garvey understood the ultimate purpose of industrialization and economic development to be the general protection and enhancement of black power in a Darwinian world of group conflict. He understood that, in the world arena, nations were required to "build up armaments of the most destructive kind," since they were the "only means of securing peace and protection. . . . Do not be deceived," Garvey advised his followers, "there is no justice but strength. In other words, in our material civilization, might is right."[21]

Thus, outside of his recognition of the immediate needs of black Americans, Garvey appreciated the fundamental role of industrialization and

---

[18] Garvey, *Philosophy and Opinions*, 1, pp. 2, 4–5, 9–10, 16, 21.

[19] Garvey reminded his followers that the black in North America would forever remain in the minority, "outnumbered by other races who are prejudiced against him." Garvey, *Philosophy and Opinions*, 1, p. 53.

[20] Here one can refer to the original Italian Nationalist and Fascist analysis. See A. James Gregor, *Mussolini's Intellectuals: Fascist Economic, Social and Political Thought* (Princeton, NJ: Princeton University Press, 2005), chaps. 2, 3.

[21] As cited in Garvey, *Philosophy and Opinions*, 2, p. 13; Martin, *Marcus Garvey, Hero*, pp. 143–4. Garvey spoke of "nationhood" as "the strongest security of any people." Garvey, *Philosophy and Opinions*, 2, p. 34.

economic development in the distribution of power on the world stage.[22] For peoples and nations, the circumstances were the same: Economic and specifically industrial power underwrote security and status.

Clearly prevailing circumstances governed Garvey's program for blacks in the United States. That program was shaped by the political realities of minority status within the confines of a well-established major world power. Industrialization and economic development for blacks so circumstanced could only involve the purchase of farm land for destitute sharecroppers, sailing vessels that would enhance the individual and collective prestige of those so desperately in need of affirmation, and the provision of employment in the variety of establishments that the UNIA was prepared to finance and sustain.

Garvey clearly understood all that, and that recognition helped mold the industrialization and economic development programs of the UNIA. For the nations of Africa, however, whose freedom he anticipated, the circumstances were entirely different.

It is certain that Garvey expected the fulsome development of technologically advanced industry on the African continent after its liberation. Nor is there any doubt that industry and technology would be used to provide the African homeland with the determinate power and authority that would inform what he unselfconsciously referred to as the "hope" of an "African Empire."[23]

In Garvey's vision, in the reasonably near future, the people of Africa would rise up against their tormentors, freeing their "Motherland" and creating a "superstate" possessed of an imperial power so formidable that Africa and Africans would be forever free – inhabitants of a empire upon which Garvey never expected the sun to set.[24] The relationship between the omnicompetent state, a united people animated by a single ideology, led by a single leader, and employing the yield of an industrially sophisticated and technologically proficient industrial base, to create a powerful

---

[22] See Garvey's characterization of his economic program in "Articles," Hill and Bair, *Marcus Garvey: Life and Lessons*, pp. 92–95.

[23] Garvey spoke of the "battles of the future" in which the "race that is able to produce the highest scientific development, is the race that will ultimately rule." Garvey, *Philosophy and Opinions*, 1, p. 14. Hence, he went on the argue, "It is advisable for the Negro to get power of every kind. Power in education, science, industry, politics and higher government. That kind of power that will stand out signally, so that other races and nations can see, and if they will not see, then *feel*." Ibid., p. 22. Garvey sought to "arouse the consciousness of four hundred million Negroes to the hope of Empire." Ibid., 2, p. 222.

[24] See the account of UNIA meetings in New York, in which members of the UNIA spoke of an African revolt against the foreign imperialists. Vincent, *Black Power and the Garvey Movement*, pp. 211–12. Compare this with Garvey's comments in *Philosophy and Opinions*, 1, pp. 11–12, 14, 68, 70; vol. 2, pp. 5–6, 16, 34–6, 235. Garvey spoke without hesitation of "making among ourselves a Racial Empire upon which 'the sun shall never set.'" Hill and Bair, *Marcus Garvey: Life and Lessons*, p. 5.

empire, was perfectly transparent to Garvey – as it was to the first Fascists.

For Garvey, all of his revolutionary program was predicated on organiza-tion.[25] Without organization, and the power that unity and planning implies, peoples, nations, or empires simply become prey to others better organized and, consequently, more powerful.

Garvey argued that organization was essential to the fulfillment of the essential needs of a *people* – a collection of persons drawn together on the basis of some similarity, such as geographic space, appearance, or culture.[26] That organization, predicated on positive ingroup sentiment, manifested itself in the functional institutions of a people, seeking to obtain, enhance, and secure satisfactions, ranging from simple survival to the psychological fulfillment of the individual as well as the collective need for self-esteem. The functional organizations, taken together in their relationships, bound in law, constitute society. Garvey identified the sovereign agency of such a law-governed community as the state.[27]

All of this mirrors the basic rationale for the Fascist state, as that ratio-nale found expression in the works of the major theoreticians of Fascism.[28] Fascists, like Garvey, saw history as the story of dynamic group relations. Groups were understood to be forever in conflict, activated by ingroup amity and outgroup enmity. Like the Fascists, Garvey admonished his followers to "never forget that all other groups ... are looking after their own individual group interest, and your interest ... is never theirs."[29] Such convictions cre-ated an individual and collective psychology forever prepared for potential

---

[25] See, for example, Garvey, *Philosophy and Opinions*, 2, pp. 111–12. The insistence on organi-zation is found throughout everything Garvey wrote. He insisted that "the fall of nations and empires has always come about first by the disorganized spirit – the disorganized sentiment of those who make up the nation or the empire." Ibid., 1, p. 34.

[26] It is reasonably clear that Garvey's notion of the "similarities" that united individuals to make of them a "people" was predicated on a form of "consciousness of kind" that was commonly understood by the social science of the beginning of the twentieth century as providing the foundation for social organization. See the comments by William A. Edwards, "Garveyism: Organizing the Masses or Mass Organization," in Rupert Lewis and Patrick Bryan (eds.), *Garvey: His Work and Impact* (Trenton, NJ: Africa World Press, 1991), p. 216. The source was probably found in Franklin Giddings who was a popular author during that period, but it might well have been Ludwig Gumplowicz, whose *Grundriss der sociologie* had been translated into English in 1899. See Ludwig Gumplowicz, *The Outlines of Sociology* (Philadelphia: American Academy of Political and Social Science, 1899). Gumplowicz's emphasis was on group dynamics and depended heavily on a notion of suitable collective consciousness. In speaking to his followers, Garvey urged them "Trust only ... those who look like you...." Garvey, "Lessons," in Hill and Bair, *Marcus Garvey: Life and Lessons*, p. 265.

[27] See Garvey, "Lessons," in ibid., pp. 211–13, 240–4.

[28] See the summary account in Gregor, *Phoenix*, pp. 27–36, 77–81, 101–11, and *The Ideology of Fascism: The Rationale of Totalitarianism* (New York: Free Press, 1969), chaps. 2–4.

[29] Garvey, "Lessons," in Hill and Bair, *Marcus Garvey: Life and Lessons*, p. 317.

conflict. Thus, Mussolini spoke of war as a predictable inevitability in a world that saw the advanced industrial nations exploiting the denizens of those less advanced. As long as such inequities existed, Mussolini was convinced, group conflict was predictable. Garvey, with equal conviction, told his followers that "man has always warred against his fellowman. . . . and [it] shall ever be so as long as man remains an unreasonable creature. No generation has shown that man intends to become wholly reasonable; therefore, in time of peace, prepare for war."[30] Since each group pursues its own interests, even "lying and stealing," in order to remain on its respective "throne," conflict must necessarily follow.[31] "Mankind," Garvey insisted, has always involved itself in "universal warfare, tribe against tribe, clan against clan, race against race, [and] nation against nation." It would be "suicidal," he went on, for any organized group of persons not to prepare itself for armed conflict.[32] While it was evident that the conditions under which blacks survived at the beginning of the twentieth century hardly allowed for the marshaling of "big guns and bombshells," the time would come, Garvey informed them, when weapons would become essential.[33] By that time, an organized community would have mounted a program of industrial development that would supply the necessary inventory.

The fact is that Fascism and Garvey's UNIA shared fundamental similarities in terms of their social and political convictions, not because one copied from the other, but because both faced a set of issues that conjured up a common response. The sustaining similarities did not end with the elements reviewed. Some other similarities were even more specific.

Both belief systems were nationalistic. Nationalism and statism were central to both.[34] For both, it was conceived that without the nation and its sovereign expression in the state, the individual could not achieve personal fulfillment. Exposed to every threat, oppressed by those "superior," the individual, without a nation and a state of his or her own, would forever remain unfulfilled.[35]

To both Fascist theoreticians and Garvey, nationalism and statism were of such critical significance that both were necessarily collectivistic – anti-individualistic in principle. Garvey, for example, attributed much of the failure of the black man in the modern world to the fact that "everywhere he

---

[30] Ibid., p. 293.

[31] See, for example, Garvey's "The Tragedy of White Injustice," in ibid., pp. 119, 134.

[32] Garvey, "A Dialogue: What's the Difference?" in ibid., p. 150. Garvey held that "Races and peoples are only safeguarded when they are strong enough to protect themselves. . . ." *Philosophy and Opinions*, 2, p. 107.

[33] Ibid., 2, pp. 111–12.

[34] Garvey's commitment to nationalism is found throughout his speeches and doctrine. See, for example, ibid., 1, pp. 6, 64, 68, 99; 2, pp. 5, 23, 37, 49, 71, 96.

[35] The position was fully articulated in the work of Giovanni Gentile. See the discussion in Gregor, *Giovanni Gentile*, chap. 4.

takes the individualistic point of view," and, lacking unity in organization, remains defenseless against his aggressors.[36]

As has been suggested, like Mussolini, Garvey held a largely negative view of the general qualities of humankind. Garvey spoke candidly of what he held to be the common properties of the entire human race. He saw humankind as intrinsically selfish, and alluded to the fact that individuals would "have no objection to even seeing an associate or friend in business die, if by [their] death it meant promotion. . . . Those of us who understand human nature know that this happens among people generally. . . ."[37]

While he recounted the frailties of the entire human race, it seems that Garvey spoke of blacks with particular disdain. He spoke of the black man as "his own greatest enemy. He is jealous of himself, envious and covetous." When the black man is caught in an infraction, Garvey continued, "the blame is always on somebody else, or else on circumstances that cannot be explained or understood." He held that virtually every black in whom he had invested confidence was prepared to betray him, personally, as well as the UNIA as an institution. The reasons involved a callous venality, a notion among some blacks that "they must become rich over night, and at somebody else's expense. . . . As far as the Negro race is concerned," Garvey argued, "we can find but few real men to measure up to the higher purpose of the creation, and because of this lack of manhood in the race, we have stagnated for centuries and now find ourselves at the foot of the human ladder."

Garvey spoke of some of his own followers, particularly those who had succeeded to the highest positions in the UNIA, as having been motivated largely by jealousy, greed, and a lust for power. He opined that disloyalty, betrayal, and selfishness – together with "sloth, neglect, indifference" – were to be found in particular abundance among members of the race.[38] Garvey was clearly convinced that neither humanity as a whole, nor its racial constituents, merited any particular respect.[39]

While it is plausible to account for such cynicism by appealing to Garvey's personal history, it is evident that such judgments are not specific to that

---

[36] Garvey, "Lessons," in Hill and Bair, *Marcus Garvey: Life and Lessons*, p. 164. Blacks were advised "to forget self and see the one big, glorious cause to which all of us should be attracted." Garvey, "Articles," in ibid., p. 108.

[37] Garvey, *Philosophy and Opinions*, 2, p. 31, and "Articles," in Hill and Bair, *Marcus Garvey: Life and Lessons*, p. 76. It was clear that Garvey did not restrict those disabilities reviewed to either race, but typical of all humankind. See Garvey, *Philosophy and Opinions*, 2, p. 134.

[38] Garvey, "Articles," in Hill and Bair, *Marcus Garvey: Life and Lessons*, pp. 62, 65–7, 69–70, and Garvey, *Philosophy and Opinions*, 1, pp. 24, 29, 37, 49, 98.

[39] The "wrong outlook" that Garvey associated with "the Negro . . . characteristically . . . everywhere in our present civilization" was not limited to blacks, but involved members of all the races. Garvey, "Articles," in Hill and Bair, *Marcus Garvey: Life and Lessons*, pp. 63, 70.

history. In much the same manner as Garvey, Fascist theoreticians similarly argued that many of the same flaws afflicted all humankind, and threatened the well-being and survival of the community. As a consequence, like Garvey, the Fascists maintained that absolute political control of populations was necessary as a defense against the manifest moral disabilities of individuals and groups of individuals.

Given the shared premises, Garvey, like the first Fascists, insisted that political government "should be absolute," an instrument in the hands of a leader who was to be "endowed with absolute authority." That would ensure the nation the strength of infrangible unity, the offset to the pernicious influence of contemporary egoism and anarchic individualism.[40]

More than that, only absolute rule could create the conditions that would fabricate a "new man" out of such flawed material. For his part, Mussolini spoke of human disabilities with the same emphasis as Garvey. Mussolini frequently spoke of the egotism, cupidity, selfishness, disloyalty, and the moral frailties of human beings. Nor was he sparing in his criticism of the moral and behavioral shortcomings of Italians.[41]

To restore their respective peoples to their appropriate place in the sun, both Mussolini and Garvey anticipated a system of rule that was not only authoritarian, but essentially pedagogical and ecclesiastical, undertaken by an elite convinced of its own incorrigibility, to provide a form of totalitarian governance with which the twentieth century became familiar. Both Fascists and Garvey expected "new men" to arise out of that singular governance – new men who would be informed by an equally new sense of competence and efficacy their immediate forebears did not, and could not, know. For as much as anything else, the authoritarian state was necessary to create the new man who would people a new world and a new reality.

For Garvey, once again as was the case with Fascist thinkers, the leadership of the revolutionary government would be composed of "a number, even though small, of active minds, ever ready and prepared to lay out the course of salvation."[42] Like the first Fascists, Garvey was an elitist and an authoritarian as well as a nationalist and a statist, whose ultimate vision directed disciplined individual and collective effort to the creation of so powerful a nation that it would serve as the foundation of empire.[43]

To achieve his ends, Garvey chose economic modalities familiar to Fascists. He rejected Marxism in all its forms. The entire notion of class struggle was repugnant to him – as it was to Fascists. Class warfare would fracture

---

[40] Garvey, "Essay," in ibid., pp. 29–30.
[41] See, in this regard, Mussolini's discussion of Machiavelli's judgments concerning human nature. Mussolini, "Preludio al Machiavelli," in *Opera omnia* (Florence: La fenice, 1954–63), 20, pp. 251–4.
[42] Garvey, *Philosophy and Opinions*, 2, p. 84.
[43] Garvey, "Lessons," in Hill and Bair, *Marcus Garvey: Life and Lessons*, p. 208; see Garvey, *Philosophy and Opinions*, 1, pp. 39, 68.

the unity of the community in its struggle for status and place. For Garvey, all blacks were workers. Even the wealthiest among them remained simple workers when compared to their oppressors. The struggle in the modern world was not, Garvey insisted, between classes, but between nations and races. In effect, Garvey conceived the entire black race circumstanced as the proletariat was in Marx's schema.[44] His concept of contemporary conflict allowed no place for the kind of struggle envisioned by Marx. As was the case with Fascist theoreticians, the struggle was not between economically defined classes, but between "proletarian communities" and those who would exploit them.

Like the Fascists, Garvey's opposition to Marxism, in whatever form, did not end with his rejection of the historic role of the class struggle. Like Fascists, Garvey advocated capitalist modalities to achieve the necessary level of industrial modernization, technological sophistication, and economic development required both by black survival and by his vision of a future African empire.

Like the Fascists, Garvey contended that "capitalism is necessary to the progress of the world, and those who unreasonably and wantonly oppose or fight against it are enemies to human advancement." In a clear sense, entrepreneurs were role models for Garvey.[45] But, again like the Fascists, Garvey sought to control capitalism through instrumentalities of the political state. Opposed to Marxism, socialism, and communism, Garvey, again like the Fascists, while accepting the market features of capitalism, sought its regulation, minimally insisting that "the state or nation should have the power to conscript and use without any obligation to repay, the wealth of . . . individuals or corporations," when that would serve the revolutionary interests of all.[46]

In practice, Garvey sought to control the investments and the enterprises of the UNIA through a variety of means (that proved to be largely ineffectual), but his tenure as leader of what was to be the largest American black political movement in the twentieth century was so brief that it would be unconvincing to attempt to outline the anticipated program of his black nation or his black empire with any conviction. All that can be affirmed is that the evidence indicates that Garvey rejected Marxism and its economic conjectures, and advocated a form of state-moderated market economy (what Fascist authors tended to identify with state capitalism).

As has been suggested, the psychic energy that shaped Garvey's political convictions arose out of an abiding sense of inefficacy and general inferiority that clearly not only afflicted him, but the millions of blacks who directly or indirectly responded to his call. Like the Fascists of Mussolini,

---

[44] See the discussion in Garvey, *Philosophy and Opinions*, 2, pp. 74–5, 111.
[45] Ibid., 2, p. 72, and "Articles," in Hill and Bair, *Marcus Garvey: Life and Lessons*, p. 103.
[46] Garvey, *Philosophy and Opinions*, vol. 2, p. 72.

who made the myth of Rome their own, Garvey, similarly situated, invoked the historic memory of an ancient Ethiopia – a half-legendary land out of which all human culture was supposed to find its origin. If Rome was the source of pride for the Italians who gathered around Mussolini during the first quarter of the twentieth century, Ethiopia was the sustaining myth of the UNIA.

For the Garveyites, Africa was "the torch of civilization, and the Negro was the teacher of the ages.... All other continents copied their civilization from Africa." Garvey believed that whatever other races have since produced was "only borrowed from Africa when it was great." It was the black man who "gave light and learning to the White man.... What the White man has done are but copies, replicas, are but duplicates, facsimiles of what the Black man originated...."[47]

Like Mussolini calling up the images of a creative Rome, the source of humankind's greatest accomplishments, Garvey's invocation of Ethiopia served the same purpose: to provide a sense of accomplishment to a people humbled by the modern history of the world. It was part of an orchestrated protest of the less developed against the oppression of the advanced nations and peoples of the time.

There was, however, something more than Fascism in Garvey's conception of the nature of the world's cultural history. Fascist theoreticians entertained a nuanced notion of the evolution of civilization in which the *nation* played a central role. As a nation, Italians were considered creative, and as having contributed to the world history of culture, but there never was a suggestion that Italians, per se, nor Romans, for that matter, were the sole creators of civilization. There was an occasional tendency to emphasize the role of Caucasians in the creation of culture,[48] but there never was a suggestion that the white race was the sole creative race. There was clear and consistent acknowledgment of Asian creativity, for example, particularly in the creation of Chinese, Japanese, and Indian civilization.

In fact, whatever racism is to be found in Fascist theory turned on the primacy of the historic nation. Fascist theoreticians argued that biological race was not a constant – it was a changing reality, modifying itself over time and in response to prevailing conditions. Thus, when Fascists addressed the entire issue of race, they spoke of "natioraces," as politically conditioned endogamous reproductive communities that, over time, manifested altered inherited traits. Race, in effect, was a derivative product of nationalism.[49]

---

[47] Garvey, "African Fundamentalism," in Hill and Bair, *Marcus Garvey: Life and Lessons*, pp. 15, 27–8.

[48] See Mussolini's comments in his preface to Richard Korherr, *Regresso delle nascite: morte dei popoli* (Rome: Libreria del Littorio, 1928), pp. 7–23.

[49] See the more ample discussion in Gregor, *The Ideology of Fascism*, chap. 6.

For Garvey, the analysis was fundamentally different. For him, race was primary, primordial, and unchanging, and the nation was derivative. Garvey seemed to believe that race was a historic constant, and the varying political communities that made up human history – tribes, confederations, city-states, nations, or empires – were derivative. Race was at the center of Garvey's belief system – and for Garvey, the black race was "the greatest and proudest race who ever peopled the earth."

Garvey believed the entire political dynamic that governed the behavior of human beings to be governed by racial concerns – and the fact that whites feared the superior achievements of blacks. In Garvey's judgment, it was that fear that left blacks "hated and kept down by a jealous and prejudiced contemporary world."[50]

It is commonplace among lay psychologists to suggest that this form of racism is a reactive product of a sense of inferiority. And that may well be the case. For our purposes, the analysis is not particularly important. What is important are the implications for individual and collective behavior.

As a case in point, the insistence upon the superiority of oneself, one's community, or one's race tends to corrupt one's capacity to make intersubjective judgments. In Garvey's case, the consequences were transparent. In guiding his followers, he advised them to dismiss whatever evidence we have of human history because "historians who have written have all twisted the history of the world so as to show the inferiority of the Blacks.... All the books...are not true." In fact, *all* the "civilization that [the white man] boasts of today is really a heritage from Africa."[51]

What is immediately evident is the consideration that if *all* books are tainted by the "White man's trick," calculated "to deceive other people for his own benefit and profit,"[52] how is one to discover and confirm the truth independently? Garvey's answer is singular, and illustrates the fundamental danger of his intransigent racism. He tells his followers that they are to judge "every thought" by the measure of

how it fits in with the Negro, and to what extent you can use it to his benefit or in his behalf. Your entire obsession must be to see things from the Negro's point of view, remembering always that you are a Negro striving for Negro supremacy in every department of life, so that any truth you see or any facts you gather must be twisted to suit the Negro psychology of things.

Garvey told his followers that they should selectively read books "to see what you can pick out for the good of the race.... Even if you cannot prove it, always claim that the Negro was great.... You must interpret anthropology

[50] Garvey, *Philosophy and Opinions*, 2, p. 82.
[51] Garvey, "A Dialogue: What's the Difference," in Hill and Bair, *Marcus Garvey: Life and Lessons*, pp. 145–6, 159.
[52] Garvey, "Lessons," in ibid., p. 192.

to suit yourself.... Things that may not be true can be made so if you repeat them long and often enough, therefore, always repeat statements that will give your race a status and an advantage."[53]

What that clearly implies is that there is no "truth" as such. There can only be *racial truths* – truths governed exclusively by racial interests. To anyone with any memory of recent history, that notion was one insisted upon by the theoreticians of Hitler's National Socialism. For the racists of Hitler's Germany, there could be no true knowledge – no objective science – there could only be a "Jewish science" and an "Aryan science." Science was understood to reflect racial psychology and racial interests.[54] It was a singular conception found nowhere among orthodox Fascists.[55]

The fact is that there were features of Garveyism that clearly distinguished it from Mussolini's Fascism. It becomes evident that however much Garveyism shared with the first Fascism, Garvey's thought could not be considered Fascist in any definitive sense.

Garvey's belief system was, at best, a member of the "family" of movements and revolutionary regimes in the twentieth century that might qualify, as did Hitler's National Socialism, as a distinct variant of a generic fascism. Any number of credible distinctions can be made, but a significant residue remains.

Garvey's absolute conviction that all of life is governed by the realities of race led him to the moral conviction, for instance, that "not until [one had] served every Negro in the world should [one] seek to be kind to others." Moreover, he counseled blacks to lie, if necessary, in the service of the race. Garvey's only caution was, that if one must lie, one should "see to it carefully that nobody knows." Among other things, he advised blacks to "lead the other fellow away from the true idea, if you are on the wrong side... build up a new argument and hold him on that until you have worn

---

53 Ibid., pp. 193–4.
54 This is explicitly and elaborately argued by Alfred Rosenberg, who as "the philosopher of National Socialism," provided its thinkers with a special "racial epistemology" in which the notion of a truth independent of race was summarily dismissed. "Truth," for Rosenberg, corresponded not only to the purposes of a given race, but was adapted to the mental and spiritual properties of that race. Art, morality, and science all served "functionally in the service of the life of the people grounded in their racial identity." Alfred Rosenberg, *Der Mythus des XX. Jahrhunderts* (Munich: Hoheneichen Verlag, 1933), pp. 683–4.
55 Some of these notions surfaced among minor Fascist thinkers in the final years of the Second World War when Fascism was overwhelmed by a Nazi presence. They were never characteristic of serious Fascist thought. See the discussion in Gregor, *Giovanni Gentile: Philosopher of Fascism*, chap. 3. While Gentile understood the functional role of the "abstract sciences," and spoke of a "national culture" associated with tradition and sentiment as influencing social science conjectures, he never argued that epistemological issues turned on matters of biological race. The fact is, he specifically objected to the suggestion. Unlike Hitler, Mussolini never suggested that there were "racial truths." Neither did any major Fascist thinker.

him out.... Always try to escape giving yes or no to any question that is important...."[56]

All of this deception was advocated in order to serve the race in its contacts with non-blacks, and was predicated on the absolute conviction that "all other races and nations will use [blacks] just the same as slaves, as underdogs." Therefore, blacks would have to be prepared to defend themselves with inflexibility, because, according to Garvey, each race, possessed of its own "outlook," inevitably seeks the exploitation of other races and peoples.[57]

Garvey was convinced that little humanity could be shared among races. Each race seeks to exploit the other, and the rationale that vindicates that conduct rests upon some set of beliefs that each race pretends is true. History, Garvey insisted, is written by each race to serve its own interests, to justify its exploitative and genocidal behavior. That, according to Garvey, is no less true of any science. Each race fabricates its own "truth" to serve in its own interest. Each race accepts only those truths that serve its needs.

So convinced of that was Garvey that he argued that if there is any "truth" that might negatively "affect [one's] cause," one is admonished to "never speak it, but go around it in every kind of ambiguous way as to justify your lie to save the cause." In fact, he advised that if "there [is] any act that [is] immoral or crooked which enables [one] to win a point..., be sure the act is done."[58] It all serves the interests of the race.

Each race is the author of its own truths. The sole measure of such "truths" is utility – service to the race. The logic of Garvey's rationale is evident. Each non-white race is involved in an implacable struggle for survival against a contemporary Western civilization that "is vicious, crafty, dishonest, immoral, irreligious and corrupt." That necessitates that the black race mount an implacable self-defense. Truth, morality, science, and religion all become hostages to the survival and uplift of one's race.[59] It was essentially for those reasons that Garvey was convinced that force, rather than reason or moral principles, was the ultimate arbiter in any clash between races.

Such an argument was not a typically Fascist argument.[60] It was common among National Socialists.[61] In fact, because of the centrality of race in the

---

[56] Garvey, "Lessons," in Hill and Bair, *Marcus Garvey: Life and Lessons*, pp. 200, 206, 246–7.

[57] Ibid., pp. 212–13.

[58] Ibid., p. 247.

[59] Garvey, *Philosophy and Opinions*, vol. 1, pp. 20, 31.

[60] Some such arguments appeared among some theoreticians at the close of the Fascist period, when National Socialist influences became increasingly prominent in Italy. Julius Evola produced a variant of these kinds of formulation, but they are not found in the works of Giovanni Gentile, Sergio Panunzio, Roberto Michels, or Ugo Spirito, major Fascist thinkers.

[61] Rosenberg explicitly rejected the "scholastic-logical-mechanical" notion of intersubjective "absolute truth." Truth, for Rosenberg, was a function of the "organically based search for truth" that is a reflection of the "racial soul" of each racial community. See Rosenberg, *Der Mythus des XX. Jahrhunderts*, pp. 691–2.

thought of Garvey, his thought, taken in its entirety, shares some of its more important properties with National Socialism rather than with Fascism.

Some of the more important features of Garvey's political thought are not to be found anywhere in the literature of orthodox Fascism, but are reminiscent of elements consistently found among National Socialists. It was a tenet of National Socialism, not of Fascism, that each race had its own "consciousness of truth." It was part of National Socialist ideology that race was a "measure of all things" – of ethics, science, art, and religion.[62] And it was part of the belief system of Nazism that one race, and one race alone, created all the world's culture and civilization. Other races might support culture, but only one could create it.

The National Socialist arguments in support of such contentions were fairly complicated, and it would serve little purpose to pursue them here. Garvey's arguments, on the other hand, were uncomplicated. We have seen that whatever was understood to serve the interests of the black race was deemed "true." That blacks were the sole creators of the world's culture and civilization was conceived true because it served black purpose. Moreover, Garvey maintained that whatever actions served the interests of the black race were morally *proper*.

Garvey was very candid. His conceptions were simple and direct. He insisted that race was the very foundation of life and the basis of everything – morals, education, science, and art. Everything was derivative of the race. As a consequence, one is admonished to do only those things that serve the "cause" – the interests of the race. Garvey's critical commandment was to serve the race. So compelling was that normative enjoinment that he derived from it an entire catalog of recommended behaviors.

The similarities shared by Garveyism and Hitler's National Socialism include an unmistakable anti-Semitism, a feature that was, at best, marginal in the totality of Fascist thought. Garvey's anti-Semitism was not particularly sophisticated, but it did increase in emphasis and intensity as he grew older.

Initially, his reflections on the Jews, as a community, expressed an admiration for their evident group solidarity, their intellectual focus, and their ability to survive under the most adverse conditions. In his full maturity, even though he advised his followers to practice the ingroup solidarity he admired among Jews, he counseled them, "Never trust a Jew. . . . [The Jew] is

---

[62] See the discussion in ibid., pp. 116–18, 697; Ludwig Ferdinand Clauss, *Rasse und Charakter* (Frankfurt am Main: Verlag Moritz Diesterweg, 1938), pp. 84–5, where we are told that "Each race has its own consciousness of truth. . . . Each racial consciousness of truth conceives a different truth and conceives it in a different way. . . . What is true for the Nordic need not be true . . ." for other races. We are informed that such is the case even with "scientific truths." None of this is found in Fascist literature, except, as has been indicated, in those rare cases, close to the end of the Second World War, when a few Italian intellectuals fell under German influence and control.

playing the odds against you all the time. He plays with loaded dice. . . . Make this a secret whispering propaganda in every commmunity where you go into a Negro home. Whisper all the time that the Jew is bad. . . . in that he believes he is the chosen of God and as such all other men must pay tribute to him."[63]

Those judgments are derivative of his worldview, his notion that the world is an arena where racial groups struggle for advantage, security, and place. The Jews were simply one prominent group among many. They were certainly no better, but probably not much worse, than any other racial or ethnic group. The difference was, apparently, that the Jews were singularly powerful.

Garvey, as a case in point, was convinced that the anti-Semitic fabrication, the *Protocols of the Learned Elders of Zion*, afforded insight into the nature of the universal Jewish plot against Gentiles.[64] By the end of the 1930s, Garvey was not only speaking of his political program as sharing features with Mussolini's Fascism, but with Hitler's National Socialism as well.[65]

At one point, Garvey even cautioned Hitler, in print, that the Jews constituted a "powerful world factor" and could wreak havoc on Germany – "to destroy [it] as they destroyed Russia" – presumably a reference to the Bolshevik revolution.[66] The Jews, for Garvey, were exceedingly dangerous.

Anti-Semitism was merely one aspect of Garvey's elemental racism. He could maintain, with the same inflexible conviction, that all races, other than black, were "full of greed, avarice, no mercy, no love, no charity. We go from the white man to the yellow man, and we see the same unenviable characteristics. . . ." Convinced of that, Garvey maintained that, given the opportunity, "all other races and nations will use [blacks] as slaves, as underdogs."[67] The Jews, as a group – although Garvey singled them out for particular emphasis – were only a fragment of the larger problem.

Satisfied as he was of the truth of his generalizations, Garvey admonished his followers that they "never allow your fellowman to rise higher than you, otherwise he will make you his slave." And as though his meaning was not evident, he went on to urge those followers to "try always . . . to master the world."[68]

Because of the relatively minor role played by the concept of race in Fascist social and political theory, very few, if any, of these views are to be found

[63] Garvey, *Lessons*, in Hill and Bair, *Marcus Garvey: Life and Lessons*, pp. 204–5.

[64] Alfred Rosenberg edited an edition of the anti-Semitic *Protocols of the Learned Elders of Zion* in 1923 for propaganda use in Germany, and Nazis generally accepted the account of Jewish aspirations as reflecting the truth about a universal Jewish plot against Gentiles.

[65] Garvey in *Black Man* (London) 2, no. 8 (December 1937), p. 12.

[66] Garvey, "Hitler and the Jews," *Black Man*, 1, no. 8 (July 1935), p. 9.

[67] Garvey, *Philosophy and Opinions*, 1, p. 81, and "Lessons," in Hill and Bair, *Marcus Garvey: Life and Lessons*, p. 212.

[68] Garvey, "Lessons," in Hill and Bair, *Marcus Garvey: Life and Lessons*, p. 270.

in standard Fascist apologetic literature.[69] International conflict was almost never attributed to racial differences. In that sense, Fascist doctrinal literature was fundamentally different from that provided by National Socialist intellectuals. In that specific sense, Garveyism was kindred more to National Socialism than Fascism.

Of course, it is perfectly true that one can find, in the collections of his writings and speeches, more than a few appeals to persons of good will of whatever race, and there were solicitations made to "humanitarians of all races," who work for the survival, freedom, and social and political equality of all humankind. In the preamble of the constitution of the UNIA, Garvey spoke, without hesitation, of pledging the organization to "respect the rights of all mankind, believing always in the brotherhood of man, and the Fatherhood of God."[70]

Unhappily, all such sentiments are compromised by several realities. First, it has been acknowledged that Amy Jacques Garvey, Garvey's second wife, a politically astute and singularly intelligent woman, took it upon herself, in the course of editing his speeches for publication, to modify her husband's thought in order to render it more palatable to non-blacks. She chose to not only moderate his tone, but to alter his text, whenever she thought necessary.[71] We have no complete account of how and what she changed.

More significant is the fact, as we have seen, that Garvey was convinced that because of the intrinsic wickedness of Caucasians, one is licensed to deceive them if deception would serve the interests of the black race. In speaking to his followers, he counseled them, whenever they found themselves challenged by foes, to quote the preamble to the UNIA as evidence of its benignity. He told them with perfect candor that the preamble "was written particularly for the purpose of winning the sympathy and support of alien races where the other objects of the Association were being threatened."[72] It seems evident that Garvey did not have any confidence in humanitarian appeals to "alien" races – neither did he have qualms about deceiving them.

He did not believe that any member of an alien race would ever extend assistance to a black person. Nor did he believe, as has been seen, that black persons should extend kindness to non-blacks, until such kindness had been shown every living member of the race. In effect, Garvey was an

[69] This would have to be qualified to the extent that after 1938, and the increasingly intimate relationship with Hitler's Germany, Fascist authors began to speak of the role of race in world politics, particularly in the semi-official publication *La difesa della razza*. For a more adequate discussion of Fascist racism, see Gregor, *The Ideology of Fascism*, chap. 6, and *Giovanni Gentile: Philosopher of Fascism*, chap. 8.

[70] Garvey, *Philosophy and Opinions*, 2, p. 10, and Amy Jacques Garvey, *Garvey and Garveyism*, p. 12.

[71] See the account in Ula Yvette Taylor, *The Veiled Garvey: The Life and Times of Amy Jacques Garvey* (Chapel Hill: The North Carolina University Press, 2002), p. 62.

[72] Garvey, "Lessons," in Hill and Bair, *Marcus Garvey: Life and Lessons*, p. 321.

irremediable and intransigent racist. He was convinced that deception was an absolutely necessary tactic in dealing with non-blacks, given the fact that, as an alien race, they are committed, in his judgment, to the exploitation and abuse of blacks. Recognizing the enormity of his recommendations, Garvey admonished his followers to conceal such counsel from non-blacks. Garvey advised blacks to be "like the Jews," and preserve the secrecy of their race training.[73] Garvey advocated dissembling and fabrication in dealing with alien races, so one must proceed cautiously in attempting to put together the elements of his belief system in which he was really invested. Clearly, Garvey did not believe that one could count on the "humanitarians of alien races" to resolve the threats to black survival, status, and place. Nor did he believe in the fundamental equality of races.

However frequently he alluded to such equality,[74] one has little confidence that he actually believed it or labored in its service. It is hard to imagine that Garvey's pronouncements concerning the equality of races and the brotherhood of man could be anything other than calculated fictions introduced to gull the innocent of alien races.

Garvey believed that the black race was, in fact, the "greatest race," responsible for all the world's creativity. As we have seen, he was absolutely convinced that culture and civilization were the exclusive product of the black race, subsequently stolen by Greece and Rome and the primitive peoples of South and East Asia. We know he held the entire Caucasian race to be the degenerate offspring of the primordial black race.[75]

In that respect, he contended that Adam and Eve had been created black. It was only after Cain slew Abel that substantial depigmentation made its appearance among humans. Garvey suggested that the shock and guilt that attended his crime caused Cain to become white. Cain then fled, with his descendants (who apparently all bore the "mark of Cain"), to Europe, where they proceeded to live in caves for centuries, thereby fixing depigmentation among themselves. Hence, we have the origins of the decadent European, greedy, vicious, and genocidal, exterminating the weaker races, and invoking "Christian love" only as a lure to deceive the black man, in order to steal his resources as well as his culture and civilization.[76]

Only his inflexible racism, with its conviction in black superiority, can explain Garvey's almost pathological preoccupation with racial purity.[77] Nor is the fact that he was fully prepared to negotiate with the Ku Klux Klan

---

[73] Ibid., pp. 183, 259.

[74] Once again, Garvey did, on more than one occasion, speak of the equality of races. See Garvey, *Philosophy and Opinions*, 2, pp. 119, 134, 347.

[75] Ibid., 2, pp. 19, 82, and "Lessons," in Hill and Bair, *Marcus Garvey: Life and Lessons*, p. 267.

[76] Ibid., p. 269, and *Philosophy and Opinions*, 2, p. 46.

[77] Garvey regularly speaks of racial purity as a primary value. See Garvey, "Lessons," Hill and Bair, *Marcus Garvey: Life and Lessons*, p. 291, *Philosophy and Opinions*, 2, pp. 62, 132, 234, 347.

and the Anglosaxon Clubs of America – white racist assocations – coun-
terevidence to any of that.[78]

Garvey was a tactician. In a nation where whites killed blacks with
impunity, and where blacks had only the most tenuous hold on security, Garvey was convinced that he could muster Klansmen and white supremacists
to black purpose by enticing them with the eventuality of black repatria-
tion to Africa. He would suffer the indignity of collaborating with white
supremacists in order to achieve his goals.[79]

None of that diminished Garvey's black racism. Toward the very end of
his life, he insisted that because the "entire physiognomy" of blacks was
"different from other peoples," those differences signaled a difference in
"outlook and ... viewpoints in life," and anyone who pretends otherwise
is "a liar and a fraud, in fact, an enemy to [the black man] and to nature."[80]
Until his death, Garvey remained an unregenerate racist.

However conceived, the convictions that Garvey entertained were the very
essence of racism. Similar convictions are not to be found in the standard
Fascist rationale for Fascist governance. They are found, on the other hand,
in all the standard apologetics of Nazi Germany.

For all of his virulent racism, none of it can plausibly suggest that Garvey
consciously entertained genocidal intent. Everything that has come down
to us indicates that he was an intelligent, sensitive, and humane person.
However much he may have been autocratic and elitist, there is virtually no
evidence that he was, in any sense, genocidal.[81] Given that reality, it is clear
that he could hardly be equated with National Socialists.

Garveyism is a variant of Fascism that featured a form of toxic racism.
With that very notable exception, Garveyism displayed many of the acknowledged properties of classic Fascism. Garvey was convinced that individual
and collective will, emotion, and action were essential to public life. Like the
Fascists, he objected to the "intellectualism" of liberalism and tolerance. All
of that was uneasily coupled with a natural suspiciousness and a readiness
to believe in the reality of complex conspiracies.[82]

Garvey's ideological convictions were very similar to those that inspired
the most dynamic revolutionary movements of the twentieth century – movements that brought grievous misery and destruction in their train. Garveyism
was a member of a class of revolutionary movements that shared many similarities. Fundamentally antidemocratic, anti-individualistic, and messianic,

---

[78] Ibid., 2, p. 71.

[79] See the discussion in Earnest Sevier Cox, *White America: The American Racial Problem
as Seen in a Worldwide Perspective* (Los Angeles: Noontide Press, 1937, revised. Originally
published in 1923), chaps. 13–15. See the introduction by E. L. Anderson, ibid., pp. viii–xii.

[80] Garvey, "Lessons," in Hill and Bair, *Marcus Garvey: Life and Lessons*, p. 268.

[81] Garvey was convinced that the majority of blacks were ignorant and that they had to be
"educated up" to his point of view. Garvey, "Lessons," in Hill and Bair, *Marcus Garvey:
Life and Lessons*, p. 329.

[82] See Lesson 11 in its entirety in ibid., pp. 260–5.

all of them mobilized humankind to arduous tasks, demanding sacrifice, commitment, loyalty, and obedience. Under the leadership of charismatics, such movements consumed the lives of millions in the service of a vision.

Most Caucasian scholars are loathe to pursue the ideologies of black protest movements of the twentieth century in that context. While, in some sense, that can be understood, it nonetheless does disservice to both blacks and Caucasians.

On the one hand, there is a refusal to acknowledge the similarities shared by Marcus Garvey's UNIA and paradigmatic Fascism. Failed in that, there is an equal reluctance to recognize Garveyism as a variant of fascism, displaying pathological features that identify it as a special subvariant, approximating traits found in Hitler's National Socialism.

It is not certain what that implies. Garveyism, as a reasonably well-defined belief system, did influence political leaders in Africa as the decolonization process commenced at the termination of the Second World War.[83] Kwame Nkrumah, the "savior" of Ghana, was particularly effusive about Garvey's influence on his own political development.[84] In fact, the political system Nkrumah contrived for postcolonial Ghana was one that reflected much of Garveyism. One interesting question urges itself upon us: Did the ideology that resulted share more features with Italian Fascism or German National Socialism?

Nkrumah's Ghana was governed by a hegemonic, single party, led by the nation's "savior," its authoritarian leader. As was the case with paradigmatic Fascism, the purpose of the entire enterprise was the rapid economic and industrial development of the postcolonial nation, the disciplined embodiment of the will of the people under the aegis of the charismatic leader and the single political party. While the system was referred to as "African Socialism," precious little socialism could be unequivocally found among its governing principles. Nkrumah's Ghana rejected political mobilization along *class* lines, for example, and insisted upon a call to *national* union. The nation, not a class, was the center of Ghana's revolutionary politics. The community sought by the system was spoken of as "communitarian," an anti-individualistic union in which the individual would find fulfillment in pursuit of "specific national goals." To achieve those goals and that unanimity of dedication, "coercion" was considered morally appropriate.[85]

Among African Socialists, in general, and among the followers of Nkrumah, in particular, there was an explicit rejection of the notion that the individual ownership of property was to be abandoned. That was

---

[83] See Martin, *Marcus Garvey, Hero*, chap. 12; Taylor, *The Veiled Garvey*, pp. 212–20.

[84] Kwame Nkrumah, *The Autobiography* (London: Panaf Books, 1957), p. 37; Michael W. Williams, "Marcus Garvey and Kwame Nkrumah: A Case of Ideological Assimilation, Advancement and Refinement," *Western Journal of Black Studies*, 7 (1983), pp. 93–5.

[85] Kwame Nkrumah, *Consciencism: Philosophy and Ideology for De-Colonization and Development with Particular Reference to the African Revolution* (New York: Monthly Review, 1965), pp. 59–60.

accompanied by an appeal to capitalist modalities in developmental programs intended to foster and sustain national renewal. An industrial base that might provide for a defense against foreign imperialism was planned. Beyond the national priorities, there was an anticipation of a Pan-Africanism that took on the appearance of Garvey's "racial empire."[86]

What was missing in the political thought of African Socialists was the overt anti-Semitism and the palpable racism found in Garveyism. The reasons for that absence are not far to seek. Racism and anti-Semitism would have thwarted liberated Africa's efforts to attract foreign capital investment. Whatever the anti-white sentiments with which Africans indulged themselves, they never attained official character in African Socialist ideology in the immediate postcolonial environment. African Socialism, as a system, remained essentially fascist in character – and might appropriately be identified as "neofascist" to accommodate the differences from paradigmatic Fascism dictated by time and circumstance. In that sense, African Socialism differed from Garveyism.

It was not only on the African continent that Garveyism worked its influence. After the federal government of the United States hounded Garvey out of the country, the UNIA gradually disintegrated. By the time of Garvey's death in 1940, hundreds of thousands of blacks felt themselves orphaned, divested not only of their leader but of their political and racial identity as well. Many, many blacks in the United States, at the time of Garvey's death, were dissatisfied by the general integrationist policies of the black civil rights movement, which promised them little more than competition with whites on what were anything but level playing fields. They sought the insulated refuge they and their parents had found in the UNIA. Within that refuge, they sought the psychological satisfactions that Garvey had provided. With the passing of the UNIA, they once more sought a masculine creed that might provide them the self-esteem that their identification as culture creators and potential "masters of the world" had delivered. In fact, what they sought was membership in an assertive community that affirmed their individual and collective efficacy.

It was not long before such an organization made its appearance and attracted many of the former Garveyites. As one among a number of political and social organizations that arose to meet the needs of so many American blacks, Elijah Muhammad's Lost-Found Nation of Islam assumed pride of place. It was to write yet another chapter in the fascinating history of neofascism.

---

[86] For a fuller account of "African socialism," particularly as it found expression in the political ideology of Kwame Nkrumah, see A. James Gregor, "African Socialism, Socialism and Fascism: An Appraisal," *Review of Politics*, 29, no. 3 (July 1967), pp. 324–53.

6

Black Nationalism and Neofascism

Elijah Muhammad and the Lost-Found Nation of Islam

Before the 1960s, when both the Black Power movement and Elijah Muhammad's Lost-Found Nation of Islam became political powers to be reckoned with, white and black liberals were quick simply to condemn any movement characterized by "fierce chauvinistic nationalism and strongly centralized leadership" as "fascist."[1] Muhammad's "Black Muslims," the heir to Marcus Garvey's Universal Negro Improvement Association (UNIA),[2] could be, and generally were, so depicted. Muhammad's Black Muslims were seen part of the "black fascist tradition" begun by Marcus Garvey. The continuity has been traced without much difficulty.

With the eclipse of Garvey's UNIA in the late 1920s, a number of candidate substitutes either made their appearance or achieved increasing prominence. They responded to the evident demands of blacks who still suffered all the disabilities common to the race – at a time when those disabilities were exacerbated by the Great Depression.

The United African Nationalist Movement and the National Movement of People of African Descent were among those organizations. The appearance of such movements was accompanied by a number of specifically religious organizations such as that of Father Divine, who announced that he was "the Son of God" – the "Messenger" to a sinful world – and Charles Manuel, "Sweet Daddy Grace," who sometimes claimed to be God, and who established "Houses of God" along the entire Atlantic seaboard of the United States. Blacks who felt orphaned by the passing of the UNIA had a choice of options in their search for its alternative.

---

[1] See Edmund David Cronon, *Black Moses: The Story of Marcus Garvey and the Universal Negro Improvement Association* (Madison, WI: University of Wisconsin Press, 1955), pp. 199–200.

[2] See Theodore G. Vincent, *Black Power and the Garvey Movement* (Berkeley, CAL: Ramparts Press, 1975), pp. 222–4.

With the disappearance of Garvey's UNIA, it would appear that many black leaders chose the path of least resistance, abandoning specifically *political* protest, to make recourse to *religious* recruitment instead. Political protest had proved very hazardous – arousing a sense of threat among whites, precipitating reactions that many Black groups found difficult to counter. Religious communities, on the other hand, that satisfied at least some of the needs of their constituents imagined themselves protected by the federal Constitution. Organizations given to religious dissidence were far easier to defend than those committed to what appeared to some persons in authority as political subversion.

All that notwithstanding, there clearly was a demand for some kind of political expression that at least allowed blacks to vent their individual and collective frustrations. The intuitive solution was for the appearance of a basically religious organization that might also address, however indirectly, the political interests of black members in a fashion that the authorities would not necessarily find threatening. Father Divine and Daddy Grace clearly served some purpose – succorance and self-enhancement needs – but so much political disquiet characterized the black population of the United States at that time that something more was clearly required.

In that context, and for our purposes, the appearance in 1913 of a relatively small group, founded by a southern black man named Timothy Drew, is of considerable interest. By the late 1920s, Drew's "Moorish Science Temples of America" began to attract some of those blacks who had previously collected themselves in Garvey's UNIA.[3] By that time, Garvey had been deported, and at least some of his followers sought other institutional identities than the UNIA. Given their individual and collective histories, what such persons sought, consciously or unconsciously, was some form of political expression better insulated from government repression than the UNIA had been.

Drew's organization apparently met at least some of those requirements. The Moorish Science organization was among the first black nationalist groups that insisted that religion, not politics, was of primary importance as a form of protest for African Americans.

The Moorish Science Temples did address, using religious pretext, the most fundamental issues of black nationalism. Drew, having changed his name to the "Prophet Noble Drew Ali," argued that the redemption of blacks could be achieved only through the establishment of their appropriate nationhood. To organize themselves effectively as a nation, Drew Ali argued, blacks had to return to their "true religion." To draw themselves together

---

[3] For a discussion of the Moorish Science Temples, see Arthur H. Faucet, "Moorish Science Temple of America," in J. Milton Yinger (ed.), *Religion, Society, and the Individual* (New York: Macmillan, 1957), pp. 498–507. Garvey was imprisoned in 1923 and deported in 1927. By that time, there was a considerable erosion of membership in the UNIA.

in a proper nation, Drew Ali insisted that blacks should renounce their identification as "Negroes" and "Christians," both having been imposed upon them by "Europeans." They should rather insist on being referred to as "Asiatics" and "Moors," or "Moorish Americans." That would make clear their affiliation with the culture creators of the Middle East, restoring their connection to the religion of Islam. For Drew Ali, identification as Asiatics and Muslims "meant everything; by taking the Asiatic's name from him and calling him Negro, black, colored, or Ethiopian, the European stripped the Moor of his power, his authority, his God and every other worthwhile possession."[4]

What Drew Ali sought to provide American blacks was that which had been offered by Marcus Garvey: natioracial pride. The difference was that, in the case of the Moorish Science Temples, the political offerings were articulated in the language of religion and the Moorish nation was to be established in North America.

Drew Ali was convinced that Morocco was the ancestral home of the American blacks, who were themselves directly descended from the Biblical Moabites and more remotely from Adam and Eve, who were the progenitors of "the human family" – which Drew Ali seemed to identify exclusively as "Asiatics and Moslems."[5] An identification with "Asiatics," culture creators of historic memory, would cancel, among whites, the common association of black Americans with slavery and jungle savagery.[6]

Irrespective of the conviction with which he spoke, Drew Ali's notions concerning Islam and almost everything else were, at best, uncertain. The geography, ethnology, history, the *Holy Koran*, and the "Moorish science," out of which he fashioned his doctrines, were largely of his own making – "divinely inspired" though they might have been. Whatever the specific content of the inspired doctrine, one of its most prominent features was its apocalyptic character. Drew Ali's Moors believed in the imminent destruction of the white race and the inevitable ascendency of a black Islam. If American blacks recognized the overwhelming material power of whites in North America, and sought not to provoke it, they took solace in the expectation that Allah would soon rescue them without the necessity of their physically challenging the "white government."

Until their redemption by Allah, according to Drew Ali, the non-white peoples of North America were required by circumstances to obey the established authorities. While they waited for the wrath of Allah to descend upon

[4] Ibid., p. 504.
[5] Cited from Drew Ali's *Holy Koran*, in Karl Evanzz, *The Messenger: The Rise and Fall of Elijah Muhammad* (New York: Vintage Books, 2001), p. 64.
[6] Garvey had offered the substance of a great deal of this, basically couched in political terms. He spoke of Ethiopia as the original homeland of blacks, but it served the same purpose as Morocco for Drew Ali. Garvey was less concerned with what blacks were called, or called themselves. He sought the substance of political equality.

their oppressors, Drew Ali's followers would not constitute a political threat to the authorities, and were not expected to draw their ire.

While awaiting the intercession of Allah, Drew Ali argued that the Asiatics of North America were required to unite themselves in solid phalanx. In the course of achieving that union, blacks would develop a "proper sense of self." A "new man" would emerge, and the hesitant, submissive black would disappear. Only then would blacks be prepared to assume their chiliastic responsibilities.

By 1928, there were seventeen Moorish Science Temples in fifteen states in the northeastern and midwestern United States doing Allah's rehabilitative work. Records indicate that membership in the temples numbered about fifteen thousand nationwide. At about that time, however, tensions mounted among members of the leadership, and Drew Ali's movement lapsed into internal crisis immediately prior to his death in mid-1929.

In the months prior to Drew Ali's death, a person by the name of David Ford joined the Chicago Temple. He was a relatively fair-skinned individual, probably of Indian-Pakistani origin, who could easily pass as Caucasian.[7] Whatever his ethnic and racial provenance, Ford rose rapidly in the ranks, and immediately before the death of Drew Ali, became Grand Sheik, leader of the Chicago Temple, as well as Drew Ali's presumptive heir.

Almost immediately after the death of Drew Ali, Ford declared himself Drew Ali's "reincarnation" and sought the succession. The consequence was a violent confrontation, which ended in bloodshed, between the various factions of the Moorish Science Temple the clash brought hundreds of Chicago law-enforcement officers to the headquarters of the movement in the effort to restore order. One of the consequences of the violence was Ford's flight from Chicago to take up residence in Paradise Valley, a black residential section of Detroit. Using the names Wallace D. Fard and Wallace D. Fard Muhammad, Ford sought to reorganize his faction under the name the Allah Temple of Islam[8]

To sustain himself during that period, Ford – or Fard, as he came to be known in Detroit – became an itinerant door-to-door salesperson. He gained entrance into the homes of Detroit's black population by selling home remedies and fabric. But more than anything else, he took the occasion to speak of his saving religion: the true, ancestral religion of the black man, Islam.

---

[7] David Ford, later to be known as Wallace Fard Muhammed, remains a mystery figure to this day. The Federal Bureau of Investigation reports on Fard are incomplete and sometimes contradictory. It is still uncertain when and where he died. Whatever the case, Fard is responsible for a good deal of Black Muslim doctrine, ranging from the character of God to the identification of the black race with the apocryphal tribe of "Shabazz."

[8] The most comprehensive account of Ford (or Fard) is that available in Evanzz, *The Messenger,* particularly pp. 398–417.

In the spring of 1931, one of the members of Fard's audience was Elijah Poole, the son of a Georgia sharecropper, born Elija Pool on the 7 October 1897.[9] Poole had lived through one of the worst periods of overt racial strife in the United States. Like, many blacks, he sought relief from threats and an inescapable sense of humiliation.

Poole had been a committed member of Garvey's UNIA, as well as the Moorish Science Temple, in which he served under his "true names": Muhammad Ah, Elim Ah Muhammad, and Muhammad Ah Fahnu Bey. With that personal history, his meeting with Fard in Detroit brought together two strands of black nationalism that had been incubating since the early years of the twentieth century: the political black nationalism of Marcus Garvey, and the religious black nationalism of Drew Ali and Wallace D. Fard.

Wallace Fard himself had been a member of the UNIA, an articulate Garveyite who was described by an informant for the Federal Bureau of Investigation as being "vehemently anti-White."[10] Although not black,[11] he shared most of the personality traits that had come to define a large segment of the urban black population of the United States during the postwar and Depression years of the first third of the last century.

The fateful meeting of Fard with Elijah Poole provided Poole the doctrinal foundations of what was to become the Lost-Found Nation of Islam, an organization that afforded a refuge for many blacks through the fateful years of the Depression, the Second World War, as well as the civil rights struggle of the 1960s and 1970s. In the course of that eventful history, Fard, long since absent, was deemed the incarnation of Allah, the God of the black man, and Poole assumed the responsibilities of his annointed "Messenger"[12] to create a black nation in the "wilderness" of North America.

Years later, Poole was to speak of his tutelage under Fard as lasting three years and some months, precisely the time that Fard was resident in Paradise Valley. Fard arrived in 1930 and departed in 1934, never to be seen again by Black Muslims.

---

[9] Although it has been established that Elijah Poole was born in October 1897, the actual day of the month remains uncertain.

[10] As cited in Evanzz, *The Messenger*, p. 403.

[11] Fard variously described himself as "Black," "Caucasian," "Maori," and "Hawaiian." His father Zared Fard was apparently a Pakistani and his mother a Caucasian. Although described as a "mulatto" in police files, Fard probably had no black ancestry. His photographs show him to have been relatively fair skinned. His hair seemed Caucasian in general form. Poole refers to Fard as half black and half white. See Elijah Muhammad, *Our Saviour Has Arrived* (Chicago: Muhammad's Temple No. 2, 1974), p. 132.

[12] It appears that Fard never claimed to be Allah. At best, he claimed to be a "Prophet" and/or the reincarnation of Noble Drew Ali. After his disappearance in the summer of 1934, Poole decided that Fard must have been Allah.

What is known of Fard indicates that he had been a member of a Masonic Lodge and the Theosophical Society as well as the UNIA and the Moorish Science Temple. His belief system was an amalgam of doctrinal snippets he had collected from all those associations. Since he was functionally illiterate,[13] most of Fard's information had been assimilated from discussions conducted among those with whom he came into institutional contact, leavened by an extremely active imagination and his hatred of whites. Fard's thought had a most singular character.

Poole, now the "Messenger," maintained that between 1930 and 1934, Fard instructed him "day and night" in the mysteries of the black man's "natural" religion.[14] It was that instruction that "saved" Poole from the seduction of Christianity. Poole had been preparing himself, precisely at that time, to take up the responsibilities of a Christian preacher.

Fard revealed to Poole that Jesus was not a Christian at all. Poole was told that Jesus had been a Muslim,[15] as had been all the so-called Jewish prophets. Whites, who were liars by nature, had not communicated that fact to the trusting blacks of North America. In fact, Poole was informed, the Christian religion itself was a deception. It was a belief system put together by whites in order to undermine the self-confidence and defense capabilities of blacks.

Christianity was a religion contrived to render the black man passive and submissive. It was, in effect, a slave religion, consciously devised by whites to render blacks ready subjects, compliant to the whims of their oppressors. Because blacks were fundamentally humane and generous, innocent in their judgment of others, they were easily confounded by pretended Christians, who used their fabricated religion to render blacks defenseless against oppression and slavery.

Fard confided to Poole that Jesus had understood all that. Not only had Jesus cursed the Jews as the deceivers they were, but the entire world of Caucasians as well, declaring that "the word of truth had no place" among them.[16] The white race was a cursed collection of beings, condemned by Allah to ultimate perdition.

Poole learned from Fard that whites had always been perverse, and congenitally inferior – both morally and intellectually – to blacks. In their inferiority, whites had lived in caves in the remote parts of Europe,

---

13 That information was solicited from Fard's common-law wife and is found in the FBI files. Cited in Evanzz, *The Messenger*, p. 401.

14 Elijah Muhammad, *Our Saviour Has Arrived*, p. 35.

15 It seems clear that the "Islam" to which the Messenger regularly alludes has very little to do with the religion founded by the Prophet Muhammad. Elijah Poole Muhammad's Islam has very little to do with the Islam of the Middle East and South or Southeast Asia.

16 Elijah Muhammad, *The Fall of America* (Chicago: Muhammad's Temple No. 2, 1973), pp. 214–15. See Elijah Muhammad, *Message to the Blackman in America* (Chicago: Muhammad's Temple No. 2, 1965), p. 78.

while the "original blacks" were creating the greatest civilization known to humankind.[17]

Poole learned that Blacks were members of a "lost Asiatic nation," some-times identified as Morocco, other times as Ethiopia, and at still other times some nation more ancient still.[18] What was evident was the fact that the white race had systematically deceived and exploited the black man, and whatever civilization and culture they possessed had been purloined.

But that was only the beginning. Poole learned a complex, if at times inconsistent and not entirely coherent, theology from Fard. Like Drew Ali, neither Fard nor Poole knew much about Islam. While his father may have been a Muslim, it appeared that Fard had learned about Islam from the members of the Theosophical Society and Noble Drew Ali, none of whom knew much that was credible about the subject. The conse-quence was that the Islam taught in the temples of the Lost-Found Nation, under the ministrations of the Elijah Poole, was forever to be very peculiar indeed.

With the disappearance of Fard, Poole became his "Messenger." He duti-fully began to preach blacks the saving beliefs of a man whom he held to be "God in Person."[19]

Throughout the remainder of the 1930s, the Messenger organized the Nation of Islam to bring together the "so-called Negroes," the "lost-found members of the Asiatic nation," to provide them succorance in a land in which "people . . . think nothing but evil," and which is "full of the blood of murdered people."[20] The doctrines calculated to hold together that embat-tled people were a strange mixture of fantasy, wish fulfillment, and resent-ment.

In the temples, blacks were taught that the age of "the present earth is around seventy six trillion years."[21] The seeming precision notwithstanding, the Messenger concedes that the exact time may be uncertain. What was certain to the Messenger was that the "heavens and the earth" were created by "Allah (God)," and that "everything has a beginning and everything has an ending except Allah (God) Himself."[22]

---

[17] That is clearly traceable to Garvey's instructions to his followers in which he outlined the process of depigmentation that distinguishes whites from blacks. He spoke of whites "hiding in caves" after God punished them as the progeny of Cain, guilty of having murdered Abel. See Marcus Garvey, "Lessons" in *Marcus Garvey: Life and Lessons* (Berkeley, CA: University of California, 1987), pp. 269–70.

[18] Marcus Garvey often spoke of Ethiopia as the source of the world's civilization, and was fond of reminding blacks that Europeans were living "in caves" while Ethiopians were members of an advanced nation.

[19] Muhammad, *Our Saviour Has Arrived*, p. 142.

[20] Muhammad, *The Fall of America*, pp. 39, 116; *Message to the Blackman*, p. 4.

[21] That means that the history of the "Black Nation" covers seventy six trillion years. Muham-mad, *Our Saviour Has Arrived*, p. 96.

[22] Ibid., p. 115.

While all that sounds perfectly orthodox, nothing said by the Messenger ever seems to mean quite what one might think. In terms of orthodoxy, there are places where Allah's Messenger insists, as one might expect, not only on Allah's self-creation, but on his oneness, as well as his self-sufficiency, omniscience, and omnipotence.[23] All of this, once again, seems eminently orthodox to anyone remotely familiar with the Bible or the Qur'an.

And yet, that orthodoxy seems to dissolve into heterodoxy almost immediately. The Messenger proceeds to articulate theological concepts that are, at best, idiosyncratic. Having lulled his followers with his apparent orthodoxy, the Messenger proceeds to surprise everyone by announcing that Allah did, indeed, have some sort of beginning. His followers were told that "there is no beginning or ending" for Allah, and yet there "must have been some kind of beginning. But how it happened, we don't know." While we are informed in one place that God "created Himself," in another it appears that we simply do not know *who* "was God's creator."[24]

All we seem to know is that at some time or another, or before there was time at all, there was "All Darkness." In that darkness, "Darkness," itself, "created an atom of life." That atom did not leave us a "record" of its own creation, "because He was the First; there was no recorders around Him."[25]

At that point, it is not clear whether the "atom of life," "Darkness," or Allah was self-created and therefore omnipotent and omniscient. Whatever the case, "He," whoever He is taken to mean, "had to wait until the atom of life produced brains to think...."[26] All of which must leave one confused. If the Darkness represents Allah, Allah had to wait until the "atom of life" produced the elements necessary for His thought. Allah, in the interim, could be neither omniscient nor omnipotent.

The Messenger speaks not of a self-sufficient, omnipotent, and omniscient Darkness creating itself, but of the "little small atom of life rolling around in darkness.... Building itself up, just turning in darkness, making its own self.... He put His Ownself turning, turning on His Own Timetable in the black womb of the Universe."[27] Allah, creator of heaven and earth, was apparently a little atom at his own creation, gradually evolving a capacity to think in accordance with "His Own Timetable." Allah is the little atom of life that was, at the same time, Darkness. But we had earlier been told that it was "Darkness" that had created the "atom of life." Remembering through all this that "the Black God produced Himself,"[28] we can only be

---

[23] Allah is spoken of as "the One God" (ibid., p. 208) and as self-sufficient (ibid., p. 153), omniscient, and omnipotent (ibid., p. 66).

[24] Ibid., pp. 39, 46, 63–4.

[25] Ibid., p. 39.

[26] Ibid., pp. 39–40.

[27] Ibid., p. 43.

[28] Ibid., p. 41.

confounded. The Messenger did, after all, tell his followers that he did not really know who created God.

What this suggests is that the theology of the Messenger is the product of an autodidact, probably the result of instructions Elijah Poole received from "Master Wallace Fard Muhammad" – the "incarnated Allah."[29] It is clear that the Messenger learned well.[30] All of his texts, while neither coherent nor consistent, are relentlessly repetitive. The same things are said over and over again – whether they approximate sense or not – almost always without change. Thus, after we have been informed that Allah (God) is self-sufficient, omniscient, and omnipotent, we are told that God is not a spirit (a "spook"), but a *man* – "nothing other than a man."[31] The self-created Being, knowing neither a beginning nor an end, the creator of heaven and earth, self-sufficient, omniscient, and omnipotent, who is somehow Darkness and a tiny atom of life turning in the vast infinity of blackness, is a human being, and his name is Wallace D. Fard.[32]

As though that were not enough, the Messenger proceeds to tell his followers that whatever Fard is understood to be – whatever his assigned attributes – "there are not any gods Who live forever.... There is no God living Who was here in the Creation of the Universe...." So Fard, incarnate Allah though he may be, was apparently not there at the creation.

There should be no surprise. If God is a man, one would hardly imagine that he would have been there at the creation. But then again – given the Messenger's stream-of-consciousness theology – we are never quite sure.

God seems to display a measure of transience that is unanticipated in a supreme being. While unexpected, it seems to be compatible with the Messenger's notions of what creation is all about. The Messenger conceives the universe itself to be transient. We are told that the universe is in a state of gradual entropy – a notion that is not, in itself, inconceivable. It seems, however, that the passing of the present universe is designed principally to allow the occasion for "a Wiser God than Them all" to come into existence in what will be "a new Universe."

[29] Wallace Fard is identified as Allah everywhere in the Messenger's texts. The identification is made too frequently to document in its entirety, but see Muhammad, *The Fall of America*, pp. 50–1, 70, 72, 81–2, 84, 105, 107, 120, 134, 142–3, 145, 156, 159, 161, 174, 181, 187, 205, 219, 224, 233, 236; *Message to the Blackman*, pp. 42, 46, 52, 96, 145, 155–6, 164, 172, 187, 233, 237, 242, 246, 259, 267, 269, 281, 298, 325; *Our Saviour Has Arrived*, pp. 6, 21, 23, 133, 141, 145, 150, 157–9, 164–5, 177–8, 187, 200, 211, 215.

[30] Nothing is more instructive of how effectively Fard taught Elijah Muhammad than the Messenger's entirely negative references to Hindus. Fard, as a Muslim in what was to become Pakistan, bore an irrepressible prejudice against Hindus. The Messenger reported that Fard had told him that if Muslims found themselves faced by a Christian and a Hindu, "kill the Hindu first because the Hindu is more poison than the Christian." Muhammad, *Our Saviour Has Arrived*, pp. 32–3.

[31] Ibid., p. 66; consult pp. 68, 71, 82, 133; see also *Fall of America*, p. 234.

[32] Muhammad, *Our Saviour Has Arrived*, p. 99; see pp. 92, 103, 110–11.

The passing of the present universe allows a wiser deity to replace the deity we were told was omniscient and omnipotent. However confused we may be, the Messenger attempts to allay our puzzlement by telling us that "once every twenty-five thousand years, another God would be given a chance to show forth His Wisdom.... This has been going on for many trillions of years...."[33]

For all that, we are told almost immediately thereafter that not only is "the Present God's (Master Fard Muhammad's) Wisdom...infinite...," but that, unlike all the gods that apparently preceded him for trillions of years, "He will set up a Kingdom (Civilization) that will live forever."[34] It is difficult to proceed with confidence with respect to any of this. One receives the impression that all this is really nothing more than a relatively thoughtless preamble to some serious business that is in the offing.

For all the talk of the trillions of years of the earth's history, it becomes evident that the Messenger comes into his own in speaking of the events that took place a mere six thousand six hundred years ago, when a black scientist named Yakub decided to "graft" a depigmented "unalike" race of creatures from the "germs" of the "Original Black Man."[35]

We are led to believe that the omnipotent and omniscient black God (or gods, as the case might be) ruled over the "Original Black race" for trillions of years, sharing a universe of complete tranquility and progressive happiness – only to allow a mad scientist, some six thousand years ago, to create an "unalike" race of creatures who would bring death, brutality, oppression, and perversity into that enduring celestial bliss. For the creature that resulted from the madness of Yakub, while a human of sorts, was clearly "not kin to [black people] at all."

The created creature revealed itself to be a being entirely "different by nature" from the blacks from whose "germs" he was cloned.[36] By their very grafted natures, the depigmented creatures that resulted were, and remain, fundamentally perverse – wickedness intrinsic to their very being. They were fashioned to be intrinsically evil, murderers, demons, barbarous, archfiends and archenemies, liars, deceivers, oppressors, tormentors, seducers, and traducers.[37] They are members of the white race, and are "beasts" by their very

[33] Ibid., pp. 96–8. It is not clear what purpose the capitalization of terms serves. Thus "god" sometimes appears lower-case, and at other times capitalized. Terms like "Who" and "Each" are sometimes capitalized and more frequently not. The quotes are provided as they appear in the original texts.

[34] Ibid., p. 99.

[35] See the discussion in ibid., pp. 12–13, 116, 120, 123; *Message to the Blackman*, pp. 50, 53, 65, 68, 128, 241, 244, 266, 300. The Messenger holds that *all* the colored races, "Brown, Yellow, and Red," somehow derive from the "Original Black Man." See Muhammad, *The Fall of America*, pp. 122–3, 174, 238–9.

[36] Muhammad, *The Saviour Has Arrived*, pp. 120–1.

[37] See Muhammad, *Fall of America*, pp. 41, 46–7, 51, 175, 181; *Message to the Blackman*, pp. 9, 23–4, 54, 60, 103, 125, 185, 215, 228, 231–2, 236, 241–2, 284, 294, 311, 320, 326, 328.

nature; even their children are "filthy," given to depravity and the molesta-
tion of the children of the "Original People." Whites are, in fact, the "beasts"
referred to in Biblical Revelation. They are "a race of devils," such that "none
of them are righteous – no not one." Born murderers, whites were created by
the lunatic Yakub to attempt the destruction of the black race. Possessed of
an irrepressible blood lust to destroy the black man, whites have wantonly
killed more than six hundred million of them over the past centuries.[38]

When the whites first realized how cursed they actually were, some
attempted to reverse the process by which Yakub had made them. They
sought to restore their original nature as well as their original pigmenta-
tion. The attempt was doomed to failure. What resulted, instead, was the
production of the entire family of monkeys and gorillas.[39]

In effect, whatever Darwinists might conjecture, humankind did not
evolve from the lesser creatures. Whites are the fathers of the lower primates,
and blacks are, and have always been, the white man's intrinsic superiors.
While Allah, in His infinite wisdom, created "Original Man," a mad scientist
fabricated whites.

Since their creation, "Black people have [had] a heart of gold, love and
mercy. Such a heart, nature did not give to the white race." Allah revealed
to the Honorable Elijah Muhammad that the races are fundamentally and
irremediably different. The black race is composed of "the mighty, the
wise, the best. . . . The white race," predictably, "is far from being able to
equal the power and wisdom of the original Black man," for blacks are
the direct descendents of the black God who created the heavens and the
earth.[40]

His followers were informed by the Messenger that it is in the very nature
of things that some creations are superior and others inferior. That is so much
more the case with whites when compared to blacks. In the case of whites,
since they were not created by Allah, but propagated through "graftings"
extracted from the Original Black Man by the scientist Yakub, they could
hardly be expected to be the equal of the original stock, any more than the
mule could be the "equal with the horse." For the Messenger, it was evident
that "there are lesser and greater in the whole of the creations."[41] By every
conceivable measure, whites are the lesser and blacks the greater. Blacks, the
"original people of the sun," are, in fact, God's elect, His chosen people.
"Black people," the Messenger informed his followers, "are by nature the
righteous."[42]

[38] Ibid., pp. 49, 102–3, 105–6, 124–5, 128, 185; *Our Saviour Has Arrived*, pp. 104, 168–9.
[39] Ibid., p. 119.
[40] Muhammad, *The Fall of America*, p. 241; *Our Saviour Has Arrived*, pp. 32, 101, 122.
[41] Muhammad, *Message to the Blackman*, p. 325.
[42] Muhammad, *The Fall of America*, pp. ix, 2, 26, 46, 132–3, 155, 159, 162, 195; *Message to
the Blackman*, p. 108; *Our Saviour Has Arrived*, p. 8. The Messenger tells us that when the
Bible refers to God's Chosen, it must be understood that it is not Israel that is the referent,
it is the black nation. *The Fall of America*, p. 159.

And yet, the Messenger is explicit in emphasizing the harrowing short-comings of the black man in America. Blacks, he laments, seem to want only to "sport and play." They are content to remain beggars at the white man's table rather than apply themselves to serious enterprise. The Messenger tells us that blacks are lamentably irresolute and "dumb."

More than that, the Messenger urged blacks to "enforce cleanliness among" themselves, in order to get "into the spirit of self-respect and the spirit of making themselves the equal of other civilized nations of the earth...." While "the white race has been very good in the way of making jobs for their willing slaves," the Messenger continued, "....they [the blacks] are far too lazy as a Nation – 100 years up from slavery and still looking to the master to care for them."[43]

While "it is not hard for the Black man in America to get rich," there is a tendency among them to revert to "the way they did in jungle life and the way you see in some uncivilized parts of Africa today" rather than pursuing the "decent side."[44] In effect, the Messenger, while identifying blacks as God's Chosen, superior to whites in every fashion, has acknowledged significant black deficiencies. How that might be possible is easily explained.

Every black moral disability, the Messenger reminds his flock, is traceable to white influence. If blacks "do all kinds of evil, murder, lying, rape, and stealing," it is "because they (white people) are like that.... By nature the Black People are good, but the Black Man is like a sheep – if the wrong people, the evil people, teach and guide him, he will become like his evil guide." For Black Muslims, it is the case that "Black people were never a wicked people until we followed the wicked one (the white man) after his wickedness."[45]

Other than giving expression to their own gross moral disabilities, whites have succeeded in making blacks ignorant, inept, and submissive so that they might be more easily ruled. To accomplish their design, whites have consciously conspired to use every strategem to destroy the black man's confidence in himself and his race. The Messenger specifically mentions the premeditated white plot to pay black women higher wages than are extended to their male counterparts in order to undermine the black man's self-confidence.[46]

"That is why you are in such conditions that you are now," the Messenger revealed, "because [the white man] actually made you like this." Every defect found among blacks is attributed to the influence of whites, the consequence of having been corrupted by a race that is naturally corrupt. "All of this,"

---

43 Muhammad, *Message to the Blackman*, pp. 170, 192; *Our Saviour Has Arrived*, p. 217.
44 Muhammad, *The Fall of America*, p. 183; *Our Saviour Has Arrived*, pp. 37, 177, 217.
45 Elijah Muhammad, *The Fall of America*, p. 27; see p. 195; *Our Saviour Has Arrived*, pp. 79–80, 107.
46 Muhammad, *Message to the Blackman*, p. 127.

the Messenger told his followers, "was done to you and me by the white race.... [T]hey taught us that which is of themselves...."[47]

With his creation of the white race, Yakub brought about "a wicked rule over righteousness." The "touch of white civilization" rendered God's Chosen "blind, deaf, and dumb..., robbed, spoiled, imprisoned, and a prey...," imagining themselves to be "nothing," to be "worthless."[48] That was the state from which the Messenger, following the instruction provided by the living Allah, Master Wallace Fard Muhammad, sought to rescue the black race.

How all this came to pass clearly left some of his following confused. In one place, the Messenger spoke cryptically of twelve enigmatic men, residing somewhere in the heart of the "Asiatic nation," who know all the mysteries of God and history. With that knowledge they controlled the future of humankind and decided to send the black man's nemesis, the white man, among them. In another place, he spoke of twenty-four "scientists" who could anticipate events thousands of years into the future – and had decided on allowing the mad scientist Yakub to embark on his adventure.[49]

Possessed of all this prescience, it remains unclear why the twelve Wise Men and the twenty-four scientists would permit the mad Yakub to graft the white race. It becomes all the more puzzling when the Messenger insists that the white race, once fashioned, would be allowed to rule for only six thousand years – to plunder, violate, and kill for only a God-allotted time. Apparently the mad Yakub had forever been under the control of the black God and the black scientists. What would be the purpose of it all?

The Messenger tells us that Yakub, and his demented plan to create a "grafted race," would visit such havoc on the Original Man and his progeny that Allah would become angry and destroy the white race. But it was Allah and the black scientists who allowed, in the first place, the manufacture of the debauched race that would rule blacks through "wickedness, enslavement, deceit, murder and death for six thousand years."

More than that, in order to allow whites to rule, "the Black Man or Gods were put to sleep." It seems that Yakub, somehow or other, assumed sovereign control over the universe and refused to permit any interference from the black God or the black scientists. The Messenger informs his Muslim brethren that "Our God was put to sleep to let the white god [Yakub] rule." That was done to provide the occasion for the white race "to build a civilization just the opposite of Righteousness, and this he has done." The white race was afforded, thereby, "superiority or supremacy over [blacks] for

[47] Muhammad, *Our Saviour Has Arrived*, pp. 28, 79, 83.
[48] Ibid., pp. 110–12.
[49] Ibid., pp. 19, 61.

a limited time in wisdom. The God who grafted them gave them a superior wisdom to qualify them to six thousand years."[50]

While all this seems to explain the moral and character defects of the contemporary black man that the Messenger laments – they are unfortunate products of the white man's evil civilization – it does not begin to explain why Allah or the black scientists, who were and are apparently omniscient, would allow it. Why would the black God (or gods, or scientists) permit such malevolence?

Clearly, the purpose served by the tale is to account for perceived black deficiencies and apparent white academic and entrepreneurial advantages. Both are apparently products of external forces over which no one, not even Allah, had any control. We are informed that the "Black god and scientists were not permitted to interfere with the people of Yakub and their civilization nor in the way they were thinking."[51] How Allah, the black God – omniscient and omnipotent – was so constrained is left to conjecture.

When he was created to be the "enemy to the Black Man," the white man "was given the gift of a creative mind. To allow him to use his own ideas, the Black Man or Gods were put to sleep in order that the Wisdom of the Black man did not interefere," for it was somehow the time for the white man to rule.[52]

Little intellectual or moral comfort is to be found in the assurance that it was "a great wisdom . . . in letting new creatures (white race) try their knowledge of mastering that which they were not made to master," when it had always been apparent to the black gods and black scientists, thousands of years before, what the outcome was to be.[53] All the violence, death, and brutality suffered by millions of blacks over six thousand years was apparently permitted for reasons that remain impenetrable.

The best that we can make of all this is that Yakub decided (apparently with the full knowledge and compliance of the other black gods and scientists) to create an evil race, the members of which, by their very nature, would be the absolute essence of depravity. They were created to be the enemies of the black race. Created without a scintilla of righteousness, every white person is evil, driven by irrepressible impulse to murder blacks.[54] Why this was to be allowed remains a mystery.

In the course of the seventy-six trillion years of history, "the Black God made the white god," Yakub, in order to initiate the entire sequence that resulted in the errant rule of the white man. The Messenger has consistently

---

[50] Muhammad, *Message to the Blackman*, pp. 325–6; *Our Saviour Has Arrived*, pp. 42, 98–9.
[51] Ibid., p. 123.
[52] Ibid., pp. 98–9.
[53] Muhammad, *The Fall of America*, p. 189; *Message to the Blackman*, pp. 110–11.
[54] See the Messenger's discussion in ibid., pp. 32, 102, 128, 185, 270, 284, 311, 320; *Our Saviour Has Arrived*, p. 104.

argued that only blacks and the black God are capable of creation. Only Allah could have created Yakub. And it was Yakub, Allah's creation, who in turn, fabricated the whites, who "were created and made for just the purpose of destroying our peace as well as our lives."[55]

Given that he was created with a specific nature, one "cannot blame the white man for what he is, you cannot blame him for being merciless, for the white people were made the people that they are."[56] Whites, as a consequence, are not responsible for their criminal conduct. Their behavior is simply a function of their contrived nature. However one chooses to understand the entire sequence of cosmic events, it would seem that Allah, the black gods (if they are, indeed, to be distinguished from Allah), and the black scientists were fully complicit in an outrage that served, and serves, no conceivable purpose.

Given that blacks are essentially without defensive arms to protect themselves against a white government – a "Pharaoh" that possesses an arsenal of weapons of mass destruction – there is nothing blacks can do but wait in quiet desperation until Allah, through his "divine plan," decides to destroy that government and its sustaining race. The "old world," blacks are informed, will be destroyed "in the twinkling of an eye. . . . by fire and other means of destruction. There is nothing of the old wicked world that can be salvaged to carry into the new world of righteousness."[57] All blacks need do is wait.

So thorough will be the devastation, that only after one thousand years will the earth bring forth the first shoots of vegetation.[58] That being the case, it would seem that all black people, themselves, would be consumed in such a conflagration. For the Messenger, the "hereafter" refers to the time after the destruction of the present cursed creation, so one can only wonder how blacks, "the original owners of the earth" would "take [the material earth] back and rule it again" after its consumption by fire – or how they would make "unlimited progress" after the conflagration, to live three times the allotted three score years and ten. All we are told is that since "Allah is going to destroy the world," blacks "should try to get out of it."[59] We are left with a great puzzlement and no little confusion.

The Messenger was consistent in maintaining that there is "no life beyond the grave." The only existence humankind can enjoy is that available on

[55] Muhammad, *Message to the Blackman*, pp. 42, 49; *Our Saviour Has Arrived*, p. 43.
[56] Muhammad, *The Fall of America*, p. 41. Blacks are counseled, "Don't hate them because they are devils. One of your Gods made them like that. I don't hate a white man just because he is a devil. He can't help himself. He was made like that. . . ." *Our Saviour Has Arrived*, p. 58.
[57] *Ibid.*, pp. 113, 186. See also pp. 168–9, 213; *The Fall of America*, p. 211; *Message to the Blackman*, pp. 158, 190, 311.
[58] Muhammad, *Our Saviour Has Arrived*, pp. 126–7.
[59] Muhammad, *The Fall of America*, p. 107; *Message to the Blackman*, pp. 233, 237, 303; *Our Saviour Has Arrived*, pp. 103, 112.

this material earth. The Messenger had revealed to his followers that the "life in the hereafter [would be] only a continuation of the present life" involving blacks who would be nothing other than "flesh and blood."[60] If that is the case, it would seem that no person, much less black people, could possibly expect to enjoy all the wonders of the new world that the Messenger promises will follow the all-consuming destruction of the cursed present. No living person, according to the Messenger's own strictures, can expect to live the thousand years required in order to experience the appearance of a new earth – whatever its glories.

This is the doleful belief system with which the Messenger, Elijah Muhammad, sought to console the black people of the United States. Why anyone should have found it a consolation is difficult to appreciate unless one is intimately familiar with the devastating life of many American blacks.

Understanding the circumstances that have fed the conviction of their oppression by whites does not, of course, justify the kind of ideological beliefs the Black Muslims have entertained and fostered. Given their unfortunate history, irrespective of the improvements in their lives over the past half-century, some blacks still find movements like the Black Muslims attractive. Such movements seem to serve some sort of therapeutic purpose.

The principal objective of the preceding review is to serve comparative purpose. In the first place, the central Black Muslim beliefs are fundamentally and profoundly racist. Irrespective of the Messenger's frequent disclaimers that his "Islamic" beliefs are *not* racist, there cannot be the least doubt of their malevolent racism. The Messenger protests that he does not teach racial hatred; he teaches only the "Truth" – it just so happens that the "Truth" is that blacks are superior and whites are inferior. If students of the Truth choose to hate as a consequence, that is *their* responsibility.[61]

It is most unlikely that any academic comparativist would judge the ideology of the Lost-Found Nation of Islam to be anything other than fundamentally racist. That is an important characterization to establish, – because racism has been taken to be a defining, if not *the* defining, property of generic fascism, and similarly a trait that identifies neofascism.[62] That granted, the question becomes, can Elijah Muhammad's Black Muslim movement be credibly classified as either fascist or neofascist?

If generic fascism is understood to rest exclusively upon the concept of the nation as a vehicle for the rehabilitation of a historic people, then Black Muslimism is a variant. If doctrinal fascism is conceived predicated on a nationalism calculated to restore, within the international community, the

---

[60] Muhammad, *The Fall of America*, pp. 14–15; *Message to the Blackman*, p. 304.

[61] John Ali, "Introduction" to Elijah Muhammad, *The Fall of America*, p. iv; Daniel Burley, "Foreword," to Elijah Muhammad, *Message to the Blackman*, p. xx; Elijah Muhammad, ibid., p. 177, and "Reply to a Judge," ibid., pp. 321–7.

[62] See the typical discussion in Mark Neocleous, *Fascism* (Minneapolis, MN: University of Minnesota Press, 1997), pp. 23–37.

standing of a given political community, to allow it to attain an appropriate "place in the sun," then the belief system of Elijah Muhammad's Lost-Found Nation is a distant variant. An argument can be made that might allow Muhammad's belief system to be spoken of as some sort of neofascism.

Like Mussolini, the Messenger regularly enjoined his followers to create a sense of infrangible unity, based on a persistent "consciousness of kind" – "the knowledge of self and kind" – so that the revolutionary community, an emerging nation, would develop the strength to wrest respect from the world community of nations. Only nationalism, in the view of the both Fascists and the Messenger is capable of providing the foundation for a people's struggle to attain its proper place.[63]

So emphatic is Black Muslim nationalism that its members entertain the notion that "every nation on earth has its own God."[64] It seems clear that the Messenger was convinced that only by uniting nationalism with abiding religious convictions might the human and material resources necessary for the demanding conflict against the black nation's oppressors be successfully mobilized.

Granted that the Black Muslim belief system conceives the redemption of the black nation the consequence of Allah's direct intervention, it remains clear that until such intervention, the respect of the world community would be forthcoming as a consequence of the manifest self-confidence of blacks that would result from their new convictions. Similar arguments were made by Mussolini's Fascists. Until their nation's ultimate rehabilitation, Fascists would demonstrate evidence of their individual and collective re-creation by making their political convictions a matter of faith. Fascist theoreticians regularly alluded to the revolutionary consequences of just such a union. The best of them spoke of Fascism as a political faith, having all the intense emotional properties of religious commitment.[65]

Coupled with just such an inspired faith, Black Muslims clearly anticipate the worldly success of the black nation before the expected apocalypse. That success would turn, at least in part, on the efficacy of the Messenger's economic plans. While awaiting Allah's intervention, the Messenger's program was calculated to make blacks materially independent producers[66] rather than dependent consumers. In his anticipation of the creation of a black

---

[63] See the following discussion in Muhammad, *Message to the Blackman*, pp. 37–8, 50, 170, 204, 222–3, 243, 301–2, 314; *Our Saviour Has Arrived*, pp. 31, 36, 141, 189.

[64] Ibid., p. 31.

[65] The sentiment was commonplace among Fascist thinkers. Sergio Panunzio made the argument clearly in *Teoria generale dello stato fascista* (Padua: CEDAM, 1939), chap. 1. He spoke without hesitation of the Fascist state as an "ecclesiastical state." Ibid., p. 59.

[66] At the time of the March on Rome, Fascist theoreticians insisted upon the necessity of Italians becoming producers. See A. James Gregor, *The Ideology of Fascism: The Rationale of Totalitarianism* (New York: Free Press, 1969), pp. 148–50, 161–2, 365–6; and *Italian Fascism and Developmental Dictatorship* (Princeton, NJ: Princeton University Press, 1979), chap. 9.

nation, independent and powerful, he urged blacks to instill in even the youngest child the will to develop the skills that would allow the extraction of resources from the earth, the manufacture of goods, and corresponding increases in employment opportunities for all. Like Mussolini's Fascists, the Messenger's blacks were enjoined to build an autarkic, a "separate," economic system among themselves, to compete effectively against other independent nations.[67]

American blacks were to separate themselves from their oppressors and establish, foster, and sustain their own economy, to "become producers and not remain consumers and employees." The black nation would "extract raw materials from the earth and manufacture" both commodities and jobs[68] to obtain the self-determination that would otherwise escape them.

To accomplish those ends, American blacks, as Italians under the Fascist regime before them, were called upon to grow their respective members in number, maintaining as high a reproductive rate as possible.[69] Other than that, they were to sacrifice, to manage their financial resources with frugality and with purpose. They were expected to contribute systematically to the accumulation of the capital necessary to nourish economic growth and industrialization.

Part of the complex process would be the creation of the financial institutions requisite to the servicing of a complex agricultural and industrial economic system. As was the case with Fascists, that would be part of the institutional structure that would underwrite the educational training critical to the articulation of the economic base. That base would provide the material strength necessary to assure the black nation its place among its real and potential opponents.[70]

Blacks should be prepared to sacrifice for the future. Blacks, the Messenger remonstrated, are disposed to waste their money on conspicuous pecuniary display when they should be saving it for investment in building a financial and educational infrastructure for the anticipated "new nation," in what could only be a recipe for "primitive capital accumulation."[71] Elijah Muhammad's program, like that of Mussolini's Fascism, was predicated on individual and collective sacrifice in the service of the revolutionary developmental community.

[67] See Muhammad, *Message to the Blackman*, pp. 56–7, 170–1. Substantial economic autarchy for Italy was among Mussolini's economic goals.

[68] Muhammad, *Message to the Blackman*, p. 56.

[69] See Muhammad, *The Fall of America*, p. 29; *Our Savior Has Arrived*, p. 209.

[70] See Muhammad, *The Fall of America*, pp. 47, 59, and pp. 16, 54, 159–60, 176–8, 201; *Message to the Blackman*, pp. 192–203; *Our Saviour Has Arrived*, pp. 47, 59.

[71] Muhammad, *Message to the Blackman*, pp. 192–8. These kinds of admonitions are found among the advocates of economic development in less-developed countries. Sun Yat-sen's speeches and writings were alive with such enjoinments. It was commonplace among Fascists.

For both Fascist Italy and Elijah Muhammad's Lost-Found Nation, their real and potential enemies were the industrially advanced nations. The Messenger, like Mussolini, identified them as the United States, Great Britain, Belgium, and Germany.[72] All industrial and economically powerful, they employed their strengths to oppress those incapable of effectively defending their own interests. For Fascists, Italy had been exploited politically and economically since before the industrial revolution itself, by what were to become the advanced industrial nations. For Black Muslims, the black nation has been subject to even more insistent and oppressive exploitation at the hands of those same powers. They were the architects of black slavery and black oppression.

If the revolutionary nation, whether industrially retrograde Fascist Italy or the Messenger's new Lost-Found Nation, were to maintain itself against such opponents, it required not only unity, but a single, hegemonic, and "totalitarian" leadership to guide it. If the revolutionary community were to survive and prevail, enduring sacrifice and self-abnegation in its process of industrial and economic growth, it would have to be reinforced by the steadfast conviction that the process was governed by a determined leadership understood to be infallible.

Thus, for Fascists, it was held that Mussolini was "always right." The regime was, in effect, an "epistemocracy" – rule by "those who know." The rationale for one-man rule in Italy was provided by a fairly elaborate philosophical argument that conceived one man capable of speaking for an entire nation.[73]

For Black Muslims, the rationale for the absolute rule of the Messenger was predicated on the conviction that Elijah Muhammad was always right, because of his peculiar relationship with Master W. Fard Muhammad – the incarnated Allah – the unimpeachable source of "absolute truth." The Messenger announced to his followers that he "had been divinely appointed by Allah" to convey impeccable truths to the Lost-Found Nation of Islam in America. He informed them that he was even better credentialed than the original Prophet Muhammad – the founder of the Islamic faith – because the Prophet had not spoken directly to Allah, or seen his face, as he, Elijah Muhammad, had. The Messenger had personally known Allah – and Allah had personally chosen him and had been his instructor for more than three years. As a consequence, he, and no other, was the purveyor of absolute truth to his long-suffering people.[74]

---

[72] Muhammad, *The Fall of America*, pp. 174, 192, 218.

[73] See, in this context, Giovanni Gentile, *The Origins and Doctrine of Fascism* (New Brunswick, NJ: Transaction, 2003), pp. 24–32; confer A. James Gregor, *Giovanni Gentile: Philosopher of Fascism* (New Brunswick, NJ: Transaction, 2001), pp. 31–4.

[74] See Muhammad, *The Fall of America*, pp. 129, 148, 185, 190–1, 234; *Message to the Blackman*, pp. 88, 232, 237, 244, 253, 256–7, 259–61, 263, 269; *Our Saviour Has Arrived*, pp. 135, 145, 194–5, 209–10.

There could be nothing remotely "democratic" about the hierarchical rule of the Messenger. He and no other determined the truth for his followers. It was he who defined their faith for them.

He denounced, among other things, the beliefs of orthodox Islam. He insisted, for example, that only the "colored" people of the world could be Muslims, whereas Middle Eastern Muslims allowed Caucasians into their fold.

Worse still, in the Messenger's judgment, was the fact that the Muslims of the Middle East refused to acknowledge that Master W. Fard Muhammad was Allah, and went on to pretend that Allah was a "spirit," something that the Messenger knew to be untrue.[75] Allah was not a "spook," but a man, a man whom the Messenger had known as Wallace Fard Muhammad.

Elijah Muhammad was equally insistent in all other matters. There was no space for dissent in the Lost-Found Nation. Symbolic of the suppression of dissent was the existence of the paramilitary Fruit of Islam – the security forces of the Messenger's movement – within the ranks of the "lost-found Asiatics of America." Like all such political movements, the elite leadership of the Black Muslims ensured its control by policing its members with trained "security forces."

All nondemocratic revolutions in the twentieth century maintained such forces both before and after their respective revolutions. The Fascists had their *squadristi*, and subsequently the voluntary militia; German National Socialism had both the SA and the SS; the Bolsheviks maintained their Red Guards and then the Red Army; while the Chinese employed their People's Liberation Army to both conduct their civil war and subsequently to suppress domestic dissidence.

To trace these features leaves one with a sense of similarity, shared by Mussolini's Fascists and the followers of the Messenger. For all that, there remains a sense of intellectual disquiet. There is something both less and more in the belief system of the Black Muslims that distinguishes them from paradigmatic Fascism.

Whatever racism one finds in Fascism, it is vastly different from that of the Black Muslims. Elijah Muhammad is an unrelenting racist. Racism is the critical center of his system of beliefs. He insists that whites, all whites, are intrinsically evil, and while some minuscule number may display some commendable properties, as a "race of devils" they are, by nature, "the enemy of Allah." All Caucasians are thus forever denied entry into "the Hereafter that is Promised to the Lost-Found Black People."[76]

---

[75] See ibid., pp. 67, 72, 134–5, 144.

[76] Ibid., pp. 89–90, 129. Whites are discriminated against even in terms of the names they are permitted to assume as Muslims. See ibid., p. 102. The Messenger elsewhere suggests that some whites might succeed in becoming Muslims: "... even though by nature they are not the real righteous, their faith will get them out of the hell that Allah (God) threatens this world with. And their time will be prolonged." Muhammad, *The Fall of America*, p. 246.

The entire creed of the Black Muslims rests on the conviction that Caucasians are not, and blacks are, a "God-created" people; Caucasians were artificially contrived by the mad scientist Yakub, who created them to be, "by nature," intrinsically homicidal, deceptive, degenerate, and "filthy."[77] These irremediably racist convictions provide the substance of the Black Muslim worldview, without which the belief system of the Messenger would no longer be what it is.

The Messenger's racism was cosmic and inflexible. Even though he regularly alluded to the "colored races" sharing affinities with the Original Black Man,[78] he so significantly qualified his acceptance of non-blacks that, in the end, only blacks remained God's Chosen.

Concerning the Native Americans, the leader of the Black Muslims informed his followers that Allah had told him that they had been expelled from India sixteen thousand years ago for having violated the commandments of Allah. The consequence was that the red man, the Native Americans, was, like the white man, "the enemies of Allah." The result was that the red man in America is fundamentally enfeebled; "Red," the Messenger insisted, "is not an equal Power" to Black.[79]

The Hindus of India do not fare any better. Although an "Original people," the Messenger deplores them, and recommends their extinction, "because the Hindu is more poison than the Christian," for it is clear that "the devil's teaching is a division of gods," and "the Hindus have many gods."[80]

Neither does the Messenger spare the Chinese, members of the yellow race, who, like the red race, are understood to be "brothers" of the Original race. We are told that the Chinese are members of "a little grafted race of people" – and like the Caucasians, are a man-made, not a "God-created," people – apparently afflicted with all the disabilities of such an artificial race.[81]

It is clear that whatever the Messenger may have said on occasion, there is no race equal to the black. It was the black God, progenitor of the black race, who created the universe and everything in it. And it was the black race that created civilization – science, art, literature, establishment or a proper faith in God – and made all that a gift to others.[82]

In effect, the Messenger systematically taught the racial supremacy of the black race to his followers. Coupled with that is a sinister anti-Semitism that is barely concealed.

---

[77] See ibid., pp. 140–2. Confer ibid., pp. 40–1, 47, 51, 122, 175, 181.

[78] See ibid., pp. 123, 174, 238–9.

[79] Muhammad, *The Fall of America*, pp. 22, 238; *Message to the Black Man*, pp. 106–7.

[80] Muhammad, *Our Saviour Has Arrived*, pp. 32–3, 67. In this context, it is not at all certain that the Messenger is a monotheist. As has been indicated, he regularly speaks of an entire series of black gods.

[81] Ibid., p. 52.

[82] Ibid., pp. 44–6, 52, 87–8.

Elijah Poole, while still a student of Wallace Fard, learned of the existence of one of the most pernicious anti-Semitic tracts known to the Western world: *The Protocols of the Learned Elders of Zion*. Having read it, he apparently continued to entertain the notion of its authenticity until his death.[83]

The *Protocols* spoke of a plot by Jews to dominate and exploit the non-Jewish world. Marcus Garvey was convinced of its authenticity and went out of his way to identify some of his specific enemies as Jews. Members of the Black Muslims have continued the practice to this day.[84]

For a time, members of the Fruit of Islam sold copies of the *Protocols* as a veridical account of an extant Jewish plot to rule the world. The Jews have been spoken of as a particularly vicious subset of Caucasians. They have been said to be guilty of the most pernicious forms of black exploitation. The Black Muslims have identified the Jews as those who, during the days of chattel slavery in North America, "used kidnapped Black Africans disproportionately more than any other ethnic group in New World History." In the course of black slavery, the "number of Africans killed" was close to "100 million murder victims." Given the circumstances, the Black Muslims argued that "the Jews ... are accountable for many of these murders."[85]

The Jews, we are told, given their commercial predispositions, were particularly important in the spread and establishment of black slavery throughout the Western Hemisphere. Beyond that, prior to, and into, the American Civil War, the Jews were almost uniformly supportive of the South's "peculiar institution" together with the Confederacy in which it was housed and by whom it was defended. Moreover, we are told that in the course of black slavery, the Jews were particularly flagrant in their sexual exploitation of their female slaves.[86]

Other than that, Black Muslim authors, who speak for the movement, communicate to us that the Jews have never been particularly attentive to "Gentile law" when it fails to serve their purpose. In fact, they have never been particularly sensitive to specifically *national* issues, since they "remained internationalists without the patriotic fervor of their Gentile countrymen," particularly in times of crisis in the early history of the revolutionary United States.[87]

These are, of course, the usual charges leveled against the Jews as a group in almost every anti-Semitic tract. In *The Secret Relationship Between Blacks*

---

[83] Evanzz, *The Messenger*, pp. 76, 202. For a discussion of the character of the *Protocols*, see Norman Cohn, *Warrant for Genocide, The Myth of the Jewish World-Conspiracy and the Protocols of the Elders of Zion* (New York: Harper and Row, 1967).

[84] See the discussion in Arthur J. Magida, *Prophet of Rage: A Life of Louis Farrakhan and His Nation* (New York: Basic Books, 1996), chap. 8.

[85] Historical Research Department, The Nation of Islam, *The Secret Relationship Between Blacks and Jews* (Boston: Latimer Associates, 1994, fourth printing), pp. vii, 177–8, 196.

[86] See "Jews, Slavery and the Civil War," in ibid., pp. 139–76, 196.

[87] Ibid., p. 25, and n. 75.

and Jews – their well-researched and-written brief against the Jews – the Black Muslims repeat all the anti-Semitic calumnies with which the twentieth century had made us all familiar. The Jews were identified as that group of persons driven, since earliest antiquity, from almost every civilized country in the world because of their ingroup clannishness and their outgroup abuse. The Black Muslim authors remind their audience that the charges lodged against the Jews included sharp economic practices and exploitative financial dealings with the unsuspecting non-Jewish populations who acted as their hosts.

In the *Secret Relationship*, the emphasis is on the relationship between the black community and the Jews during the period of black slavery. The research that produced the work is impressive. The difficulty lies in the authors' use of unrestricted generalizations that imply that *all* Jews are responsible for the behavior of some. More than that, there is a suggestion that whatever culpability might be assigned to the Jews of the period prior to and through the Civil War, contemporary Jews might somehow be considered, in whatever measure, equally culpable.

It seems evident that the Lost-Found Nation of Islam tolerates this kind of anti-Semitic material because it reflects the sentiments of its leaders. The Messenger himself argued that the Jews had tampered with the true religion and had killed its prophets so that others could be deceived. The Messenger informed his followers that this was so apparent that Jesus himself had cursed the Jews as the children of Satan.[88] All these claims have regularly surfaced in anti-Semitic tracts since time immemorial.

Not much of this is to be found in the doctrinal literature of Italian Fascism.[89] Whatever malevolent racism and anti-Semitism there was manifested itself only in the final days of Mussolini's regime, when Fascism became hostage to Hitler's National Socialism. To those whose wont it is to search out similarities, racism and anti-Semitism are characteristic more of National Socialism than Fascism.

Almost all the Black Muslim arguments reviewed have their analogs in the work of Alfred Rosenberg, the acknowledged "chief ideologist for the Nazi Party."[90] His *Der Mythus des XX. Jahrhunderts* provides a catalog of racist arguments, almost every one of which is to be found, in one form or

---

[88] See Muhammad, *The Fall of America*, p. 214; *Message to the Blackman*, p. 71; *Our Saviour Has Arrived*, p. 181.

[89] After 1938, when Fascism committed itself to its fatal alliance with Hitler's Germany, a journal appeared in Italy, *Difesa della razza*, that contained very similar material as a poor copy of that which characterized the ideological notions of National Socialism. It was not typical of the doctrinal literature of the Fascist "mainstream."

[90] Robert Pois, "Introduction" to *Race and Race History and other Essays by Alfred Rosenberg* (New York: Harper and Row, 1970), p. 13. Albert Chandler speaks of Rosenberg as "the most influential and representative intellectual leader of the [Nazi] party." Albert R. Chandler, *Rosenberg's Nazi Myth* (Ithaca, NY: Cornell University Press, 1945), p. 3.

another, in the thought of Elijah Muhammad or in the published works of the Lost-Found Nation of Islam.

Rosenberg, like Elijah Muhammad, is advocate of a *racial* religion, a belief system predicated on a "myth of the blood." It was a religion that would give expression to the genius of a peculiar "race soul" – that of a culture-creating, "solar" race that had mysterious origin in the fabled spaces of Hyperborea and Atlantis.[91]

It was the worldwide *Wanderung* of that "divinely gifted race," infilled with "creative blood," that provided the lesser beings *(Untermenschen)* of earth with culture, science, and humanity. In their travels, Rosenberg's creative race – gifted with a sense of honor, generosity, heroism, a thirst for exploration, loyalty, creativity, and nobility – ranging over the globe from China, through the Mediterranean, North Africa, to North and South America, bringing civilization in its wake, found itself confronted by "demonic" subraces, given over to chthonian divinities, phallic worship, sexual frenzy, temple whores, personal preoccupations, collective malevolence, and attendant degeneracy.

In the course of its contacts, the members of the creative race, because of their innocence and spontaneous generosity, failed to appreciate the differences between themselves and their real and potential opponents, to find themselves savaged by the inferior races. Millions of the creative race were massacred by "spiritually alien, 'unalike [*fremdartig*]' beings" impelled, as those beings were, by "dark satanic forces."[92] Elijah Muhammad had said nothing less. The only difference was the race selected as superior.

For Rosenberg, the time for the rebirth of the creative race was at hand. It was to draw together in "folkish" unity to uplift itself. A new mysterium would manifest itself as a felt need to defend the divine in humanity, as the divine more and more materializes itself in the consciousness of the superior race. The race might then strike back at its subhuman, netherworldly antagonists, to "open the way for a new age," peopled by "new men" who would bring forward, "shining brightly, a new dawn of creation."[93] Elijah

---

[91] See the discussion in Alfred Rosenberg, *Der Mythus des XX. Jahrhunderts: Eine Wertung der seelisch-geistigen Gestaltenkämpfe unserer Zeit* (Munich: Hoheneichen Verlag, 1933), pp. 1–3, 114, 116–17, 258.

[92] See the account in ibid., First Book, chap. 1, and pp. 167, 698. In one place, Rosenberg gives a figure of 9 million for the number of Nordics mass murdered by their racial enemies. Ibid., p. 167. In other places, he speaks of "blood baths" in which Nordic blood was spilled. So much Nordic blood was lost that the entire character of France was altered. See ibid., pp. 99–101. Since Rosenberg considered the 2 million Germans fallen in the First World War as having been slaughtered by the contrivances of a deceitful "racial enemy," he imagined that the number of Nordics lost in racial conflict could exceed tens of millions.

[93] Alfred Rosenberg, "Preface to the 1933 Edition," in *Die Protokolle der Weisen von Zion und die jüdische Weltpolitik* (Munich: Hoheneichen Verlag, 1933); *Der Mythus des XX. Jahrhundert*, pp. 114–15.

Muhammad had said nothing less. All that was different was the selected race.

Rosenberg saw in Christianity one of the major obstacles to the anticipated resurgence of the superior race reborn. Like the Black Muslims, he saw Christianity a Semitic excrescence, preaching submission and docility to a proud, independent, and assertive people for whom self-defense was a critical necessity. For Rosenberg – as was the case with the Messenger – Christianity was a religion fit only for slaves, consciously employed by the enemies of the "children of the sun," to create a world of "racial chaos" in which only the Jews might rule.[94]

Although Rosenberg admitted that the evidence was inconclusive, he chose to see Jesus as other than a Jew,[95] whose mission was obscured by the workings of the Jew Saul – the apostle Paul – who consciously sought to shape Christianity to the purposes of his race.[96] All of the "effeminate excesses" of the Sermon on the Mount, the nonresistance to evil, the turning of the other cheek, the entire doctrine of "cowardice," are attributed to the influence of the Semites, who know nothing of inner strength and physical courage.

A German church, to truly serve the enduring interests of the race, could only reserve the love that is essential to religion to members the German community – its own kind.[97] Like Garvey and Elijah Muhammad, Rosenberg argued that love and charity are to be extended beyond the race only after the last member of one's own race has enjoyed a surfeit of both.

Given all the elements of his belief system, Rosenberg, like the Black Muslims, saw miscegenation, the mixing of unlike blood, the ultimate threat to "palingenesis," the rebirth of a new and better world. For his part, and given the divine nature of blacks as opposed to the satanic nature of whites, the Messenger advised his followers that racial intermarriage could only succeed in taking blacks to hell and thwarting the plans of Allah. He insisted that it was critical for blacks "to keep [the] nation pure."[98]

Beyond these racist essentials, Rosenberg, like the Black Muslims, conceived the "international Jew" as the principal enemy of the "divine race." For Rosenberg, the *Protocols of the Learned Elders of Zion* provided a blueprint of their satanic designs. The charges leveled against the Jews by those convinced of the authenticity of the *Protocols* included everything from failing to defend the Fatherland in its struggles against its enemies, to

---

[94] Ibid., pp. 69–81, 105–7, 113, 158.

[95] Rosenberg believed, with Houston S. Chamberlain, that Jesus of Nazareth, given his aristocratic character and his origin, among peoples with a tradition of "Nordic" provenance, was, more likely than not, a "Nordic" himself. See ibid., pp. 26, 76, n. 604.

[96] Ibid., pp. 605–6.

[97] Ibid., p. 608.

[98] Muhammad, *Our Savior Has Arrived*, pp. 87, 201. Compare, for example, Rosenberg, *Der Mythus des XX. Jahrhundert*, pp. 37, 43, 46, 56, 70–1.

imposing communism on the unsuspecting, to the sexual exploitation of Gentile housemaids. Such charges are, and have long been, the common coin of anti-Semitism.

All things considered, there is more National Socialism in the beliefs of the Black Muslims than there is Fascism. Fascists, National Socialists, and Black Muslims all share the common commitment to some form of nationalism and national development in the effort to restore their oppressed nation to its rightful place in the international community. All share the conviction that only an inspired charismatic, at the head of a "vanguard elite," could lead an oppressed people to renewal. Unlike Italian Fascism, National Socialism, Garveyism, and the creed of the Black Muslims conceived race the irreplaceable core of their respective systems. And yet, Elijah Muhammad's Black Muslims fail to convey the impression that they are nothing other than a black variant of Hitler's National Socialism. The Black Muslims, unlike Hitler's National Socialists, are possessed of "cold zeal" – given to inflammatory "toxic speech," but ill-disposed to racial violence.

The Messenger always carefully communicated to his followers that the white devils were in possession of an overwhelming inventory of weapons against which essentially defenseless blacks could not prevail. Blacks, the Messenger reminded his followers, have neither weapons nor the means to fashion them. The destruction of White civilization was the task not of blacks, but of Allah. Master Wallace Fard Muhammad would, in his own time, rain fire on the United States of America. Elijah Muhammad advised blacks never to fire a shot nor raise a sword against the government of the white man. It is Allah who would somehow ultimately deliver the entire earth to blacks, to enjoy as their own.[99]

Thus, the racist "toxic speech," the inflammatory rhetoric commonplace among some Black Muslims, does not presage actual violence against the so-called white devils. The function of racist rhetoric among Black Muslims appears to provide the opportunity for the venting of frustration and the psychological affirmation of manhood. The zeal that actually informs such speech is "cool," that is, the speaker does not expect his audience actually to undertake violence to destroy the racial enemy; that is left to divine providence.[100]

Unlike National Socialists, in their own time and place, black revolutionaries in the United States have rarely sought to achieve their aspirations through organized political or racial violence.[101] Under any and all

---

[99] See Muhammad, *The Fall of America*, pp. 17, 184, 211; *Message to the Black Man*, pp. 36, 315; *Our Saviour Has Arrived*, pp. 65, 87, 103, 105, 112–13, 168, 206–7.

[100] See the discussion in Robert Jewett, *The Captain America Complex* (Philadelphia, PA: Westminster, 1973), pp. 76, 90–2.

[101] There are clearly some exceptions. Malcolm X is well-known for having appealed to "any means necessary" to achieve black purpose, but there is evidence that the Messenger opposed any such strategy.

conceivable circumstances, blacks would constitute no more than a small minority of the entire population, and it is extremely unlikely that any armed activity they would initiate could long operate effectively against the security forces of the United States.

An indisposition to invoke violence characterizes the Black Muslims. Although they have been known to direct deadly force against their own apostates,[102] there is very little credible evidence of any organized intention to attack whites either as individuals or as representatives of the "white government."

That feature renders the Black Muslims distinct in the family of twentieth-century revolutionary movements. Its specifically religious institutional form, and its indisposition to revolutionary violence, renders it a singularly peculiar member of the collection.

The Messenger's general developmental plans, both agricultural and industrial, are really marginal to his entire system of beliefs. Unlike Fascists, who were to invest heavily in the industrialization of their nation, the Black Muslims seem to address the issue of the technological and manufacturing bases of their prospective nation with considerable insouciance. In fact, economic and political matters really occupy very little of the energies of the Lost-Found Nation. The Messenger's principal purpose seems to have been to serve the psychological needs of his flock, to the general exclusion of their material, that is, the economic and political, needs.

In that sense, the Black Muslims are neither Fascists nor National Socialists. They rather share some prominent features with marginal religious eccentrics like the "Anglo-Israelites," who imagine that the British and Americans are the *real* Israelites, chosen by God and destined to rule the world. The real emphasis is doctrinal, and the major goals psychological. Even the heirs of the Anglo-Israelites, among the followers of contemporary "Christian Identity" movement who are more political and violent in their advocacy, hardly qualify as Fascists or National Socialists.[103]

The belief system of Elijah Muhammad shares with the Christian Identity movement some of the same structural features. It is the content that varies.

---

[102] Malcolm Little, the charismatic "Malcolm X," was assassinated by members, or former members, of the Lost-Found Nation of Islam. There are other recorded incidents of black-on-black violence involving members of the Nation. Conversely, there is very little evidence of violence directed against whites.

[103] Many members of the Christian Identity movement do not believe that the Jews are Hebrews at all. They consider them the descendants of a heterogeneous mixture of Turko-Finnish and Mongoloid peoples from Khazaria, converted to Judaism in or around the eighth century. Black Muslims entertain such notions. Popular among them is a book by Michael Bradley, *Chosen People from the Caucasus: Jewish Origins, Delusions, Deceptions and Historical Role in the Slave Trade, Genocide and Cultural Colonization* (Chicago: Third World Press, 1992), which echoes many of the convictions of Christian Identity concerning the origins of the Jews.

With the substitution of blacks for Anglo Americans, one finds a surprising congruity between the belief systems of the Black Muslims and Christian Identity – including their respective anti-Semitisms.

Again, the major distinction between contemporary American white racist groups and the Black Muslims is their apparent readiness to make recourse to violence.[104] Granted that, it would still be difficult to identify white racist groups such as the Aryan Nation, patriotic militias, apocalyptic millennialists, pro-gun advocates, and fundamentalist Christians, no matter how disposed to employ violence, as neofascist. Still less do the Black Muslims qualify.

Italian Fascists were committed to a syndrome of essentially secular political traits that were interconnected and specifically goal-related. Little of that is found among American racists, religious fanatics, and survivalists. Even Hitler's National Socialists shared some affinities with Mussolini's secular Fascists, however occult the beliefs of Alfred Rosenberg may have been. That is not saying a great deal. It affords us little, if any, cognitive advantage to identify any and all groups that entertain racist notions, even if supported by a disposition to violence, as neofascist.

The entire history of the Church of Jesus Christ of Latter Day Saints (LDS) in the United States is laced with racism and violence.[105] Until 1978, official Church doctrine held that a dark skin was a divine sign that the person had sinned grievously in the spiritual realm before his or her material birth. Blacks, with their dark skin, were "justly cursed by God." All peoples so afflicted were to be essentially shunned and were not permitted to participate fully in Mormon liturgy or leadership. Even in death they were to be denied full participation in the celestial kingdom. Mormonism, at its origin, and long into its history, was fundamentally racist, although the leaders of the Church were to deny the fact for most of its existence. Nonetheless, until the "revelation" of 1978 that ended some of the principal racist practices, anti-black racism was a constant within the Church and among its members.[106]

Together with that, a long and doleful history of violence attended the founding, establishment, and fostering of the Church. In addition, there was a clear effort at nation building, with all the features we have here reviewed. Nonetheless, little purpose would be served in identifying the Church of the Latter Day Saints as neofascist.

[104] See Richard Abanes, *Rebellion, Racism and Religion: American Militias* (Downers Grove, IL: InterVarsity Press, 1996), particularly Parts 4 and 5. It would be hard to imagine that the Black Muslims would circulate the black equivalent of a book like Andrew Macdonald's *The Turner Diaries* (Hillsboro, WV: National Vanguard, 1999, originally published in 1978).

[105] See the entire discussion in Richard Abanes, *One Nation Under Gods: A History of the Mormon Church* (New York: Four Walls Eight Windows, 2002). Most of the discussion of race in this discussion follows that of Abanes; see ibid., chap. 16.

[106] Ibid., pp. 63, 110, 357–9, 362–4, 370–2, 420.

In effect, the characterization "neofascist" should be reserved for those revolutionary movements that satisfy at least the major entry criteria into the category. Again, the term "neofascist" refers to a family of political movements. As Ludwig Wittgenstein contended, there are terms in our ordinary speech that allude to classes of referents that share a "family resemblance." They are terms whose use is governed by neither formal nor lexical definition. "Neofascist" seems to be just such a term – all the more reason that one should be careful in its employment.

Racism is neither necessary nor sufficient to identify neofascists nor their movements. Neither the Ku Klux Klan, Christian Identity, nor Elijah Muhammad's Lost-Found Nation of Islam, nor the Church of Latter Day Saints[107] is neofascist. Racism is a contingent variable in the classification of a political movement.

Neither is the invocation of violence necessary or sufficient, in and of itself, to identify a political organization as neofascist. The term "neofascist" requires a criterial, range, or syndromatic definition – one that refers to an indeterminate, but finite, number of properties that provide the grounds for counting something as a member of a class of things.[108]

It may be politically expedient to identify as neofascists those who have earned our disapproval, but other than the psychological satisfaction that attends such use, the exercise has very little substantive merit. We may deplore the toxic speech of Elijah Muhammad and his Black Muslims, but we would be hard pressed to identify him, or his organization, as neofascist or "nazi" by any credible social science criteria.

Curiously enough, the entire issue of the role that Islam is to play in the twenty-first century has forced itself on the Western world however one interprets Elijah Muhammad's Lost-Found Nation of Islam or whatever its future. Quite independent of the Messenger and his Lost-Found Nation, Islamic fundamentalists have taken it upon themselves to cloud the horizons of the twenty-first century with worldwide terrorist acts that have exacted both Gentile and Jewish victims in appalling numbers. As a consequence, there are those who appear prepared to identify Islamic fundamentalism as neofascist.[109] That is so important an issue that it requires sober consideration – and should not be derailed by a readiness to abbreviate the process by prematurely settling on a politically useful, but cognitively uncertain, designation.

---

[107] The Church of Latter-Day Saints has mended its ways with respect to race relations, so that much of the preceding discussion applies exclusively to its past.

[108] See the discussion in A. James Gregor, *Metascience and Politics: An Inquiry into the Conceptual Language of Political Science* (New Brunswick, NJ: Transaction, 2003), pp. 127–46, and the term's definition in the "Glossary," pp. 368–9.

[109] For example, Walter Laqueur speaks of a "clerical fascism" that includes Islamic fundamentalism; *Fascism: Past, Present Future* (New York: Oxford University Press, 1996), part 3.

7

Islamofascism

Neofascism in the Middle East

The search for neofascism in the Middle East reveals a great deal about the general character of the search itself, as well as its putative content. It makes evident the prevailing notions that shape the inquiry, making clear the uncertainty of many of its underlying premises. The consequence is reflected in the tortured results one finds in the contemporary analyses devoted to what has come to be known as "Middle Eastern fascism," and its more recent incarnation, "Islamofascism."[1]

There is a loosely structured argument that identifies some of the secular Arab regimes in the region as "fascist-style dictatorships," and contemporary radical Islamist[2] groups as somehow representing its "religious variant."[3] Some have suggested that historic Fascism was intrinsically "fundamentalist" and, as a consequence, shared some of the most negative properties of the religious fanaticism of contemporary Islamism.[4]

The identification of Middle Eastern political movements as neofascist did not simply arise as a consequence of the terrorist attack on the World Trade Towers on 11 September 2001. Academicians early employed the notion in their efforts to understand something of the first independent political

---

[1] Daniel Pipes, *Militant Islam Reaches America* (New York: W. W. Norton, 2003), pp. 40, 47, 68–9.

[2] The term "Islamist" is used to distinguish the radical form of Islam, the subject of the present chapter, that inspires those Muslims who have chosen to employ violence and terror against both the West and Muslims who oppose them. For a discussion of the distinction, see A. G. Noorani, *Islam and Jihad: Prejudice Versus Reality* (London: Zed, 2002).

[3] Robert Spencer, *Islam Unveiled: Disturbing Questions About the World's Fastest-Growing Faith* (San Francisco: Encounter, 2002), p. 98; see the reference in Gilles Kepel, *Jihad: The Trail of Political Islam* (Cambridge, MA: Harvard University Press, 2002), p. 5.

[4] See the discussion in Walter Laqueur, *Fascism: Past, Present, Future* (New York: Oxford University Press, 1996), pp. 147–78. Mussolini's Fascism was, of course, a "political religion," a peculiar form of revolutionary politics characteristic of the twentieth century. As such, it shared features with fundamentalist religions. That does not make it a fundamentalist religion. Fascism's value system was preeminently secular.

responses made by those "decolonized" peoples in Africa, Asia, and the Middle East following the end of the Second World War. Amid those responses, certain political features appeared with some impressive regularity.

Immediately following the decolonization of those sectors of the less-developed world that had previously been subject to the control of nations more industrially advanced, one witnessed the advent of industrializing and modernizing movements led by self-proclaimed revolutionary "anti-imperialist vanguards." Those vanguards charged themselves with the responsibilities of restoring the dignity and status of their retrograde communities in the face of a rapacious imperialism.

To accomplish their ends, they sought to mobilize masses and marshal their sentiment to revolutionary purpose. They made appeal to the past grandeur of their respective nations – and promised its restoration in exchange for unqualified obedience and a readiness to labor and sacrifice. Kwame Nkrumah, for instance, spoke of the glories of ancient Akan society, and Gamal Abdel Nasser recalled the majesty of Pharaonic Egypt – an Egypt he held to be the ultimate source of the world's civilization.

To succeed in their purposes, both Nkrumah and Nasser advocated a political system governed by a single-party state, a "true democracy" that could succeed in its pursuit of "freedom" only when "directed according to the principles of the Revolution."[5] Both, together with Mussolini's theoreticians, rejected the "semblance" of democracy found in Western representative systems for the "reality" of democracy in a one-party state. In the case of Egypt, such a democracy was sought in a political system "whose tendency toward totalitarian controls" had become increasingly obvious over the years, with its suppression of "dissident" political associations, a controlled press, and educational policies that reflected the wisdom of the charismatic leader.[6] In Nasser's Egypt, three years after the seizure of power, the Revolutionary Command Council had intimidated, dispersed, or destroyed its political competitors.[7] If one scrutinizes Nasserism in more detail, the similarities shared with paradigmatic Fascism become something more than superficial.

Unlike the quaint Marxism of the Bolshevik revolution, with its confused notions of "proletarian dictatorship" and the suppression of the

---

[5] See the discussion in "The Charter of National Action," in Nissim Rejwon, *Nasserist Ideology: Its Exponents and Critics* (New York: John Wiley, 1974), p. 217. The Charter was the ideological rationale for the Nasser regime and was published in 1962. For a discussion of the Nkrumah regime, see A. James Gregor, "African Socialism, Socialism and Fascism," *Review of Politics* 29, no. 3 (July 1967), pp. 324–53.

[6] See the comments in George Lenczowski, "The Objects and Methods of Nasserism," *Journal of International Affairs* 19, no. 1 (1965), p. 68.

[7] It is interesting to note that in 1925, three years after his seizure of power in 1922, Mussolini, having dispersed, exiled, and defeated his opponents, declared that Fascism would assume "totalitarian" control of the peninsula.

entrepreneurial "bourgeoisie," Nasser advocated a form of class collaboration, through functional representation, that rejected "class warfare" as
inimical to the nation's industrial and economic development. As was the
case with Fascism, rapid economic growth and industrial development were
critical to Nasser's program of Egyptian renewal. Like Mussolini, Nasser
spoke of masses rather than classes as the foundation of the revolution, the
engine of production, and the basis of governance.[8]

Nasser's Arab socialism embodied an ideology animated by an urgent
demand for redress, not on behalf of an oppressed proletariat, but to rectify
the shame of generations of Egyptians who suffered at the hands of foreign
imperialists – the "plutocracies" of then-recent Fascist memory.[9] Like the
first Fascists, Nasser's Arab socialists sought to efface the history of humiliation that clouded the glorious memory of an ancient civilization that had
once dominated the known world.

Arab socialists sought rapid industrialization and the "building of a powerful national army" to assure the security of the nation against any impostures and attendant humiliation, including any emanating from Israel – that
"aggressive racial movement" – that served as a weapon against Arabs in
the hands of imperialists.[10] Israel was an opponent because it was seen as
another humiliating intrusion by foreigners into the historic space of the
"Arab nation." It was perceived as an effort to sever the organic links that
bound the Arab Middle East in unity.

Like the first Fascists, Nasser's Arab socialists acknowledged that they
could not embrace the theories of nineteenth-century Marxism, but salvaging
the kernels of truth to be found there, they put together a more modern system of socialist beliefs better calculated to answer contemporary problems.
Like those socialist revolutionaries who made up the intellectual leadership
of the first Fascism, Nasser's ideologues argued that traditional socialism
failed to address the sense of national unity that inspired revolution in the
twentieth century, and proved incapable of appreciating the requirements of
revolution in retrograde economic circumstances. Like Fascist intellectuals,
Nasser's followers were prepared to transform the internationalism of classic Marxism into a national socialism that would acknowledge the central
role of the nation in the evolving developmental revolution.[11] Like the first
Fascists, Nasser's Arab socialists were advocates of production rather than
socialist redistribution. They, like the Fascists before them, recognized that
classical Marxism, with its expectation that the state would "wither away"
after the revolution, failed to understand the critical role the state would

---

[8] See the Charter of National Action, in Rejwan, *Nasserist Ideology*, pp. 199, 216–17,
   223–4.
[9] See the discussion in A. James Gregor, *Young Mussolini and the Intellectual Origins of
   Fascism* (Berkeley, CA: University of California Press, 1979), chap. 9.
[10] The Charter of National Action, in Rejwan, *Nasserist Ideology*, pp. 196–7, 212.
[11] See the discussion in ibid., chap. 6.

discharge in an accelerated program of economic and industrial development in less-developed nations.

With their programs of productive growth and technological advance,
both Mussolini's Fascists and Nasser's Arab socialists were hard task-masters
who sought to invoke commitment, sacrifice, labor, and skill in a mixed economic system composed of both public and private sectors, all under expanding state-supervised industrial production, influenced by market signals and
shaped by indicative planning. Like Fascism, Arab socialism advocated state
dominance over the nation's transport, communications, and educational
infrastructure, its financial institutions and credit allocation, together with
industries or activities critical to national defense.[12]

It was in the "battle for production" that the new "Arab socialist man"
would "justify his worthy position under the sun." Like Fascism, Arab socialism promised a people, oppressed for centuries by the wealthy arrogance of
the West, a proper "place in the sun" – and a "new man" who would be its
proper denizen.[13]

Like the first Fascists, Nasser sought to restore territorial integrity to his
nation. He saw Egypt as the core of a renewed "Arab Nation" that would
once again stretch from the Mediterranean to the Indian Ocean. While his
"Pan-Arabism" stretched nationalism much further than anything standard
in Mussolini's Fascism, his was an insistent irredentism that shared traits
with Mussolini's thirst to return to Italy, once again, territories that had
once been elements of the empire of Rome.[14]

In its contest for the allegiance of the masses, Nasser's Arab socialism,
like Italian Fascism, sought to domesticate a powerful religious competitor.
Mussolini contained Roman Catholicism as Nasser sought to contain Islam.
Both allowed religious expression, recognizing the powerful influence of
religious convictions among their followers, but both sought (with varying
degrees of success) to maintain ultimate political control over institutional
religion.[15]

---

[12] For a full discussion of Fascist economic policy, see A. James Gregor, *Mussolini's Intellectuals:
Fascist Social and Political Thought* (Princeton, NJ: Princeton University Press, 2005). Compare with the Nasser's Charter of National Action, in Rejwan, *Nasserist Ideology*, section 6.

[13] Ibid., p. 235.

[14] Fascists regularly invoked the Roman Empire when they advanced claims in the Balkans, in
North and East Africa. See, for example, Fernando Gori, *Roma nel continente nero* (Rome:
Editoriale Tupini, 1940). Nasser did not seek empire, he sought the reconstitution of an
"Arab Nation." That "Nation" was understood to include virtually the entire Middle East.

[15] The form this took under Fascism was expressed in the official *Dottrina del fascismo*, in
which a secular idealism, the Actualism of Giovanni Gentile, was chosen to represent the
philosophical foundation of Fascism. The Roman Catholic Church publicly objected to the
role of Actualism in the rationale for the regime. See the discussion in A. James Gregor,
Giovanni Gentile: Philosopher of Fascism (New Brunswick, NJ: Transaction, 2001). Fascism forever remained at odds with the hierarchy of the Roman Catholic Church, just as
Nasser, throughout his life, remained at odds with the fundamentalist Muslims of the Muslim
Brotherhood.

Both Fascism and Arab socialism found it necessary to deal with monarchial institutions, Mussolini with the inherited House of Savoy, and Nasser with the royalist regime in Saudi Arabia, as well as the Hashimite royal house and the emirates of the Gulf. Together with traditional religion, both Mussolini and Nasser sought to marginalize traditional royalty (once again with varying degrees of success).

In effect, Nasser's Arab socialism shared substantial features with the Fascism of Mussolini. Nor were Egyptian intellectuals disposed to conceal the fact. It was not uncommon for regime intellectuals, in their discussions concerning socialism, to refer to its generic form as encompassing not only the system then prevalent in the Soviet Union, but also that which flourished in Hitler's Germany and Mussolini's Italy.[16]

For Arab socialists, the term "socialism" thus included an indeterminate array of variants. Nasser's ideologues made evident that his socialism had very little if anything to do with Marxism. Marxism was rejected, at least in part, because it was materialistic and deterministic, failing to take the measure of human will and determination. It was rejected because it was wrong in its premises and misguided in its objectives.[17]

It is clear that Nasser, like Mussolini in Italy, suppressed all organized expressions of Marxism and revolutionary communism in Egypt, not only because they threatened the political integrity of the single-party state, but because they created dysfunctional stresses within the nation's multiclass program of rapid industrial and economic development. The form of socialism that animated Nasser's ideology was essentially the same that one finds in Fascist apologetics. Like Fascism, Nasser conceived his socialism as a "third way" to the future, a future neither capitalist nor Marxist-Leninist.

In its principles, its most elemental purposes, and in much of its institutional form, Nasser's Arab socialism shared some essentials with Mussolini's Fascism. Its practice, of course, was conditioned by circumstances, and its international behavior was a function of opportunity. It is a commonplace that no two political systems in history are ever identical. Nonetheless, for classificatory and didactic purposes, it would be plausible, with some qualification, to speak of Nasserism as a neofascism.

Maurice Bardeche, as a fascist intellectual himself, acknowledged as much. In the course of his account, he referred to Nasserism as a fascism with Islam at its back – and then went on to argue that all fascisms were somehow "religious" in character.[18] Bardeche seemed to believe that fascism, as a political religion, might, without altering its essentials, simply accommodate the prevailing religious institutions it found in its environment.

---

[16] See the citations in Rejwan, *Nasserist Ideology*, pp. 100–2.

[17] Ibid., p. 102.

[18] Maurice Bardeche, *Qu'est-ce que le Fascisme?* (Paris: Les Sept Couleurs, 1961), Part 2, chap. 2.

Actually, established religion has always been fascism's competitor. Nasserism could no more simply accommodate Islam than Mussolini's Fascism could simply accommodate Roman Catholicism. Like Fascism, Nasserism acknowleged the role organized religion might play in the political program of the regime, but, once again as in Fascism, Nasser was not prepared to allow religion to influence the regime's policies significantly. Like the Arab socialism of Hafiz al-Asad in Syria, modeled after that of Nasser, Islam was to be made to serve the secular purposes of the regime.[19] As long as institutional religion did not create obstacles for the revolution, it was permitted to exist as a tactical ally of the single-party state. The historic fact is that organized religion, in general, has always been a competitor, to one degree or another, of Fascism and its variants.[20]

Nasser, like Mussolini, undertook to suppress religious expression when it assumed dissident political form. Mussolini suppressed those agencies of the Roman Catholic Church, the Catholic political parties, and Catholic Action, as well as those clandestine "Guelph" factions, that opposed the regime in any sense or measure. As a consequence, relations with the Church of Rome continued to be confrontational, although contained, throughout the history of Mussolini's regime.[21]

For his part, Nasser, like Asad, forcefully suppressed Islamic "fundamentalists" when their beliefs, in any way, threatened the political system. Like Mussolini, Nasser sought an ally, a belief system that would support and sustain, rather than compete with, the ideology of the state. Like Mussolini, Arab socialists were content to have the nation religious, but neither controlled nor significantly influenced by clerics. Religion was to serve as an *instrumentum regni* in these systems, to be used for the political ends of the one-party state. When it became clear that religion did not so serve, it was confined or suppressed. For Arab socialism – with the passage of time – the nation's relationship with Islam, as both a religion and a political force, was to take on more and more omnious features that were, ultimately, to have fateful historic consequences.

By the end of the 1950s, Nasser's prestige among Arabs had attained dramatic heights. His decision in the late 1950s to assume control over the Suez Canal, at the cost of France and Great Britain, certified Nasser's

[19] See Moshe Ma'oz, *Asad: The Sphinx of Damascus* (New York: Grove Weidenfeld, 1988), chap. 12.

[20] There are few convincing cases in which religion was the ally of a "true" fascism. The instances that often have been cited require assessment and review. The discussion will be reserved for later, in Chapter 10.

[21] For a convenient collection of documents concerning the relationship between Fascism and the Roman Catholic Church, see Pietro Scoppola, *La Chiesa e il fascismo: Documenti e interpretazioni* (Bari: Laterza, 1971). In this context, see Renzo De Felice, *Mussolini il fascista: L'organizzazione dello Stato fascista 1925–1929* (Turin: Giulio Einaudi, 1968), particularly chap. 5.

anti-imperialist credentials for many Arabs. Few seemed to notice that in the course of the brief hostilities that accompanied Egypt's successful move, the small Israeli army had succeeded in defeating a large Egyptian force armed with the most modern Soviet weaponry. Nasser had twisted the tail of foreign imperialism.

In February 1958, the proclamation of a Syrian–Egyptian unitary state electrified many throughout the Middle East. The Ba'ath revolution in Iraq, in July that same year, appeared to signal a further articulation of a proposed unified Arab nation. Pro-Nasser forces in Lebanon, supplied by Egypt, took the initiative in what was anticipated to be yet another success for pan-Arab socialism.

By 1963, Nasser signed an accord that anticipated a federal union between Egypt, Syria, and Iraq. It soon became clear, however, that such a federation could not take place. Each government had reservations that alienated the others. Ultimately, Syria and Iraq were to evolve into competitive revolutionary centers within the conjectured "Arab Nation."

By that time, it appeared that Nasser's pan-Arabism was unraveling. More than that, the British and the Americans had undertaken interventions in the region that augured problems in the immediate future. In May 1967, having reorganized his armed forces and refurbished them with the most advanced Soviet weaponry, Nasser declared that history demanded nothing less than the physical obliteration of Israel.[22] Threatened by Egyptian, Jordanian, and Syrian forces, Israel launched a preemptive attack that devastated its opponents, driving them out of the West Bank, the Golan Heights, and Sinai.

The war was a humiliating defeat for Arab socialism – from which it was not destined to recover. It seemed to demonstrate the impotence of the secular Arab regimes. It cost the "Arab Nation" the loss of major Muslim holy sites, as well as Jerusalem, the third holiest city of Islam. With the Israeli occupation of Old Jerusalem, the Dome of the Rock and the al-Aqsa Mosque fell into the hands of the Jews, rendering the struggle with Israel no longer simply an Arab nationalist concern, but, more emphatically, an Islamic one.

Nasser survived the humiliation, but died a scant three years later. In fact, with Nasser's death, and the further humiliation of the Arab Nation, the experiment in Arab socialism was, in substantial part, over. Whatever temporary successes surfaced thereafter, they were to prove largely ephemeral.

Almost immediately after Nasser's death, Anwar Sadat, his successor, affirmed Islam as the state religion of Egypt – in a transparent move to attract and accommodate Islamic support. He identified himself as the "Believer-President," but failed to convince his most critical audience. What had become increasingly evident was the fact that Islam had begun to fill the space vacated by the flawed secular aspirations of Nasserism in all its forms.

---

[22] As quoted, Paul Johnson, *Modern Times: The World from the Twenties to the Nineties* (New York: Harper, 1991, revised edition), p. 666.

It was clear that there was restiveness throughout the Middle East. In 1972, Sadat abandoned the alliance with the Soviet Union and in October 1973, on the festival of Yom Kippur, he launched a combined Egyptian–Syrian assault on Israel. After brief initial success, the assault was defeated.

In the years immediately following the Yom Kippur War, the oil-producing nations of the Middle East organized themselves in an enterprise intended to employ the "oil weapon" to punish the advanced industrial nations for their foreign policy offenses – primarily for their support of the Jewish state. In the course of that effort, during the years between 1974 and 1977, price manipulation brought into the coffers of the Arab oil-producing cartel revenues that amounted to about half the available financial liquidity of the world. That was the time of maximum Arab power. But whatever the use of the oil weapon was intended to accomplish, it failed. Not only did Israel survive, but the advanced industrial nations continued to prosper – and they proceeded with their domination of the international environment.

In the ferment that resulted, in 1979, Iranian Shi'ite fundamentalists swept away the "apostate" Peacock Throne of the Shah. In its place, the Ayatollah Ruhollah Khomeini proclaimed the establishment of an "Islamic Republic," which then proceeded to seize the American embassy in Tehran, taking sixty Americans hostage and holding them for 444 days until they were ransomed. The Ayatollah had committed himself to the destruction of the "satanic" American government. Islamic fundamentalism had scored its first revolutionary success.

In general, the fundamentalist Muslims of the region welcomed the Iranian revolution as a long-awaited response to Western impostures. The revolution in Iran provided evidence that a militant Islam could defeat not only a secular monarchy, defended by a modern security force, but one of the world's most powerful nations – the United States – as well. Khomeini's revolution held out the promise of a restoration of Muslim dignity to those most sorely in need. Pictures of Khomeini took the place of those of Nasser, and the call for revolution in the Middle East took on more and more of the features of an antisecular fundamentalist religious restoration.[23]

It was within that political environment that in October 1981 fundamentalists of the Muslim Brotherhood assassinated Sadat. Sheikh Omar Abdel Rahman, who served as mufti of the Brotherhood cell responsible, was subsequently charged with conspiracy to commit murder. It was he who provided the *fatwas*, the justificatory religious judgments, that argued that the assassination of Sadat conformed to the prescriptive strictures of the *Qur'an*.

What was becoming clear was the increasing disillusionment that had begun to fester among Arabs. Muammar al-Qaddafi in Libya, Saddam Hussein

---

[23] See Walid M. Abdelnasser, *The Islamic Movement in Egypt: Perceptions of International Relations 1967–1981* (New York: Kegan Paul International, 1994), pp. 65–7.

in Iraq, and Asad in Syria all attempted to continue their efforts as "Arab socialists," but to very little purpose. In the eyes of very many Arabs, the program embodied in the ideology of secular Arab socialism had, in large part, failed.

With the failure of Arab socialism, Muslims have been called to *jihad*, to take up arms for the survival, enhancement and glory of Islam. Largely without distinction, Muslims are called to rise up against their own "apostate" leadership, the "crusaders" of the West, and their allies in the region – to carry *jihad* to all who oppose the pristine religion of the Prophet.

Secular leadership in the Middle East, Americans, and Europeans, together with Jews in general, and Israelis in particular, all became increasingly targeted by those who would restore the community of the faithful – the *ummah* of the Prophet Muhammad, as it had been at the time of its founding in the seventh century. A new force had made its fulsome appearance in the troubled Middle East: what students of neofascism were to identify as "Islamofascism." The Islamic faith, in its most fundamentalist expression, was no longer seen as ancillary to a local secular fascism, but had supposedly become a neofascism itself.

Actually, whatever it was, or whatever it was to become in the eyes of its critics, fundamentalist Islam – whose *salafist*[24] sectarians were most rigorous in the traditionalism of the faith – was far, far older than any fascism. A red thread of continuity leads almost all contemporary Islamists, those *salafists* most committed to "original" Islam, back to the theological work of a thirteenth-century sage, Taqi al-Din ibn Taymiyya (1268–1328).

Ibn Taymiyya lived during the troubled times of the Mongol invasions of Arab lands. By that time, the expansive and triumphal Muslim community, the *ummah*, which had swept over the Christian and pagan lands that surrounded it, had suffered the depredations of the Christian Crusaders. The most serious Christian incursions of the period were turned back by the end of the twelfth century.[25] Nonetheless, even their temporary success proved traumatic to a community that had grown accustomed to the idea of its own invincibility.

For their part, the Mongol invaders – although they converted, in time, to Islam – persisted in many of their pagan traditions, often relating to the laws of the *Qur'an*, the *shari'ah*, more in breach than honor. For ibn Taymiyya, the antinomian behavior of the Mongol rulers reduced Muslims once again

---

[24] The term *salafiyya* has had variable meanings over time. As *salafi*, it refers to the first generations of Muslims, whose proximity to the Prophet is held to confirm both their pristine virtue as well as the authenticity of their beliefs. In contemporary Islam, the term *salafist* refers to the fundamentalist, most extreme, anti-Western sectarians.

[25] Whatever Crusader efforts were undertaken in the thirteenth century were on a small scale, and after the fall of Acre in 1291, no further attempts were mounted.

to that state of "spiritual darkness *(jahillyya)*" from which the revelations of the Prophet had rescued them. In 1258, not only had the Mongols destroyed Baghdad, killing three-quarters of a million persons, together with the last caliph of the Abbasid empire, they subsequently embarked on the conquest of established Muslim dynasties elsewhere in the Middle East. Against the proscriptions of the *Qur'an,* Muslim killed Muslim.[26]

Amid the chaos, the Taymiyya family fled from the onslaught that not only threatened Taqui al-Din Ibn Tamiyya, but humiliated Islam. Ibn Tamiyya condemned the Mongol converts for their perfidy. Any Muslim who took up arms against another Muslim was to be considered an unbeliever and a hypocrite. However artfully they posed as Muslims, the Mongols were seen by ibn Taymiyya as worthy only of punishment in this life and torment in the next.[27]

It was in those circumstances that ibn Taymiyya urged a return to Muslim origins. He became the first *salafist.* He seemed convinced that the judgment of Allah lay behind the frightful afflictions that beset the entire Muslim family of his time. Muslims were being punished because they had allowed the purity of the faith to become contaminated.[28] In the effort to restore the dignity and power of Islam, he became obsessed with the need to reestablish the original purity of its beliefs.

Critical to the pursuit of that purity was the restoration of the role of *jihad,* holy warfare, alongside the five defining "pillars" of Islam. He argued that together with daily prayers, the pilgrimage to Mecca, the provision of alms for the needy, the declaration of Muslim faith, and fasting during Ramadan, one must give evidence of true Islamic belief by striving, not only with one's wealth but with one's weapons, in the service of Allah.[29] To ibn Taymiyya, the redemption of Islam required nothing less than a reaffirmation on the part of every Muslim to commit himself, without qualification, to struggle to the death in Allah's cause.

Until that time, there was relatively little dispute among Muslims about the nature of *jihad,* generally spoken of as a "striving" in the service of Allah. Other than a reference to "holy warfare," the term carried connotations in its train that suggested internal struggle against indecent impulse and selfish interest. Traditionally, however, the term was generally understood to

---

[26] In his discussion of the faith, ibn Taymiyya reminded Muslims of the proscription against killing a fellow Muslim. Ibn Taymiyya, *Kitab Al-Iman: Book of Faith* (Bloomington, IN: Iman, 1999), p. 270.

[27] Ibn Taymiyya defined the hypocrite as one who inwardly rejects belief, but outwardly pretends to behave as a Muslim. Eternal damnation is their due. Ibid., p. 66, confer pp. 193–4.

[28] Ibn Taymiyya regularly cited *surahs* such as 2:5 and 20:123 to make the point that only those who are true Muslims prosper. See, for example, ibid., p. 35.

[29] He cites *surah* 49:15, which affirms that "believers" must "struggle hard with their wealth and their lives in the way of Allah." Ibid., p. 192.

mean fighting *(qital)*, undertaking organized violence – making war – against the enemies of Islam, either to protect its territorial integrity or extend its reach.[30]

Ibn Taymiyya cited the Prophet in arguing that *jihad* was a Muslim duty. For him, *jihad* was a collective obligation, much like *zakat*, the giving of alms that was one of the prescribed "Five Pillars" of Islam. Every believer, he insisted, was required to undertake "at least one aspect of *jihad*." In fact, when ibn Taymiyya spoke of the "best deeds" a Muslim might perform in this world, he listed *jihad* among the first. In response to the question as to what *jihad* might best be understood to be, he replied that it was the "collective duty. . . . to fight against unbelievers wherever you find them. . . ." Since it was evident that by the time he wrote his *Book of Faith* the term *jihad* had multiple meanings, it seems clear that, of all the alternative meanings, ibn Taymiyya chose to emphasize armed conflict. Thus, when speaking to his audience concerning the "best death" that a Muslim might seek, he characterized it as one "in which your blood is spilled and your horse is wounded."[31]

Equally evident was ibn Taymiyya's injunction that the devout struggle – that is, undertake *jihad* – against *all* sin, disbelief, and hypocrisy – including that of their own impious rulers. In 1303, at the behest of a Mamluk sultan, he drafted a *fatwa*, a religious brief, to justify a *jihad* against Muzaffar, prince of Mardin, an "apostate" Muslim leader. In his *fatwa*, ibn Taymiyya admonished Muslims to take up arms against any Muslim who failed to pass the test of strict adherence to doctrine. He had planted the seed of revolutionary violence at the very heart of Islam. Thereafter, any Muslim government, perceived as apostate by any Qur'anic scholar, was open to the threat of violence by its own subjects.

By the time the Ottoman Turks substituted themselves for the Mamluks in the sixteenth century, ibn Taymiyya's views had lost favor, to remain marginalized until the eighteenth century, when Muhammad ibn Abd al-Wahhab (1703–92) once again enlisted them to the service of fundamentalist Islam. They were once again of utility because changes in Europe had altered the familiar relationship between Muslim and non-Muslim peoples.

In 1683, the Ottoman armies, after having penetrated into the Balkans, were stopped at the gates of Vienna by European military power. In 1686, a century and a half of Muslim rule in Hungary was brought to an end with the fall of Buda. While neither of these events proved of major consequence to the attitudes of many in the court of the Ottoman Caliph, other changes

---

[30] See the discussion in John L. Esposito, *Unholy War: Terror in the Name of Islam* (New York: Oxford University Press, 2002), chap. 2.

[31] Ibn Taymiyya, *Kitab Al-Iman*, pp. 30, 269, 271, 273. See ibid., chap. 21 for the discussion concerning "collective duties."

were taking place that, all together, were to affect the substance and posture of Islamic rule.

Throughout the same period, it became increasingly evident that the Europeans were outflanking Islam, and new sea routes around Africa threatened the South and Southeast Asian commerce of Muslim traders. As early as the beginning of the sixteenth century, the Republic of Venice had already signaled the danger inherent in the European domination of the seas, and by the mid-seventeenth century, the navy of tiny Venice defeated Ottoman ships of the line. By the seventeenth century, the danger of European command of the seas had matured into the presence of the Portuguese, Dutch, and other Europeans in East and South Asia. With that intrusion came the local establishment of naval facilities that gradually transformed host territories into European dependencies. The Muslims had lost initiative to Western "imperialism."

Russian expansion and general European hostility cost the Ottomans dearly by the end of the seventeenth century – exactions that continued into the eighteenth. By that time, there was a sense among the political and military leaders of Islam that it would be prudent to mount an overall defense against the "infidels."[32]

One of the suggestions made early in the seventeenth century was that Muslims, in collecting their resources to resist foreign incursion, be prepared to learn something of modern science and military tactics from their opponents. There was a sense that something was going very wrong with the system created by the Prophet a thousand years before, and perhaps there was something to be learned from Islam's tormentors.

Muslim leaders asked the *ulema*, the doctors of Islamic law, to authorize their followers to accept the teachings of "infidels" in the effort to protect the future of the caliphate. The Treaty of Carlowitz of 1699 had precipitated a searching discussion of survival strategy among Muslims. Only the seriousness of the situation had driven the Ottoman rulers to so radical a course. They were prepared to learn from the West.

At the same time that learning from the infidels recommended itself as a defense, one of the most frequently recurring collateral enjoinments was a return to the original purity of the faith.[33] The means of ultimately assuring the survival and prevalence of Islam were to be found in the return to the pious ways of their forebears on the part of all Muslims. It was within

---

[32] Bernard Lewis, *What Went Wrong? The Clash Between Islam and Modernity in the Middle East* (New York: Harper Collins, 2002), Introduction and chap. 1.

[33] This remains constant in the literature of the Islamists. In the twentieth century, Sayyid Qutb made the same point. See Sayyid Qutb, *Milestones* (Cedar Rapids, IA: Mother Mosque Foundation, n.d.), pp. 108–12, 115, 133, and *Social Justice in Islam* (Oneonta, NY: Islamic Publications International, 2000), pp. 287–8.

that particular intellectual and spiritual environment that the thought of Muhammad ibn Abd al-Wahhab took form.

It was the fundamentalist interpretations of ibn Taymiyya that urged themselves on ibn Abd al-Wahhab in what seemed to be an effort to explain the declining fortunes of the religion of Muhammad. Like ibn Taymiyya before him, ibn Abd al-Wahhab saw Islam's decline as evidence of Allah's disfavor.[34] Muslims had brought down the wrath of Allah because they had allowed their faith to be compromised by past success, present indifference, and foreign influence. Ibn Abd al-Wahhab sought to restore Islam to its pristine purity, free of all accretions that originated in indifference or impiety. To save Islam, he advocated a puritanical, militant, and uncompromising faith.[35]

Animated by two central themes – the ideal of the Islamic state in piety and glory together with the invocation of *jihad* for its realization and furtherance – ibn Abd al-Wahhab mobilized the *Ikhwan*, a militia of warriors drawn from the tribes of central Arabia. By the end of the eighteenth century, the entire central Arabian plateau had fallen to their arms. While the Ottomans were making their modest efforts to modernize in the face of the Western challenge, the "Wahhabists," as they came to be called, insisted on their intransigence and fundamentalist reform of Islamic beliefs. Thus while Muslims throughout the Middle East attempted to adapt themselves to the increasingly insistent demands of the eighteenth, nineteenth, and early-twentieth centuries, the Wahhabists continued to lament Islam's descent into *jahiliyya*, that barbarism and ignorance that preceded the coming of the Prophet. Islam's poverty, vulnerability, and ignorance were attributed not to the absence of economic development, attendant military sophistication, or educational and scientific achievement, but to the lack of sufficient Muslim piety. In all its unconvincing brevity, the argument was that having fallen away from authentic Islam, Muslims had lost their former greatness. Allah had withdrawn His favor. More and more regularly, intransigent Muslims insisted that only a return to *salafiyya Islam*, the "pure" Islam of their forefathers, would restore the Muslim nation.

It was Muhammad Rashid Rida (1866–1935) who carried these ideas into the turbulent twentieth century.[36] Deeply influenced by Wahhabi doctrines, he insisted that the decline of the Muslim *ummah* could be halted only if Islam were purged of all the impurities with which its followers, over the

---

[34] The same relationship continued to be argued in the twentieth century by Sayyid Abul A'la Mawdudi, one of the major ideologues of today's most radical Islamists. See his *Fundamentals of Islam* (Jahore: Islamic Publications, 2000), pp. 160–2, and chap. 28, together with his *Witnesses unto Mankind: The Purpose and Duty of the Muslim Ummah* (Leicester, UK: Islamic Foundation, 1994), pp. 37–9, 62.

[35] See Hamid Algar, *Wahhabism: A Critical Essay* (Oneonta, NY: Islamic Publications International, 2002).

[36] Abdelnasser, *The Islamic Movement in Egypt*, pp. 32, 83, 120–1, 126–7.

years, had allowed it to be contaminated. While Rida's arguments were less stark than those of ibn Abd al-Wahhab, he did invoke *jihad* against those "who do not rule by that which God has revealed." He advocated inspiration from antiquity, when "the rightly guided caliphs" ruled Islam.[37] Against the importuning of the Western industrialized democracies, he sought the rehabilitation of the traditional Islamic state, the restoration of the caliphate, and the pious obedience of its citizens.

One of the students in Rida's circle was Hasan al-Banna (1906–49), who was to found the Egyptian Muslim Brotherhood. From a tiny rented room initially providing space for a small membership, the Brotherhood was to go on, over the years, to expand both its membership and its ideological influence throughout the Muslim world – to Libya, Iraq, Jordan, Syria, and the Sudan – and to establish fraternal connection with Muslims in India and what was to become Pakistan.[38]

Al-Banna formed the Brotherhood and undertook the responsibilities of leadership after a contingent of workers came to him, as a religious scholar, and asked whether he could advise them on how the glory of Islam might be restored in an age that brought only "humiliation and restriction" to Muslims. Without "status or dignity," they felt themselves nothing more than "mere hirelings belonging to foreigners." Possessing nothing but their faith, they felt utterly abandoned and helpless.

It was on that night, deeply moved by their appeal, that al-Banna administered an oath that committed them to service in the struggle for the redemption of Islam. The Muslim Brotherhood was born in March 1928, when al-Banna was a scant twenty-two years old.[39]

The belief system of the Brotherhood, while intrinsically religious, was politically inspired.[40] Its members took an oath to pursue the establishment of a truly Islamic state, restore the caliphate, redeem the Muslim *ummah*, and reanimate the community of believers. Members were enjoined to be prepared to act, to sacrifice, and to be obedient in the service of Islam – and to be forever prepared to respond to the call for *jihad*.

Al-Banna was convinced that only a return to authentic Islam would bring Muslims the political and economic power requisite to their survival and prevalence in the contemporary world. To provide for the defense of Islam and for its success, members were admonished to "struggle for the revival of forgotten Islamic customs and the elimination of practices alien to Islam in all areas of life." One was to be Muslim in "greetings, language,

---

[37] Daniel Benjamin and Steven Simon, *The Age of Sacred Terror: Radical Islam's War Against America* (New York: Random House, 2002), pp. 56–7.

[38] Abdelnasser, *The Islamic Movement in Egypt*, p. 57.

[39] Noorani, *Islam and Jihad*, p. 69.

[40] Islam is considered intrinsically political. No effort is made to distinquish the religious from the political responsibilities of the members of the *ummah*.

the calendar, dress, household furnishing, times of work and rest, food and drink, arriving and departing, expressing joy and sorrow, etc." The creed of the Brotherhood was "God is our objective, the *Qur'an* our constitution, the Prophet our leader; struggle our way." But more than all that, members of the Brotherhood were counseled to be prepared for "death for the sake of God" as their "highest aspiration." By the early 1930s, Hassan al-Banna had begun to lay the foundations of the belief system of the *jihadist-salafists* of our time.[41]

Because of the undercurrent of violence implicit in its doctrines, the Muslim Brotherhood was, at the time, sometimes characterized as "fascist,"[42] but since the ascription was not supported by anything other than the fact that its membership anticipated violence as a political necessity the attribution seemed hardly sufficient to so characterize the Brotherhood. The ascription seems to have been made almost exclusively on the basis of bias. Almost every revolutionary party, whatever its political persuasion, anticipated at the time, and anticipates today, that violence may well be necessary in the course of seizing state power. The appeal to political violence is no more specifically fascist than it is Leninist or Maoist.[43] Almost every revolutionary movement in the twentieth century has invoked violence in the pursuit of its political ends.

Whatever the case, al-Banna's ideas were fostered and expanded by two of his contemporaries who were to outlive him by some years: Sayyid Qutb (1906–66) and Sayyid Abul A'la Mawdudi (1903–79). Qutb was Egyptian in origin and was to be al-Banna's ideological and institutional heir in the Muslim Brotherhood. Mawdudi, in Lehore, India, was to be founder of the Jama'at Islami in 1941. A *jihadist*, he was to develop the *salafist* core of Islamism in order to mobilize the Muslims of South Asia.

The ideas of al-Banna, Qutb, and Mawdudi were to influence significantly the revolutionary thought of the Ayatollah Ruhollah Khomeini (1902–89), the Shi'ia leader of the Iranian Islamist revolution of 1979. The first of the Islamist revolutions to succeed in establishing a radical Qur'anic state, Khomeini's ideas were to transform the traditional quietism of Shi'ia Islamism into an activist, voluntaristic, and revolutionary creed given to the employment of violence and terror in the effort to accomplish what was taken to be the original political vision of the Prophet.[44]

---

[41] See S. M. Hasan al-Banna, *Imam Shahid Hasan Al-Banna: From Birth to Martyrdom* (Milpitas, CA.: Awakening, 2002), passim, but particularly pp. 36, 46–7, 53–4, 56.

[42] Left-wing critics argued that the Brotherhood sought to distract the Egyptian proletariat from their class interests, just as Fascists were supposed to have done in Italy. See Kepel, *Jihad*, pp. 28–9.

[43] See the discussion in A. James Gregor, "Fascism, Marxism and Some Considerations Concerning Classification," *Totalitarian Movements and Political Religions* 3, no. 2 (Autumn 2002), pp. 61–82.

[44] See Ayatollah Ruhollah Khomeini, *Islam and Revolution: Writings and Declaration of Imam Khomeini* (Berkeley, CA: Mizan Press, 1981).

Before the *jihadist* and *salafist* ideas of Islamism could fully mature among the Sunnis of the Middle East, Ali Shariati (1933–77) was articulating the ideas of al-Banna, Qutb, and Mawdudi in modern Shi'ia format. While their Islamist convictions provide the background for his exposition, Shariati's Islamism was, and often in substantial part remains, concealed in an idiom that is more secular than religious.[45]

Nonetheless, Shariati's genuine Islamist convictions are very close to the surface in his account. While it is true that there are Marxist elements to be found in his work,[46] they are largely confined to the conviction that the Islamist revolution would have to address what are generally identified in leftist literature as class interests – the interests of the "disinherited" as opposed to those of the "arrogant."

Thus, in an echo of the essays of the young Karl Marx (so popular in the 1970s), Sariati spoke of modern workers as being "alienated" and "deformed" through exploitation by capitalists, who were themselves reduced to "worshippers of gold" and nothing more.[47] But other than employing some of the familiar Marxist rhetoric of the student unrest of the period, Shariati's work is fundamentally anti-Marxist.

Like all Islamists, Shariati rejected both Marxist as well as capitalist materialism, for very real philosophical and sociological reasons. Marxists and capitalists, he contended, saw human beings motivated exclusively by material concerns. Both Marx and capitalist economists sought to explain human behavior by exclusive reference to material considerations. Shariati maintained, instead, that human will, ideals, sacrifice, and personal determination served as irreplaceable determinants in individual and collective behavior.

He saw political democracy under either capitalist or Marxist auspices a snare and an illusion. He saw humanity "deformed" and deluded by the "fake veneer" of political democracy in both its capitalist and "proletarian" expression.[48]

At the center of his objections was the conviction that both capitalistic liberalism and Marxist communism worship at the same shrine: that of industrialism. Both capitalists and Marxists concern themselves obsessively with "production" – at the expense of the "transcendental" – Allah and

---

[45] Consult Ali Shariati, *On the Sociology of Islam: Lectures by Ali Shariati* (Berkeley, CA: Mizan Press, 1979).

[46] See Mangol Bayat, "Iran's Real Revolutionary Leader," *Christian Science Monitor*, 24 (May 1979), p. 24.

[47] Ali Shariati, *Marxism and Other Western Fallacies: An Islamic Critique* (Berkeley, CA: Mizan Press, 1980), pp. 104–5. Shariati's prose vaguely suggests the "postmodernism" that became so popular at the end of the twentieth century. See, for example, his insistence that there can be no evaluative standards for humans without God. Ibid., p. 101.

[48] See ibid., pp. 26–31, 92–3. Compare the similar views of Mawdudi, *Witnesses unto Mankind*, p. 42, and those of Qutb, *Social Justice in Islam*, pp. 265, 318. The same argument was standard Fascist fare. See, for example, Bruno Spampanato, *Democrazia fascista* (Rome: Politica nuova, 1933).

human values.[49] It was out of such objections that the uncertain notion of "Islamic socialism" emerged.

According to Muslim fundamentalists, it is that "socialism," rather than any Western ideology, Marxist or capitalist, that is essential to humanity, its liberation, and its ultimate fulfillment. That liberation requires the full commitment of the individual and the mobilized masses to its service, a commitment that requires the abandonment of the arrant individualism that typifies the modern world. For Shariati, only a collectivism predicated on a community of belief could supply the strength essential to the success of enterprise.[50]

Shariati's account of Islamism was perhaps the most "secular" of the versions that began to make their fulsome appearance in the 1970s. Most of his writings were addressed to Westernized Muslims, those educated in the universities of Europe and the United States. Perhaps for that reason, one might expect elements of generic fascism to have surfaced in his thought. Fascism, like the Islamism of Shariati, sought the mobilization of citizens against Western democracy and Marxist socialism by appealing to a "third way." And yet, there was very little that one might identify as specifically "fascist" in his exposition. There is little appeal to the redress of past grievances through present aggression, and there is virtually no advocacy of a program of rapid economic growth and technological development to resolve a communal sense of inefficacy and inferiority.

Shariati explicitly rejects the impulse to that industrial development he identifies with the capitalist West, Marxist dictatorship, and fascism. He tells us that "protestantism, capitalism, Marxism and Fascism . . . [are] brothers born of the same materialism. . . . Fascism, arising in the same social setting as Marxism, was basically a movement of the technocrats and bureaucrats."[51] He clearly conceived Fascism as a political orientation developmental in intent – a preoccupation he does not recommend to militant Islam.

However idiosyncratic within the tradition, Shariati's discussion emphasizes the differences between the secular political doctrines of our time and that of revolutionary Islam. Radical Islam is neither developmental in intent nor nationalist in inspiration.[52] The only nationality with which Muslims

---

49 Shariati, *Marxism and Other Western Fallacies*, pp. 70–3. Thus, Shariati dismisses Marxism as assessing humanity as nothing other than a product of technology and its machines. See ibid., p. 35.

50 Ibid., pp. 114–17. Shariati refers to the Muslim concept of *tauhid*, oneness, to provide an Islamic sense to the discussion. See ibid., p. 67. Elsewhere he simply speaks of the "precedence of society over the individual" as preferential. See ibid., pp. 63–4.

51 Ibid., p. 50. Shariati's ready association of Marxism with Fascism is part of his analysis. It reappears in critical places in his account. See ibid., pp. 106–8.

52 Standard among Islamists is the conviction that there is only one "nation" to which Muslims must surrender their allegience, and that is the nation of the faith. See Mawdudi, and *Fundamentals of Islam*, p. 4; *Witness unto Mankind*, pp. 34, 43. Qutb, *Milestones*, pp. 36, 51, 95, 118–19, 123, 125, 129.

identify is Islam – an Islam captured neither in geography nor politics.[53] Islam is a religion, and politics is one of its byproducts. Geography is important only in so far as Islam expects to be *the* world religion of the proximate future. Geographic expansion is its form of life.

The configuration of radical Islam that emerges from all this, however secular the idiom, is that to be found in the unmistakably religious work of Hasan al-Banna, Sayyid Qutb, and Abul A'la Mawdudi.[54] The Islamic Republic of Iran was, in identifiable measure, animated by their ideas.

Although it soon lost favor among militant Islamists, Khomeini's revolution did serve as evidence that a dedicated religious community could defeat the superpower of the West. At about the same time, the Soviet occupation of Muslim Afghanistan produced a crisis that was to transform the politics not only of Southwest Asia but the Middle East as well. The Soviet incursion galvanized Afghanistan's religious and tribal leadership. There was a call for *jihad*. The Soviet Union had prompted the diversity of tribal and ethnic groups – Pashtuns, Uzbeks, Tajiks, and Hazaras – to come together as dedicated and committed Muslims in order to resist the infidel. They called upon Muslims everywhere to take up the sword against the invader. By 1984, thousands of volunteers from the Muslim nations in the Middle East had joined the *jihad* against the Soviet Union.

With massive assistance from the United States, Pakistan, and Saudi Arabia, the Afghan *mujahidin* fought the Soviet Union to a standstill in a bitter and protracted contest of arms. By 1992, the Soviet military had been driven out of Afghanistan, the local communists had been defeated, and the victorious *mujahidin* had founded an Islamic state in what had been a Soviet satrapy.

The armed struggle in Afghanistan brought tens of thousands, perhaps hundreds of thousands, of Muslims together, to train and fight against one of the world's most formidable superpowers – and win. That the United States, through Pakistan, supplied the *mujahidin* the wherewithal to engage the Soviets was largely dismissed in the assessment of factors leading to victory. Victory against the frightful might of the Soviet Union was attributed, almost entirely, to the purity of faith among the the the "soldiers of God."[55]

Mujahidin victory in Afghanistan inspired the *jihadist* and *salafist* Muslims from Morocco to the Philippines to greater efforts in the service of a reunited and regenerate Islam. By 1992, the ideology that would sustain them had been cobbled together. It was frequently referred to as "Islamic socialism" and was a composite of elements drawn from the thought of ibn Taymiyyah, ibn Abd al-Wahhab, Rashid Rida, Hasan al-Banna, Sayyid Abul A'la Mawdudi, and Sayyid Qutb.

---

[53] See Mawdudi, *Fundamentals of Islam*, p. 95.
[54] Abdelnasser, *The Islamic Movement in Egypt*, pp. 147–50.
[55] See the instructive account in Robert D. Kaplan, *Soldiers of God: With Islamic Warriors in Afghanistan and Pakistan* (New York: Vintage, 2001).

It was a kind of socialism having very little, if anything, to do with the socialism associated with Karl Marx or even the "fascist socialism" sometimes found in the tracts written by specialists.[56] Islamic socialism was predicated on the Qur'anic commitment to wealth redistribution that would follow from the collection and parsing among the faithful of the obligatory *zakat*[57] – the alms required of the faithful to underwrite the needs of the poor. The *zakat*, collected by the religious leaders of the community, was a means by which the material differences among members of the faith could be mitigated. The amelioration of poverty, as well as the reduction of differences in wealth, was calculated to enhance the sense of community and reduce any disposition to individualism and egoism that might survive among believers.[58]

Even the more secular among the fundamentalists refer to the redistribution of wealth, effected by *zakat*, as assuring that class strife would not trouble Islamic society. We are told that the fundamental concern of "economics in Islam," based exclusively on the *Qur'an* and the traditions, is the provision of "safeguards for the distribution of . . . wealth . . . among all members of the nation." The concern is not with "developing and increasing wealth, but rather the just distribution of . . . wealth." Its preoccupation was not with the generation of wealth, per se, but with the establishment of a "just economy," one that is "compassionate and free from conflict."[59]

There is a seeming indifference to "modernization and economic progress" among the ideologues of radical Islam.[60] There is an insistence that irrespective of the secular pursuit of economic and industrial development, "degradation and humiliation, ignominy and powerlessness" will continue to stalk the *ummah* until such time as Muslims begin faithfully to "fulfil the covenant that God has made with them."[61] Modern industry is largely a matter of only contingent concern. While there is an occasional recognition that without an industrial base capable of supplying arms the *ummah* must necessarily remain defenseless against its enemies, there is little in the way of a consistent developmental policy to be found in the doctrinal literature of radical Islam.[62] There is much talk of "equity and justice, reform and upliftment, caring and efficient administration, social welfare, peace

---

[56] See, for example, Drieu La Rochelle, *Socialismo fascista* (Rome: Edizioni Generali Europee, 1973).

[57] The *zakat* is one of the Five Pillars of Islam, together with the avowal of belief in one God and his Apostle, the pilgrimage to Mecca, daily prayers, and fasting during Ramadan.

[58] See the ample discussion in Mawdudi, *Fundamentals of Islam*, chap. 21.

[59] See Samih Atef El-Zein, *Islam and Human Ideology* (New York: Kegan Paul International, 1996), pp. 74, 320–1, 342; Mawdudi, *Witnesses unto Mankind*, p. 32.

[60] See, for example, ibid., pp. 21–2, 40.

[61] Khurram Murad, "Introduction" to ibid., p. 22.

[62] It is evident that al-Banna and Qutb both acknowledged the necessity of an industrial base for a modern Muslim community, surrounded as it would be by enemies, but there is little that might pass as developmental planning, and still less that sounds like enjoinments to

and order, virtue and righteousness..., honesty..., civilized conduct..., integrity and loyalty...," but precious little about capital accumulation, growth and export policies, labor management, or economic planning.[63] We are informed that problems of "economic progress and development" are "not the primary problems" that beset Muslims. Their problem is to "follow Islam totally and devotedly." Only then would there be the lifting of the burden of "defeat,... fear and impotency." Muslim peoples suffer the "yoke of colonial rule and domination,... degradation, humiliation, gross backwardness and utter powerlessness," not because they have failed to develop industries but because they have failed to be true to "the principles and teaching of Islam." Only then would Muslims enjoy "prestige and reputation,... influence and authority [and] hold sway over the world."[64] Political success would not be a function of material, but of spiritual, power.

There is sometimes talk of the need for "heavy industry" in future Islam, but almost nothing is advanced in terms of specifics. In one case, when the subject was broached, amid almost four hundred pages of text, we find it said, on the one hand, that "in Islam, factories do not fall under public or State ownership," and on the other, it is the "State" that is the "only party capable of building factories."[65] It seems reasonably clear that the subject is not central to the discussions of Islamists.

Since guidance is sought exclusively in the *Qur'an* and the traditional *hadith* and *sunnah*, written hundreds of years ago, there is very little counsel to be found therein that might serve a developmental program. In its relative indifference to economic growth and industrial development, Islamism distinguishes itself from almost all the revolutionary movements and regimes of the twentieth century – including paradigmatic Fascism.

The indisposition to occupy itself with rapid economic growth and industrial development clearly distinguishes Islamist ideology from Fascism and the variants of Marxism-Leninism with which the twentieth century was familiar. "Productivism" was at the very heart of Fascist economic thought. Fascist thinkers argued that only industrial expansion and product sophistication could provide the capabilities required to challenge the existing hegemony of the advanced industrial nations.[66]

Other than its peculiar posturing with respect to economic growth and industrial development, Islamist ideology shares features in common with any number of the revolutionary doctrines of the twentieth century. Almost all rose out of the sense of humiliation and inefficacy suffered by

---

marshal the energies that would be requisite to such a task. See the account in Abdelnasser, *Islamic Movement in Egypt*, pp. 125, 148–9.

[63] Mawdudi, *Witnesses to Mankind*, p. 32.

[64] Ibid., pp. 37, 40–1.

[65] El-Zein, *Islam and Human Ideology*, pp. 327, 329.

[66] See A. James Gregor, *Italian Fascism and Developmental Dictatorship* (Princeton, NJ: Princeton University Press, 1979).

less-developed economic communities in their protracted contact with the advanced industrial powers. As a consequence, and again like almost all of them, ranging from Mussolini's Fascism to Mao's Marxism, Islamism is "anti-imperialist."[67]

A great deal of the discussion surrounding "imperialism" in the twentieth century was tendentious, driven more by bias than defensible scholarship. Fascism was always "anti-imperialist," if anti-imperialism is understood to mean objection to the international dominance of the industrial democracies. The very logic of Fascist international policy was predicated on the conviction that the "plutocratic" nations of the world conspired to obstruct the economic and industrial development of those "proletarian" nations that were "late developers." From its first doctrinal statements to its rationale for entry into the Second World War, "proletarian" Fascism argued that its enemies were the "plutocratic" imperialists who had exploited Italy for centuries and who then obstructed its efforts to attain equality in a world of unbridled Darwinian competition.[68]

When Fascism expanded into Dalmatia, Albania, Greece, North Africa, and Ethiopia, its ideologues argued that what was transpiring was not "imperialism," but the simple restoration of lands that had properly belonged to the Roman Empire.[69] Much the same posture is assumed by "anti-imperialist" Islamists when they insist that any "reconquest" by the faithful of Spanish Andalusia, in the Balkans, and in South and Southeast Asia, as well as in the Philippine islands, is not "imperialism," but a restoration to *dar el Islam* of lands "usurped" by infidels centuries ago.[70]

Centuries-old grievances and irredentist passions were the stuff of revolution in the twentieth, and now the twenty-first, centuries. More frequently than not, the "imperialism" that fuels resentment is largely in the eye of the beholder.

What does distinguish the Islamic fundamentalists from Fascism, as well as most of the revolutionary movements of the twentieth century, is their candid rejection of nationalism in whatever form. While the Marxism-Leninism of the twentieth century pretended to be "antinationalist" in character, there is very little contemporary disagreement with the assessment that revolution, governance, and international relations in Marxist-Leninist states were animated by nationalist, "patriotic" sentiments. Like Fascism, Marxist-Leninist

---

[67] Al-Banna, *Imam Shahid Hasan Al-Banna*, p. 18.

[68] See Mussolini's discussion in Benito Mussolini, "Atto di nascita del fascismo," *Opera omnia* (Florence: La fenice, 1964 [hereafter cited as Oo]), 12, pp. 322–3; "Gesto di rivolta," "Governo vile," "Il bavaglio," "Decidersi o perire!" "Il discorso," "Il nostro dovere e quello di liberarci dal giogo della plutocrazia internazionale," "Per rinascere e progredire: Politica orientale," ibid., 14, pp. 5, 8–9, 12–13, 28–31, 222–3, 225–7. Such citations can be multiplied, but doing so is hardly necessary.

[69] See, for example, Fernando Gori, *Roma nel continente nero* (Rome: Editoriale Tupini, 1940).

[70] See the discussion in Kepel, *Jihad*, p. 222.

movements and regimes have been nationalistic in spirit and behavior if not in doctrine. More than that, Fidel Castro speaks without embarrassment of demanding of his followers commitment to "the fatherland or death." Similarly, contemporary Chinese communists have made traditional nationalism their source of legitimacy.[71]

The difficulty we have is that there have been too few Islamist governments available for inspection, and they have endured for too brief a period, to allow confident judgments to be made concerning their respective nationalisms or lack thereof. We know that the major ideologues of *jihadist-salafist* Islam have explicitly rejected nationalism and consistently sought to make religious faith, not secular identity, the foundation of their future society.[72]

Muslims are specifically admonished to remember that they do not "belong" to their "country and motherland," but to the "community of Allah." Identification with the nation could lead only to apostasy – corruption of the faith.[73] Devotion to the motherland would detract from that owed Allah. Many, if not most, observers are convinced that Islamism, as an alternative political ideololgy, has supplanted what had been their nationalism among critical populations in the Middle East, the former Soviet dependencies, South and Southeast Asia, as well as the southern Philippines.[74]

Many of Islamism's remaining traits – its antidemocratic disposition,[75] its conviction in the infallibility of its belief system, its elitism, its readiness to invest unqualified faith in its leadership, together with its apocalyptic expectations for the near future – are shared with all the major revolutionary movements and regimes of the twentieth century.

Muslims are admonished to "follow the commandments of God, enforce these on all people and make them submissive." There should be one among them, a "chief of the Muslims equipped with correct knowledge," who "with the strength of them all . . . should enforce the laws of Islam and prevent the people from violating them."[76] All of this is familiar to those who have observed revolution in the twentieth century.

Muslims, because there can only be "one aim of life for [them] all," are enjoined to develop a "spirit of singleness of purpose," abandon "individualism," and unite behind a leader, for a "party cannot be a party at all unless

---

[71] See Maria Hsia Chang, *Return of the Dragon: China's Wounded Nationalism* (Boulder, CO: Westview Press, 2001).

[72] Mawdudi, *Witnesses unto Mankind*, p. 34; see the comments on Mawdudi's position in Abdelnasser, *The Islamic Movement in Egypt*, p. 150, and that of the Islamic student association, ibid., p. 81.

[73] Mawdudi, *Fundamentals of Islam*, p. 256; see also pp. 257–9, and *Witnesses unto Mankind*, p. 34.

[74] See the discussion in Kepel, *Jihad*, p. 118; see also pp. 62–5.

[75] See the insightful discussion in Fatema Mernissi, *Islam and Democracy: Fear of the Modern World* (Cambridge, MA.: Perseus, 2002).

[76] Mawdudi, *Fundamentals of Islam*, pp. 130–2.

[there is] an *Imam*," an inspired master. Muslims "should have a unified aim. They should obey one chief," precisely as they would "in the army."[77]

It is clear that obedience, sacrifice, and submission are required of Muslims who conceive themselves the "slaves of Allah." A community organized on the basis of that obedience, sacrifice, and submission is subject to *shar'iah*, Divine Law, requiring that one submit to its demands, carry out its orders, and submissively accept its decisions. It is the government, as Allah's earthly agent, that is legitimated by divine authority, and the obligation of obedience to its will falls to the members of the *ummah*. *Shar'iah* becomes "the law of government and *ibadaat* [obedience], compliance with its laws and regulations," becomes incumbent on all Muslims.[78]

Sayyid Qutb relentlessly pursues the logic that informs these convictions. His argument is that there is but *one* true law of life and being, eternal and immutable, and it finds expression exclusively in the *Qur'an*. The truth, one and indivisible, is with Islam – and that truth constitutes the "essence" of the universe.[79]

Those who would live a life that is both fulfilled and free are counseled to obey the laws of Allah. Obedience to the truth is in itself freedom and fulfillment. Anything else would propel one into an abyss of "filth and rubbish," for anything else is *jahiliyyah* – barbarism, immorality, and darkness. For Muslims, their duty is to enforce Islam's way of life on those who, for whatever reason, found themselves denizens of *jahili* societies – those immersed in darkness and barbarism. We are told that "the foremost duty of Islam in this world is . . . to take . . . leadership in its own hands and enforce the particular way of life which is its permanent feature."[80] Only then can humankind profit from the truths and freedoms of Islam.

Jewish and Christian societies are, by definition, *jahili* communities, the proper objects of *jihad*. Qutb is emphatic in affirming that Islamic *jihad* is not simply a defensive responsibility – to protect Muslims from aggression. *Jihad* is "dynamic."[81] It is obliged to seek out Islam's enemies and "annihilate" them, for "in the world there is only one party of God; all others are parties of Satan and rebellion."[82]

While non-Muslims cannot be coerced to accept Islam, Allah requires that they live under its laws. Without consigning themselves to Allah, they are permitted to live as "protected" minorities under *shar'iah*, under a law governing all aspects of their behavior. Non-Muslims, in effect, would be

---

[77] Ibid., pp. 121–2, 124–5.
[78] Ibid., pp. 81, 89, 254.
[79] Qutb, *Milestones*, pp. 85, 90, 105.
[80] Ibid., pp. 94, 131, 139.
[81] Ibid., pp. 62, 71.
[82] Ibid., pp. 61–2, 117. We are told that the reasons for *jihad* include "to establish God's authority in the earth; to arrange human affairs according to the true guidance provided by God; to abolish all the Satanic forces and Satanic systems of life. . . ." Ibid., p. 70.

compelled to enjoy the "freedom" of obeying Islamic law. Muslims would be licensed to employ "force against those who deviate from it, so that those who have wandered from the true path may be brought back to it."[83]

The logic sustaining such a notion is singularly Hegelian. Since God is both good as well as the author of all things, living in obedience to his laws could only benefit humankind. A fully rational human being, understanding that, would comprehend that obeying God's laws, as they find expression in *shar'iah*, would be in his or her interest. Any fully rational human being would choose to so behave without compulsion. Thus, to obey the law, under whatever empirical conditions, would be an expression of his or her informed freedom. Anything else would be an act produced by "false consciousness."

One finds the analogy of such arguments in the Marxist and Fascist apologetics of the not-too-distant past. The difficulties that attend it are equally familiar. The "laws" presumably fashioned by God,[84] or "History," or philosophical insights have to be articulated, interpreted, and applied by flesh-and-blood humans, circumstanced in a given environment and a given time. The putative "laws" provided by some higher agency or greater wisdom have to be deciphered in order to serve any mundane purpose – and there does not seem to be any objective criteria that can certify that any *imam, emir, khilafa, vozhd, massimo lider, duce,* or *führer* has correctly interpreted cosmic, historic, or moral law. We are simply expected to obey without resistance. Among the Islamists, the best we are offered is that we are assured that Allah will somehow be our protector against any abuse, for it is clear that citizens may well require protection from "a ruler ... invested with full and unlimited powers within the bounds set by God's law."[85] How Allah might protect us from a ruler who might violate the bounds of His law remains unclear.[86]

We are informed that the purpose of our life is to prepare for *jihad*, the destruction of all non-Muslim societies. We are told, with absolute

---

[83] Qutb, *Social Justice in Islam*, p. 41. In this context, see the account provided by Mawdudi in his *Witnesses unto Mankind*, p. 246, where we are told that in a Muslim society, the "force of the government" is used to "exterminate" all of society's evils, ranging from "indecent dress" to "unethical education." God's laws are to be enforced on *all*, whether Muslim or non-Muslim. Ibid., pp. 130–2.

[84] "Only God, and no one else, can provide man with the knowledge of the right guidance.... Only God can give man a guidance which will be applicable universally and for all times." Ibid., p. 56.

[85] Muhammad Qutb, *Islam: The Misunderstood Religion* (New Delhi: Markazi Maktaba Islami, 2001), p. 101. Muhammad Qutb is Sayyid Qutb's brother.

[86] We are told that the ruler in Islamist society is provided "wide powers." But, we are further informed, no ruler may "oppress the souls or the bodies of Muslims, nor dare he infringe upon their sanctities, nor touch their wealth.... Allah Himself protects them from his power...." Qutb, *Social Justice in Islam*, p. 124. We are not informed just how that might be accomplished.

confidence, that "the real objective of Islam is . . . to establish the kingdom of God on Earth." Only through *jihad* can "the main objectives of Islam" be fulfilled.[87] For that reason, human beings are inured to multiple daily prayers, obligatory alms-giving, required pilgrimages, and all the rest. "The truth of the matter," we are told, "is that these functions were made obligatory to prepare you for a big purpose and to train you for a great task." That purpose and that task is to destroy all *jahili* governments and *jahili* societies, to "take power . . . and end their mischief by force."[88]

Since "all Jewish and Christian societies today are . . . *jahili* societies," it is clear that Muslims are obligated to take up arms against them until they submit. Islam cannot leave them unmolested in their geographic confines even if they pose no threat. Muslims and non-Muslims alike are obliged to submit to the authority of Islam. Islam enjoys "a God-given right to step forward and take control of . . . political authority so that it may establish the Divine system on earth."[89]

The Islamic government that would follow successful *jihad* would be one in which all authority would be "genuinely and exclusively" invested, and any opposition duly "subdued," in order to be assured obedience from a suitably "pious" population. Such objectives can be achieved only when the *jihadist* revolutionary party is *one*, for "Truth" is one. "The very nature of Truth demands unification and cohesion, unity and harmony. Dissension and sectarianism appear only when falsehood is mingled with the Truth, or when Truth is used as a mask to cover evil."[90]

Victory requires that party factionalism be suppressed. He who follows the call of Islam is required "to give his complete loyalty to the new Islamic movement and to the Muslim leadership."[91] The partisans of Islam must be

---

[87] Mawdudi, *Witnesses unto Mankind*, p. 48.

[88] Mawdudi, *Fundamentals of Islam*, pp. 243, 246. "These *Salah*, fasting, *Zakat* and *Hajj* are in reality meant for this very preparation and training. . . . You are the most pious slaves of God on the surface of earth. So go ahead and fight, and remove the rebels of God from the government and take over the powers of caliphate. . . . Then bar all avenues of illicit earning, lewdness, oppression, indecency and immorality" ibid., pp. 250–2. Sayyid Qutb makes manifestly clear that all this applies to every society and government that is not now Islamic. We are told that "there is nothing beyond Islam except *jihiliyyah*, nothing beyond the truth except falsehood." Qutb, *Milestones*, p. 127.

[89] Qutb, *Milestones*, pp. 72, 76, 81. Qutb felt that *all* the Muslim societies of his time were *jahili* societies as well, so that *jihad* was an anticipated conflict that was universal in its demands. See ibid., p. 82.

[90] Mawdudi, *Fundamentals of Islam*, p. 259, and *Witnesses unto Mankind*, pp. 49–50. In his *Fundamentals*, Mawdudi cites, on p. 259, the *Qur'an*: "And they were not enjoined anything except that they should serve Allah, being sincere to Him in obedience. . . ." 98:5. Qutb takes every opportunity to remind his readers that "truth is one and not many. . . . Truth is indivisible, and it is the name of that general law which God has ordained for all affairs; and everything in existence either follows it or is punished by it." Qutb, *Milestones*, p. 90.

[91] Ibid., p. 48.

united and organized in a single, vanguard party,[92] each member prepared to "voluntarily lay down his life in the way of God" in order to be a "witness *par excellence* to his faith and the Truth he has received."[93] For fundamentalist Islam, there is one God, one truth, one leader, one *ummah*, one party, and one purpose.[94]

Given those convictions, we have the rationale for totalitarian controls.[95] A government that is the sole possessor of "Truth" is licensed to control the behavior of all its subjects.[96] The behavior that results – engendered by pious conviction, or coerced by the state – is necessarily in the "best interests" of all. As has been suggested, such a rationale shares the essentials of a Hegelian conception of the nature of morality, and elements are to be found, throughout the twentieth century, in the apologetics of Fascist intellectuals, and classical Marxists, together with the justificatory arguments of Stalinists and Maoists.

It is a philosophical and moral posture that is fundamentally antidemocratic. Fascist and Marxist-Leninist intellectuals dismissed representative democracy, with its tolerance of alternative opinions, as intrinsically deceptive and manipulative, the product of antinational conspiracy or "false consciousness." As is now the case among *jihadist, salafist* Muslims, truth in the twentieth century could find its embodiment only in a unitary, vanguard party, martial in character and led by charismatic leaders. It was embodied in a party that expected individuals to be prepared to die for its purposes, and in dying to find their ultimate moral fulfillment.

The prima facie feature that distinguishes Islamists from Fascists or Marxist-Leninists is their unrelenting and irrepressible anti-Semitism. While anti-Semitism served tactical purpose for both Fascists and Stalinists,[97] it was not essential to doctrine. In fact, in a significant sense, anti-Semitism was antithetical to their respective doctrines.[98]

---

[92] Ibid., p. 80.

[93] Khurram Murad's "Introduction," to Mawdudi, *Witnesses unto Mankind*, p. 13.

[94] See Mawdudi, *Fundamentals of Islam*, pp. 121–2, 124, 127.

[95] See Mawdudi's characterization of "righteous Muslims." "Their sentiments, their desires, their ideologies, their thoughts and opinions, their hatred and inclinations, their likes and dislikes, everything is subservient to Islam.... Your sleep, your wakefulness, your acts of eating and drinking, your moving about, in fact, each of your actions should be strictly in obedience to the law of God." Ibid., pp. 69, 102.

[96] Ibid., p. 132.

[97] See Renzo De Felice, *Storia degli ebrei italiani sotto il fascismo* (Turin: Giulio Einaudi editore, 1962); Gennadi Kostyrchenko, *Out of the Red Shadows: Anti-Semitism in Stalin's Russia* (Amherst, NY: Prometheus, 1995); Arkady Vaksberg, *Stalin Against the Jews* (New York: Alfred Knopf, 1994).

[98] See the discussion in A. James Gregor, *Giovanni Gentile: Philosopher of Fascism* (New Brunswick, NJ: Transaction Publishers, 2001), chap. 8; V. I. Lenin, *Über die Judenfrage* (Berlin: Verlag für Literatur und Politik, 1932).

For the *jihadists*, the Jews are considered cursed by Allah – down through the ages, they have been treasonous and perfidious, bringing their "ritual impurity" into the most sacred places – and it seems evident that they might lift that curse only by becoming pious Muslims. Alternatively, some of the more rabid Islamists have suggested that Jews must be destroyed "to the very last one."[99] Some radical Muslims are convinced that the Jews, as a continuing biological community, have entered into a historic and malicious covenant:

... to eliminate all limitations, especially the limitations imposed by faith and religion, so that the Jews may penetrate into the body politic of the whole world and then may be free to perpetuate their evil designs. At the top of the list of these activities is usury, the aim of which is that all the wealth of mankind end up in the hands of Jewish financial institutions....[100]

Jews are understood to be part of an international and long-standing program dedicated to the fostering of "infidelity, immorality, corruption and oppression." They are understood to be involved in a plot aimed at subjugating humanity to their rule, thereby to arrogate to themselves all the world's wealth. They are the chief architects of a plan that intends to employ Marxism as a weapon against Islam. Founded by a Jew, and supported by international Jewry, Marxism has been used against Islam since the beginning of the twentieth century.[101]

The anti-Semitism of contemporary *jihadists* shares more affinities with Hitler's National Socialism that with almost any revolutionary movement of the twentieth century.[102] Anti-Semitism was at the core of Nazism – and, at best, on the margins of Mussolini's Fascism and East European Marxism-Leninism.

More than all of that, unlike Fascists and Marxist-Leninists of whatever stripe, Muslim fundamentalists, as *salafists*, conceive themselves as essentially restorationists, not revolutionaries. They seek to restore, not transform, the *ummah*. Unlike the major revolutionaries of the twentieth century, who were almost all essentially secular,[103] the contemporary *jihadists* are religious fundamentalists.

---

99   Mawdudi, *Fundamentals of Islam*, pp. 161–2. See the account in Dore Gold, *Hatred's Kingdom: How Saudi Arabia Supports the New Global Terrorism* (Washington, DC: Regnery, 2003), p. 175.
100 Qutb, *Milestones*, p. 111.
101 See the allusions in Abdelnasser, *The Islamic Movement in Egypt*, pp. 122–3, 226–7.
102 The anti-Semitism of the Romanian "Iron Guard" of Corneliu Z. Codreanu made the movement the kindred of National Socialism rather than generic fascism. See the introduction to Corneliu Zelea Codreanu, *Guardia di ferro* (Padua: Edizioni di Ar, 1972), particularly p. 13.
103 Codreaneu's Iron Guard, which shared the intense anti-Semitism of National Socialism, was essentially a religious rather than a revolutionary movement, and in that sense was more like radical Islam than Fascism.

The revolutionaries of the twentieth century dealt with religion in a variety of fashions. Some sought its extirpation (but generally failed in their efforts). Others sought to coerce or cajole collaboration. The original Bolsheviks killed clergymen, China's post-Maoists have regimented them, and Castro has sought to emasculate them. For all that, almost all the mass-mobilizing, revolutionary movements of the twentieth century took on religious features, with their quasireligious symbolisms, martyrs, saints, and inspired doctrines. Italian Fascism was certainly not alone in possessing a peculiar "religious" character.

Mussolini approved of the developmental and secular nationalism of Mustafa Kemal Ataturk – the Nasser of the period – who sought to transform Islamic Turkey into a modern nation. Mussolini saw Ataturk, leading the modernizing and armed vanguard of the Muslim world against the Western plutocracies, as a natural ally of modernizing and revolutionary Italy. He saw a secular Turkey making impressive progress toward modernity under the "illuminated guidance" of Ataturk – a guidance that shared some "general political affinities" with Fascist Italy.[104]

In his pursuit of modernity, Ataturk abolished the caliphate, the spent institution that radical Muslims even today conceive as having represented the unity of the faith. In general, Ataturk is reviled by contemporary *jihadist-salafists* for precisely the same reasons that Mussolini, and paradigmatic Fascism, found him attractive. Modern revolutionaries have shown little tolerance for otherworldly religions.

Beyond that, what seems to distinguish the Islamic *salafists* of our time from the vast majority of modern revolutionaries is their ready disposition to invoke *jihad* indiscriminately – in the form of terrorism – at the least provocation. Terrorism – making acknowledged innocents the random targets of deadly force – would seem to identify *jihadism* as representing a particularly virulent form of political violence.

Many revolutionary movements in the recent and more remote past have not only employed violence, but prophylactic, demonstrative, and punative terror, as well, to effect their purposes. Political terrorism and violence typified much of the twentieth century. Innocents were killed and incarcerated in large numbers in order to convey the message that political rule would tolerate no departures from strict obedience. Fascists, National Socialists, and Marxist-Leninists all systematically employed instrumental violence and terror.

Hitler, Stalin, Mao, and Pol Pot used violence to destroy human beings in incalculable numbers. The first case was an attempt literally to destroy an entire people; the others, to destroy ill-defined classes, those who failed to evince "proletarian consciousness" or who had embarked on a "capitalist

---

[104] See the discussion in Mussolini, "Insegnamenti," *Oo*, 18, pp. 431–2, "Italia e Turchia," *Oo*, 24, p. 38, "Brindisi al Presidente Turco," *Oo*, 25, p. 105.

road." However morally reprehensible, all these employments seem to have been governed by some specific purpose – however perverse.[105]

Contemporary *jihadists*, on the other hand, seem to employ simple terror, the arbitrary destruction of innocent human beings, for purposes that appear obscure even to themselves. It is hard to imagine how Osama bin Laden, having "declared war" against the United States, Jewry, and Christendom in their respective entireties, imagined that destroying the World Trade Towers in New York, killing almost three thousand innocents, including Muslims, might advance the cause of Islam. Terrorism, together with conventional military operations, might further a cause, but terrorism, in and of itself, hardly seems an effective tool.

Terror tactics are very frequently used in conventional international war and revolutionary politics. When they are used, the death of innocents is usually attributed to unavoidable "collateral damage." The Islamists, on the other hand, appear to be among the few revolutionaries to use terrorist tactics without apology and seemingly without specific purpose.[106]

The killing of noncombatants in the course of conflict has almost always been undertaken with a palpable degree of moral discomfort. Even Hitler

---

[105] It is sometimes argued that the violence invoked by Marxist-Leninists (as distinct from Fascist violence) was intended ultimately to ensure universal peace and/or material abundance for all. It is not clear how much comfort one should take from such a distinction. As for the promised "universal peace," Maoists have been very forthright. They informed us that "class warfare" and its attendant international warfare could be expected to continue for "perhaps 100 million years"! It appears that the anxiously awaited peace would be a very long time in coming. See Gregor, "Fascism, Marxism and Some Considerations Concerning Classifications," particularly pp. 62–3.

[106] On 6 October 2001, after the destruction of the Trade Towers, Sheikh Wajdi Hamzeh al-Ghazawi affirmed that "the [kind of] terror that is permissible according to Islamic law is terrifying to cowards, the hypocrites, the secularists, and the rebels, by imposing punishments [according to the religious] law of Allah. . . . The meaning of the term 'terror' that is used by the media . . . is the jihad for the sake of Allah. Jihad is the peak of Islam. Moreover, there are religious scholars who view it as the sixth pillar of Islam." As cited, Gold, *Hatred's Kingdom*, p. 190.

Mussolini argued that while violence was unavoidable, it should be employed with surgical precision, without "bestiality," and "intelligently," for a publicly identifiable and credible purpose, in order not to alienate those who remain undecided in the course of conflict. The issue became one of institutional discipline. See Mussolini, "Ancora la disciplina," *Oo*, 18, pp. 399–400. Sergio Panunzio, who was intimately associated with the Fascist *squadristi* of northern Italy, had written an entire volume on the use of violence in war and revolution and had ruled out terrorism, the wanton murder of innocents, as a revolutionary instrument, not only because it was, in his judgment, immoral, but because it would alienate potential allies. See Sergio Panunzio, *Diritto, forza e violenza: Lineamenti di una teoria della violenza* (Bologna: Licinio Cappelli, 1921). Clearly many Fascists and Fascist squads conducted themselves in a bestial manner and killed innocents indiscriminately. The distinction seems to be that the Fascist leadership was not prepared to justify that behavior. Islamist terrorists are armed with *fatwas* from their religious leaders that provide moral approval of terrorist actions.

and Stalin concealed the mass murder of innocents from their own people. The civilized world continues to be appalled by the deliberate mass murder of innocents for whatever purpose – but when such murder appears to have no discernible purpose, the mind reels. The readiness of Islamists to embark publicly on the mass murder of noncombatants, women and children, would seem to distinguish them at least in degree, if not in kind, from the revolutionaries of the twentieth and twenty-first centuries. They have issued doctrinal affirmations and *fatwas* that announce their readiness to kill women and children – irrespective of the *Qur'an*'s explicit injunctions against such acts.[107]

In February 1998, bin Laden issued a short *bayan*, a doctrinal statement, containing quotations from the *Qur'an* and from Ibn Taymiyya. In it, he affirmed that "every Muslim who is capable of doing so has the *personal duty to kill Americans* and their allies, *whether civilians or military personnel*, in every country where this is possible."[108] How bin Laden expected such individual acts of criminal assault to serve Islam's ultimate purpose remains obscure to this day.

After the destruction of the World Trade Towers, bin Laden circulated a videotape in which he cited the "beautiful *fatwa*" provided by Sheikh al-Ulwan, that informed the world that the victims of Al Qaeda's terrorism "were not innocent people." Somehow, even the children who died in the attack on the World Trade Towers were guilty in the eyes of Allah.[109] In effect, their deaths were not the consequence of "collateral damage." They deserved to die – a judgment whose callousness would seem to earn contemporary *jihadists* a singular place among the most heartless agents of violence in modern times.[110]

Initially, it would seem, the radical Islamism of the twenty-first century belongs to an inclusive class of revolutionary movements that might best be identified, didactically, as antidemocratic – one of an indeterminate number of movements that include a wide variety of related forms – among which one might find a subclass of neofascisms. For the purposes of our analysis, however, Islam's *jihadist-salafists* hardly qualify for membership in the

---

[107] The traditional Islamic literature enjoins Muslims, "Neither kill the old..., nor children and babes nor the females." The Prophet "admonished his men and warned them against killing women and children." We are told that "Islam has forbidden [the] killing altogether [of] women and children, the aged and the infirm, the blind, the imbeciles, the travellers, and the man devoted to monastic services." Abdul Hameed Siddiqi, *Jihad in Islam* (New Delhi: Islamic Book Service, 1998), p. 35.

[108] As cited, Kepel, *Jihad*, p. 320. Emphasis added.

[109] As cited in Gold, *Hatred's Kingdom*, p. 283, n. 5.

[110] Mussolini's Fascism, often identified as "terroristic," actually had little use for political terror, comparatively speaking, either in its revolution or its governance of the nation. See the discussion in Stanley G. Payne, *A History of Fascism 1914–1945* (Madison, WI: University of Wisconsin Press, 1995), pp. 408–9.

latter category. Today's Islamists are religious eccentrics, antinationalists of conviction, political reactionaries, indifferent to economic growth and industrial development, and committed to terrorism as their principal method of restoring the dignity and glory of their *ummah*. They simply do not satisfy the criteria that would make them credible neofascists.

The twentieth century witnessed the emergence of religious movements that might conceivably be considered neofascist; Islamic fundamentalism, struggling to restore an Islam of yesteryear, happens not to be of their number. That granted, there were other religious movements that, like Islamic fundamentalism, had their roots in the twentieth century, but which have a fundamentally different political story to tell.

An example of such a movement is Hindu nationalism. Born in India about the time of the appearance of the Muslim Brotherhood, Hindu nationalism as a politicized religion has exercised influence in Indian politics to a degree totally unanticipated a few decades ago. By the end of the twentieth century, Hindu nationalism had become one of the most important political movements on the Indian subcontinent. Its critics identify the movement as revolutionary, as a mortal threat to Indian democracy. They choose to speak of it as a "saffron fascism."

8

Hindutva

The Case for a Saffron Fascism

Since the 1990s, the Bharatiya Janata Party (BJP, National People's Party) has emerged as the largest single, and perhaps the most influential, political party in India. Founded in April 1980, the heir of antecedent political efforts, the BJP has steadily increased its appeal among the Indian electorate. In the nationwide parliamentary elections of 1984, of the total of 545 seats in the Lok Sabha (the People's Assembly), the party succeeded in winning only 2. In 1998, it succeeded to an unprecedented victory by winning 180 seats, a commanding 26 percent of total votes cast. Together with its allies, the party controlled 248 seats, supported by 37 percent of total popular votes.[1] "Hindu nationalism" had become a significant, and potentially a determinant, factor in the contemporary politics of the Indian subcontinent.

Commentators have characterized that phenomenal success as the rise of "Hindu fundamentalism," "religious nationalism," and "Hindu supremacism." The BJP is spoken of as the "party of choice of the upper caste conservative Hindus." Less-constrained critics speak of "Hindutva," the ideology of the BJP, "as a modern variant of Brahmanism, a virulent ideology of hatred and fascism that seeks to establish an ethnically pure Hindu *Rashtra* [nation] inhabited only by white-skinned Aryans."[2] Should such characterization be true, one is clearly speaking not of neofascism, but of neonazism, a lineal descendent of Adolf Hitler's racism.

The political and social implications of such a depiction are obvious. Equally arresting is the fact that not only political partisans but some credible Indian social scientists have expressed something of the same judgments

[1] Partha S. Ghosh, *BJP and the Evolution of Hindu Nationalism from Periphery to Centre* (New Delhi: Manohar, 2000), p. 15.

[2] There are any number of sites on the Internet devoted to "India/Hindutva" that supply an endless stream of commentary. The quotation given in the text originates with "Hindutva: The Brahmin Conspiracy," which features the standard of the National Socialist SS division Liebstandarte Adolf Hitler directly under the title, followed by the subject quotation.

about the successes of the BJP – if in less inflammatory fashion. K. N. Panikkar speaks of a "fascist agenda" being pursued by the proponents of Hindutva. More cautious perhaps, others speak of the "seeds of fascism," rather than Hitlerian racism, to be found in the ideology, or among the followers, of the BJP.[3] More than half a century after its extinction, some are prepared to argue that generic fascism has made its appearance in a major political community of about one billion inhabitants, a nation armed with nuclear weapons and with more than one million men in uniform. The claims tendered involve matters of very serious consequence and deserve more than superficial assessment.

Beyond dispute is the fact that the Bharatiya Janata Party is the heir of a long ideological tradition that finds its origins in the first decades of the last century. The ideology that informs the BJP is largely, if not exclusively, the result of the labors of three intellectuals: Vinayak Damodar Savarkar (1883–1966), Keshav Baliram Hedgewar (1889–1940), and Madhav Sadishiv Golwalkar (1906–73).[4] Throughout the relatively long and complicated history of Hindu nationalism, there has been remarkably little departure from the essentials of their thought. Savarkar's *Hindutva* (published in 1923), together with Golwalkar's *We or Our Nationhood Defined* (1939) and his *Bunch of Thoughts*[5] (1966), remain central to the normative and political convictions of the millions of followers of the BJP and its affiliated organizations.

Hindu nationalism grew in circumstances that have now become familiar. In its time, the Indian subcontinent suffered about a thousand years of foreign invasion and collective subjection, ultimately to submit to colonization at the hands of an industrially more advanced nation. By the early-nineteenth century, India had fallen largely under British control, and millions upon millions of Indians found themselves subject to the political dictates of relatively small numbers of Britons who made up the "Raj."

In that atmosphere of defeat and subordination, intellectuals such as Savarkar, Hedgewar, and Golwalkar were to respond as intellectuals in similarly circumstanced communities have done for generations. By the early-twentieth century, the first efforts of Hindu nationalists to organize movements of rehabilitation and renovation were undertaken to restore their

---

[3] K. N. Panikkar, *Before the Night Falls: Forebodings of Fascism in India* (Bangalore: Books for Change, 2002), p. xii. See also Manini Chaterjee, "Seeds of Fascism," *Seminar* (New Delhi), no. 399 (November 1992), pp. 18–19.

[4] There is no serious dispute about the ideology of the BJP. It is a combination of the thought of the three intellectual founders of Hindutva. By the 1990s, all three thinkers were accepted as the intellectual founders of Hindu nationalism. See the comments of Pralay Kanungo, *RSS's Tryst with Politics: From Hedgewar to Sudarshan* (Dehli: Manohar, 2002), p. 139, n. 184.

[5] M. S. Golwalkar, *We or Our Nationhood Defined* (Mahal, Nagpur: Harihareshwar, 1945, third edition), and *Bunch of Thoughts* (http://www.hindubooks.org, 2004, third edition); V. D. Savarkar, *Hindutva* (New Delhi: Bharti Sahitya Sadan, 1989, sixth edition).

nation to the station it had once enjoyed. To the masses of India, Hindu nationalists recounted the tales of India's grandeur in antiquity, when the subcontinent, animated by a "great and divine mission" to bring civilization and righteousness to a benighted world, constituted "the very heart – the very soul – of almost all the then known world." Hindu nationalists spoke of a time when the nation's influence radiated outward in an arc that stretched from what is now Mexico to Japan.[6] The beginning of the twentieth century saw Hindu revolutionaries committed to the regeneration of their nation – to restore its lost preeminence. They sought to overcome their oppressors and once more assume their proper place in the community of nations. Hindus were no longer to be modern-day "helots" or "coolies." They pledged themselves to once again "attain to the heights of greatness and of strength as in the days of yore."[7] Hindus were no longer to consider themselves "degenerate, down-trodden uncivilised slaves,... hewers of wood and drawers of water," but denizens of "a free Nation of illustrious heroes, fighting the forces of destruction," rallying to the *Bhagawa Dhwaja*, the Hindu standard, in order to achieve a "national renaissance" aimed "at rebuilding, revitalizing, and emancipating from its present stupor, the Hindu Nation."[8]

In pursuit of those ends, Savarkar served the Akhil Bharatiya Hindu Mahasabha (the Great Conference of Hindus) as its president from 1937 through 1942. The Mahasabha had been founded in 1922, and Hedgewar served as secretary from 1926 through 1931, having founded at almost the same time, in 1925, the Rashtriya Swayamsevak Sangh ([RSS] National Volunteer Corps).[9] Both organizations, affording themselves mutual support, significantly influenced Indian political thought. Savarkar was a major influence on the thought of Hedgewar, and on Golwalkar,[10] who was to succeed Hedgewar upon his death as *Sarsanghchalak* (leader) of the RSS in 1940.

As early as 1925, the Hindu Mahasabha had formulated a program of action predicated on an emphatic nationalism. While it charged itself to "represent the communal interests of the Hindus in all political controversies," it sought to serve not only Hindus, but to "promote good feelings with Mohammedans and Christians" in order to recruit all Indians to the labors at hand. It intended to mobilize the youth of the nation to industrial

---

[6] Golwalkar, *Bunch of Thoughts*, chap. 14, p. 3.

[7] Savarkar, *Hindutva*, pp. 17, 76

[8] Golwalkar, *We or Our Nationhood Defined*, pp. 17, 49, 64, 68.

[9] See the discussion in Kanungo, *RSS's Tryst with Politics*, pp. 38–44.

[10] Kanungo affirms that "Golwalkar takes Savarkar's *Hindutva* as his starting point." See the discussion in *ibid.*, p. 112; confer pp. 108–113. *Rashtra Meemansa*, by Savarkar's brother, apparently served as a major influence as well. See the account given in Sitaram Yechuri, in his "What is Hindu Rashtra?" to be found on <http://www.jaihoon.com.the antifascist campaign>.

pursuits, to foster their physical health, and to better the life circumstances of women, all in the service of the nation's rebirth and renewal.[11]

For its part, the RSS, as an organization, was inspired by the conviction that Hindus, as a nation, were cultured, prosperous, and mighty long before recorded history. Their flag flew "over many lands," and their benign influence "extended over vast regions of the earth."[12] That they had succumbed to invaders in historic times was attributed to the debilitating effects of a lack of challenge and a life that was too abundant.

In the course of time, the RSS organized a family of kindred organizations, the Sangh Parivar (SP), that extended its influence throughout society. The affiliated organizations of the Sangh Parivar include the Akhil Baratiya Vidyarthi Parishad (ABVP), a students' organization founded in 1948 and which now includes branches in more than 121 universities in more than 415 districts throughout the nation. In 1955, the Bharat Mazdoor Sangh (BMS) was founded as an RSS-affiliated labor union, to become one of the largest labor organizations in India by the end of the century. At the same time, the RSS supervises the Vidya Bharati, an independent national educational system that serves over 1.2 million students and employs about forty thousand teachers. Clustered around these organizations are those like the Seva Bharati and the Vanavasi Kalyan Ashram ([VKA] Center for the Welfare of Tribals), devoted to the uplift of the "scheduled castes" and backward "tribals" – population elements that have been long subject to discrimination in the traditional society. Together with those, there is the Bharatiya Kisan Sangh (the Indian Farmers' Union) and the Rashtriya Sevika Samiti (National Women Workers' Council), among others.[13]

It was out of these cultural and service organizations that the popular ideology of the BJP emerged. By the time the party succeeded as heir of the Bharatiya Jana Sangh ([BJS] National People's Union) in April 1980, it enjoyed the collateral support of the entire family of organizations affiliated with the RSS. The political environment was alive with the ideology of Hindutva, "Hinduness," the rationale for the rebirth of India.

In 1984, the Bajrang Dal was formed to serve as the security wing of the BJP. Reportedly with a membership of over one hundred thousand the Dal serves as a defense and security agency for the party. In the 1990s, in order to secure control over the Dal, the BJP imposed a more rigid institutional structure in which trained cadres from RSS headquarters introduced

---

[11] Ghosh, *BJP and the Evolution of Hindu Nationalism*, pp. 63–4.
[12] Hedgewar left very little in fully articulated writings. Most of his ideas are found in his public speeches. See *Sangha Darshan* (Bangalore: Prakashan Vibhag, RSS Karnarak, 1964), pp. 5–8.
[13] Pratap Chandra Swain, *Bharatiya Janata Party: Profile and Performance* (New Delhi: A.P.H., 2001), pp. 86–9, provides a convenient catalog of collateral support organizations of the BJP affiliated with the RSS.

something akin to military discipline among its members in 350 training camps held nationwide.

By that time, the BJP was prepared to contest national elections with the conviction that it was equipped to assume firm leadership within the community. In the elections that followed, the leader of the BJP was called upon to form a government – a government that was to survive into the new century.

Even before the electoral successes of the BJP at the end of the past century, and even before its very founding in the early 1980s, critics were quick to identify its political features and its economic program with some kind of generic fascism. As has been suggested, some went so far as to speak of the ideology of the BJP as "Hitlerism under Hindu garb." Another maintained that from its very origins, Hindu nationalism looked to Fascist Italy and National Socialist Germany for inspiration, and yet another identified the RSS, its affiliated organizations, and the BJP (its "political front"), as fascist – by identifying its essential traits as nothing other than "intolerance, hatred, brutality, and [the] urge for ethnic cleansing." The BJP is held to be fascist because it advocates "an exclusivist concept of nationalism, practices politics based on hatred and violence and promotes obscurantism, superstition, and irrationality."[14]

It would be more than difficult to make taxonomic distinctions based on any such criterial list. Is the nationalism of the BJP more "exclusivist" than that of the Khmer Rouge of recent memory? Are the politics of the BJP more hateful and violent than that of the Khmer Rouge? Were the politics of the Khmer Rouge not obscurantist, superstitious, and irrational? In reviewing the political thought of Enver Hoxha, Fidel Castro, and Kim Il Sung, would one find it more inclusive, less hateful and violent, and more rational than that of the BJP? Either fascism is far more prevalent than most analysts are prepared to consider, or the criterial traits offered to identify its presence are excessively vague and ambiguous.

All things considered, the general arguments invoked to sustain the identification of the BJP as "fascist" are not particularly persuasive. The more specific arguments, are hardly more so.

One argument that appears with some frequency among the critics of the BJP is that the party is held to be the creature of the RSS,[15] and it is

---

[14] See Marzia Casolari, "The Fascist Heritage and Foreign Connection of RSS: Archival Evidence," in Chaitanya Krishna (ed.), *Fascism in India: Faces, Fangs and Facts* (New Delhi: Manak, 2003), pp. 111, 125, 135; K. K. Gangadharan, *Sociology of Revivalism: A Study of Indianization, Sanskritisation and Golwalkarism* (Delhi: Kalamkar, 1970), pp. 99–102; Panikkar, *Before the Night Falls*, pp. 62, 119, 140.

[15] The leadership of the RSS has always held that the organization is concerned with the *culture* of Hindus, not their *politics*. The BJP is understood to be the politically active expression of Hindutva. While the theoretical distinction is consistently argued, in practice the distinction between *culture* and *politics* is hard to discern. See the discussion in H. V. Seshadri (ed.), *RSS: A Vision in Action* (Bangalore: Jagarana Prakashana, 1988).

claimed that the hierarchical and nondemocratic form assumed by the RSS is intrinsically fascist – a disability with which it infects the party. While the argument is more complex than the more general alternatives, on inspection it is no more persuasive.

The leadership of the RSS has always required undivided loyalty and unequivocal discipline from its members. It has argued that the struggle for political power in India would be difficult for a variety of reasons – and in order to ensure the survival and ultimate success of the RSS in such an atmosphere, discipline and obedience recommended themselves.

As a consequence of the demanding requirements of the struggle, the *Sarsanghchalak*, the leader of the RSS, to whom all obedience is owed, is characteristically appointed by his predecessor rather than elected by the membership. The practice is defended by the argument that only appointment of the leader precludes the increasing internal tensions, sectarianism, and fractious struggles that almost inevitably attend electoral contests, weakening organizational effectiveness.

There was, and remains, a general tendency among Hindu nationalists to advocate unity and discipline among members of their various organizations, in order to maximize organizational strength in the struggle against advantaged opponents. The real question is whether such a disposition is convincing evidence of an antidemocratic, *fascist*, essence, and whether the BJP can be identified as fascist by association.

There is little persuasive testimony that any of this is the case. The architects of Hindu nationalism, for example, have traditionally supported political democracy. Savarkar was insistent that voting was the sole recourse to which Hindus could turn in their struggle for an India reborn. Even before the nation attained its independence from the British, it was clear that Savarkar conceived the ballot as the means that would "revolutionise...the Indian State."[16]

Thus, while Golwalkar later lamented that democracy in India remained essentially rule by the few, and that it had allowed the rise and expansion of communist parties that Hindu nationalism found objectionable, the ideal of all Hindus was a "single, democratic and unified *Bharat*." He went on to remind his followers that "the spirit of democracy at its best, which confirms the right of freedom of speech, thought and action upon individuals is nowhere more fully recognised and practised than in the age-old Hindu tradition."[17] Golwalkar – while he was prepared to argue that Indian democracy

---

[16] Savarkar, *Hindu Rashtra Darshan* (Bombay: S. S. Savarkar, 1984, second edition), pp. 63, 66, 88–90.

[17] Golwalkar speaks of Hinduism, as it finds expression in the Vedanta, as providing a "higher basis for democracy" than any modern ideology, predicated as it is on the conviction that "individual souls [are] sparks of a supreme cosmic spirit." Golwalkar, *Bunch of Thoughts*, Introduction, p. 4; see ibid., chap. 3, p. 5; chap. 16, p. 11; chap. 25, pp. 5, 13.

required some reform – conceived Hindu nationalism as intrinsically democratic.[18]

The rejection of political democracy is nowhere to be found in the ideological rationale of Hindu nationalism. Within that rationale, there is a fairly
standard rehearsal of the difficulties that attend parliamentary democracy.
Modern parliaments, we are told, are almost inevitably host to special interests and ideologically motivated participants who influence the legislature's
deliberations and compromise its results. Nonetheless, there is nowhere in
Hindu nationalist literature the advocacy of revolutionary violence or the
recommendation that Hindus opt for an authoritarian or dictatorial alternative.[19] Arguments mounted to affirm the antidemocatic essence of the BJP
find no support in the ideological literature of the party itself or the intellectual tradition upon which its ideology is based. Much the same can be said,
as we shall see, concerning the other evidences of "fascism" found by the
BJP's opponents in the political thought that animates the BJP party.

It is clear that many critics find the conceptual language of Hindu nationalism particularly disturbing. Many find the very concepts employed by Hindu
nationalism objectionable. Its language is alive with talk of struggle or sacrifice, of battle, and of victories to be won. Golwalkar, for instance, regularly
told his first followers that they should count themselves blessed for having
been born in the wretched circumstances of oppression and humiliation, for
such circumstances could do no less than drive them to seek redress, to forge
forward in order that India "stand before the world a colossal personality,
full of grandeur, in triumph as well as defeat." Threatened by enemies from
within and without, India must necessarily seek "national regeneration":
it had no option, he argued, but to seek its remaking, "independent and
glorious."[20]

Many find such talk disconcerting, but it is not difficult to find similar
sentiments, and the emotions that fuel them, in the ideologies of many other
revolutions undertaken in many other places. The imagery is familiar. Both
the nineteenth and twentieth centuries were filled with similar characterizations by peoples who conceived themselves oppressed and humbled by
the pretense of others. It is not surprising, for example, to find Savarkar,
as a Hindu ideologue, making allusions to the revolutionary activities of
Giuseppe Mazzini.[21]

---

[18] Golwalkar clearly appreciated the problems that attend democracy in an environment of
corruption and venality. But there is little doubt that he conceived political democracy to
be the most defensible form of government. See the account in Ritu Hohli, *Political Ideas
of M.S. Golwalkar: Hindutva, Nationalism, Secularism* (New Delhi: Deep and Deep, 1993),
pp. 53, 59–60, 119–20.

[19] Later in the discussion, the assessment of political totalitarianism by Hindu nationalist intellectuals will be specifically considered.

[20] Golwalkar, *We or Our Nationhood Defined*, pp. 5–7.

[21] Savarkar, *Hindutva*, p. 94.

Like Savarkar, Mazzini, in his time, spoke to a divided and despised nation of its past glories and present humiliations to advocate revolution and rebirth. Like the ideologues of Hindutva, Mazzini called for a union of dedicated followers who would devote their time, treasure, and, if necessary, their lives to the restoration of their nation, to achieve once again, in liberty, the grandeur enjoyed in antiquity. Fascists were to shape these enjoinments into an antidemocratic doctrine that contributed to the advent of one of the most devastating wars in the history of human kind.

While that can be said, one need only recall Marcus Garvey's ideology of black rebirth, with its similar recall of the oppression suffered by the race, and his inspiring invocation of the memory of ancient Ethiopia in order to elicit energy and sacrifice in the effort at collective rebirth, to recognize that not all such perlocutionary speech need move people to dictatorship, violence, or mass destruction.

Sun Yat-sen made similar appeals for similar reasons. He reminded his audiences of the wretched conditions of the China of his time. He appealed to the glories of China's past to remind them that China had once been the Central Kingdom, the center around which the world gravitated. He sought to inspire his followers to pursue the path of self-sacrifice, discipline, and labor in order to foster not only a rebirth of that community that each held to have been the source of the world's civilization and culture, but to secure its ultimate future in democracy.

It would be difficult to argue that all such ideologies were fascist or neo-fascist in principle or substance. Burdened by the disabilities that attend less-developed communities when they find themselves in competition with the more advanced nations, one finds the respective responses of all such renovative revolutions sharing some properties in common. There is, for instance, an exaggerated sensitivity to any perceived affront to personal and collective honor. There is the repeated injunction that the community system-atically pursue strength, manhood, virility, courage, and accomplishment. The pages of Savarkar and Golwalkar are dotted with such enjoinments.[22] None of that, in and of itself, is "fascist."

More often than not, such posturing is accompanied by a political pro-gram intended to initiate and/or sustain the rapid economic and indus-trial growth of the less-developed community. Fascist Italy initiated just such a program. Whatever changes were suffered with the passage of time, Fascism attempted to implement a comprehensive program of economic growth in general and industrialization in particular. That, in and of itself, is not enough to identify a political system as "fascist." Most revolutionary

---

[22] See Golwalker, *Bunch of Thoughts*, chap. 4; chap, 5, pp. 4, 6; chap. 6, p. 5–6; chap. 8, p. 7; chap. 9, pp. 5–6; chap. 12, p. 9; chap. 13, p. 3; chap. 17, p. 1; chap. 19, p. 8–9; chap. 20, pp. 3–4; chap. 22, p. 13–14 and *We or Our Nationhood Defined*, pp. 5, 70; Savarkar, *Hindutva*, pp. 21, 23–25, 38, 76, 139.

movements of the twentieth century, both of the right and left, pursued such programs.

Thus, it is perfectly true that Savarkar insisted that critical to the rebirth of the Hindu nation was its industrialization and militarization. He spoke of the rapid development of the chemical and paper industries and of large industrial complexes that might satisfy the demands of an Indian military. He spoke of protecting domestic infant industries and import substitution that might render the nation as self-sufficient as possible.[23] In and of itself, none of that is particularly fascist.

Golwalkar, who fully appreciated Savarkar's argument, spoke not of Fascist Italy or National Socialist Germany but of post–World War II Japan as his model of economic and industrial development. Democratic Japan served him as an exemplar because it had mobilized its energies through patriotic appeals – an irrepressible desire to restore the nation's place in the world community.

It was evident that Golwalkar rejected any suggestion of a nonmarket "socialist" command economy, arguing that the market served as the basis for rational pricing for a community in the course of economic development. Rational pricing was essential for the program of industrial expansion and deepening required by the military defense of the homeland. Golwalkar, like Savarkar, advocated the rapid development of large-scale and technologically proficient industries in order to provide the weapons platforms for the Indian military. Together with that general program, he also emphasized, the role of cooperative enterprises and small-scale production, largely labor-intensive, in order to absorb available labor. The pattern he suggested was one that had demonstrated its efficacy not only in democratic Japan but would be confirmed by the economic histories of democratic South Korea and Taiwan,[24] where essentially agrarian economies, within the space of a quarter-century, were transformed into modern technologically based economies, transferring and absorbing a rural labor force into a modern urban work environment.[25]

Decades later, Atal Bihari Vajpayee, leader of the BJP, serving as prime minister of India, argued a similar case. He advocated what he held to be a "nonsocialist" developmental program, predicated on rapid economic and industrial development. The program was to be based on the principle of *swadeshi*, Indian economic independence. The features of that program, once again, were remarkably similar to those found in the earlier writings of

---

[23] Savarkar, *Hindu Rashtra Darshan*, pp. 155, 161.

[24] Both South Korea and Taiwan went through periods of authoritarian rule that gradually transformed itself into basically democratic form.

[25] Golwalkar, *Bunch of Thoughts*, Appendix, pp. 8–10. For the outlines of the program of economic development in Taiwan, see A. James Gregor, *Ideology and Development: Sun Yat-sen and the Economic History of Taiwan* (Berkeley, CA: Institute of East Asian Studies, 1981).

Savarkar and Golwalkar,[26] and the program would be undertaken under fundamentally democratic auspices.[27]

Vajpayee's program explicitly opposed both a "command economy" as well as one that represented "unrestrained economic liberalism." Both were seen inadequate to the needs of India at the end of the twentieth century. In Vajpayee's judgment, India required the existence of a functioning market to ensure the essential rationality of prices, but the market was not to be allowed to impoverish those Indians already handicapped by poverty and a dearth of skills. With 70 percent of India's population involved in agricultural pursuits, the government, in Vajpayee's judgment, was obliged to provide some assurance of returns on crops and predictability in terms of prices. Increasing income, in a climate of price stability, would allow a corresponding increase in the domestic savings rate to an anticipated 30 percent of the gross domestic product – a rate typical of economies on the trajectory of sustained industrial and agricultural growth.

The general program of economic development featured in the ideological pronouncements of the party is familiar. It is essentially anti-Marxist, market-oriented in practice, and intended essentially to provide the material foundation for the restoration of the nation's military and material grandeur, the prerequisite for its acceding to an independent place in the world as an agent fully the equal of others.

Against a rate of economic growth of 3.5 percent per annum for most pre-BJP governments, Vajpayee sought an accelerated growth rate of between 8 and 9 percent per annum. That would be accomplished, it was argued, by reducing the size of government and dismantling much of its control and administrative infrastructure. The BJP argued that those government agencies, created by past administrations, represented little more than encumbrances that impaired Indian economic enterprise. The general disposition was opposed to state centralization,[28] as distinct from the creation of a strong government.[29]

Vajpayee spoke of expanding and modernizing the transport and energy delivery systems, of standardizing and improving the educational system, and facilitating the provision of credit to the broad middle class upon whom much of the economy depended. For Vajpayee, the proposed program found its central convictions in the works of the founders of Hindu nationalism, and its confirmation in the successes of the "little dragons" of East Asia.

---

[26] See "Swadeshi Approach," in Sanjay Kaushik, *A. B. Vajpayee: An Eloquent Speaker and a Visionary Parliamentarian* (New Delhi: APH, 1998), pp. 169–99.

[27] See A. B. Vajpayee's comments in ibid., pp. 16, 30, 35, 156, 241, 278–9, 281, 295.

[28] Ibid., pp. 12, 17–18, 29, 174, 182–3.

[29] Ibid., p. 177.

Following the example of the newly industrialized nations of East Asia, Vajpayee advocated the linking of large- and small-scale industries in a web of mutually supportive enterprises. As in Japan, South Korea, and Taiwan, he expected small-scale establishments to contribute to the maintenance of high levels of employment throughout the process of rapid agrarian and industrial development.

In a strategy that seemed a function of India's peculiar circumstances, the BJP has advocated selective direct foreign investment and the transfer of technology from the advanced industrial powers, with the focus on India's needs rather than satisfying the interest of foreign multinational corporations in gaining access to a large market supplement for their exports. Having rejected socialist nostrums that had failed by the end of the twentieth century in the Soviet bloc, China, North Korea, and Cuba, the BJP had put together a reasonably coherent economic policy for one of the largest nations on earth.

At this juncture, one might comment that the BJP program contains echoes of the economic programs implemented by Fascist Italy during the first years of the regime.[30] That would tell us very little, however, for many economies, developing under democratic political auspices, share the same features.[31] Certainly, very few would pretend that such general features would license one to characterize the economic program of the BJP as "fascist."

There are other issues that attend the programs of the BJP and find their inspiration in the ideological work of Hindu nationalists. Given the circumstances of its origins, its commitment to the rebirth of the nation, as well as its judgments concerning the challenges of the international environment, the BJP's lack of specificity concerning its defense policies has caused surprise among its critics. The fact is that deliberations concerning defense policy have occupied little space in the public statements of *any* of India's political parties throughout the fifty years of the nation's independence. Acknowledging that, the general defense policy of the BJP seems reasonably clear and essentially grows out of insights provided by the ideological founders of the Hindu nationalist movement.

Savarkar long lamented the fact that India was unarmed and irresolute in its own defense.[32] Like Golwalkar, and largely for the same reasons, he advocated the expansion of India's industrial base in order to support

---

[30] See, for example, the works of Alberto De' Stefani, Mussolini's first Minister of Finance, particularly *L'Ordine economico nazionale* (Bologna: Nicola Zanichelli Editore, 1935); *La restaurazione finanziaria: I risulati 'impossibili' della parsimonia* (Rome: Volpe, 1978, reprint of the 1927 edition); *Una riforma al rogo* (Rome: Volpe, 1963).

[31] Compare the developmental suggestions contained in the works of Friedrich List, written more than a century and a half ago in 1844. Friedrich List, *The National System of Political Economy* (London: Longmans, Green, 1916).

[32] See Savarkar, *Hindu Rashtra Darshan*, pp. 153, 155–6, 158–9, 161, 164–5, 167–8; see Golwalkar, *Bunch of Thoughts*, chap. 24, p. 3; chap. 25, pp. 8–9.

an anticipated growing and increasingly proficient security establishment.[33] Consistent with those generic policy directives, the BJP has supported increased military defense expenditures as well as the development of nuclear weapons together with suitable delivery systems, making India one of the world's seven acknowledged nuclear-armed powers.[34]

In general, then, the policies that the BJP brought with it to office in India reflected the convictions of the founders of Hindu nationalism. Its entire economic program reflects the thought of the founders of the movement. That having been acknowledged, none of its programs unequivocally qualifies it as "fascist." Similar programs are to be found throughout the developing world. The current policies of a contemporary "Marxist-Leninist" China, with its increasingly liberal domestic economic arrangements, together with its openness to foreign direct investment, shares some important features with the growth and industrialization strategy of the BJP.[35]

The entire political, economic, demographic, and defense policies of the BJP reflect the convictions of Hedgewar and Golwalkar, who understood that India was a latecomer to the process of industrialization. India, when it achieved its independence, was largely agrarian in character – unarmed in a world that was armed, without the productive industrial base that would allow it to defend itself effectively. To compound its problems, an unarmed agrarian India was burdened by a cultivated tradition of nonviolence. The nation, the authors of the ideology of Hindutva reminded their audience, found itself threatened in a world in which the laws of the jungle continued to prevail, in which each nation sought advantage, often, if not always, at the expense of others.[36]

India, as a nation, required not only accelerated industrialization, but a rekindling of its martial spirit, a sense of unity and commitment.[37] As early as

---

[33] Golwalkar, like Savarkar, saw the world as beset by conflict, and ruled by the "law of the jungle," in which only strength assured survival. The world, composed of predators, respected only "invincible strength," discipline, and military power. See Golwalkar, *Bunch of Thoughts*, chap. 22.

[34] See Ghosh, *BJP and the Evolution of Hindu Nationalism*, pp. 352–65. During a brief period, when those who would lead the BJP were temporarily allied with the Janata Party, Vajpayee served as minister of external affairs in the Morarji Desai government, and he publicly affirmed its nonnuclear policy. (See Kaushik, A. P. *Vajpayee*, pp. 298–9.) Once the BJP was firmly established, its nuclear policies conformed more consistency to the general strategic injunctions of Savarkar and Golwalkar.

[35] See the discussion in A. James Gregor, *A Place in the Sun: Marxism and Fascism in China's Long Revolution* (Boulder, CO: Westview Press, 2000). Of course, significant differences distinguish the two developmental programs. Beijing, as a case in point, is pursuing an export-driven growth pattern, while the BJP advocated a relatively restricted employment of export incentives. China has allowed far more foreign direct investment than the BJP anticipated. But the similarities are evident.

[36] See Savarkar's comments in *Hindutva*, pp. 138–40.

[37] Savarkar, *Hindu Rashtra Darshan*, pp. 152–3, 156, 161, 163–4, 167–8.

the first decades of the twentieth century, Savarkar renounced "weakness," and called upon Hindus to reopen "the mines of Vedic fields for steel," and with that steel to fashion weapons "on the altar of Kali the Terrible." He argued that so "long as the whole world was red in tooth and claw," the nation was compelled to conjure up not only the weapons, but the "valor and strength" that were once its most prominent features. No longer afflicted by the "opiates of universalism and nonviolence," the nation would resist all forms of aggression, military and cultural, and restore to Hindudom the dignity to which it was qualified by history. Only in some such fashion might right once more be sustained by might.[38]

Some critics have found all this singularly "fascistic." Hindu nationalists, they maintained, seek to render Indians violent and aggressive. India was to be transformed into a "fascist" power, and Fascism, they insisted, was a unique regime of violence and brutality.[39] Hindu nationalists, it is said, seek to make India nothing less.

Such notions are predicated on a number of questionable assumptions. However confident such critics may be in their judgment, almost everyone seriously concerned with the classification of political systems finds such loosely framed contentions less than credible. Most sovereign nations now, and have in the past, shared many of the features that typify the foreign policy and defense postures of the BJP.

The fact is that Hindu nationalism has essentially indigenous roots. Sharing generic features with nationalism and its attendant economic developmentalism as universal phenomena, Hindu nationalism is no more fascist than it is Maoist or post-Maoist.[40] India's colonial past, when it was "the diadem in the crown of the British Empire," created the impetus for the appearance of an assertive nationalism. Similar nationalisms have arisen everywhere in postcolonial Africa and Northeast, East, and Southeast Asia.

Emerging from the constraints of colonialism, the masses of India had an uncertain awareness of their historic past, a past that stretched back into the recesses of time to the very beginnings of organized life on the subcontinent.

---

[38] Savarkar, *Hindutva*, pp. 21, 23–25. See the poetry quoted on pp. 50–1, and the comments on pp. 63–4, where we are told only "the sword," "strong force," can assure protection against foreign impostures. Golwalkar makes a particular point of the effects of "cultural imperialism" on the Hindu nation, rendering its population a defenseless, "deculturised, denationalised people." Golwalkar, *We or Our Nationhood Defined*, pp. 64–5.

[39] Thus, for Mark Neocleous, "for Fascism, violence and war are *absolutes*." *Fascism* (Minneapolis, MN: University of Minnesota Press, 1997), p. 17.

[40] Marzia Casolari attempts to make a case for a *direct* Fascist connection for the RSS in "The Fascist Heritage and Foreign Connection of RSS: Archival Evidence," in Krishna, *Fascism in India*, pp. 106–41. The attempt remains unconvincing. It seems clear that the leadership of the RSS sought insights from wherever available. They used visits to England, France, Germany, and Italy to put together programs for building a defense system for India. They took cues from pre–World War II Russia, Japan, and Germany when they anticipated, at that time, a more authoritarian India emerging from the trammels of colonialism.

Native intellectuals sought to provide a historic identity for the people of India that would inspire them to meet the challenges of the twentieth and twenty-first centuries. Savarkar, Hedgewar, and Golwalkar put together an interpretation of India's past that would serve as a principal component of the ideology that would infill, about a half-century later, the political convictions of the leaders of the Bharatiya Janata Party.

The history of the BJP, like that of the individual histories of similar revolutionary, mass-mobilizing, developmental movements of our time, is necessarily unique. Whatever features it shares with paradigmatic Fascism, it shares with all similarly disposed contemporary developmental movements of the right and left, democratic as well as antidemocratic. Beyond that, the critics of the RSS, the BJP, and the entire Sangh Parivar, insist that there are singular traits that distinguish Hindu nationalism from the general category of developmental systems that render it specifically fascist. One way through which they attempt to accomplish that is to identify Hindu nationalism with racism – and racism with Hitler's Germany.

Other than its putative antidemocratic and violent predispositions, its commitment to rapid industrialization and its programmatic efforts to militarize the Motherland, critics insist that the BJP and all its support organizations are characterized as irretrievably racist, compelled by convictions that must inevitably result in a nationwide debauch of racial discrimination and mass murder. There is an unrelenting repetition of such charges by the opponents of Hindu nationalism in all its expressions.

As indicated, some commentators speak, without qualification, of Hindutva, in all its manifestations, as fostering "the ominous spread of the cobrahood of fascism" throughout India. The entire Sangh Parivar, the constellation of organizations that provides the ideology and governs the group behaviors of Hindu nationalism, is spoken of as possessing "fascist and genocidist credentials." We are informed, with absolute confidence, that "a form of genocide or ethnic cleansing is implicit in the programme of every fascist movement, as it is in that of the RSS." We are told, with the same assurance, that Golwalkar argued that "the entire nation is identified with a particular race, similar to other Nazi race theories."[41] Such critics proceed to inform their readers that the RSS, the "moral and cultural guild" of the BJP, not only admired "Hitler and his methods" but has inspired the BJP to enter into "the business of genocide."[42]

That such charges can be leveled with impunity is testimony to India's British tradition of freedom of speech. The central charge, that Hindu nationalists advocate a "racially pure" *Rashtra*, peopled exclusively by "White Aryans," can be immediately dismissed. Entailed by that is the equally

---

[41] Chaitanya Krishna, "Fascism in India: Faces, Fangs and Facts," in Krishna, *Fascism in India*, pp. 3–4; Jairus Banaji, "The Political Culture of Fascism," ibid., pp. 24, 28.

[42] Arundhati Roy, "Gujarat, Fascism and Democracy," ibid., p. 34.

immediate dismissal of the notion that Hindu nationalism is the contemporary heir to Hitler's National Socialist race theories.

In the early 1920s, when Savarkar wrote *Hindutva*, the book that would serve as inspiration for the Hindu nationalist movement, the belief that much of the world's culture was the product of a singularly gifted race of blue-eyed, blond Aryans enjoyed considerable currency in Northern Europe and the United States, amply reflected in selective immigration policies and racist politics. It would not have been unusual had Savarkar simply accepted a racist interpretation of history, popular as it was at the time among British imperialists. The fact is that Savarkar did not accept that particular bit of conjecture concerning humankind.

Savarkar was perhaps prepared to accept (with considerable caution) the claim that an "intrepid" band of people called Aryans, thousands of years ago, had migrated from somewhere into India. There, along the banks of the seven rivers, the Sapta Sinhus, they encountered different peoples with whom they became "incorporated." In time they became a nation, composed of a "people that had welded Aryan and non-Aryans into a common race."[43]

What becomes immediately evident, in the first pages of Savarkar's exposition, is the realization that he entertains a *populationist* conception of race – a conviction that race is a dynamic constant, the result of the fusion of different breeding communities within a politically defined space. Thus, when Savarkar spoke of the Aryan nation in the course of his exposition, he specifically defined the term to mean "all those who had been incorporated as parts integral in the nation and people." Hindus, in effect, are a "family of peoples and races ... individualised into a single Being." Under favorable conditions, animated by a sense of community, and given sufficient time, such a "new polity" composed of a "family" of races and peoples would grow into a "new race." That was the homogeneous race of which Savarkar was to speak – the consequence of the "Aryans and Anaryans knitting themselves into a people [to be] born as a nation."[44]

Savarkar articulated a conception of race formation and nationhood that involved a complex process of dynamic evolution. He held that all nations have a similar history, proceeding through a process that is one of politically fostered group building. All human communities are drawn together and increasingly fused by affinities, be those affinities "religious, racial, cultural, or historical." Those affinities may turn on beliefs, social visibility, custom, or challenges survived and victories shared.[45]

The ingroup sentiments that sustain the community promote intermarriage, creating a "breeding-circle," out of which a new race is created. The race is thus, for all intents and purposes, coextensive and coterminous with

[43] Savankar, *Hindutva*, pp. 4, 8–11.
[44] Ibid., pp. 12, 28–9, 33, 45, 48; see pp. 108, 115, 119–20, 134, 138.
[45] See his explicit exposition in Savarkar, *Hindu Rashtra Darshan*, p. 48.

the politically defined nation to become "one homogeneous national unit."
He described the "organic" process that resulted in the formation of the
nation in the following fashion: "By an admirable process of assimilation,
elimination and consolidation, political, racial and cultural, [the Aryans]
welded all other non-Aryan peoples whom they came in contact with or
conflict with through this process of their expansion in this land from the
Indus to the Eastern sea and from the Himalayas to the Southern sea into a
national unit."[46]

Thus, when Savarkar speaks of Hindus as a "race," sharing a "common
blood" and a "common origin," the allusions are not ominous; they refer to
a common history, a common culture, and a common sense of fraternity. The
"common blood" refers to the intermixture, "assimilation," and "fusion"
necessary for the creation of a "natiorace." Savarkar spoke of such processes
as part of the creation of nations. There were no nations that were uniracial;
all nations were the result of the intermingling of different racial groups ultimately to stabilize as Englishmen, Irishmen, Germans, or Italians. All viable
nations are "race-*jati*" – each a dynamic "racial brotherhood," prepared to
mix blood and share destiny.

Thus, Savarkar explained, Hindus are both "Aryans and Anaryans" in
origin, but have come to share a common blood because all Hindus *feel*
themselves members of a brotherhood committed to the sharing of love,
life, and destiny. Each nation is just such a historic product, the result of a
community united by a common sense of destiny.

All of this transpires with the entire human race as its foundation. In fact,
Savarkar reminded his followers, there is "but one single race – the human
race kept alive by one common blood. . . . All other talk is at best provisional,
a makeshift and only relatively true."[47] Nations are evolutionary products,
fragments of a history of the human race infinitely more vast. Races are
provisional, makeshift, and evolving – constituents of nations that are critical
to humanity's fulfillment. Nations are not only the vehicles of race formation,
but of our self-realization as persons.

These conceptions of raciation and the intrinsic association of raciation and the formation of nations became part of the ideology of Hindutva. It became a conspicuous component of the political ideology of M. S.
Golwalkar. His *We or Our Nationhood Defined*, published first in 1939,
when Golwalkar was thirty-two years old, was to become the "Bible of the

---

[46] Ibid., p. 48. "It will be clear from this hurried peep into our history that ever since the
     Vaidic ages, for some 5,000 years at least, in the past our forefathers had been shaping the
     formation of our people into a religious, racial, cultural and political unit. As a consequence
     of it all, growing organically the Sindhus of the Vaidic time have grown today into Hindu
     Nation. . . ." Ibid., p. 35.
[47] Savarkar, *Hindutva*, pp. 86–7, 90.

RSS."[48] Like the work of Savarkar, it contains the same tenets concerning raciation and nationhood.

In *We or Our Nationhood Defined*, Golwalkar speaks of "race" as a "hereditary society having common customs, common language, common memories of glory or disaster; in short, it is a population with a common origin under one culture. . . . Even if there be a people of foreign origin, they must have become assimilated into the body of the mother race and inextricably fused into it." There is no talk of "pure races" to be found anywhere in the discussion. As the occasion arises, foreign peoples and alien races can and must be "fully assimilated in the nation" to share a sense of "common origin and common fellow feeling," to develop an appreciation that they "are related together in common traditions and naturally by common aspirations." All that taken together, the "ideas of common origin, religion, culture, language and so forth . . . make of a people, a race strictly so called."[49]

What is eminently clear in all of this is the priority of the nation – the vessel in which a race in formation is borne. Out of the commitment to the nation, a brotherhood is formed and a mission is undertaken. Within that brotherhood, no one is rejected and all are respected. That creates the conditions necessary for the molding of human beings into exemplars of virtue – prepared to sacrifice themselves, selfless and disciplined in service, courageous under threat, heroic in battle, and patriotic by natural disposition – to become "new men," the proper denizens of a nation in the process of rebirth.[50] The governing principle is the recognition that the nation is the means by virtue of which human beings can achieve great things in common. The people are no longer a mass, subject to the whimsies of political leaders, but have become a "homogeneous community," which means that they have "evolved a definite way of life molded by common ideals, culture, feelings, sentiments, faith and traditions."[51] Sharing a life in common, they share a common blood, in an intermingling that seals their community of destiny.

The entire complex of ideas that provides structure to Hindu nationalism is common to the nationalism of the twentieth century. One can find similar convictions among other revolutionary nationalist movements that have left evidence of their passing. Sun Yat-sen, for example, spoke of nations as race-cradles, in which different peoples and races would find a common life and a common destiny – and from which would emerge a "new race."

---

[48] See J. A. Curran, *Militant Hinduism in Indian Politics* (New York: Institute of Pacific Relations, 1951), p. 39.

[49] Golwalkar, *We or Our Nationhood Defined*, pp. 25, 54, 58–9.

[50] See Golwalkar, *Bunch of Thoughts*, chap. 3, p. 7; chap. 4, p. 5; chap. 32, p. 2; chap. 333, pp. 1, 12, 15.

[51] See the discussion in Kohli, *Political Ideas of M. S. Golwalkar*, pp. 17, 19.

Sun spoke of an "American race" that was emerging from the hetero-geneity that resulted from the inmigration of peoples and races from all countries and continents into North America. That diversity was destined to "undergo a process of fusion...to be 'welded in the melting pot,' [to] form a new race."[52] For Sun, like Savarkar and Golwalkar, the nation was a community of destiny, the environment in which a true confraternity was formed. A similar concept is found among Russian nationalists, who after the collapse of the Soviet Union have sought a collection of convictions that would give form to their beliefs.[53]

Lev Gumilev, who articulated his views before the final collapse of the Soviet Union, spoke of *ethnoi* as populations that have settled over several generations in a geographic space to practice endogamy. Inspired by a sense of community, such a union develops functional responses to environmental challenges, ultimately to become historic nations. Nations arise to "historical unity and community" through the working of history.[54]

For Gumilev, an *ethnos* is a "stable collective of individuals that opposes itself to all other similar collectives." Affinities govern the formation and persistence of such collections with the recognition that "we are such-and-such and all others are different," reflecting selected ingroup similarities as opposed to outgroup differences. *Ethnoi*, infilled with a sense of commu-nity, share a sense of common destiny, made manifest in traditions, rituals, ceremonies, and customs – stored in historic memories and myths of heroes past.[55]

All these concepts are found, in their various formulations, in nationalist ideologies in Europe, in Africa, in Asia, and on the Indian subcontinent. They probably originate, in substantial part, in a common source: the nineteenth century work of the Austro-Hungarian sociologist Ludwig Gumplowicz.[56]

The English anthropologist Arthur Keith employed Gumplowicz's notions in his *Nationality and Race from an Anthropologist's Point of View*,[57]

---

52 Sun Yat-sen, *The Triple Demism of Sun Yat-sen* (New York: AMS Press, from the Wuchang English Edition by the Franciscan Press, 1931), pp. 64–70, 79.

53 For the present discussion, the best contemporary spokesperson for these views is Lev N. Gumilev, *Ethnogenesis and the Biosphere* (Moscow: Progress, 1990). The elements of the position can be traced back to the nineteenth century.

54 Ibid., p. 246.

55 Ibid., pp. 95–8, 248, 256.

56 The primary source of these ideas is Ludwig Gumplowicz, *Der Rassenkampf: Sociologische Untersuchungen* (Innsbuck: Verlag der Wagner'schen Univ.-Buchhandlung, 1883). Some of these same ideas are reviewed and expanded upon in Gumplowicz, *Outlines of Sociology* (New York: Paine-Whitman, 1963, from the first German edition of 1885). Golwalkar refers to Gumplowicz in *We or Our Nationhood Defined*, p. 22, and was clearly familiar with his work.

57 Arthur Keith, *Nationality and Race from an Anthropologist's Point of View* (London: Oxford University Press, 1919). A more ample account is to be found in Keith, *A New Theory of Human Evolution* (New York: Philosophical Library, 1949).

published about the same time that Savarkar was writing his *Hindutva*. Golwalkar makes specific reference to Gumplowicz's work in *We or Our Nationhood Defined*.[58] The central conceptions originate among those who sought to provide an account of race formation, employing the evolutionary concepts of endogamy and selection to explain genetic drift and phenotypic change in populations. Among the Darwinists of the end of the nineteenth and the beginning of the twentieth centuries, there was almost continual discussion surrounding such notions. Influenced by just those circumstances, the concept "race" recurs frequently in the exposition of the theoretical framework of Hindu nationalism. It would be surprising had it not.

Within that framework, the nation is seen as the instrument of dynamic change and development, itself the evolutionary product of a natural biopsychological disposition to identify with one's similars and show diffidence to those who are dissimilar. In history, those dispositions sustain communities, whether tribes, castes, clans, confederations, city-states, nations, or empires. The specific form they take is shaped by historic circumstance.

Given such an account, it is perfectly comprehensible why Savarkar could speak of only one human race, with variations being a function of endogamy, territorial separation, and an abiding sense of group identity.[59] New races were a function of evolutionary mechanisms, territorial isolation, endogamy, and natural selection. What becomes of critical importance to nationalists is the fact that such a conception of evolutionary development identifies the psychological mechanisms that render human beings prepared to serve and sacrifice for their communities – to see community as an extension of themselves – to merge with others without the distractions that follow from their specific individual interests.[60]

Among nationalists, race is rarely, if ever, the central concern. The nation is the issue, together with the behavior of individuals in the face of their conceived responsibilities to that specific community of destiny. The implications are reasonably clear. Consistent nationalists, in general and in principle, are not expected to discriminate against members of the national community for any reason, much less because of their race – and that appears to be the case among Hindu nationalists. As early as his presidential address before the Hindu *Mahasabha* in 1937, Savarkar made explicit that in a future independent India, all "countrymen of whatever religion or sect or race they belong are [to be] treated with perfect equality and none allowed to dominate others or is deprived of his just and equal rights of free citizenship." He went on to insist that Hindu nationalism sought to "create an Indian state in which

---

[58] Golwalkar, *We or Our Nationhood Defined*, p. 22.
[59] See Savarkar, *Hindutva*, p. 90.
[60] Golwalkar speaks of the community as a "corporate personality" in which the individual merges with the group. See Golwalkar, *Bunch of Thoughts*, chap. 3, pp. 4, 6; chap. 5, pp. 4–5.

all citizens irrespective of caste and creed, race and religon are treated all alike."[61]

The rationale for such a position is obvious. The work of "national regeneration" required that everyone commit himself or herself to sacrifice, selflessness, and enduring collective labor. To Golwalkar, every member of the community deserved the assurance that such an ethic could be sustained. To ensure that, the spirit animating the nation must be one in which "none are rejected and all are respected." Golwalkar insisted that Hindu nationalism pledge itself to the binding conviction that "all individuals are ... equally sacred and worthy of our service."[62]

What becomes clear, in considering these convictions, is that the social philosophy of Hindu nationalism differs in fundamental fashion from that which provided the rationale for nineteenth-century liberalism. Hindu nationalism does not conceive society and politics a simple product of a hypothetical social contract,[63] by virtue of which collective life is disaggregated into the calculated decisions on the part of individuals to protect and pursue their personal interests – their security and their private property. Hindu nationalists recognize the social contract theory of the state to be a product of a peculiar form of European individualism.

The concept of a Hindu *Rashtra*, *Barat Rashtra*, embodies an entirely different notion of social life and responsibility. The *Rashtra* conception rests on the sociophilosophical notion that individuals are, in and of themselves and in an important sense, collective beings. Hindu nationalists remind us that everything we know of animate life suggests that all creatures in nature are group beings – human beings no less so. Golwalkar refers to that reality when he speaks of the relationship between the individual and his community. He reminds us that "the 'I' in me, being the same as the 'I' in ... other beings, makes me react to the joys and sorrows of my fellow living beings just as I react to my own. This genuine feeling of identity born out of the community ... is the real driving force behind our natural urge for human unity."[64]

As has been intimated, Hindu *Rashtra* is predicated on the conviction that the individual, in actuality, is not "individual" at all; he or she becomes an individual only as part of a corporate reality. While the social contract theory of society and politics is predicated on the notion of an inherent

---

[61] Savarkar, *Hindu Rashtra Darshan*, pp. 5, 22. Savarkar repeated these convictions in a number of places. He sought a "an independent and strong and mighty Hindu nation ... based on perfect equality of citizenship for all loyal and faithful Indian citizens irrespective or race and religion...." He insisted on equality, with advantages based on "merit alone and the fundamental rights of freedom of worship, language, script, etc., guaranteed to all citizens alike...." in a society in which "all minorities should be given effective safeguards to protect their language, religion, culture, etc...." Ibid., pp. 66, 183, 196.

[62] Golwalkar, *Bunch of Thoughts*, chap. 5, p. 3.

[63] See the account in Kohli, *Political Ideas of M. S. Golwalkar*, p. 21.

[64] Golwalkar, *Bunch of Thoughts*, chap. 1, p. 3.

conflict between the individual and others, Hindu *Rashtra* is inspired by the philosophic conviction that we are all parts of one living reality that finds expression in "the common inner bond" that fuses all members in a given historic community.[65]

Until that final resolution in which we all merge into some ultimate reality, human beings will be functional members of a corporate unity, a *Rashtra*,[66] a community through which destiny manifests itself and in which individuals find the only true fulfillment available to them in this creation. Understanding that, individuals voluntarily and in appreciation are prepared to assume the moral obligations attendant on felt gratitude – the performance of duty, the willingness to sacrifice and labor in the service of the *Rashtra*, and an "absolute loyalty to the Hindu nation" – the permanence against which individuals are but transient.[67]

What is eminently clear is that Hindu nationalism turns on the *nation*. Race was only a contingent byproduct of a process now identified widely in the literature as a populationist conception of race and raciation. In that process, the nation serves as a "race cradle," a vehicle in which genes, mutations, endogamy, natural selection, and geocultural circumstances collaborate to foster racial variations that were part of the secular mechanism of human evolution. It was the nation, not the race, that was the critical center of *Rashtra*, as *Rashtra* was understood by the advocates of Hindutva.

That understood, it becomes equally evident that Hindu nationalism has very little, if anything, to do with Hitler's race theories. The racism that was central to National Socialist convictions was fundamentally different from anything found in the ideological works of the founders of Hindu nationalism.

For Hitler, races were understood to be historic constants that existed in the primordial past as pure, pristine biological realities that were debased over time by intermixture with lesser races. Among the primordial races, the "Germanic" or "Nordic"[68] race was endowed with capabilities that rendered

---

[65] Ibid., chap. 3, p. 4.

[66] The *Rashtra* is revealed in the "consciousness of a single reality running through all ... individuals. The individual is a living limb of the corporate social personality. The individual and the society supplement and complement each other with the result that both get strengthened and benefited." Ibid., chap. 3, p. 6.

[67] Ibid., chap. 5, p. 4; chap. 6, pp. 3, 5.

[68] The terms "Germanic" and "Nordic" were used interchangeably by National Socialist race theorists. Those who were most consistent spoke of "Nordics," but it was common for Hitler to refer to the privileged race as "Germanic." The easiest access to National Socialist race theory is through the literature available in English. Hans F. K. Günther's *Racial Elements of European History* (London: Methuen, 1927) was early translated. He was to receive the first National Socialist gold medal for his research production. References to the abundance of German literature are to be found in A. James Gregor, *Contemporary Radical Ideologies: Totalitarian Thought in the Twentieth Century* (New York: Random House, 1968), chap. 5.

it the world's sole culture creating agent. Its intermixture with lesser races impaired its abilities and threatened humankind with the total collapse of culture.

Hitler's followers saw it as their responsibility to "purify" the chosen race and restore it to its conjectured original genetic superiority. At the same time, they were to protect such culture creators from those races or peoples who not only neither produced nor sustained human culture, but constituted nothing other than a "ferment of decomposition" in an increasingly decadent world.

All of this is fundamentally alien to Hindu nationalism. Nowhere in the literature of Hindu nationalism does one find the suggestion that Aryans, "white-skinned" denizens of the Vedic world of Hindu antiquity, were the sole culture creators on the Indian subcontinent. By entailment, no other race or people is identified as inferior. There is explicit rejection of the notion that non-Aryans, Dravidians, tribal groups, or migrants into India were or are intrinsically inferior and are for that reason to be the objects of discrimination or abuse.[69]

For Hitler, race was the primary historic variable. It was the community in which the individual found his true self. For Hitler, the race was that biological entity that determined the individual's behavior and shaped his or her destiny. For National Socialist theorists, there was a "law of the race" that dictated the qualities of "soul" and "character" for the individual, revealed in an empirical "science" called "psychoanthropology."[70] For most, if not all, National Socialist race theorists, a person's somatotype was an indicator of that person's psychological and moral character. In general, it was held that the principal elements of character and spirit were largely, if not entirely, determined by genetic endowments.

These kinds of notions are to be found not among Hindu nationalists, but as has been indicated, among some black nationalists, particularly the followers of Elijah Muhammad. For Black Muslims, *all* whites bear the moral defects that resulted from the genetic manipulations of the mad scientist Yakub. In that case, a white skin is a certain indicator of depravity. The followers of the Lost-Found Nation of Islam are clearly, irretrievably, and malevolently racists. Like some of the major National Socialist race theorists,

---

[69] Golwalkar explictly rejects the racist interpretation of Indian history in which the Aryans enter India bringing culture and civilization and become "contaminated" by the inferior blood of pre-Aryan peoples (including the Dravidians). He insisted that the term "Aryan" "was always a sign of culture and not the name of a race." Golwalkar, *Bunch of Thoughts*, chap. 10, p. 7.

[70] See, for instance, the work of Ludwig Ferdinand Clauss, *Rasse und Charakter* (Frankfurt am Main: Verlag Moritz Diesterweg, 1938), and *Rasse und Seele: Eine Einführung in den Sinn der leibliches Gestalt* (Berlin: Büchergilde Gutenberg, 1937).

they are biological determinists, denying, in the final analysis, the responsibility of human beings for their own conduct.

None of this was, or is, true of Hindu nationalists, of Sun Yat-sen or Lev Gumilev. Nationalist beliefs might very well include one or another form of racism, but nationalists are not necessarily racists.[71] For "true" nationalists, it is not the race, but the "organic" community of which he or she is part, that is the critical historic reality – the object of loyalty and devotion. As that reality, the nation provides the stage for the undertakings of the individual – behaviors that are all deliberate and chosen. Individual performance for nationalists is behavior that is never determined, but the result of moral calculation and ethical judgment. Like "true" nationalists, Hindu nationalists conceive human behavior as composed of acts that are essentially chosen by the individual – never determined by his or her race. "True" nationalists tend to be voluntarists,[72] understanding behavior as a function of character. For such nationalists, behavior is never determined, but always chosen. Thus, Savarkar spoke freely of an alien who chose to adopt Hindu culture and came to adore India as a "Holyland." That person was no longer an alien, but a Hindu. Savarkar went on to say, "any convert to Hindutva of non-Hindu parentage can be a Hindu, if *bona fide*, he or she adopts our land as his or her country . . . thus coming to love our land as a real Fatherland. . . ."[73]

For Savarkar, it clearly was not race but moral choice that shaped the destiny of individuals. Persons were free to choose, even on the occasion of life's most important decisions.

In the illustrative circumstances described by Savarkar, one chooses to be a Hindu, just as one chooses to be courageous, selfless, idealistic, and committed. All acts are the consequence of willed decision, the product of choices made as a result of living in a brotherhood in which values are shared and principles sustained.[74]

Hindu nationalists are "true" nationalists. Race constitutes no more than a feature of the object world that is a matter of relative indifference. "Race" was a matter of some considerable theoretical interest at the turn of the twentieth century and it would have been odd if Savarkar had not addressed it at all.

Savarkar did address the subject, but in a fashion that rendered it subsidiary to the reality and historic significance of the nation. Race would not be allowed to undermine the integrity of the nation – or the sentiment of

---

[71] See George L. Mosse, *The Fascist Revolution: Toward a General Theory of Fascism* (New York: Howard Fertig, 1999), chap. 3.

[72] See Golwalkar, *Bunch of Thoughts*, chap. 23, p. 6.

[73] Savarkar, *Hindutva*, p. 130.

[74] See some of Golwalkar's reflections in Golwalkar, *Bunch of Thoughts*, chap. 22, p. 6.

brotherhood that sustained it. Hindu nationalists would allow nothing, not the European theory of Aryanism, nor the notion that Dravidians or other Indian subpopulations were somehow "inferior," to impair the "organic homogeneity" of the *Barat Rashtra*.

What is perhaps more interesting than all of this – surely something that requires some reflection – is the fact that the conceptions that provide substance to the ideology of Hindutva share some significant features with the belief system of Italian Fascism. By the time that Mussolini's Fascism reached its ideological maturity, it had adopted notions of raciation and the relationship of race to nation similar to those of the spokespeople for Hindutva.[75]

For much the same reasons as Hindu nationalists, Fascist theoreticians articulated convictions concerning raciation that made "new races" the consequence of the influence of reproductive isolation in geographic space over varying lengths of time. In that discussion, one finds documented traces of the thought of Ludwig Gumplowicz and Arthur Keith – elements of the same social science conceptions that surfaced in the ideological statements of Savarkar and Golwalkar.

Together with shared notions of raciation, one finds Hindu nationalists articulating some of the same criticisms leveled against representative democracy to be found in Fascist literature.[76] Golwalkar was candid in listing some of the failures of representative democracy. He spoke of the parochialism and special interests that seem to thwart the unity of the nation under the circumstances that attend the major forms of Western political democracy.[77]

Golwalkar proceeded to suggest that in order to reduce the propensity to lapse into the parochialisms and special interests of "groupism and casteism," representative democracy in India might choose an alternative manner of representation: functionalism. The representative houses of India might be divided into two categories: representatives of professions and avocations in one, while representatives for the other might be chosen on a territorial basis. It was anticipated that direct representation of functional interests might reduce the occasion for corruption in a national legislature in which professional and business interests are only indirectly represented.[78]

---

[75] See the discussion in A. James Gregor, *The Ideology of Fascism: The Rationale of Totalitarianism* (New York: Free Press, 1969), chap. 6.

[76] See the discussion in Bruno Spampanato, *Democrazia fascista* (Rome: Edizoni di "Politica Nuova," 1933).

[77] Golwalkar, *Bunch of Thoughts*, chap. 4, p. 1; chap. 16, p. 11. See Golwalkar's discussion of the search for "oneness" in so diversified a nation as India. Representative democracy, he seemed to argue, contributes to the difficulty of creating one homogeneous community. Ibid., chap. 18, pp. 1–5.

[78] Ibid., chap. 4, pp. 1–3.

One can hardly avoid appreciating the similarity with the corporativism that became one of the defining institutions of Fascist Italy. Mussolini spoke of the functional representation of the productive elements of the Italian economy as one of the central features of Fascism. He described the *stato corporativo*, the corporative state, as the revolutionary fulfillment of the promises of both liberalism and socialism. Mussolini seemed to imagine that the corporative state, with its functional representation, was perhaps Fascism's greatest single accomplishment.[79]

What emerges from this kind of discussion is the impression that although the critics of Hindu nationalism are wrong in attempting to identify the movement as heir to Adolf Hitler's race theories, they may be correct in loosely associating Hindu nationalism with Italian Fascism. Such a conclusion could only be warranted by a more careful consideration of everything surrounding the judgment.

It is conceivable that the founders of Hindu nationalism might have been influenced by Fascist thought, and even that they might have found some aspects of Fascism attractive in the late 1920s and early 1930s.[80] Emergent India, like post-Risorgimento Italy, was a nation only then emerging from hundreds of years of foreign oppression and colonialism. The possibility that some Hindu nationalists saw similarities in the circumstances governing the two nations – and imagined that Italian revolutionaries might somehow offer insights into a promising program of Indian revival – cannot be cavalierly dismissed.

That such may have been the case, however, is hardly sufficient to make the case that Hindu nationalism is a variant of Fascism – a contemporary "neofascism." It would be much more relevant to consider the sustaining ideologies of both movements in their respective entireties in order to render a judgment based on best evidence.

Mussolini himself would seem to be a credible source if, for comparative purposes, one seeks an authority on the nature and content of Fascism as an ideology as well as a political system. In one of his major statements on Fascism, Mussolini insisted on corporativism as a central set of institutions providing substance to the system. But corporativism, in and of itself, is hardly sufficient to identify a political system as fascist. Corporativism was a tool to be employed to accomplish some specific purpose. Fascists argued that the rapid industrial development and economic growth of the peninsula could best be accomplished by controlling the nation's productive system by imposing corporative discipline on both capital and labor alike. How that

---

[79] Benito Mussolini, "Discorso per lo Stato corporativo," in *Opera omnia* (Florence: La fenice, 1964), 26, pp. 94–6.

[80] See the discussion in Casolari, "The Fascist Heritage and Foreign Connection of RSS," in Krishna, *Fascism in India*, pp. 109–14.

discipline was to be effected provides insight into the differences between Fascist and nonfascist systems.

In Mussolini's judgment, in order to establish and sustain the requisite discipline, three critical conditions had to be met: (1) The system had to be structured by a single, hegemonic political party that would provide for (2) the extension of totalitarian controls through a state that would (3) "mobilize the energy, interests, and aspirations of the nation in its entirety.... in an atmosphere of strong ideal tension."[81]

That succinctly describes the surface features of the system in which Fascism lived out its tenure in Italy. It must also be remembered that in the course of that tenure, Fascism allowed its relatively benign conception of raciation to devolve into anti-Semitism, to make Italy complicit in the National Socialist crimes against the Jews.[82]

It was very soon clear to observers that, given some set of incentives, the originally relatively benign racial and corporative constituents of the ideology of Fascism could be readily transformed into violations of civil liberties and crimes against humanity. With respect to the racial notions of Fascism, when Mussolini chose to ally Italy with National Socialist Germany, he created conditions that precipitated an Italian accommodation for Hitler's anti-Semitism. The tragic consequences are too well-known to warrant review.

To many, the devolution of the Fascist system was the consequence of its totalitarianism – its entire dependency on the single, hegemonic party for its operations – and the centralization of control through the institutionalization of the "charismatic leader." Only under such circumstances could Fascist Italy, which had abjured anti-Semitism throughout its history,[83] suddenly reverse itself without political cost. Whatever virtues that the system of sustained discipline may have had were paid for at exorbitant cost – the consequence of the absolute ascendency of the totalitarian state and the unassailable paramountcy of its leader.

Given the clear admonitions of history, what one finds in the ideological recommendations of the intellectual leaders of Hindu nationalism is an explicit rejection of all those features of the Italian system that not only compromised whatever virtues it may have had, leading not only to the ruin of Fascism, but to the egregious crimes against the nation's citizens.

---

[81] Mussolini, "Discorso per lo Stato corporativo," p. 96.

[82] Clearly Fascist complicity in National Socialist crimes never reached the same criminal level. Until Mussolini became captive to Hitler's forces, Fascist anti-Semitism had "very little in common with that of the Nazis." Renzo De Felice, *Storia degli ebrei italiani sotto il fascismo* (Turin: Einaudi, 1993, enlarged new edition), p. 236; see ibid., "The Introduction to the New Edition," and chaps. 1, 7.

[83] See Mussolini's comments in Emil Ludwig, *Colloqui con Mussolini* (Verona: Mondadori, 1932), p. 72.

There are several features to be found in the thought of the founders of Hindu nationalism that suggest either that they had learned from the Fascist experience – or that they had never countenanced the fabrication of a totalitarian state under the inflexible control of an absolute leader. As early as 1939, Savarkar was prepared to commit the Hindu nationalist movement to the defense of traditional democratic rights – a commitment that would preclude both the totalitarian state and its "Leader." Savarkar spoke of an active defense of the "fundamental rights of liberty of speech, liberty of conscience, of worship, of association, etc., [to be] enjoyed by all citizens alike.... [in a] united Hindusthani State in which all sects, and sections, races and religions, castes and creeds, Hindus, Moslems, Christians, Anglo-Indians, etc. [would] be harmoniously welded together into a political State on terms of perfect equality."[84]

In effect, even before India won its independence from Great Britain, the Hindu nationalist movement was prepared to reject any intimation of totalitarian rule,[85] a hegemonic party, or a paramount leader.[86] Unlike Fascism, which held that the nation is a product of the state[87] and, by implication, its leader, Hindu nationalists held that "all questions regarding the form of the state," as well as its leadership, would be entrusted to the nation.[88]

The authors of Hindutva, as a doctrine, expressed grave reservations concerning an "all-powerful state." They committed themselves to the vision of the state to be found in the works of the ancients. The explicit function of the state was confined "to the protection of the people against foreign invasion and internal strife.... A state," Golwalkar continued, "which transgresses these limits... cannot be the friend of the people."[89]

Hindu nationalism insists that any system that anticipates the "concentration of all power in the state" threatens its citizens with "blood baths [and] mass massacres as have no parallel even in the darkest and least civilized periods of human history." Golwalkar went on to point out that "the enslavement of the average human being, the regimentation of ideas, thought and sentiments, the total suppression of all freedoms... [are its] frightful effects." Together with all that, the leaders of Hindu nationalism, while they

---

[84] Savarkar, *Hindu Rashtra Darshan*, p. 94.

[85] See Golwalkar, *Bunch of Thoughts*, Appendix, p. 20.

[86] Ibid., chap. 24, pp. 3–4.

[87] "It is not the nation that generates the state.... Rather the nation is created by the state which endows a people... with a will, and in so doing, with an effective existence." Mussolini, "La dottrina del fascismo," *Opera omnia*, 34, p. 120.

[88] Hindu nationalists always gave primacy to the nation, then to society and only then to the state, which was seen only as an instrumentality. Compare M. A. Venkata Rao, "Introduction" to Golwalkar, *Bunch of Thoughts*, p. 7, and ibid., chap. 8, p. 7; Appendix, p. 20.

[89] Golwalkar, *Bunch of Thoughts*, chap. 4, p. 3; chap. 8, p. 6. See the comments in ibid., chap. 15, p. 6. Golwalkar explicitly rejects dictatorship as violative of the "dignity of man." Ibid., chap. 38, p. 2.

spoke of the necessity of "adamantine will" on the part of the nation's leaders, maintained, with equal insistence, that it must be the people who retain ultimate control.[90]

In effect, it is difficult to argue with much conviction that Hindu nationalism is a variant of Mussolini's Fascism. Whatever its philosophical rationale, its political and economic behaviors overall bear more resemblance to the nationalist liberalism of nineteenth-century England than to twentieth-century Fascism. Hindu nationalists have consistently advocated a limited state. Granted the increased responsibilities assumed by the government as a consequence of developments in the twentieth century entirely unanticipated by our antecedents, the BJP has continued to insist on a reduction in those functions of the state that limit political and economic freedom. Even its reactive nationalism shares more properties with the nineteenth-century developmental program of Friedrich List than with that of Benito Mussolini.[91]

What gives Hindu nationalism its contemporary political cast is its complex organizational structure. Built around the Rashtriya Swayamsevak Sangh, (RSS), the Sangh Parivar is the mother organization of the entire Hindutva cultural and political family. The revolutionary twentieth century made such developments not only possible, but perhaps inevitable. That does not alter the practical content of Hindu nationalism – that owes more to nineteenth-century British political and economic traditions than it does to twentieth-century mass-mobilizing, totalitarian movements.

In fact, it can be argued that those elements of the ideology of Hindu nationalism that many find particularly threatening – its allusions to the relationship of race to nationalism, in particular – were equally of nineteenth-century British and Continental origin, from a time when racism, however it was understood, had not yet taken on those pathological features that rendered it a rationale for mass murder. The residual racism one finds in Hindu nationalism bears only the most remote kinship to the racism of Adolf Hitler. Its kinship is rather with the Anglo-American Darwinism of the late-nineteenth century. At that time, persons spoke, without the least embarrassment, of British and American "races."

The real problem that besets Hindu nationalism arises not out of its putative racism, but out of its insistence that all the citizens of India commit to an unqualified "devotion" to the Motherland. A Hindu nationalist demands of others, should they wish to an equal among equals, that they not only adopt Hindu culture, respecting the history of the nation, but that the Motherland be both the land of their love as well as the land of their worship.[92] None of this can be taken to mean that Muslims, Jews, or Christians would not be permitted to practice their own respective faiths in the India of the

---

[90] Ibid., chap. 24, p. 2; Appendix, p. 20.
[91] See the discussion of A. B. Vajpayee, in Kaushik, *A. B. Vajpayee*, pp. 12, 18, 169, 182–3.
[92] See Savarkar, *Hindutva*, pp. 84, 99–116.

twenty-first century. The Hindu nationalist argument is that Hinduism has traditionally been so generous a cultural current that it could accommodate all sects, religions, and practices. Tolerant of all religious expression, what Hindu nationalists have insisted upon is that all conationals put the nation first, before Mecca, Jerusalem, or Rome. Whatever their religious convictions, all are to be equal in a renewed India, "irrespective of caste or creed, race or religion – provided they avow and owe an exclusive and devoted allegiance to the Hindusthani State."[93]

That has created special difficulties for Muslims, who interpret devotion to the nation to be a form of idolatry, proscribed by the doctrinal monotheism of the *Qur'an*. The tensions generated by such reservations have contributed to the religious conflicts that have fueled the homicidal violence that has marred India's history for centuries, long before the advent of Hindu nationalism. It is abundantly clear that the religious violence that has tainted Indian history over time is neither exclusively nor primarily the responsibility of Hindu nationalism, although it is evident that the insistence that Muslims love India as a "holy land" contributes to the overall ill-will that, to this day, kindles it.

There is an evident problem insofar as Hindu nationalists are apparently not prepared to tolerate a sect within the community that looks outward, beyond the political boundaries of the nation, for its spiritual home. It is a problem of the same order that created anti–Roman Catholicism in the United States and Great Britain in modern times, or anti-Semitism in a host of nations in the ancient and modern world.

The critics of Hindu nationalism have simply chosen to identify any form of religious or racial intolerance as "fascist" – and are thus prepared to identify Hindutva as one of its expressions. Given that notion, they are prepared to argue that the Hindu religion itself has been "fascist...from its very beginning"[94] – thousands of years ago.

In fact, the term "fascist" is used with such abandon by some Indian academics and journalists that any instances in which "power" is employed at anyone else's expense is immediately dubbed "fascist." As a consequence, instances of "fascism" in India include "marital rape, sexual preferences,... uranium dumping, unsustainable mining, weavers' woes, [and] farmers' worries."[95] Everything and anything one deplores is identified as "fascist."

There is little if any evidence that Hindu nationalism is responsible for marital rape, or sexual preferences, in India. Neither weavers' woes nor farmers' worries can be reasonably laid at the door of the advocates of Hindutva.

---

[93] Savarkar, *Hindu Rashtra Darshan*, p. 94. Savarkar insisted that "Hindutva is not... determined by any theological tests." Savarkar, *Hindutva*, p. 125.

[94] Arundati Roy, "Gujarat, Fascism and Democracy," in Krishna, *Fascism in India*, p. 143.

[95] Mukesh Manas, "Fascism in India: Hypothesizing a Dalit Perspective," ibid., pp. 40–1.

More serious are the charges that Hindu nationalists have incited and directed anti-Muslim riots in the recent past in which hundreds, if not thousands, have perished. Critics of Hindu nationalism speak of local leaders, without the least hesitation, as "practising Nazis."[96] Religious riots in India have been attended by unspeakable violence with the murder and violation of women and children – all accompanied by looting and the massive destruction of property – and Hindu nationalists have been charged with culpability.

Such serious charges should be addressed by the Indian courts. To date, neither the RSS, the BJP, nor any of their affiliated organizations have been indicted, tried, or found guilty of these obscenities. But even if individuals or organizations were be tried and found culpable in such cases, that would not establish their credentials as fascists or neofascists. Barbarisms of similar or worse magnitude have occurred, in the recent past, in Central Africa and the Sudan, in the Balkans and the Middle East, and in the islands of Southeast Asia. If tribal or confessional violence is, by its very occurrence, evidence of "fascism," then fascism is inordinately widespread in both space and time. The mass murder of innocents by any perpetrator or perpetrators can hardly count as certification of their fascism.

In substance, the search for a saffron fascism has gone largely unrewarded. In power the Bharatiya Janata Party has scrupulously obeyed India's constitutional prescriptions. It has taken up power and surrendered it in accordance with the electoral choices of the Indian people, Hindu and non-Hindu alike. The BJP has consistently made efforts to uplift disadvantaged castes and tribal groups. It has mobilized women in their own defense. It has organized Indian workers into one of the largest labor unions in the nation.

As early as the 1930s, Hindu nationalists sought to mobilize not only Hindu youth, but the Rashtra Sevika Samiti, the woman's affiliate, later to be joined by the Seva Bharati and the Vanavasi Kalyan Ashram, intended to provide assistance to women, "scheduled castes," and tribals – as well as slum dwellers – administering nearly ten thousand centers calculated to meet the welfare needs of all the disadvantaged.[97] By the last decade of the twentieth century, all these groups were constituent parts of the BJP and delivered the votes necessary to make the party one of the largest and most influential in India.

None of this appears cosmetic. The ideology with which the party identified itself sought the creation of a true community in which individuals and groups could identify without reservations. Pandit Deendayal Upadhyaya wrote the BJP's *BJP Philosophy: Integral Humanism* in the late 1960s and provided contemporary Hindu nationalism a studied rationale for the equality of all citizens and their identity with the community.

[96] A. G. Noorani, "A Practising Nazi Trampling on India," ibid., p. 281.
[97] See the account in Swain, *Bharatiya Janata Party*, chap. 5.

It is difficult to imagine what evidence might adequately support the claim made by the critics of Hindu nationalism that "the Hindutva movement is a violent sectarian movement seeking to create a Hindu *Rashtra* (an ethnically 'pure' Hindu nation) in India, in many ways similar to the Nazi idea of a pure Aryan Germany."[98] There is very little, if anything, that might warrant the identification of Hindutva with Nazism. The argument for a Hindu fascism is no more persuasive.

What seems evident is that Hindu nationalism will continue to occupy a critical position in the twenty-first century politics of India – a nuclear-armed nation of more than a billion people at the crossroads of international tension, sitting astride some of the most important sealines of communication in the world. India gives every evidence of becoming a major industrial power in the near future. It has every right to expect a place in the council of nations second to none. To speak of India or any of the political parties that make up its roster of domestic contenders as "fascist" without convincing evidence to support the characterization is to irresponsibly poison the future of international relations. In almost all its aspects, the search for neofascism on the Indian subcontinent does not present an edifying spectacle.

---

[98] Sabrang Communications, *The Foreign Exchange of Hate: IDRF and the American Funding of Hindutva* (http://www.stopfundinghate.org/sacw, 2004), chap. 1, p. 2.

9

Post-Maoist China

Fascism with Chinese Characteristics

Of all the efforts that make up the contemporary search for neofascism, academic discussions devoted to the politics of the People's Republic of China have been among the most disappointing. For an extended period of time, particularly during the long years of the Second World War, a number of important Anglophone journalists and academics somehow chose to distinguish the "fascism" of Chiang Kaishek's Kuomintang from the "progressive" politics of Mao Zedong's Chinese Communist Party.[1] It was a distinction that was to persist doggedly for decades after the war.

Edgar Snow was perhaps the most notable among those who convinced Americans of the benignity of Mao Zedong. In the years immediately preceding the Japanese attack on Pearl Harbor, Snow devoted his time and considerable talent to providing his readership with informed conjectures concerning what a communist revolution might bring to China. His work was considered so credible that it was recommended by some of America's most informed Sinologists. We were told that Snow was, in some real sense, "prophetic" – that he had accurately foreseen China's future. After a successful revolution undertaken by the Communist Party, that future would be one that included a "brief period" of "controlled capitalism" in which the "bourgeois democratic revolution" would be a preamble to the final "heroic democracy" to follow. According to Snow, the Chinese communist revolution was inspired by the "democratic Socialist ideas" for which so many Chinese had sacrificed themselves – ideas that presumably included the "rights of freedom of speech, assembly, [and] organization"

---

[1] In his introduction to the English translation of Chiang Kaishek's *China's Destiny*, Philip Jaffe writes of the Kuomintang enforcing its "reactionary philosophy" on the people of China, while the "Communists and their supporters" are characterized as "forward-looking groups." Philip Jaffe, "The Secret of 'China's Destiny,'" in Chiang Kaishek, *China's Destiny and Chinese Economic Theory* (New York: Roy, 1947), p. 15.

that had previously been denied them by Chinese "fascism" and its agents.[2]

For much of the twentieth century, many Sinologists viewed the political history of China through just such a prism. The Communist Party of Mao Zedong was seen as well intentioned and somehow fundamentally democratic. The "liberation" of China by Mao's forces was understood to have brought "solid benefits to all." Beyond that, it was said, the nation was lifted from the level of one of the most backward in the world to one, "perhaps the only one," in which economic and industrial development was "really going on."[3]

Western intellectuals held those convictions so firmly that they were even affirmed in the years immediately following the tragedy of the Great Leap Forward (1958–61), one of the most devastating periods in recent Chinese history. It was during the Great Leap Forward that the Chinese people suffered famine of Biblical proportions – perhaps the most catastrophic in their history.[4]

Academics and journalists largely dismissed the reports by refugees of starvation, cannibalism, and all manner of privations as lacking credibility. Most Westerners appeared ill-disposed to consider the possibility that Maoism was anything other than a progressive solution to retrograde China's social, economic, and political problems.

Among many, there was a persistent refusal to consider China's circumstances with anything like the objectivity required. Few if any commentators were prepared for what would follow the economic disaster of the Great Leap Forward. Immediately following that calamity, Mao was compelled by his party colleagues to loosen his control over the system – only to organize a counterattack almost immediately – by mobilizing student masses against the Communist Party itself, together with its bureaucracy. Students were mobilized to "attack the headquarters" and "destroy those representatives of the bourgeoisie who have sneaked into the party," in what was identified as an imperative "struggle [to] . . . liquidate the bourgeoisie."[5]

---

[2] Edgar Snow, *Red Star Over China* (New York: Grove Press, 1944), pp. 481, 483, 494. In his analysis, Snow spoke of the insights he obtained from the "accomplished social scientist" V. I. Lenin, together with information provided by Joseph Stalin. Ibid., pp. 478, 480, 494. Professor John K. Fairbank, at that time perhaps the foremost Sinologist in the United States, specifically spoke of Snow's "prophetic" assessments of what the communist revolution would bring to China. See John K. Fairbank, "Introduction," ibid., p. iv.

[3] Joan Robinson, Foreword to E. L. Wheelwright and Bruce McFarlane, *The Chinese Road to Socialism* (New York: Monthly Review Press, 1970), p. 8.

[4] Refugees from the Chinese mainland reported the devastation, but most Western Sinologists refused to believe them. For the extent of the catastrophe, see Philip Short, *Mao: A Life* (New York: Henry Holt, 1999), pp. 502–5.

[5] *Circular of the Central Committee of the Chinese Communist Pary: A Great Historic Document (16 May 1966)* (Beijing: Foreign Languages Press, 1967), p. i; "Hold High the Great Red Banner of Mao Tse-tung's Thought and Actively Participate in the Great Socialist Cultural

Western intellectuals attempted to understand the disturbances in China in the course of which Mao unleashed his fanatics to attack those in the Chinese Communist Party deemed to be "capitalist roaders." Mao's Red Guards went forth to destroy all the traces of tradition, its artifacts, and its ideologies. The horrific series of outrages precipitated by Mao's revolutionaries are now identified as those of the Great Proletarian Cultural Revolution (1966–9).

While China was in the throes of anarchic violence and bloodshed, some Sinologists could describe the chaos that gripped China as a laudable attempt to "reconcile democracy with good order" so that the people might be better served.[6] Most Sinologists were genuinely confused as to what had transpired.

In the course of the Cultural Revolution, the Chinese Communist Party suffered a purge unprecedented in the history of the People's Republic of China. Of the 169 members of the Eighth Central Committee of the party in 1966, 115, or 68 percent of the total, had been purged by the middle of 1969. Seventy-three percent of the membership of the ruling Politburo were relieved of their responsibilities along with 75 percent of the 316 leaders who held positions of assistant ministerial rank or higher in the economic ministries of the central government.

Given the lack of direction amid the prevailing disorder, between the years 1966 and 1969, together with an incalculable waste of funds and resources, there was a steady and systematic decline in the total output value of industry and agriculture. The waste of resources and human capital was appalling. Together with the decline in output, there was an erosion in overall quality of product.[7] Material losses were accompanied by unspeakable human costs. Hundreds of thousands of Chinese died in the violence, which often included acts of brutality by elements of the People's Liberation Army.

Whatever the Western interpretation of events in the People's Republic, the Chinese themselves, witnesses to what was transpiring under the "dictatorship of the proletariat," were driven to question the very "socialism" of the Maoist revolution. In the early 1970s, three years before Mao's death on 9 September 1976, young Chinese intellectuals in Beijing affixed "big character posters" to what had spontaneously become the city's "Democracy Wall." Those posters gave voice to the complaint that socialism in China was no more than a mockery of what had been promised. Rather than liberty and equality, Maoism had brought with it an entrenched and privileged stratum of false revolutionaries who arrogated to themselves control over the lives of all Chinese.

Revolution," *The Great Socialist Cultural Revolution in China* (Beijing: Foreign Languages Press, 1966), 1, p. 1.

[6] Joan Robinson, *The Cultural Revolution in China* (Baltimore, MO: Penguin, 1969), pp. 43–4.

[7] See the more detailed discussion in A. James Gregor, *Marxism, China and Development* (New Brunswick, NJ: Transaction, 1995), pp. 82–5.

Legitimized by the pretense that all property had become the possession of the Chinese people in its collectivity, the members of an "emergent new class" assumed the right to its control and administration. What followed, the argument proceeded, was exploitation of those who were not entitled members of the "proletarian dictatorship."[8] Some of the Red Guards – who had fought so assiduously against "capitalist roaders" for "socialism" – suddenly realized that for which they had sacrificed themselves gave every evidence of being a form of "social fascism."

They spoke of such a fascism as the product of a system that "sanctified" a "bureaucratic-military machine" that in turn succeeded in maintaining hegemonic control over an oppressed and exploited population, with every enormity concealed "from view by a screen of socialist verbiage." It was said that under the banner of "proletarian dictatorship," those possessed of both "political leadership and economic control" bang the "drums of narrow-minded patriotism and nationalism" in order to make of what had been Chinese Communism a "fascist dictatorship."[9]

This interpretation surprised Westerners. They had not expected that citizens, subject to the constraints of "proletarian dictatorship," might deliver themselves of such views. At about the time the critical "big character posters" were being publicized, Chou Enlai, as Mao's spokesperson, warned that the critics themselves, those undisciplined "exceptionalists," were threatening China with the transformation of the "Marxist-Leninist Chinese Communist Party" into a "revisionist fascist party."[10]

Thus, Maoism was seen as fascist by its domestic critics and as a bulwark against fascism by its defenders. Many in the West were genuinely, and understandably, puzzled by developments. More than twenty years after its extinction in Europe, fascism had become a living issue on the mainland of China.

To complicate the interpretation of events in China still further, it must be remembered that in the Soviet Union, for years after 1965, it had become standard intellectual fare to interpret Maoism as a variant of fascism. The Sino–Soviet dispute had produced an abundance of Soviet literature critical of the leadership of the People's Republic of China. Mao's Soviet critics had pointed out, with considerable conviction, that Mao pretended to have made a "proletarian socialist revolution" in a country innocent of proletarians, lacking the "concentration of capital" and the corresponding "declining

---

[8] See the account in Li Zhengtian, Chen Yiyang, and Wang Xizhe, "On Socialist Democracy and the Legal System," in Anita Chan, Stanley Rosen, and Jonathan Unger (eds.), *On Socialist Democracy and the Chinese Legal System* (Armonk, NY: M. E. Sharpe, 1985), pp. 31–85.

[9] Chen Erjin, *China Crossroads Socialism: An Unofficial Manifesto for Proletarian Democracy* (London: Verso, 1984), pp. 72–75.

[10] Chou Enlai, "Report to the Tenth National Congress of the Communist Party of China," in Raymond Lotta (ed.), *And Mao Makes 5: Mao Tsetung's Last Great Battle* (Chicago: Banner Press, 1978), p. 83.

rate of profit" that Marxist theory insisted would have to attend highly industrialized economies. Throughout the history of Marxist speculation, all Marxists understood just those eventualities to be the necessary if not sufficient conditions for socialist revolution. Without the existence of those prerequisite conditions, Soviet intellectuals warned, revolutions could only fail and produce little more than caricatures of what Marx and Engels had anticipated.[11]

Given the analysis, the only result could be, in the judgment of Soviet academicians, that Maoists had orchestrated a revolution produced by the "pseudorevolutionary petty bourgeois" that would inevitably give expression to a "peasant based nationalism," characterized by "subjectivism, voluntarism, and obscurantism." Soviet scholars argued that what would, and in fact did, emerge was a dictatorial system, the product of Maoist "demogogy," sustained and fostered by a "cult of personality," supplemented by the use of terror and control over the flow of information. All of this succeeded in confusing the "most backward section of the Chinese working class and...peasantry," enlisting them in the service of the aggressive and violent nationalism of "Great Han chauvinism."[12] We were told that what had transpired in China, with mass mobilization undertaken under the doctrinal auspices of a single, hegemonic party, with the economy and the population disciplined behind the charismatic leadership of an inerrant "Chairman," to pursue the ends of aggressive, irredentist nationalism, was "in no way different from fascism."[13]

By the time of Mao's death, it would seem, not only the economy, but the ideological rationale for a "communist" China, had been hopelessly compromised. Both domestic and foreign critics found fascism in its past institutions as well as its Maoist ideology, together with intimations of fascism in its emerging post-Maoist institutions as well as its post-Maoist ideology.

The study of the economics and politics of Communist China continued in this fitful and distracted fashion after the death of Mao. The very nature of the regime on the mainland of China became a central concern for Western scholars only after the Chinese Communist Party leadership itself denounced the Great Leap Forward and the Great Proletarian Cultural Revolution as "grave blunders," lamented the frequent purges within the party as "entirely wrong," and informed the nation that many of the policies rejected by Mao as "revisionist or capitalist" during his tenure "were actually Marxist and socialist."

[11] See the discussion in A. James Gregor, *A Survey of Marxism: Problems in Philosophy and the Theory of History* (New York: Random House, 1965), chaps. 5, 6.
[12] See the accounts provided in V. A. Krivtsov and V. Y. Sidikhmenov (eds.), *A Critique of Mao Tse-tung's Theoretical Conceptions* (Moscow: Progress, 1972), particularly pp. 8–9, 11, 27, 50–1, 63–4, 144–7, 212–13.
[13] A. Malukhin, *Militarism: Backbone of Maoism* (Moscow: Novosti Press Agency Publishing House, 1970), p. 33.

Westerners were told by Mao's successors that Mao Zedong had, in large part, misled the Chinese people. Failing to provide "a correct analysis of many problems, he confused right and wrong." While he "urged the whole party to study the works of Marx, Engels and Lenin...and imagined that his theory and practice were Marxist," his notions about Marxism were fundamentally in error. Therein, we were told at the time, "lies his tragedy."[14]

The Chinese leadership revealed that Mao had never really been a proper Marxist. He had misunderstood the theories of Marx, Engels, and Lenin. He had "divorced theory from practice." He was arbitrary, dogmatic, and willful in his interpretations. He became convinced of his own inerrancy. He sponsored a "cult of personality" through which he came to dominate Chinese life in its entirety. The consequence was "the over-concentration of Party power in individuals and for the development of arbitrary individual rule and the personality cult in the Party."[15]

By the time of Mao's disappearance into history, it really was no longer credible to speak of his revolution and his rule as "Marxist." The question was, how might Maoism be correctly depicted?

Many Westerners were uncertain as to what Maoism had been. Dedicated Maoists in the West were uncertain what Maoism was to become. Some of the most dedicated began to speak of the possible emergence of a "fascist China" out of the ruins of Maoism.[16] If Maoism had not been so before, post-Maoism gave every evidence of becoming "fascist." The great, liberating proletarian revolution that had been expected to uplift China – so much anticipated by so many in the West – had dissolved into great confusion. Some would argue that Maoism, as a Chinese socialism, had not really been defeated; it had never really been either Marxist or socialist.

The discussion concerning the relationship of fascism to Maoism has remained in that parlous state since the rise of a post-Maoist China. Some have been content to deal with developments in China as they might with any developing country – in the dynamic terms of the interaction of institutional structures and bureaucratic personalities.[17] Very few have ventured into the uncertain domain of comparative ideology.

For all that, the Chinese experience is instructive. While its long revolution has featured constituents that have been characterized as "fascist," the

---

[14] *Resolution on CPC History (1949–81)* (Beijing: Foreign Languages Press, 1981), pp. 17, 29–34, 41.

[15] Ibid., pp. 44–47.

[16] Charles Bettelheim, an American Maoist, saw the leadership of Communist China repudiating not only Maoism but Marxism as well. He anticipated the emergence of a "counterrevolutionary fascism" emerging from the post-Maoist reforms. See Neil Burton and Charles Bettelheim, *China Since Mao* (New York: Monthly Review Press, 1978), pp. 42, 73, 112.

[17] Typical of these is the excellent study by Kenneth Lieberthal and Michel Oksenberg, *Policy Making in China: Leaders, Structures, and Processes* (Princeton, NJ: Princeton University Press, 1988).

term is used without much discrimination. More often than not it is used simply to identify political dictatorship, political oppression, and economic dislocation.

For an extended period of time, the Kuomintang was spoken of as "fascist."[18] That continued until Kuomintang rule on the island of Taiwan transformed itself into an operative, competitive democracy in the 1980s and 1990s. Conversely, as the Kuomintang became the sponsor of Taiwanese democracy, the Communist Party on the mainland of China lapsed, over time and in a variety of circumstances, into what observers identified as "fascism." Again, the term was employed to refer to any system that could be described as dictatorial, irrational, obscurantist, brutal in one or another form, and given to the general exploitation of its subject population. The term, in effect, was generally used to convey a general and emphatic disapprobation. It was rarely advanced primarily as a cognitive distinction.

The unfortunate implication of such a strategy is that it brings in its train the view that the term "fascism" is appropriately employed only to apply to those political systems that are dictatorial, brutal and disposed to conflict. That is not particularly helpful. Many political systems, – not only those of the nineteenth and twentieth centuries, but almost all those of antiquity as well – could be so characterized. What all this is supposed to tell us about contemporary China or fascism is not immediately evident. The issue is too important to allow it to languish without further scrutiny. Interestingly enough, we have expert testimony from Fascist intellectuals themselves that has particular relevance concerning these issues.

In the early 1960s, Ugo Spirito, who had served Mussolini as one of his principal ideologues,[19] having survived the Second World War, was given the opportunity to visit Mao's China. On his return he produced a number of essays that, taken together with some of his earlier thoughts, bear on the issue of a Chinese fascism. Particularly pertinent is his substantial essay on "Chinese Communism."[20]

Spirito found much to admire in Mao's China. Almost immediately, the reasons for his admiration become apparent.

Spirito argued that Chinese communism fundamentally distinguished itself from the communism with which the West had become familiar. Communism in Europe, he argued, was the product of Western thought. It was a byproduct of Enlightenment liberalism. Its principal focus, and its ultimate purpose, was the material well-being of the individual. Its characteristic

---

[18] For a treatment of the scholarship devoted to the identification of Chiang Kaishek's Kuomintang as fascist, see Maria Hsia Chang, *The Chinese Blue Shirt Society: Fascism and Developmental Nationalism* (Berkeley, CA: Center for Chinese Studies, 1985).

[19] See A. James Gregor, *Mussolini's Intellectuals: Fascist Social and Political Thought* (Princeton, NJ: Princeton University Press, 2005), particularly chaps. 5, 6.

[20] Ugo Spirito, "Comunismo russo e comunismo cinese," *Il comunismo* (Florence: Biblioteca Sansoni, 1965), pp. 225–67.

strategy and corresponding tactics were essentially and invariably reformist – meliorative.[21]

The communism found in the Western nations, Spirito reminded his readers, was predicated on and nurtured with an irrepressible individualism – a kind of philosophical narcissism that found life's ultimate purpose exclusively in the pursuit of personal happiness. Spirito saw that as unworthy of human beings, individually or collectively.

None of that was the case, in his judgment, in the People's Republic of China. There, the sociophilosophical ideal was that the individual could succeed to happiness only in the company of others – if all could achieve it as well. Happiness could not be attained in isolation, or at the expense of others, and could not be realized if others were somehow excluded from its pursuit.[22]

In that sense, Spirito argued, the communism of Mao and of China was a different kind of communism than the communism with which Europeans had grown familiar. Chinese communism was nationalistic in inspiration. Its nationalism was born of humiliations suffered because of the pretense of foreigners. It was productivistic, as all reactive nationalisms must be in those less-developed communities suffering depredations at the hands of others.[23] We were reminded of the logic of revolution made manifest in the twentieth century.

It was particularly significant for Spirito that Chinese communism found expression in agricultural communes and collectively owned and operated enterprise. In those institutions, he argued, the private blurred into the public. It was within those institutions that persons were taught to appreciate that the "collectivity enjoyed priority over the individual. . . . [and that] it is necessary that the individual subordinate himself to that life which is social. To think together, act in concert, and share life in unity." To live otherwise, Spirito informed his readers, would be incomprehensible in Mao's China.[24] What Spirito found in revolutionary China was familiar to him. It echoed things he had come to know in Fascist Italy.

As in Mussolini's Italy, Spirito found a urgent sense of community in communist China, a pervasive sense of discipline, order, and sacrifice that arose out of a common faith and a sense of necessity dictated by past indignities and the present threat of enemies within and without. Under the "attentive control of the regime," Spirito wrote, the opinions of the individual serve only to "support the merits of collective decisions once taken."[25]

---

[21] Spirito was particularly distainful of European communism. See his discussion in Ugo Spirito, *La fine del comunismo* (Rome: Volpe, 1978).

[22] See the discussion in Spinto, *Il comunismo*, pp. 225–8.

[23] Ibid., pp. 246–8, 264–5.

[24] Ibid., pp. 240, 248–9.

[25] Ibid., pp. 254, 258, 260–1.

In a reformulation of an argument with which he had been long familiar, Spirito insisted that the arrangements found in Mao's China were neither tyrannical nor despotic. What Westerners fail to understand, he argued, is that tyranny and despotism are possible only when conduct is imposed on persons, not when they voluntarily lend their consent to it. When a person chooses to be a Christian, and submits to Christianity's regimen, he or she is not imposed upon. One obeys one's conscience. One acts in liberty.

This is possible, Spirito argued, because one is, in a fundamental sense, the product of one's life circumstances. One is fashioned by one's family, by one's peers, by one's education, and by a thousand silent influences, all bound together by principles of reason learned at the same sources. One's tastes, one's preferences, and one's morals are all the complex products of that education that begins at birth in a community – and that never ends. Everything that we count as "personal," particularly "individual," is a function of life lived in an intricate web of social interactions. When all these interconnected, if occult, influences mutually reinforce each other, we find individuals who are unequivocally "collective beings." In that most profound sense, the individual becomes the community – the particular merges, without remainder, into the universal.[26]

What Spirito outlined in his discussion of Mao's China is the rationale for totalitarianism. For Fascists, the concept had only superficial resemblance to that bruited about and debated by academicians during the Cold War. For Fascists, the concept found its full expression in the works of Giovanni Gentile,[27] the author of the philosophical portion of the official *Doctrine of Fascism*, which served as justificatory foundation of Fascist practice.

In the "Fundamental Ideas" of the *Doctrine*, in the section that provides the normative grounds for Fascist political conduct, Gentile wrote:

For Fascists...the human being is not a separate, self-sufficient being independent from all others, governed by a natural law that instinctively renders him disposed to live a life of egoistic and fleeting pleasure.... Fascism is an historical conception that conceives individuals the result of their functional role in a family and social group, in the nation and in history.... Fascism is opposed to all abstract individualism....[28]

Under Fascism, as under Maoism, the individual can attain full humanity only in an organic, articulated community. Conceiving the individual in such fashion, both Fascism and Maoism opposed that political and economic liberalism that pretended that society was an aggregate of individuals, each

---

[26] Spirito, "Il totalitarismo," in *La filosofia del comunismo* (Florence: C. C. Sansoni Editore, 1948), pp. 33–65.

[27] For an account of Gentile's Actualism, see A. James Gregor, *Giovanni Gentile: Philosopher of Fascism* (Transaction: New Brunswick, NJ, 2001).

[28] Benito Mussolini, *Dottrina del fascismo*, in *Opera omnia* (Florence: La fenice, 1965), 34, pp. 118–119. Although the "Fundamental Ideas" were written by Gentile, they appeared over Mussolini's name, making them formally part of the ideological rationale of Fascism.

moved by his or her own interests and desires, given to cooperation only as a consequence of self-interest or coercion.

In opposition, both Fascism and Maoism portrayed themselves as a special form of "democracy" in which individuals spontaneously identified with the community to which they were inextricably bound. Without contrived distinctions, the natural organicity of communities would find expression in the identification of individuals with each other and of all with the community. Together, they would share sentiment, preferences, convictions, and aspirations. So constituted, the individuals who are members of such an organic community would identify with others, and find full representation in a single spokesperson – a leader who could speak for all.

For both Fascists and Maoists, living individuals – not the "abstractions" of liberal social theory – find their reality in "organic," concrete, historical communities. In that reality – united in national communion – they find their liberty as well.[29] When the community is free of oppression and exploitation, no longer subject to the economic, cultural, political, or military impostures of foreigners, the individual, no longer servile in any sense, enjoys not only true freedom, but a genuinely "spiritual" and "ethical" life. Multitudes, united by an idea that expresses a collective will to existence and empowerment, constitute in their solidarity a historic personality – in which the individual finds his or her true self.[30]

The detailed presentation of this conception of totalitarianism is found in Gentile's major political and philosophical works,[31] and finds its echo in Spirito's analysis of the political circumstances in Mao's China. To complete the outline, one must reference the role of the state in such a rendering. For Fascists, the state is the conscious will of the organic, historic community. It is the political state that is at the epicenter of all the constituent associations, groups, syndicates, federations, and related collectivities – and it is doctrine that provides its ethical substance.[32]

Doctrine, for both Fascists and Maoists, emerges out of historic circumstances – what Mao called "concrete conditions" – mediated by rare individuals, endowed with intellectual and spiritual integrity, who see further

---

[29] In the "Fundamental Ideas" of the *Doctrine of Fascism*, Gentile specifically states that while those who make up nations share "ethnic" affinities, those affinities are *not racial*. "Ethnicity," for Gentile, refers to a shared history, and a common sense of collective destiny. Ibid., p. 120.

[30] Ibid., pp. 119–20.

[31] The most readily available account of Gentile's social and political philosophy is to be found in the English translation of his last work as Giovanni Gentile, *Genesis and Structure of Society* (Urbana, IL: University of Illinois Press, 1960).

[32] "The ethical state of Giovanni Gentile, with its idealism, was the indispensable core of corporativism. . . . The idealism of Gentile was the life-blood that permitted the realization of a new order that made citizens aware that they were not simply economic, but social creatures as well, concerned more with others than themselves." Anthony Galatoli Landi, *Mussolini e la rivoluzione sociale* (Rome: ISC, n.d.), pp. 86–7.

and with greater precision than others. They, and those who follow them, are tested by time and challenged by events. They become the historic figures spoken of by Hegel and Emerson, and alluded to by Marx when he spoke of those few who constitute "the most advanced and resolute section" of revolutionaries that "pushes forward all others," because it enjoys the "advantage of clearly understanding the line of march, the conditions, and the ultimate general results of the...movement."[33]

Spirito called attention to this legacy in speaking of the ideology that sustained Maoist China's political system. He spoke of the "affinities" shared by Hegel and Marx, and of the elements of Fascist totalitarianism to be found there.[34] He spoke of the role of a self-conscious minority, identified with the community, infusing masses with a conscious faith in order to meet the needs of the revolution.[35]

In speaking of the Chinese political system, Spirito specifically cited those features of minority rule and the attendant guidance of masses through the use of slogans, enjoinments, and control over the flow of information – features with which he was most familiar.[36] Together with its antiliberalism and anti-individualism, it seems clear that Spirito found the political culture of Communist China reminiscent of Fascist Italy. Like Fascism, Maoism refused to entertain the notion that individuals be allowed, under any circumstances, to compromise the unity, integrity, and discipline of the community. To accomplish the historic tasks that time and circumstances had imposed on their nation, individuals were to identify themselves with that historic community, their lives and their interests inextricably fused with that of their compatriots.[37]

The concept of "totalitarianism" that emerges in Spirito's discussion of Communist China is substantially different from the concept that occupied the attention of scholars during the years after the Second World War. Both Fascists and liberals were agreed on the institutional features of totalitarianism: presence in the system of the charismatic leader, the formal ideology, the dominant single party, the near monopoly control of information, the extensive intervention of the state into the economy, and the infrastructure of surveillance.[38]

33 Karl Marx and Friedrich Engels, *The Communist Manifesto* (New York: Monthly Review Press, 1998), pp. 25–6.

34 See Spirito's discussion in Ugo Spirito, *Critica della democrazia* (Florence: Sansoni, 1963), particularly pp. 18–46.

35 Spirito, *La filosofia del comunismo*, pp. 12–13, 20.

36 Spirito, "Comunismo russo e comunismo cinese," in *Il comunismo*, p. 262.

37 See the discussion in Spirito, "Dall'economia liberale al corporativismo: Critica dell'economia liberale (1938 revised edition of 1930)," and the entire section identified as "L'identificazione di individuo e stato," in "I fondamenti dell'economia corporativa (1936)," all in *Il corporativismo* (Florence: Sansoni, 1970), pp. 78–79, 195–208.

38 See the account in Leonard Schapiro, *Totalitarianism* (New York: Praeger, 1972), chap. 2. Compare this with the Fascist understanding of "totalitarianism," found, for example,

Granted that, the differences between Fascists, Maoists, and liberals are instructive. For liberal academics, the term "totalitarianism" refers, by and large, to institutional features of a class of nondemocratic political systems calculated to deny individuals their civil and human rights. For Fascists, while they acknowledged that the term "totalitarianism" referred to a set of institutions, they denied that those institutions were designed to deny individuals their liberty. They argued that in order to understand that, one would have to consider the worldview or the set of sociophilosophical presuppositions that informed both systems. Unlike philosophical liberals, both Fascists and Maoists held sociophilosophical presuppositions that provided the basis of the argument that envisioned the state, the conscious will of the community, as the central agency promoting and sustaining human individuation – in the existential process of making self-conscious human beings. As such, the state had not only a pragmatic but a moral concern with everything that transpired within its confines.[39] None of that implied that the state was morally obliged, or disposed, to intervene in everything that transpired within its confines, but the rationale provided the moral ground for just that eventuality should intervention be deemed necessary.

What is notable in considering all this is the fact that the Maoist rationale for state intervention in all aspects of the lives of the citizens of the People's Republic shares the informal logic of Mussolini's *Dottrina del fascismo*. Like Fascism, Maoism is rooted in Marxist concepts that saw human beings as "group animals,"[40] entirely capable of finding their individual interests fulfilled in those of the community. In the Marxist case, the community was a class, the proletariat. That conviction supplied the logic at the core of the Maoist rationale for the omnicompetent party and/or the omnicompetent leader provisioned to speak for all members of the community. Given the logic of what was basically a Hegelian argument, one person was equipped by history to speak for all members of the community.

Conversely, philosophic, political, and economic liberalism conceives the state a necessary evil – to perform only those functions that exceed the capacity of the individual. Individual freedom, for liberals, means essentially freedom from interference. Fascists and Maoists see the individual identified with the community, and what the state does is what the individual would do if possessed of universal right reason. Totalitarianism rests on that

in Sergio Panunzio, *Teoria generale dello stato fascista* (Padua: CEDAM, 1939), pp. 452–64. See the more general account in Guido Bortolotto, *Die Revolution der jungen Völker: Faschismus und Nationalsozialismus* (Berlin: R. Kittlers Verlag, 1934), pp. 111–14.

[39] See the account offered by Gentile: "The state [as the will of the integral community] includes, unifies, and fulfills every human activity, every form or element of human nature; so that every concept of the state that omits some element of human nature is inadequate." Gentile, *Genesis and Structure of Society*, p. 135. See ibid., chap. 6.

[40] See the discussion in Karl Marx, *Economic and Philosophic Manuscripts* (Moscow: Foreign Languages Press, n.d.), pp. 109–14, 145–9.

fundamental postulate. Sharing a rationale built around that postulate as a
Hegelian inheritance, Maoism and Fascism were both totalitarianisms.

For the leadership of the People's Republic of China, to this day, "bourgeois liberalism" has remained one of the principal sources of "ideological
pollution." Like Fascists, both Maoists and post-Maoists see philosophic and
political liberalism as a threat to unity and discipline. Like Fascists, the leaders of post-Maoist China understand both to be absolutely essential to any
program of economic growth and industrial expansion. And, like Fascists,
the leaders of post-Maoist China recognize that economic growth together
with industrial expansion and sophistication is critical to the military defense
and status of the nation.[41]

When one focuses on the normative logic that sustains both antiliberal systems, one immediately understands why Ugo Spirito, an Actualist and one of
Fascist Italy's foremost spokespersons, might find the political environment
in Maoist China, not to speak of post-Maoist China, in some fundamental
sense appealing. It is clear that for their advocates, the specific institutions
that characterize one or another totalitarian system are less important for
analysis than the underlying rationale advanced to vindicate them.

Thus, Spirito refers to Mao's communes and the absence of private property as evidence of Maoism's totalitarianism. In the post-Maoist period, the
communes have been abandoned and some of the rights of private property
have resurfaced in Communist China. Other "rights" and "liberties" have
made their appearance. As a consequence, China is now rarely spoken of
as "totalitarian." One of the more favored portrayals is to see China as a
"fractured authoritarianism."[42] There is regular, if somewhat awkward, talk
of the development of a "civil society" in post-Maoist China.

What "civil society" is understood to imply varies with each author. It is
often taken to mean some sort of independent sector that exists somehow
between the political state and the market. For Hegel, the term referred
to that collection of individuals, characteristically withdrawn from their
community, whose interests, necessarily partial and selfish, were pursued
outside the governance of the society.[43] For Marxists, the term referred to
those circumstances in which individuals, because of the existence of private
property, pursued their selfish, rather than community, purposes. As members of civil society, they fail to appreciate that "their true freedom consists
in the acceptance of principles" that foster and sustain the "synthesis of

---

[41] See, for example, the injunctions of Deng Xiaoping, "Bourgeois Liberalization Means Taking
the Capitalist Road," *Selected Works of Deng Xiaoping* (Beijing: Foreign Languages Press,
1994), 3, pp. 129–30.

[42] See Kenneth G. Lieberthal, "The 'Fragmented Authoritiarianism' Model and Its Limitations," in Kenneth G. Lieberthal and David M. Lampton (eds.), *Bureaucacy, Politics, and
Decision Making in Post-Mao China* (Berkeley, CA: University of California Press, 1992),
pp. 1–30.

[43] See G. W. F. Hegel, *The Philosophy of Right* (Oxford, UK: Oxford University Press, 1977).

universal and particular interests" that make up a truly human social order. In a truly human community, the egotism of civil society would no longer be possible.[44]

The logic, once again, is familiar. Fascist revolutionaries, most of whom had received their initial political training as Marxists, made the same case for totalitarianism. That the logic remains binding is evidenced by the fact that although some practical "liberalization" has taken place in post-Maoist China, the polity remains more than simply "authoritarian." It is a liberalization that reaffirms the central logic of totalitarianism. Much of the discussion of the liberalization of China, deals with the decentralization of economic and political control and the abandonment of central planning. In their effort to rescue the nation's economy from total collapse after the passing of Mao, the post-Maoist leadership in China appealed to market modalities in order to restore some rationality to the nation's price structure.[45] Given the need for local decision making, the necessity of dealing with government and party agencies, together with the exigencies that attend supply and demand, citizen and business associations began to make their appearance throughout the system. Some Sinologists saw those associations as the rudiments of an emerging civil society.

The presence of civil society is generally seen as necessary, if not sufficient, for the existence of a truly liberal and democratic polity. Given what is taken to be a fledgling civil society, Communist China is sometimes seen as entering a transition that will take it from the totalitarian and dictatorial system of Maoism to a democracy distinguished only by some Chinese characteristics.

Many specialists remain unconvinced. Many point to the associations created in response to the reforms on the Chinese mainland as bodies that must not only be officially sponsored, but which the government employs as instruments of policy and control. The new citizens' and business associations that have arisen enjoy only limited autonomy. In general, Communist Party officials tend to be patronizing concerning these associations, viewing them largely as adjuncts to the party's complex control apparatus.[46]

Circumstances in Fascist Italy were analytically similar. Both society and the economy featured a multiplicity of organizations ranging from church and educational groups to relatively formal entrepreneurial and workers' associations. The autonomy of all was systematically compromised by the physical presence of party representatives or organizational ties to

---

[44] See the "Editor's Introduction" to Karl Marx and Friedrich Engels, *The German Ideology* (New York: International Publishers, 1988), pp. 5–11.

[45] See Maria Hsia Chang, *The Labors of Sisyphus: The Economic Development of Communist China* (New Brunswick, NJ: Transaction, 1998), chaps. 5, 6.

[46] Bruce J. Dickson, *Red Capitalists in China: The Party, Private Entrepreneurs, and Prospects for Political Change* (New York: Cambridge University Press, 2003), pp. 72–83; J. Unger, "'Bridges': Private Business, the Chinese Government and the Rise of New Associations," *China Quarterly*, no. 147 (September 1996), pp. 795–819.

corporative federations or confederations. By the time the Fascist regime had attained full maturity, the political and economic landscape was clogged with citizens' groups and business associations all linked to the central government by a wide array of state, semistate, parastate, and ad hoc entities that made manifest the totalitarian impulse of the system.[47]

Totalitarianism can take on a variety of institutional embodiments. What is important for the present discussion is to recognize its fundamentally anti-individualistic and antiliberal rationale, which, in China, manifests itself in principled opposition to any form of western representative democracy.[48] In the People's Republic, in the final analysis, it is the government that holds sway over the behavior of all constituents of the national community, and it is "the [Communist] party [that] exercises leadership over the government,"[49] producing a totalitarianism with Chinese characteristics.

In Fascist Italy, the configuration of control was different. The Fascist revolution had inherited a state structure from the precedent liberal regime, and the nationalist movement that inspired much of Fascist ideology made the state the very linchpin of the nation. In the last analysis, however, the state in Fascist Italy, via a series of substitutions, fell under the real or potential control of the party. The Grand Council of Fascism and the Central Corporative Council, whose respective agendas were dominated by Mussolini, head of the government and leader of the Partito nazionale fascista, could intrude into the political and economic life of the nation at any time,[50] producing a totalitarianism with Italian characteristics.

In both contemporary China and Fascist Italy, citizens could operate with considerable independence within a range of activities that did not impinge on the state's prerogatives as established by the unitary party. In both systems, the ownership of private property is or was conditional, always qualified with the proviso that its use forever remain subordinate to the superior interests of the community.[51] In both systems there are or were associations of citizens

---

[47] See the account in Giulio Scagnetti, *Gli enti di privilegio nell'economia corporativa italiana* (Padua: CEDAM, 1942).

[48] See Deng Xiaoping, "Bourgeois Liberalization Means Taking the Capitalist Road," and "Address to Officers at the Rank of General and Above in Command of the Troops Enforcing Martial Law in Beijing," in *Selected Works* (Beijing: Foreign Languages Press, 1994), 3, pp. 129–30, 294–9.

[49] Deng Xiaoping, "Help the People Understand the Importance of the Rule of Law," ibid., 3, p. 167.

[50] Gregor, *Mussolini's Intellectuals*, pp. 162–3.

[51] See the qualifications governing the use of private property as they appear in *La carta del lavoro* (with a commentary by Giuseppe Bottai), (Rome: Diritto del lavoro, 1928), paras. I, II, IV, VII, IX. The general considerations were regularly affirmed as "the individualistic conception of private property has been eclipsed; property no longer is an instrument to be used by the individual in his own egoistic service.... Fascist doctrine entirely overthrows the individualistic conception [of private property]. Under Fascism, the ownership of property assumes a social function and a corresponding responsibility.... The private organization

that pursued parochial interests, but always under the supervision of the state in what is aptly described as a "state-corporatist" arrangement – an array of overlapping interventions into the activities of subject groups that involved everything from official sponsorship, the withdrawal of support, to punitive sanctions.[52] In both systems, public law – while much to be recommended when compared to law in National Socialist Germany, Stalin's Soviet Union, or Mao's China – still invariably represented or represents the will of the state or the party.[53]

In totalitarian polities, the rationale by virtue of which citizen rights are extended and/or amended is invariably presented as inerrant. The system's supporting grounds are advanced in the form of a set of mutually reinforcing empirical or logical truths. However variable and "dialectical" that set might be over time, the pretense is that the system-sustaining ideology is unalterable and commanding, a constellation of beliefs that the individual is expected to accept without reservation.[54] Once the sociophilosophic grounds legitimating the system are accepted as impeccable, the leader speaks with the voice of truth, and his enjoinments become binding on all.[55] For Fascists, all this found expression in the insistence that "Mussolini is always right," and for Maoists, that "Mao Zedong's thought [is] the greatest truth ever known since time immemorial. . . . to be put in command of everything."[56]

The informal logic of these systems is evident. Totalitarianism is the end result of a series of entailments: Human beings are group animals; a

of production is undertaken in the national interest . . . and those who engage in production remain responsible to the state." Franco Angelini, "Prefazione," in *La concezione fascista della proprietà privata* (Rome: Confederazione fascista dei laboratori dell'agricoltura, 1939), pp. 17, 31, 35.

[52] Gordon White, "Prospects for Civil Society in China: A Case Study of Xiaoshan City," *Australian Journal of Chinese Affairs*, no. 29 (January 1993), pp. 63–87. See also Dickson, *Red Capitalists in China*, pp. 23–8, 61–9.

[53] See the discussion in Maria Hsia Chang, *The End of Days: Falun Gong* (New Haven, CT: Yale University Press, 2004), chaps. 4, 5.

[54] In this context, see the comments of Fang Lizhi, a prodemocracy dissident in post-Maoist China. Fang Lizhi, "A Natural Scientist Views the Reforms," and "Democracy, Reform, and Modernization," in *Bringing Down the Great Wall: Writings on Science, Culture, and Democracy in China* (New York: Alfred A. Knopf, 1991), pp. 126–34, 157–88.

[55] See the discussion in A. James Gregor, "Fascism, Marxism and Some Considerations Concerning Classification," *Totalitarian Movements and Political Religions* 3, no. 2 (Autumn 2002), pp. 61–82.

[56] "Long Live the Great Proletarian Cultural Revolution," Editorial, *Hongqi*, no. 8, 1966, and "Mao Tse-tung's Thought is the Telescope and Microscope of Our Revolutionary Cause," Editorial, *Jiefangjun Bao*, 7 June 1966, reprinted in *On the Great Socialist Cultural Revolution in China*, 4, p. 13; 3, p. 11. "Mao Zedong's thought is an ideological weapon of unlimited revolutionary force which makes all monsters tremble with fright. . . . Armed with Mao Zedong's thought, the Chinese people are invincible." Yao Wen-yuan, "On 'Three-Family Village,'" and Chi Pen-yu, "On the Bourgeois Stand of *Frontline* and the *Peking Daily*," in ibid., 1, p. 48; 2, p. 65.

community shares a common interest; a doctrine that provides a true account
of that collective interest speaks in the interest of all; and any person or group
of persons possessed of that true account speaks with the voice and in the
ultimate interest of all, possessing, thereby, the moral authority to command
allegiance. The logic is familiar. It is a variant of Hegelianism, and is to be
found in the public defense of Stalinism, Fascism, and Maoism, together with
all their varieties.[57]

Post-Maoist China has been loathe to abandon "Mao Zedong Thought,"
however much it laments its errors. The "Four Cardinal Principles" that
inform the political governance of post-Maoist China include the injunction
that the nation submit to the rule of "Mao Zedong Thought."[58] Once "Mao
Zedong Thought" becomes the impeccable truth of the system, the vanguard
party and the charismatic (or pseudocharismatic) leader have their warrant
to rule, and the totalitarian system is grounded.

For the purposes of the present discussion, the term "totalitarian" refers
to any polity that legitimizes state intervention in the lives of citizens whenever the state itself deems such intervention necessary. It is the fact that the
system has a legitimation to which it can appeal that makes totalitarianism distinctive. More than that, the legitimating ideology of totalitarianism
affirms that obedience to the state is essential to the fulfillment of the individual self. More important than all that, perhaps, is the fact that contemporary
technology allows the state to pursue the individual virtually everywhere and
anywhere should that be considered necessary. There are no longer private
places than can serve as sanctuary.

The checks and balances familiar in liberal democratic systems is characteristically absent in totalitarian polities. Deng Xiaoping, for his part, explicitly rejected such a protection for citizen rights in post-Maoist China, and did
not hesitate to insist that a truly revolutionary system "cannot do without
dictatorship."[59]

Within totalitarianisms, the political arrangements are, in principle, fundamentally antidemocratic and antiliberal. Totalitarianism may accommodate a variety of institutional forms, some more enabling and "open" than
others – the consequence of tactical responses to external demands or internal exigencies – but the system that results can hardly be described as democratic in any sense recognizable to Westerners. The variant cases, those less

---

[57] See the discussion in A. James Gregor, *Contemporary Radical Ideologies: Totalitarian
Thought in the Twentieth Century* (New York: Random House, 1968), chap. 1.

[58] As Deng stated in an interview on 2 September 1986, "Mao Zedong Thought Is Still Our
Guiding Ideology." Deng Xiaoping, "Replies to the American TV Correspondent Mike Wallace," *Selected Works*, 3, p. 176.

[59] Deng, irrespective of his revolutionary intention to transform post-Maoist China, refused
to countenance any possibility of a "Western system" of "checks and balances" within the
political system, because the possibility of any such restraints would negatively impact the
party's ability to "exercise leadership." Deng, "On Reform of the Political Structure," "Take
a Clear-Cut Stand Against Bourgeois Liberalization," ibid., 3, pp. 178–9, 194–5.

permissive, may be spoken of as "totalistic," and those more permissive as "administered," or "fragmented authoritarian" societies. Whatever the differences, the system's core remains totalitarian.

A variety of systems in the twentieth century would seem to qualify as totalitarian. The products of various times and circumstances, they have all been different in a variety of ways, but all remain totalitarian in the sense indicated. They all accord primacy to the community and/or its agent, and understand individuals to be, in some significant sense, derivative products of community life.

Other than the fact that Communist China and Fascist Italy shared, and share, some discernable ideological similarities, what is perhaps of more interest in the present context is the fact that both Maoist and post-Maoist China share some of the central program imperatives of Fascism, in that Mao and the post-Maoists have committed the nation to rapid economic growth and industrial development. Just as Mussolini made agricultural and industrial production one of the major policy goals of the system, China's Maoists and post-Maoists have pursued the same ends.

Fascists insisted that anything that negatively impacted production weakened the nation in a Darwinian world of threatening "plutocratic" powers – a thesis argued not only by Mao but even more emphatically by his heirs.[60] The reasons for such a posture are not difficult to understand.

The revolutions of the twentieth century were largely undertaken by communities that were economically retrograde. To achieve the status they sought, and to create a military capable of defending that status once attained, the communities needed rapid economic and industrial development.

Once convinced of the necessity of such a program, the communities had to meet its collateral conditions, which included the inculcation of a work and sacrifice ethic among the masses. Fascist Italy, Mao's China, and post-Maoist China all sought or seek to instill in their peoples an abiding sense of unity, discipline, and self-sacrifice in the effort to initiate and sustain rapid economic development in a retrograde, capital-poor, but labor-rich environment.

Virtue becomes a central theme in such systems. There is a constant emphasis on frugality, selflessness, labor, diligence, cooperation, and obedience – all particularly instrumental in the development and deepening of an

---

[60] See Gregor, *Mussolini's Intellectuals*, chaps. 2, 3, 4; and the comments by Galatoli Landi, *Mussolini e la rivoluzione sociale*, p. 180. Similar statements recur in the writings of Mao and Deng. See, for example, Deng, "We are Building a Socialist Society with Both High Material Standards and High Cultural and Ethical Standards," "Building a Socialism with a Specifically Chinese Character," "The Army Should Subordinate Itself to the General Interest, Which Is to Develop the Country," "The Reform of the System for Managing Science and Technology Is Designed to Liberate the Productive Forces," "Unity Depends on Ideals and Discipline," "We Shall Expand Political Democracy and Carry Out Economic Reform," *Selected Works*, 3, pp. 38, 75, 105, 115–17, 121, and passim.

industrial system under conditions of capital scarcity. "Rational low wages" typify such systems, in which capital is extracted from peasants and workers in order to fuel the growth plans of the revolutionary state.

None of this is particularly difficult to understand. What is more relevant to our purposes is to reflect on how a "Marxist" system such as that of Communist China should come to share so many similarities with a presumably anti-Marxist Fascism.

Because of the long tradition of conceiving Fascism to have been of the "right," there has been a systematic neglect of its intellectual patrimony. The fact is that Mussolini, and many of the most important intellectuals who made up the first Fascism were knowledgeable and influential Marxists. Before, during, and after the First World War, they individually and collectively sought to revise traditional Marxism to better conform to the realities of their time and circumstances. They proceeded to undertake the "revolutionary amendments" of the inherited doctrines advocated by Mussolini in the years immediately preceding the war.[61] Those who survived the carnage of the war went on to collect themselves around a "heretical" Mussolini to form the first Fascism.[62]

One of the critical factors that influenced policy construction among the first Fascists was the painfully evident failure of the Bolshevik experiment in Russia. At the time that emergent Fascism was putting together its revolutionary belief system, not only had Russia suffered an all but total collapse of its economy, but Lenin appeared to lack any plan for its rehabilitation. Bolshevism gave every evidence of being totally incompetent to carry its revolution to anything but a disastrous conclusion. Not only did the economy unravel, the immediate aftermath of the revolution brought famine to millions of Russians. Lenin became so desperate that he embarked on the New Economic policy (NEP) that saw the ad hoc restoration of some of the critical features of capitalism, including the reappearance of a commodity market and the private ownership of property.

The Fascists were not alone in condemning the failed experiment. Some of Italy's most accomplished economists, including Vilfredo Pareto and Maffeo Pantaleoni, pointed out the failure of Marxism to provide even the rudiments of an economic system for an underdeveloped economy.[63]

---

[61] See Mussolini's comments in the opening editorial of his journal devoted to "revolutionary socialism," "Al largo!" *Utopia* 1, no. 1 (22 November 1913), pp. 1–4.

[62] See the more extensive account in A. James Gregor, *Young Mussolini and the Intellectual Origins of Fascism* (Los Angeles: University of California Press, 1979).

[63] See Pantaleoni's preface in Maffeo Pantaleoni, *Bolcevismo italiano* (Bari: Gius, Laterza, and Figli, 1922), in a work in which he applauded the Fascists for rejecting Marxism-Bolshevism as offering a viable economic system. See also Luigi Montini, *Vilfredo Pareto e il fascismo* (Rome: Volpe, 1974). In 1920, Pareto warned that the imposition of Marxism on the Russian economy might well be a harbinger of a new Middle Ages. He advocated, instead, an investment in a program of economic stimulation. Ibid., pp. 119–120.

What had transpired was evident to anyone who chose to consider dispassionately the intellectual history of classical Marxism. The nineteenth-century thought of Karl Marx and Friedrich Engels was addressed almost exclusively to well-developed industrial systems – those distinguished by heavy rates of capital investment, high measures of concentration, and a population composed of proletarians in its "vast majority" – none of which applied to either postczarist Russia or post–World War I Italy.

Fascists argued that since the requisite conditions for a "socialist revolution" did not prevail, it would be suicidal for an economically backward nation to attempt its undertaking. What was really required for nations languishing in underdevelopment was to embark on a program of accelerated economic growth and industrial development. That arduous task required national unity, a recognition by all classes, sectors, factions, and parochial interests that only through a disciplined solidarity might the nation survive and prosper. Italy did not require a revolution that would provide for the pretended distribution of the nonexistent abundance of an advanced industrial system. What it required was the systematic and expeditious expansion of its productive forces. At the time, the Fascist position was apprized as apostasy by Marxists, and willingly acknowledged as heresy by Fascists. It was within those intellectual parameters that the first Fascism fabricated its program.

After Mao's death, the Chinese communist leadership decided that he, like Lenin in another time, had in fact impaired the nation's agricultural and industrial growth. The decision was made to embark on a program of "modernization" that turned on the abandonment of some of the more dysfunctional distributionistic policies of the past in order to commit the nation to a program involving the rapid development of the productive base. Deng Xiaoping was candid in describing the fundamental post-Maoist economic reforms he sought to impose on China. Taken together, the reforms constituted Communist China's NEP.

In referring to the plans outlining those systemic reforms at the Third Plenary Session of the Central Advisory Commission of the Communist Party of China in October 1984, Deng said that the document on the reform was a "good one, because it explains what socialism is in terms never used by the founders of Marxism-Leninism. There are some new theories.... We could never have drawn up such a document without the experience of the last few years. And even if it had been produced, it would have been very hard to get it adopted – it would have been regarded as heresy."[64] Deng had discovered what Fascists had divined six decades earlier. Marxism, in whatever variant, was totally unsuited for the development of a retrograde economy. Classical Marxism was an ideology designed for a postindustrial revolution.

[64] Deng, "Speech at the Third Plenary Session of the Central Advisory Commission of the Communist Party of China," *Selected Works*, 3, pp. 97–8.

What retrograde China required was a program for rapid economic and industrial growth. Deng proposed just such a program. The result was what Deng correctly identified as a "revolution." It was a revolutionary program that shared fundamental similarities – given all the differences in scale and circumstance – with that of the Fascism that emerged out of the First World War, and sought the industrialization of the Italian peninsula.

In August 1993, the Communist Party of China spoke of "Deng Xiao-ping's theory" as the "fountainhead for realizing China's socialist modern-ization." Between the late 1970s and the 1990s, much if not all of Maoist economic policy had been swept aside. In a specific sense, Dengism was a return to classical Marxism – at least insofar as Deng was prepared to acknowledge the primacy of the role of the nation's productive forces in its future. It had been Marx who had insisted that it was "the multitude of pro-ductive forces accessible to men" that determined the nature of the society in which they dwelt. And it was Marx who had insisted that successful commu-nist revolution could follow only the fullest development of the productive forces.[65]

Dengism, like Fascism, is perhaps best understood as a Marxist heresy. It has sought to make revolution in an environment unripe for socialism. Like Fascism, post-Maoist China has assumed responsibilities that classical Marx-ism had assigned not to the working class, but to the entrepreneurial national bourgeoisie. As a consequence, by the turn of the twenty-first century, the Communist Party of China was inviting members of the entrepreneurial bourgeois to join the "party of the proletariat," and had extended to the entire possessing class constitutional protection for their property and profits.

All the features of accommodation with the "capitalist class" that pro-voked scorn from leftist critics when undertaken by Fascism are now to be found in the "Marxist-Leninist" system of post-Maoist China. It is a per-fectly comprehensible response to the realities of less-developed countries in a world environment dominated by competitors that are fully, and sometimes more than fully, industrialized.

Challenged by some of the same threats as those directed against Italy during the first quarter of the twentieth century, China, in the twenty-first, displays some of the other criterial properties of "antiplutocratic" Fascism. Like Mussolini's Fascism, post-Maoist China has insisted on its irredentism. It has meticulously identified all the "lost territories" wrested from China during the "century of humiliation" by the "plutocratic powers."

Everyone in China – party members, functionaries, intellectuals, and sim-ple citizens – will recount, with the least provocation, the humiliations suf-fered by their nation at the hands of foreign powers throughout the nine-teenth and the beginning of the twentieth centuries. The most humiliating

---

[65] Marx and Engels, *The German Ideology*, pp. 42–3, 56.

among a host of humiliations was the loss of Chinese territory. At one time, China's effective control extended over Outer Mongolia, Tibet, and, at times, Korea, the Ryukyu islands, and northern Vietnam. Tributary states included those as far away as Ukraine, Iraq, Iran, and Burma. "Voluntary" subjects of imperial China encompassed Taiwan, Laos, Benghal, Bhutan, and Nepal.

At one time, all the extent of what is now counted as the Russian Far East was Chinese territory. Chinese authors consider western Siberia, the Altay Mountains, Lake Baikal, and the Yenisey River as features of "lost Chinese territories." Beijing similarly identifies the Diaoyutai/Sengaku islands off the Japanese home islands as such. In the southeast, Chinese territorial claims extend over the entire South China Sea, across the major sealines of communication, traversed by almost all the bulk carriers of fossil fuels so essential to the industries of Taiwan, Japan, and Korea.[66]

Researchers report that it is common for contemporary Chinese to "hold a normative vision of a China with boundaries that correspond with the borders of the Manchu empire at the height of the Qing dynasty." It is a vision of a prospective "new" China that would have recovered the entire array of ex-imperial territories and tributary irredenta that were lost to the nation in the defeats that followed the Opium wars of the early- and mid-nineteenth century.[67]

In addition to stating the general conviction that the nation has a right to its lost lands, Chinese strategists have argued that in order for the People's Republic to be truly secure, significant portions of those lost territories would have to be restored to the sovereign control of Beijing as expeditiously as possible to serve as parts of its forward defense perimeter. Correspondingly, when provoked, Beijing has used its armed forces to contest the territorial pretensions of others in those sectors of the region in which it insists on the priority of its own claims.

Over the years, in the course of territorial disputes, the People's Republic has employed military force against Tibet, India, socialist Vietnam, the North Korea of Kim Il-Sung, Taiwan, and the former Soviet Union. It has threatened the future use of military force against the Republic of the Philippines and Taiwan for all the same reasons. To leave no doubt concerning its seriousness of purpose in Southeast Asia, Beijing has declared, in domestic law, the waters, islets, cays, and banks of the South China Sea all legally parts of the "national territory" of the People's Republic.

---

[66] See the more extensive account in Maria Hsia Chang, *Return of the Dragon: China's Wounded Nationalism* (Boulder, COL: Westview Press, 2001), chap. 9.

[67] Eric Hyer, "Chinese Irredenta: Continuity and Change in Elite Views of Mongolia," in Edward H. Kaplan and Donald Whisenhunt (eds), *Opuscula Altaica: Essays Presented in Honor of Henry Schwarz* (Bellingham, WA: Western Washington University, 1994), pp. 333–48.

To reinforce the impression of its seriousness and its readiness to pursue all its claims with force, Beijing has embarked on a program of military modernization that includes the off-the-shelf purchase of some of the world's most advanced weapons platforms. With the requisite power projection capabilities provided by guided ballistic missiles, an increasingly capable submarine and surface blue-water navy, and the readiness to purchase and build aircraft carriers, China is now in the process of integrating some of the world's most lethal weapons into its inventories. China, already a nuclear weapons power, deploys what is rapidly becoming one of the world's most formidable conventional military forces.[68] All of this is reminiscent – acknowledging, once again, the differences in time, dimension, and circumstances – of Fascist planning and behavior in the Mediterranean during the years between the two world wars.[69]

Collateral with all that, the nationalism of the People's Republic has become increasingly strident. Usually referred to as "patriotism *(aiguo zhuyi)*," the sentiment shares all the operational features of an insistent nationalism.[70] As a consequence, some have no difficulty in speaking of Beijing's strategy of popular control as including an appeal to "hypernationalism."[71]

As is the case in many instances of revolutionary Marxism in power, Chinese communism always harbored an element of nationalism within its internationalism – and, like many other revolutionary Marxist regimes, ultimately became more nationalist than internationalist. Before its extinction, the Soviet Union became increasingly nationalistic until, at the end, the Communist Party of the Russian Federation was openly nationalistic, with its myth of national origins, its appeal to an imagined primordial national culture, and its panoply of semilegendary national heroes.[72]

No one pretends that Castro's Cuba or the Khmer Rouge are or were animated by anything other than fervid nationalism. From its very commencement, Maoist China was clearly nationalistic in its conceptions of itself and its anticipated relationship with the external world. The "two traits of

---

[68] See A. James Gregor, "Qualified Engagement: U.S. China Policy and Security Concerns," *Naval War College Review* 52, no. 2, sequence 366 (Spring 1999), pp. 69–88.

[69] See the discussion in Robert Mallett, *The Italian Navy and Fascist Expansionism 1935–1940* (London: Frank Cass, 1998).

[70] In survey research conducted in China, researchers found a high correlation between "nationalist" scores and "patriotic" scores among Chinese respondents. See Ronald Kosterman and Seymour Feshbach, "Toward a Measure of Patriotic and Nationalist Attitudes," *Political Psychology* 100 (1989), pp. 257–74.

[71] Tani Barlow, "*Zhishifenzi* [Chinese Intellectuals] and Power," *Dialectical Anthropology* 16 (1991), p. 214.

[72] See, for example, Yitzhak M. Brudny, *Reinventing Russia: Russian Nationalism and the Soviet State 1953–1991* (Cambridge, MA: Harvard University Press, 1998).

nationalism and of emphasis on the martial virtues" were forever at the heart of Maoism.[73]

With the passing of Mao, Deng Xiaoping made the inculcation of "patriotism" – and the unity, sacrifice, and discipline it invoked – the responsibility of the Communist Party.[74] The patriotism that emerged from Deng's post-Maoist efforts was explicitly "antileftist," rejecting the artificial egalitarianism of Maoism as well as its drumbeat of class warfare. Egalitarianism weakened the incentives that sustained development, and class warfare not only undermined disciplined unity, but dissipated both resources and energy.[75]

Together with rejecting leftist nostrums, renouncing class struggle, and invoking the deepest nationalist sentiments, Deng appealed to market modalities and capitalist strategies to foster the economic and industrial development central to the program to restore the nation to its proper grandeur[76] – programmatic features shared with the "heretical Marxism" of Benito Mussolini. By the end of the last decade of the twentieth century, Communist China had taken on properties that share an undeniable similarity with the criterial traits of Fascism. That acknowledgment introduces another aspect of post-Maoist ideological development that is of comparative interest: the gradual, but discernible, drift from a "state nationalism" to some variant of "racial nationalism."[77]

The preoccupation of China's intellectuals, as well as its political leadership, with the mercurial notion of "race" has a long and tortured history reaching back to the first years of the twentieth century.[78] Initially a generic Chinese concern with the "superiority" and "inferiority" of one or another race, Chinese interest soon addressed the race issue with conceptions far more sophisticated and nuanced. The discussion found in Sun Yat-sen's

[73] Stuart Schram, *Mao Tse-tung* (Baltimore, MO: Penguin, 1967), p. 44.

[74] Deng, "The Party's Urgent Tasks on the Organizational and Ideological Fronts," "Speech at the National Conference of the Communist Party of China," *Selected Works*, 3, pp. 50, 147.

[75] Deng, "The Party's Urgent Tasks on the Organizational and Ideological Fronts," "One Country, Two Systems," "We Must Follow Our Own Road in Economic Development as We Did in Revolution," "We Shall Expand Political Democracy and Carry Out Economic Reform," "Reform Is the Only Way for China to Develop Its Productive Forces," "Speech at the National Conference of the Communist Party of China," "Let the Facts Speak for Themselves," "Keeping to Socialism and the Policy of Peace," ibid., 3, pp. 48, 57, 68, 100, 121, 140–1, 144, 148, 158, 160.

[76] Deng, "There Is No Fundamental Contradiction Between Socialism and a Market Economy," ibid., 3, pp. 151–3.

[77] I am indebted in the following account to the work of Barry Sautman, entitled "Racial Nationalism and China's External Behavior," presented as a paper to the American Political Science Association annual meeting in San Francisco in August 1996.

[78] See the account in Frank Dikotter, *The Discourse of Race in Modern China* (Stanford, CA: Stanford University Press, 1992).

Sanminzhuyi (the Three Principles of the People), written for his followers
in the Kuomintang in 1924, for example, advances a surprisingly modern
conception of race, race formation, and its relationship to nationhood – a
conception that is not entirely unfamiliar.[79]

Sun conceived human races the "natural" product of human evolution, the
consequence of endogamy practiced over extended time periods – the result
not only of geographic separation but of self-induced isolation, the consequence of ingroup amity and outgroup diffidence. Sun spoke of these natural
dispositions as finding political idiom throughout human history, producing
not only conflict between human groups but also creating a disciplined and
dedicated unity among their members. That discipline and that unity are a
function of a shared cultural, political, and experiential history. Successful
groups prosper and extend their authority over adjacent territories. Over
time, they assimilate those who have fallen under their political control. The
result is a gradual "fusion" of members, whatever their personal or group
histories. Originally distinct, groups merge to become a single "racionation."

Implicit in such a conception is the argued belief that such a politically
defined community becomes, in time, composed of members who proceed
to share "bloodlines." The nation is the vessel of a "new race" that shares a
consciousness of kind, a sentiment of kinship that unites all in an extended
brotherhood. Chiang Kaishek, who assumed responsiblity for the Kuomintang after the death of Sun, argued precisely such a thesis. He argued
that China had emerged from a millennial history as one "stock" – the product of the physical union of culturally and politically distinct communities
until all shared the "same blood," the same sense of community, and the
same destiny.[80]

Throughout the modern period, many nationalists have argued similar
theses. It has not been uncommon for Marxists, when faced not with the
international revolution anticipated by Karl Marx and Friedrich Engels, but
with national revolution, to make a case for ethnic nationalism in which
primordial ingroup sentiment is reinforced by a concept of a "community
of blood." Political nationalism becomes a form of "ethnonationalism" suf-
fused with vague intimations of race. One finds its traces among some of
the most important Marxist theoreticians of the nineteenth century, including Moses Hess, the "communist rabbi" who reportedly converted Marx to
communism, and Ludwig Woltmann, who ultimately succumbed to the siren
call of biological racism.[81]

---

[79] The subsequent discussion follows Sun's thought as it finds expression in Sun Yat-sen, *The
Triple Demism of Sun Yat-sen* (New York: AMS Press, n.d., a reproduction of the Wuchang
edition of the Franciscan Press, 1931), Part 1, First Lecture, pp. 63–85.

[80] See the account in Chiang Kaishek, *China's Destiny and Chinese Economic Theory* (New
York: Roy, 1947), chap. 1, particularly p. 40.

[81] See the discussion in A. James Gregor, *The Faces of Janus: Marxism and Fascism in the
Twentieth Century* (New Haven, CT: Yale University Press, 2000), chap. 8.

What is important for the present discussion is the fact that post-Maoist China has taken up all the elements of an ethnonationalism that is largely indistinguishable from those found in the works of Sun and Chiang – long rejected as "fascistic" by both interwar Marxists and the Anglophone left.[82] Today, scholars in the People's Republic speak of the nation as "an organic community" sharing a common history, culture, language, territory, economy, and self-awareness, and ultimately "mixed bloodlines," in an echo of Sun and Chiang.[83]

The scholars of the People's Republic speak of the common descent of all Chinese, including those communities – Tibetans, Uighur, Hui, Yi, Miao, Yao, Bai, Zhuang, Tujia, Gaoshan, among others – long identified as minorities. All the citizens of China, we are told, are united by "blood" – people of the same "race, blood and culture" – with consanguinity established by contemporary seriological research.[84] All, it is seriously claimed, ultimately trace their ancestry to the Yellow Emperor, Huang Di (purportedly born around 2700 B.C.), now celebrated on the Chinese mainland as the "first ancestor."

It serves little purpose to pursue such lucubrations. It replicates similar views found among reactive nationalists over the last century and throughout the world. Very similar notions are found among German nationalists, Hindu nationalists, and Italian nationalists. In the Italian case, Fascist intellectuals fully articulated the conception of a "natiorace" in a long series of publications that ultimately appeared in summary as the official "Manifesto of Fascist Racism."[85]

Fascist racism was predicated on group sentiment – tribal, clan, moiety, city-state, confederation, or national – understood at minimum as nurturing a natural ingroup amity. Raciation, the gradual hereditary changes among people, was a product of the persistence of such ingroup amity over time, inevitably leading to admixture and assimilation. Confined by geographic as well as political boundaries, such a process, with its attendant endogamy, natural and artification selection, as well as genetic mutation, would produce new races – the degree of uniformity of type the consequence of the extent of isolation, the measure of inbreeding, and the selective pressures operative in the environment. It was within that theoretical framework that Fascist intellectuals could speak of an "Italian race" – the product of a millennial

---

[82] See the comments of Philip Jaffe to Chiang's *China's Destiny*, pp. 11–25, as well as his notes throughout, particularly n. 17 on p. 40 as well as his comparison of *China's Destiny* with Adolf Hitler's *Mein Kampf* on p. 19.

[83] See Sun, *The Triple Demism*, pp. 70–1 and compare with the review of present scholarship concerning the formation of the Chinese natiorace in Chang, *The Return of the Dragon*, pp. 182–3.

[84] He Xin, as quoted by Sautman, "Racial Nationalism and China's External Behavior," p. 27.

[85] See the translation in Gregor, *The Ideology of Fascism: The Rationale of Totalitarinism* (New York: Free Press, 1969), Appendix A.

history in which the different populations of the peninsula could "fuse" into the contemporary natiorace.

Fascists could speak without theoretical embarrassment of the "British," "French," or "German" races. Each nation was the dynamic product of a politically defined endogamous breeding circle. Sovereign independence and internal mobility would, over time, relate all constituent members of such a circle to a common gene pool. The relatively new, or "geographic," race would distinguish itself as a variant of a "great race," one of the five or so major races identified by overt physical features such as skin color or epicanthic eye folds.[86]

Fascists saw their notion of raciation providing essential support for the nation traversing an extremely exacting period of its existence. The conception of the nation as an extended family, united not only by history and destiny but blood as well, was expected to kindle the warmth of kinship among millions of conationals – distinguished by differences of religious, political, philosophical, and moral conviction, as well as employment, income, station, locale, and taste – spread over the great variety of the peninsula.

For Fascists, whatever distinctions were to be found among conationals was a matter of no consequence. Unlike the National Socialists across the Alps, race was not to be used to undermine the unity of the nation – making some Germans superior to others because of observable physical traits. Fascist racism insisted that there were no a priori grounds for the claim that one race was superior to another.[87] National unity and integrity would not be compromised by either class, confessional, regional, or racial differences.

Fascist theoreticians were convinced that such convictions would help foster the obedience, selflessness, commitment, and sacrifice necessary for the rapid development of the nation in the taxing circumstances in which Italy found itself at the end of the First World War. The Communist Party of China in the twenty-first century conceives of its version of ethnonationalism, tracing the biological origins of the nation back into the dim recesses of the Pliocene and lower Pleistocene,[88] as serving precisely the same purposes in a different time and under vastly different circumstances.

The post-Maoist People's Republic of China seems to have emerged as an exemplar of the only form that neofascism can assume in the twenty-first century. However different in detail, however variable in institutional feature, the unmistakeable features of a generic fascism seem evident. In the unfurling of flags, in the hegemonic, unitary party, in the dominance of the paramount

---

[86] See the more exhaustive account in ibid., pp. 252–60.
[87] See the first paragraph of the "Manifesto of Fascist Racism," in ibid., p. 383.
[88] Jia Lanpo and Ho Chuan Kun, "Lumiere nouvelle sur l'archaeologie paleolitique chinoise," *L'Anthropologie* 94, no. 4 (1990), pp. 851–60, as cited in Sautman, "Racial Nationalism and China's External Behavior," pp. 30–1.

leader (however personally uncharismatic), in the corporatist structure of the economy, in the role of private enterprise within the constraints of a "directed economy," in the importance of the military, in the commitment to restore the lost territories to the nation, and in the conviction that the twenty-first will be the "century of China," one cannot mistake the echoes of Mussolini's Fascism.

10

Conclusions

There are many reasons why so many academics have spent so much time in the search for neofascism. For some it simply involved a pursuit of an old enemy. Their number includes all those proper thinkers who as liberals and democrats have made it their purpose to expose all who would violate the civil and human rights of others. It includes all those who still suffer the memory of the mass murders done for political reasons – and who seek to foreclose any possibility that such horrors might befall humanity again. All of these reasons are entirely understandable and commendable. The difficulty is that the focus of such inquiry is much too narrow. If the object of the enterprise is to identify those forces responsible for the carnage and violation of human rights that have darkened the twentieth century, limiting our scrutiny to Fascism, generic fascism, or neofascism would hardly serve the purpose.

Commencing with the Armenian genocide at the turn of the century, the entire twentieth century has witnessed the mass murder of innocents at the hands of a variety of revolutionary governments, all attended by grievous violation of civil and political rights. Neither Mussolini's Fascism, generic fascism, nor neofascism could possibly be made responsible for all that.

If the motive behind the search for neofascism is the desire to preclude the advent of antidemocratic, antiliberal, and xenophobic political forces in the modern world, the scope remains too narrow, for even the nonexistence of Mussolini's, or Hitler's, regimes would have neither saved the lives of millions upon millions of innocents lost in our time nor preserved democracy. There would still have been those millions of lives consumed by the policies of mass murder that stained the modern history of the Soviet Union, the People's Republic of China, and Democratic Kampuchea. Nor would the absence of Fascism or National Socialism provide for the civil or political rights of persons living under the auspices of Marxist-Leninist regimes, common kleptocracies, military authoritarianism, or religious fanaticism.

Some, of course, have pursued neofascism because they are somehow convinced that any "right-wing" movement, must be, intrinsically and irremediably, an enemy of humankind. Throughout much of the long history of neofascism studies, Marxist systems have been showcased as the moral alternative to antidemocratic and racist systems. By the end of the twentieth century, we learned that Marxist-Leninist systems were as given to the violation of human rights and the mass murder of innocents as any twentieth-century fascism. Today, one cannot, with intellectual honesty, make a case for the superiority of left-wing regimes in the protection of human rights. Either what has been considered "left-wing" for about a hundred years is really "right-wing" and "fascist" or the distinction is hollow. It has become impossible to continue the pretense.

The unhappy reality of our time is that mass murder and the violation of human rights cannot be ascribed exclusively to Fascism, National Socialism, generic fascism, or neofascism. The twentieth century is filled with the doleful history of the massacre, incarceration, and torture of millions – under the auspices of "left-wing" as well as "right-wing" revolutionary regimes. In our own time, terrorists have taken it upon themselves to murder innocents in the name of religion. In the effort to tidy their enterprise, those who study neofascism have decided to identify such terrorists as "neofascists." But if the sole entry criterion into the class of "neofascists" is the readiness to kill and wound innocents, why would not the Marxist-Maoist Khmer Rouge, or the Marxist-Leninist Stalinists, qualify?

The fact is that Mussolini's Fascism is important in all of this, but not for the reasons usually advanced by those in search of contemporary neofascism. Mussolini, and those intellectuals around him, anticipated a great deal about revolution in the twentieth century that remains of cognitive significance in the twenty-first.

It was Mussolini, and those around him, who saw the twentieth century as a century of conflict – not between economic classes, but between "proletarian" and "plutocratic" nations. It was not the Enlightenment or the French Revolution that provided the ideological impetus for the revolutions of our time. It was, in the studied judgment of the first ideologues of Fascism, the inequities that result from the protracted diplomatic, economic, and military contact between those nations that were industrially developed and those that were not. It was the industrial revolution that created the circumstances in which some nations might lord over others – and it was that poisoned relationship that precipitated the reactive nationalism that would fuel transformative change.

Fascism's rationale was the composite product of the thinking of revolutionary syndicalists and nationalists. The nationalists – who were ultimately to merge with Fascism – provided some of the basic components of its doctrine. They identified the moral, psychological, political, economic, and security concerns that arose out of the asymmetrical relationship among industrially advanced and basically agricultural communities.[1] Part of their insights rested on the work of Friedrich List, a nineteenth-century developmental economist whose work – dismissed by Karl Marx as inconsequential – was influential in the growth policies of the West throughout the nineteenth and into the twentieth century.[2]

List published his major works at about the same time that Karl Marx and Friedrich Engels were doing the preliminary studies that would result in the *Communist Manifesto*. At that juncture, the intellectual substance that academics were to seize upon to distinguish the left from the right in the revolutionary politics of the late-nineteenth and twentieth centuries was already fixed.[3] The "right" was nationalistic, and sought rapid industrial development that would take place with the human and material resources available within the nation. The "left" was preoccupied with the human costs of the industrial development that had already taken place. As a consequence, Marx and Engels dismissed List's work as irrelevant because they argued that he was concerned with national industrial and economic development at a time when an antinationalist international proletarian revolution was imminent.[4]

The leftist argument, as it was given expression by Marx and Engels, was that the world would see not nation-based economic growth and industrial development, but the international uprising of a worldwide industrial working class. Such a revolution, in its universal entirety, would eliminate oppressors everywhere. The proletariat would rise up in unison in all the advanced industrialized nations, and then uplift all those who languished in underdevelopment.[5] The future, the Marxists predicted with absolute assurance, was proletarian and internationalist. The twentieth century was to prove them to have been woefully in error.

The twentieth century was to see revolutions made by those outraged by the soul-deadening cost exacted from everyone around them because of the economic and industrial backwardness of their nation. There was the outrage born of humiliation and inefficacy. There was very little talk of "to each according to his needs." The talk was of "from each according to his abilities." The revolutionaries in economically backward nations sought

---

[1] See the account in A. James Gregor, *Mussolini's Intellectuals: Fascist Social and Political Thought* (Princeton, NJ: Princeton University Press, 2005), chaps. 2, 3.

[2] See the introductory essay by J. Shield Nicholson, in Friedrich List, *The National System of Political Economy* (London: Longmans, Green, 1916, translation of the 1844 German edition), pp. xiii–xxvii.

[3] See the insightful exposition in Roman Szporluk, *Communism and Nationalism: Karl Marx Versus Friedrich List* (New York: Oxford University Press, 1988); see also Alfred Meusel, *List und Marx: Eine vergleichende Betrachtung* (Jena: Gustav Fischer Verlag, 1930).

[4] Karl Marx, "Draft of an Article on Friedrich List's Book *Das nationale System der politischen Ökonomie*," in *Collected Works* (New York: International Publishers, 1976), 4, pp. 265–83.

[5] See Szporluk, *Communism and Nationalism*, chaps. 3, 4, 11, 12. See also A. James Gregor, *A Survey of Marxism: Problems in Philosophy and the Theory of History* (New York: Random House, 1965), chap. 5.

dedication and labor from everyone in order to reduce the distance between themselves and the advanced industrial powers.

The revolutionaries of the twentieth century sought to establish equality between themselves and more materially advanced nations. The revolutionaries of those less-developed nations, convinced of their own cultural superiority and their ancient glories, sought to extract recognition from others. No longer content to live in the shadow of those industrially advanced, suffering their distain, many, if not most, of the revolutionaries of the twentieth century committed themselves to the rapid economic and industrial growth of their respective nations as the material foundation of their redemption. Revolutions did not take place in the advanced industrial nations, but in those nations failing to thrive in the backwardness that left them prey to those capable of projecting power throughout the world.

When revolution came to Czarist Russia and postimperial China, they proved not to be the revolutions of leftist vision. The "oppressed" would remain oppressed – if oppressed in a novel fashion. Peasants and workers in both Communist Russia and Communist China were to suffer low, "exploitative" wages for decades as their respective leaders undertook *national* economic and industrial development. They were regimented, coerced, and exploited in order to satisfy the demands of what Soviet Marxist-Leninists euphemistically called the "primitive socialist accumulation" of capital necessary for rapid development. Independent worker and peasant organizations were destroyed and everyone regimented to the purposes of the "workers' state." Compliance was assured by the control of education and information and the inculcation of a formal ideology from which no departures were tolerated.

Suddenly, in all of this, the outlines of Mussolini's Fascism make their unmistakable appearance. The doctrine of Fascism said little more than that Italy, as a backward nation – imposed upon by advanced industrial nations for decades – was compelled to develop its economy, in general, and its industrial base, in particular, in order to survive and prevail in the modern world. From that point forward, there was the advocacy of all those instrumentalities with which we are now fully familiar. There was the rationale for the charismatic leader, the unitary party, as well as its infallible ideology – all calculated to inspire an ethic of labor and sacrifice among a people that would have to undertake the daunting ascent to industrialization – so that the nation could go forth armed with the weapons necessary to face their industrialized tormentors.

Fascism and the corresponding Marxist-Leninist "left-wing" revolutionary regimes of the twentieth and twenty-first centuries shared, and share, profound and irrepressible imperatives – imperatives that were neither of the left or the right, imperatives understood in some fundamental sense by Friedrich List, the contemporary of Karl Marx. In time, the leftists of the Soviet Union and Maoist China came to learn what the revolution of the twentieth and twenty-first centuries really involved – and neither Karl Marx nor V. I. Lenin anticipated any of it.

Fascists understood their task. There were others who understood the task as well. Many – including, as we have seen, Mussolini himself – recognized the affinities between the revolutionary intentions of Kemal Ataturk and those of Fascism. Marxists early in the twentieth century recognized those same affinities between the ideology of Sun Yat-sen and those of Italian Fascism. What has been suggested here is that those same affinities obtain between the various forms of Marxism-Leninism in Eastern Europe and Asia and paradigmatic Fascism as well. Each has been an instance or special subset of a developing system inspired by what has been aptly called "ideologies of late industrial development."[6]

What distinguished the members of such a class of ideologies of late industrial development were variations in their respective goal cultures. Sun Yat-sen, for example, anticipated that the phase of "political tutelage," composed of one-party control under the leadership of a charismatic leader, would ultimately grow into the phase of "constitutional government"[7] to bring democracy to China. Fascists anticipated no such evolution.

Clear in their every behavior was evidence that Marxist-Leninists were themselves advocates of late industrial development. The Marxists of Stalinism and Maoism could only jerry-build a suitable ideology and corresponding institutions as they proceeded. Stalin spoke of the "dialectical" path that the "internationalists" and "socialists" of Bolshevism would have to traverse. In the course of this path, they would have to undertake the construction of "socialism in one nation," which would involve rapid industrialization under the auspices of the charismatic leader, the unitary party, and the totalitarian state.

The revolutionary Marxism of the Bolsheviks devolved into the elitist-dominated, single-party state, driven to industrialize a backward economy in order to furnish its military forces adequately so that they might contend with the formidable inventories of "international imperialisms" – the analog of Fascism's "plutocratic nations." Time, circumstances, and the imperatives of rapid industrialization had transformed "leftist" revolution into an analogue of its "rightist" adversary.

Few today fail to recognize the institutional similarities that united the various forms of Marxist-Leninist revolution with those of Mussolini's Fascism. The best of the Fascist intellectuals recognized the affinities, as did Mussolini

---

[6] See A. James Gregor, *The Fascist Persuasion in Radical Politics* (Princeton, NJ: Princeton University Press, 1974), pp. 411–13. Mary Matossian, "Ideologies of Delayed Industrialization: Some Tensions and Ambiguities," in John Kautsky, *Political Change in Underdeveloped Countries* (New York: Wiley, 1962), pp. 252–64.

[7] See Sun Yat-sen, *Fundamentals of National Reconstruction* (Taipei: China Cultural Service, 1953).

and Giovanni Gentile, the "philosopher of Fascism."[8] Whatever remained of Marxism-Leninism as an ideology after the "creative developments" of Stalin and Mao looked very much like a primitive form of Fascism.[9]

Hitler's National Socialism, as an exotic variant of the developmental ideologies of the twentieth century, arose in a nation that had already achieved a broadly based industrialization. Unhappily, it was a nation that was treated as though it were underdeveloped and of no consequence in the arena of those nations already developed. Germany's treatment after its defeat in the First World War mimicked that accorded the lesser nations of Europe and the Third World nations of the less-developed periphery. Hitler's Germany proceeded to behave as though it were underdeveloped. National Socialism drove the nation to undertake a massive acceleration of industrial production, marshaling everyone, in the space of six years, to the discipline and sacrifice that sustained the program of constructing a military that would conquer Europe in two years.

Besides its basic development, what distinguished Germany was the singular ferocity with which it pursued its goal – the restoration of the nation to its place at the forefront of nations. In that ferocity, the conviction that Germany had been denied its place in the competition among nations inspired superhuman effort on the part of Hitler's followers. The conviction in their own superiority supplied the energy that fueled their effort. The obverse was the ready identification of inferiors together with the incorrigible belief that there were those who would obstruct the realization of the revolutionary goals of the leadership. Out of all that emerged the homicidal racism that came to characterize National Socialism in history.

We cannot pretend to understand the etiology of such a disorder. That it is in part the result of collective pain and humiliation suffered at the hands of others, an abnormal exaggeration of the sense of ingroup amity and outgroup enmity, seems reasonably clear. But that does not begin to account for the readiness to murder innocents in the numbers consumed by Nazi Germany. Why the dispositions that are regularly found among those communities long treated as inferiors should become so inflamed in some cases rather than others is difficult to determine with anything like clinical assurance. All that is available to us is informed speculation.

We find traces of similar pathologies among communities that feel themselves ill used by outsiders. It is found among some blacks, long afflicted by the psychological and social impostures of racism. It is found among some forms of religious fundamentalism. It is found among the followers of one

---

[8] See the discussion in Gregor, *The Fascist Persuasion in Radical Politics*, pp. 183–5, for the apposite documentation.

[9] See the discussion in A. James Gregor, "Fascism, Marxism and Some Considerations Concerning Classification," *Totalitarian Movements and Political Religions* 3, no. 2 (Autumn 2002), pp. 61–82.

or another religious creed. It is found in contemporary instances of tribal conflict – and it was manifest in the mass murders in the Soviet Union, in Maoist China, and in Pol Pot's Kampuchea. The general psychology behind the pathological form is reasonably well understood. What is not as well-known is what factors might trigger its pathological expression in particular cases.

The most common of reactive nationalisms observed in the twentieth century is that found in paradigmatic Fascism. In its original form, it found expression in impassioned ingroup amity and solidarity. Italians saw themselves as members of a millennial community, sharing history, values, and political goals. The pathological variant of that kind of nationalism is found in the history of National Socialism and Marxism-Leninism in almost all its manifestations. The pathological variant of ingroup amity and solidarity limits amity and solidarity to only some groups of the preexisting national community. Distinctions are made not on the bases of shared political citizenship, values, history, or goals, but by virtue of some fixed political, class, or ascriptive features that are understood to signal the superiority or inferiority of subnational groups.

In the worldview that results, the members of such subnational communities receive the treatment, positive or negative, that they are understood to deserve in light of the sustaining revolutionary ideology. Whether such subnational communities are composed of Nordics, blacks, Jews, proletarians, the bourgeoisie, or capitalists is a matter of little consequence for our analysis. What is important is that entire collectivities are so characterized and, as a consequence, can be made subject to discrimination and abuse.

In dealing with enormities of the kind that have cost the lives of millions upon millions of innocents, it is difficult to speak with any conviction of the necessary and sufficient or contingent conditions that might be responsible. What can be said with confidence is that such pathology is clearly not limited to the political right.

For the purposes of the present analysis, Fascist nationalism is treated as the norm. Calculated to inspire members of the community to enterprise and self-sacrifice, it fostered compliance and commitment. It also threatened punishment and ostracism to those who would not conform or obey, so that the potential for violence was always present. That violence, at no time, approximated the willful destructiveness of life of which one finds National Socialism and Marxist-Leninist systems equally guilty.

Fascist violence nowhere approximated, in kind or number, the level of violence one finds in Hitlerism, Stalinism, Maoism, or Polpotism.[10]

---

[10] Fascists were guilty of the inexcusable mistreatment of their own citizens who happened to be Jews, and complicit in the murder of Jews at the hands of the Nazis occupying Italy during the final months of the Second World War, when Fascism was hostage to Adolf Hitler. Why Fascist anti-Semitic behavior was so markedly different from that of the Nazis

The Fascist treatment of Italian Jews was ignoble, and immoral, abusing citizens who were innocent of offense, but a far cry from the treatment of Jews at the hands of the Nazis, or the treatment of the "bourgeoisie" at the hands of Marxist-Leninists.[11] None of this can be taken to mean that Fascist behavior in their mistreatment of their Jewish conationals was anything other than abhorrent – only that the distinction must be made if we are to understand reactive nationalism in all its manifestations.

All of this must be considered in the context in which Marxist-Leninist systems hunted down and murdered persons for being "bourgeois." At times, such persons were guilty of nothing other than the possession of certain ascriptive traits – being the offspring of landowners or being children of members of "black classes." At times, it was not at all clear what properties one must possess to mark one for destruction. Millions were swept into the maelstrom of violence and death in Marxist-Leninist states without knowing why they were being destroyed. Randomly applied demonstrative terror consumed innumerable lives in the Soviet Union, in Mao's China, and in Democratic Kampuchea.

Some of those regimes with which our time has become familiar, animated by ideologies of late industrialization, were incarceration or exile regimes, disembarrassing themselves of real or fancied dissidents by imprisoning them or sending them abroad. Fascist Italy and Castro's Cuba would seem to meet the entrance criteria for just such systems. Those that haunt our memory are those polities that were essentially mass-murder regimes. Millions, guilty of little if anything, were slaughtered by such regimes as imagined enemies and in instances of prophylactic and demonstrative terror. It is hard to imagine we will ever have an adequate explanation for their behavior. However ill understood, they make up an important subset of those revolutionary regimes spoken of as involved in the systemic tensions of late development.

For at least these reasons, it seems that the search for neofascism, as such, can be of only limited significance unless we are prepared to acknowledge that while Mussolini's Fascism constitutes a paradigmatic instance of such regimes, it is to serve as a classificatory norm from which other regimes, similarly identified, are a harrowing departure.

That is, Italian Fascism serves as a paradigm insofar as the system was clearly aware of its goals and the instrumentalities understood to achieve them. Fascism did not pretend to be embarking on a world revolution that would satisfy all humanity's needs and wants. It understood its task to be

is difficult to explain. For the experience of an inmate of a Fascist internment camp for Jews, see Salim Diamand, *Dottore! Internment in Italy, 1940–1945* (New York: Mosaic Press, 1987).

[11] As has been indicated, the most instructive account of the treatment of Jews by the Fascists remains that of Renzo De Felice, *Storia degli ebrei italiani sotto il fascismo* (Turin: Giulio Einaudi Editore, 1993, the new enlarged edition).

the creation of an economic, particularly industrial, base for the provision of a military inventory that would restore the nation's prestige in a world that had all but dismissed the nation's very presence. The ideology that animated the program was consistent with the goals and provided the rationale for the anticipated instrumentalities necessary for their achievement. Unlike most of its left-wing variants, Fascism had a clear understanding of its goals and the means it imagined necessary to achieve them. Only its involvement in the Second World War and its subordination to Hitler's National Socialism obscured all of that to some degree.

Mussolini's Fascism provides a classificatory norm for the assessment of the alternative members of the class of revolutionary regimes to be considered. Thus, the ideology of National Socialism is seen as an aberration against that norm. National Socialism, as an illustrative difference, never really provided an account of what its ultimate goal might be. More than that, Hitler's insistence on racism as the critical center of National Socialist ideology compromised its nationalism and augured ultimate and inevitable problems for the regime. Racism cast itself athwart the sentiment of national unity so important for mass mobilization. It was, in effect, a dysfunctional variant of Fascism, creating invidious distinctions among Germans and undermining the unity and discipline of the nation.

Fascist theoreticians recognized much in National Socialism as deviant. They specifically argued against the intrusion of the form of racism advocated by Hitler's National Socialists into any nationalist program.[12] Nationalism, not racism, was at the core of Mussolini's Fascism.

Given our current knowledge of revolution in the twentieth century, we can draw distinctions among nondemocratic developmental movements and regimes with considerable confidence. We also appreciate that those systems that invoked Marxism-Leninism as the legitimizing rationale for their respective rule very quickly and literally abandoned all of it. We appreciate that those revolutions led by declassed bourgeois intellectuals were made without proletarians in economically backward environments. The state did not "wither away," nor did political leaders become subject to "democratic control." The systems failed to bring peace, fraternity, equality, or abundance. Over the span of a decade, Stalinism created institutions to govern "Marxist" Russia that bore impressive similarities to those fashioned by Fascism to govern Italy. By the time of its disappearance, the Soviet Union saw major factions within the ruling elite arguing for protection and maintenance of the "ethnos" – that biological community that was understood to constitute

---

[12] See Aldo Capasso, *Idee chiare sul razzismo* (Rome: Augustea, 1942), p. 27; L. Franzi, *Fase attuale del razzismo tedesco* (Rome: Istituto nazionale di cultura fascista, 1939), pp. 44–45; Guido Landra, "Il concetto di razza," *Difesa della razza*, 2, no. 9 (5 March 1939), p. 12.

the foundation of the nation.[13] At that juncture, Soviet Marxism gave every appearance of being a deviant form of Italian Fascism.

The ideological decay of Marxism-Leninism in power is perhaps best illustrated in the case of the performance of the Khmer Rouge. Their rule, we are told, was governed by "a philosophy of racial superiority and purity that resembled that of Nazi Germany.... The idea of pure Kampuchean blood or a pure Kampuchean race was a combination of European racism and Marxist science fiction."[14] As a pathological variant of Fascism, the Khmer Rouge shared some unmistakable features with Hitler's National Socialism.

The decay of Marxist-Leninist systems into something totally unanticipated by social science was foreseen, as has been suggested, by Fascist theoreticians. Mussolini himself had early argued that if the Soviet Union wished to survive, it would have to abandon Marxism in its entirety – appealing to nationalism, and ensuring itself of overall discipline and collective effort through the agencies of a totalitarian state. In speaking of a work published by a young Fascist theoretician, Mussolini agreed with the author in saying that if the Soviet Union wished to survive over time, "the leaders of Bolshevism must reassess their enterprise and abandon Marx in favor of the principles of Fascism."[15] What was not anticipated were the grotesqueries that would result.

Fascists had articulated a system of beliefs calculated to service the needs of economic development and industrialization – something that fell outside the theoretical purview of the founders of traditional Marxism. Once that is appreciated, the involution of the ideology of the Soviet Union, as well as its fabrication of the totalitarian state and all its adjuncts, becomes comprehensible.

All these systems are dangerous. They maintain controls over their respective populations through elaborate surveillance and security forces. They incarcerate and exile almost at will – and far too many, with little if any provocation, have murdered untold numbers. If the victims were not members of a proscribed race, they were members of a proscribed class. In all too many cases, those to be killed were simply selected at random.

Beyond that, if the "infallible" leaders of such systems were not directly responsible for the deaths of millions of their own citizens, they became guilty of irresponsibly involving their nations in conflicts, or assuming tasks, that

---

[13] See the discussion in A. James Gregor, *The Faces of Janus: Marxism and Fascism in the Twentieth Century* (New Haven, CT: Yale University Press, 2000), chap. 8, and *Phoenix: Fascism in Our Time* (New Brunswick, NJ: Transaction, 1999), chap. 7.

[14] Elizabeth Becker, *When the War Was Over: Cambodia and the Khmer Rouge Revolution* (New York: Public Affairs, 1998), pp. 155, 243.

[15] Benito Mussolini, "Segnalazione," *Opera omnia* (Florence: La fenice, 1958), 26, p. 84. Mussolini's comments served as a preface to Renzo Bertoni, *Russia: Trionfo del fascismo* (Milan: "La prora," 1937), p. 6.

far exceeded their capabilities – and that was as true of Hitler's Germany as it was of Mussolini's Italy, as it was of Maoist China. While the conviction that leaders were infallible may have served to provide psychological and emotional reserves during times of crisis and duress, it afforded leaders, at the same time, the power to mislead the nation to disaster. Any rational person, for example, could have seen Italy's declaration of war against the United States in December 1941 as the piece of madness that it was. No less mad was Mao's "Great Leap Forward," which cost China perhaps as many as 30 million victims.

For at least those reasons, the identification of any movement or regime as "fascist" or "neofascist" is very serious. Thus, the insistence that Hindu nationalism is fascist is fraught with implications. The very ascription carries potential international consequences in its train.

There is every indication that India will emerge as one of the world's largest economies in the twenty-first century. Its strategic location in South Asia, beside the major ship routes that extend from the Middle East carrying fuel to all the major industrial nations in East Asia, renders India of special international importance. Its position between Pakistan and the People's Republic of China, two regions of critical importance to the United States, make India a nation of importance. The very suggestion that one of its major political parties, the Bharatiya Janata Party (BJP), might be fascist or neofascist could well have extremely serious implications for U.S.–Indian relations.

Unlike those revolutionary systems we have considered, India is one of those nations that has proceeded to develop economically under essentially democratic auspices. Against enormous pressure, the Indian political system has managed to retain its essentially democratic character – and the BJP has not sought its change. The party has respected the constitutional responsibilities that it assumed as a representative member of the Indian democracy that emerged from colonialism. There is very little in its ideology or its behavior that would identify it as fascist or neofascist.

In political democracies, scholars, essayists, journalists, and commentators have the right to express their opinions freely about almost every subject. Granted that, the easy identification of movements and governments as fascist or neofascist can work considerable mischief with the interests of everyone involved. The Bharatiya Janata Party is neither fascist nor neofascist by any reasonable definition.

Much the same must be said of the Muslim fundamentalists who have brought so much pain to the United States. Identifying them as "Islamofascists" certainly serves propaganda purpose, to reinvoke all the negative connotations that have, over time, collected around the terms "fascist" and "neofascist." By characterizing Muslim fundamentalists as fascists or neofascists steels the resolve of Americans. For the foreseeable future, Muslim fundamentalists will wreak considerable pain and exact enormous cost – but they are not fascists or neofascists for all that. However hateful, however devoid of moral principle, however destructive of innocent life, they are not fascists, neofascists, or nazis. They are Muslim fundamentalists convinced that their religion obligates them to act as they do. The ready availability of weapons of mass destruction makes them a threat to civilized life on the planet. They must be neutralized, and they will be – but not because they are fascists, neofascists, nazis, or Marxist-Leninists. Their neutralization will require dedication, the sacrifice of life, and the expenditure of treasure. All that notwithstanding, to depict them as fascists or neofascists does not really help, and cannot be defended by best evidence.

There is no reason to imagine that the difficulties in the Middle East will soon be resolved. The Middle East is change-resistant. There is currently little that could pass as economic growth or industrialization and, under prevailing conditions, there is little prospect of such development in the proximate future. The consequence is that most of the population of the vast region has scant opportunity and less hope for betterment. The increasing wealth of the industrialized states can only appear to such despairing persons as an insult and an increasing threat to the integrity, independence, and cultural autonomy of a region that continues to fall further and further behind the advanced industrial nations.

More than half the population of the Middle East is less than twenty years of age. That age group has historically constituted the most important demographic for transformative change anywhere, and everywhere, in the world. By the end of the next decade, the population of the Middle East will be more numerous, poorer, more urban, and more frantic. Change will be sought. Caught up in religious fundamentalism, there is little prospect that anyone, with any hope of success, will seek rapid economic growth or industrialization. Immediately after the Second World War, secular Arabs attempted to mount mass-mobilizing, developmental regimes specifically committed to those ends. Having failed with Gamal Abdel Nasser, Muammar el Qaddafi, and Saddam Hussein, it is not likely that another indigenous effort will be mounted within the next decades. Without some fundamental change in the prevailing constellation of forces, the Middle East, in all probability, will languish in its present impasse for the foreseeable future. The result will be an increasingly volatile region – with the greatest threats extending to Saudi Arabia, Jordan, and Egypt – with a nuclear-armed Israel living in what would be tantamount to a perpetual state of siege.

The ready availability of weapon systems of fearsome lethality will make anti-Western terrorism particularly threatening. The Middle East will probably spawn international terrorist cartels committed to the senseless murder of Christians and Jews. Without very fundamental change, even with no real prospects of victory, such combinations will probably persist, in one state of effectiveness or another, for an incalculable time – membership being fed by the surplus youth produced by the high birth rates of the region. Without sustained economic growth and development, the indigenous circumstances are not likely to change. All of this is probable without the presence of any neofascism.

Unless there are basic changes in the region, what will emerge from that cauldron will continue to threaten the peace. Living standards for the bulk of the population in the Middle East will probably deteriorate for some time, with the advanced industrial nations being seen as bearing full responsibility. With the populations of the industrialized nations declining because of low birth rates, waves of immigrants from the Middle East will tax the social services of the West. They will be welcomed by industries requiring cheap labor, but objected to by domestic populations. At least in the short term, one can expect an increase in resistance to uncontrolled immigration in potential host nations. The resistance to foreign immigrants will generate cries of "neofascism," because there will be a predictable growth in the number of, and membership in, the organizations resisting liberal immigration policies. For all that, none of it will be "fascist" or "neofascist."

There have been and there will continue to be armed efforts to staunch the continued terrorism bred in the region. By the first decade of the twenty-first century, the population of Algeria had been repulsed by the unspeakable atrocities committed by fundamentalist violence; by the end of the previous century, moderate Muslims sought to reestablish civilized life by repressing criminal fundamentalists, reintroducing the semblance of democracy, and allowing the emergence of a market system for the nation.

In Egypt, the government has systematically suppressed fundamentalists in the effort to control events. In Libya, Muslim fundamentalists are allowed little opportunity to organize. And, of course, the United States, with its coalition of nations, has sought to suppress any possibility that Muslim terrorists might obtain sanctuary and/or material support in Afghanistan or Iraq. All of these efforts aim to neutralize the wide-ranging terrorism spawned by the long-standing conditions in the Middle East.

Of all the candidate "neofascisms" here considered, post-Maoist China shares more properties with paradigmatic Fascism than any of the others. That is a matter of considerable importance both for China as well as the industrial democracies. In the twenty-first century, China will be challenged by difficulties that will test the strength and viability of its economy as well as the resilience and responsiveness of its government. These challenges will influence both China's domestic and its international behavior.

Since the passing of Mao Zedong, the leadership of China has reintro-duced all the market modalities that Marxism, in principle, had traditionally opposed. The nonstate sector of the Chinese economic base, released from the unforgiving constraints of a command structure, has proven itself. It is the private sector that sustains the continued spectacular growth and increasing sophistication of the Chinese economy.

Since stabilization was achieved after the death of Mao and the sup-pression of his most ardent followers, the Chinese Communist Party has introduced reforms that have made a fiction of its Marxism. Nonetheless, the system that has taken the place of the pretended Marxism of the first years of Mao's rule continues to draw the same inspiration and sustenance from the abiding sense of collective humiliation, the irredentism, the national sensitivity, the masculine protest, and the thirst for lost grandeur that sustained Maoism at its inception. It is the same clutch of properties that inspired and sustained the Fascist revolution.

At some time in the twenty-first century, barring serious internal political and/or economic dislocation, the People's Republic of China will be among the world's most productive economies. With that will come increasing assertiveness. Other than the expected difficulties that accompany the drive to economic maturity in less-developed nations, the People's Republic will face specific problems. With a population that taxes the support capacity of the soil, and with energy demands escalating at an annual rate that threatens the very possibility of supply, China will be entering critical times. At those times, China may become most dangerous.

Conditions within China are precarious. More than 100 million Chinese are essentially rootless, peasants seeking the more profitable and attractive jobs in the burgeoning private sector of the mainland economy. They constitute a restless, sometimes volatile mass. There are frequent reports of unrest, of dissidence among urban and rural dwellers. There have been episodic attacks on government offices. There has been a notable proliferation of criminal gangs throughout China. The measure of corruption that accompanies business and government activities is arresting.

While reliable statistics are difficult to obtain, there are persistent reports of urban underemployment and unemployment that tax the social welfare facilities and provoke potential unrest. The Chinese government has forbidden the organization of independent unions and citizens' associations that might address such issues.

The most common estimate among developmental economists in the United States is that China must maintain a sustained rate of economic growth at 7 percent per annum in order to contain the restlessness of its population. Given the perceived inequities in income in the urban sector and the general poverty in the rural areas, China is precariously balanced. It must maintain its current rates of spectacular economic growth in order to gratify the expectations of its new entrepreneurial classes, allow for the support of the urbanized general working class, and provide for the most fundamental needs of the peasantry.

Government surpluses are used to extend support to the rural areas, some of which endure the starkest of poverty. The costs of the construction of an increasingly elaborate infrastructure are offset by the profits supplied largely by the impressive rate of export growth. In effect, a great deal is riding on China's continued economic expansion. The principal difficulty that attends that process is the exponential rate of growth of resources needed to sustain that growth.

Given the waste and inefficiency of Chinese factory production, China has required a continuous and rapid increase in available resources – particularly energy resources. From an economy that was originally nearly self-sufficient, China has become a net importer of fossil fuels and raw materials. That means that in order to survive, China will require access to a ready and expanding source of resupply.

Because of its ideological conviction that the nation is threatened by "imperialism," China seeks to be essentially autarkic with respect to its growth, sustenance, and defense needs. With the rate of growth it has enjoyed over the decades since the death of Mao Zedong, China is unlikely both to achieve or sustain such a goal. In the relatively near future, it will have to abandon either autarky or the rate of growth that many economists judge critical to its political stability.

Given its irredentist impulse, all things being equal, China might seek to reach out and control resources in regions that it has claimed since imperial times. While it is not clear how abundant the oil reserves located beneath the waters of the South China Sea might be, for example, nor clear how soon the technology for deep-water drilling will be fully available to Beijing, it seems certain that, at one time or another in the relatively near future, China will demand exclusive economic control over the offshore subsoil resources throughout the entire geographic region in southeastern Asia. That can be done only at the expense of its neighbors and as a threat to United States interests in Asia.

There is the further promise of recoverable energy resources in the lightly populated Russian Far East – lands claimed by China. The Russians have been long cognizant of the Chinese claims, having addressed them directly as early as the 1970s and 1980s.[16] With the continued decline in Russian military capabilities, and with China's industrial needs rapidly increasing, Beijing will be subject to corresponding temptation.

Almost all the developed regions in the Russian Far East are host to large and increasing Chinese populations. As more and more Russians return to European Russia, the population of the Russian Far East becomes increasingly Chinese. The evidence of history suggests that when regions abut and one is population-poor and resource-rich, and the other is population-dense and resource-poor, the outcome is predictable. At some point in time, a rapidly growing China will seek to expand into regions rich in resources and possessed of empty space. China no longer makes any pretense of pursuing goals of international solidarity and peace. Its international behavior has become increasingly ominous. Some responsible Chinese military specialists publicly speak of "living space" in the Russian Far East, and of expanding the defense perimeter of the nation to the "second island chain," to Guam in the Mid-Pacific, in order to secure strategic depth for the Motherland.

---

[16] See, for example, G. Apalin and U. Mityayev, *Militarism in Peking's Policies* (Moscow: Progress, 1980), especially chap. 6.

It is that China that has been described as "heavy handed...with a siege mentality and a presumed mandate of history. A China that grows strong while remaining an imperial state. It threatens Taiwan, locks up democrats, makes a vassal of Myanmar (Burma), crusades against religion in Tibet...and refuses to negotiate a settlement of disputed islands in the South China Sea." Such a "repressive empire cannot be stable, comfortable with its own...vigor, or a friend to the United States or [its] neighbors."[17]

That is the "neofascist" China that has grown out of the reform of Maoism. Its features are unmistakable. Because of its imagined future, Beijing has embarked upon a program of military expansion and modernization that has attracted the attention of strategists and defense planners in Washington.

Since the early 1990s, U.S. intelligence agencies have become increasingly concerned about China's next generation nuclear weapons – more sophisticated, road-mobile, solid propellant–fueled, intercontinental ballistic missiles. The People's Liberation Army has developed small, more efficient designs intended to allow its rocket forces to employ missiles armed with multiple independently targetable reentry warheads.

China has supplemented that development with the purchase of high-performance computers, capable of performing from 1,500 to 40,000 millions of theoretical operations per second. Such computing power is essential for modern weapon design – in nuclear weapons, advanced aviation equipment, complex detection devices, and command-and-control installations for military operations. Together with massive upgrades in combat aircraft, submarines, armor, surface combatants, and increasingly sophisticated training for its personnel, the People's Liberation Army is rapidly becoming a major, modern military power. The process is not unfamiliar. We recall similar developments in Europe in the interwar years before the Second World War.

How important the ideological convictions of the leadership in Beijing actually are can be illustrated by a comparison of the Chinese and Indian armed forces. India is a democratic polity, committed to economic growth and industrialization, suffering many of the population and resource problems of China. What is absent in India is a neofascism that might inspire the kinds of international sensibilities or the irredentist claims that precipitate conflict. As a consequence, India neither underwrites nor deploys a military that possesses aggressive capabilities.

Comparatively speaking, the Chinese People's Liberation Army is an impressive military force about twice the size of the Indian military. Together with its raw manpower advantage, its airforce is about five times the size of that of India. The airpower inventory of the Chinese People's Liberation Army consists of air superiority aircraft that compare favorably with the

[17] Ross Terrill, *The New Chinese Empire and What It Means for the United States* (New York: Basic Books, 2003), p. 340.

best deployed by the United States. China's nuclear capabilities are intercontinental. For its part, India deploys about 125 intermediate-range missiles and a modest airforce.

While India has 130 naval vessels, including 1 aircraft carrier, about 16 conventional submarines, 8 destroyers, 12 frigates, and 6 fast-attack, coastal, and inshore patrol craft, together with about 17 minesweepers in inventory, China deploys about 750 naval vessels, involving 65 submarines, including nuclear-powered attack boats and at least 1 nuclear-powered vessel capable of the independent launch of nuclear missiles, 20 destroyers, and at least 40 frigates, together with over 100 fast-attack craft (both missile and torpedo) and 200 coastal and inshore patrol craft as well as about 40 minesweepers and 200 amphibious and support craft. The differences are dramatic and suggest something of the difference in political attitude between the two countries.

India has suffered foreign invasions over centuries and increasing European penetration from the sixteenth and seventeenth century until Great Britain's accession to paramountcy after the Final Maratha War at the beginning of the nineteenth century. Nevertheless, India has never developed that form of reactive nationalism that has made nations bellicose in the past. Unlike China, India does not regularly reiterate its fear of "imperialist" imposture, nor does it seek to recoup "lost" lands through the use of force.

India had suffered every humiliation to which a people might be made subject, and yet one finds a reactive nationalism that displays little of the hostility and injured pride that typifies China's response patterns. Compared to China's sense of grievance, India is the model of moderation.

India's Hindu nationalists seem to channel all the reactive nationalism of which the nation is capable. And they display relatively little hostility against the "oppressor nations" of their recent past. The reactive nationalism of the Bharatiya Janata Party is moderated by its presence among a variety of political parties operative in its political environment. Functioning in a broadly democratic environment, the advocates of Hindutva express a form of developmental nationalism not incompatible with the prevailing Indian ethos.

The differences between India and China in terms of their international posturing could hardly be more emphatic. Authors can produce, for example, credible books entitled The China Threat,[18] while such a book about India would be, at its best, unconvincing.

In the future, it will be probable that the leader of the Bharatiya Janata Party will once again assume the responsibilities of head of government. However firm his commitment to Hindu nationalism, the very ideology of

---

[18] Bill Gertz, *The China Threat: How the People's Republic Targets America* (Washington, DC: Regnery, 2000).

Hindutva, together with the institutional constraints of a multiparty democracy, would not allow any radical changes in Indian foreign policy that might threaten neighbors or the interests of the United States.

The principal threat to stability in the region and to U.S. interests turn on relations between India and Pakistan. The measure of hostility between these nuclear-armed powers, has fluctuated over the years – and could combust at almost any time.

The war against international terrorism has made Pakistan a major, if fragile, ally of Washington. Escalating tensions between Islamabad and New Delhi could only impair the efforts to suppress organized terrorism. The possibilities of increased tension and armed conflict always percolate close to the surface. Hindu nationalism has little, if anything, to do with that. Those realities obtained at the very moment India became a nation and would continue even if the BJP had never existed.

The tensions that exist on the subcontinent do not arise because of the presence of Hindu nationalism. The conflict that divorced Pakistan from India after decolonization dates back into remote history. It has nothing to do with the nationalism of the BJP. While China's neofascism is the core of its potential threat to United States interests in Asia, whatever troubles arise in terms of those interests on the subcontinent will not have been caused by Hindu nationalism – much less an imagined "neofascism."

What all this suggests is that there are circumstances in which the existence of fascist or neofascist political systems is of importance in the world configuration of forces. It also means that terms such as "fascist" and "neofascism" should be employed with circumspection. The terms should refer to political substance rather than serving as terms of simple derogation. The terms do refer to cognitive distinctions. They have application among movements and regimes that most characteristically arise among those communities trying to negotiate late industrial development in an environment of challenge.

Among such late developers, movements and regimes that share traits with paradigmatic Fascism constitute a distinct subset. There are late-developing nations that undertake the exacting process of a drive to economic maturity under fully democratic auspices – India among them. Only when the late-developing community chooses to pursue its ends by mass mobilizing populations behind the elite leadership of a single party – to control information, inculcate a formal ideology, and ultimately fashion a totalitarian political structure to house it all – can one begin to speak of fascism or neofascism. The psychology that inspires and fuels the enterprise arises out of a sense of frustration and inefficacy born by people that who too long have been consigned to inferior status by those more powerful.

In instances when reasonably powerful nations, because of military defeat or economic collapse, are reduced to the station of less-developed nations, one may observe a similar response. Germany, after the First World War, was reduced to the level of a less-developed community by the victors of that war. The nation's economy collapsed under the burdens of reparations, the loss of colonies, and the costs of a four-year conflict against the major industrial powers of the world.

The reaction on the part of the Germans was to mimic the febrile nationalism of Italian Fascism.The economic and political collapse of the Soviet Union at the outset of the 1990s of the last century precipitated a very similar response among Russians – and "neofascism" made its abundant appearance there in impressive, if variable, and probably unsustainable, form.[19] There has been such mimicry in the past, and we shall probably see more of it in the future. In those circumstances, such revolutionary movements will probably display some of the critical traits of revolutions of delayed development.

Revolutions of late development can be pursued under both democratic or nondemocratic auspices. Each can find expression in a variety of institutional patterns. Paradigmatic Fascism was only one major configuration among nondemocratic alternatives. Sun Yat-sen's program anticipated traversing three stages: the stage of military rule, the stage of political tutelage, until finally the stage of constitutional, democratic rule. Sun imagined that nondemocratic rule would endure for a relatively brief period. It endured for half a century.

There were, in fact, both similarities and differences between the Fascist and Chinese revolutions. Fascist intellectuals always acknowledged as much. They documented the similarities shared by Kuomintang rule in China and Fascist rule in Italy. More than that, Mussolini himself outlined the historic factors that shaped both revolutions.

In late 1933, Mussolini addressed Asian students in Rome, and he spoke to them of the reactive nationalism that inspired the revolutionary unrest in their homelands. He told them that Fascists "saw themselves" in the "resentments and reactive responses" that roiled Asians, subject to the abuses imposed upon them by the "capitalist" powers. He told them that Fascists understood the humiliation generated by the consciousness of being used by the plutocratic powers of Europe as nothing more than a market for their surplus manufactures and a source for raw materials.

Mussolini told them that Fascists had made a similar response to similar circumstances. He told them that the revolution that had begun to manifest itself throughout Asia may "differ from Fascism in form and detail, but [both] share the same foundation."[20] He argued that both revolutions found

---

[19] The discussion devoted to neofascism in the former Soviet Union has been long and complicated. See, for example, A. James Gregor, "Fascism and the New Russian Nationalism," *Communism and Post-Communist Studies* 31, no. 1 (1998), pp. 1–15; Stephen D. Shenfield, *Russian Fascism: Traditions, Tendencies, Movements* (Armonk, NY: M. E. Sharpe, 2001).

[20] Mussolini, "Oriente e Occidente," *Opera omnia*, 26, pp. 127–8.

their motive energies in the inequalities that were the inevitable consequence of international relations between the advanced and the less-developed nations.

The identification of political movements and regimes of delayed development as "fascist" or "neofascist" means that they share features of the ideology, goal culture, and/or some of the critical institutional properties of the Fascism of Mussolini. Most Fascist intellectuals maintained as much. If that is granted, most of the political phenomena identified in contemporary Anglophone literature as "neofascist," hardly qualify.

What we find in many if not most of the contemporary volumes devoted to neofascism is a catalog of small and ineffectual European or North American groupuscules that generally represent public display of the frustrations suffered by malcontents in the psychologically taxing environment of postindustrial and postmodern society. Those are the groups spoken of as "radical right-wing" and "extremist." They are almost invariably composed of clinically disturbed racists, antigovernment fanatics, conspiracy mongers, occultists of every conceivable persuasion, sadomasochists, and exhibitionists of one or another sort. They are a problem for psychotherapy and law enforcement, more a subject of study for psychologists than social scientists, not candidates for the study of neofascism.

More likely than not, neofascism in the twenty-first century will be associated, just as it was in the twentieth, with revolutions of late industrial development, and will share certain properties made familiar by the Fascism of Mussolini, manifest in the institutions they tend to create, with the population management ancillaries they advocate, as well as the rationale utilized to legitimize them. Even as aspirants to power, they will make clear their revolutionary intentions – just as did Maoism even before Maoism came to power.[21]

Some considerable time before V. I. Lenin came to power in Czarist Russia, Rosa Luxemburg warned that Lenin's "ultracentralist" views would concentrate power in the hands of a self-selected minority of political leaders imposing "blind obedience" and "mechanical subordination" on everyone else. She warned that Lenin sought to make the few, and not the democratic masses, the "rulers of history." And she warned of the potential "militarism" implicit in Lenin's position.[22]

The Marxist critics of Leninism before Leninism came to power in Czarist Russia recognized the features of neofascism before they knew its name. Karl Kautsky aroused Lenin's ire by predicting that the Bolshevik revolution would only lead to a form of state dominance and all the attendant

---

[21] Among the many Sinologists who have discussed Mao Zedong, Stuart Schram is among the most insightful. See Stuart Schram, *Mao Tse-tung* (Baltimore, MO: Penguin, 1966).

[22] See Rosa Luxemburg, *The Russian Revolution and Leninism or Marxism* (Ann Arbor, MI: University of Michigan Press, 1961), pp. 6–7, 17–23 and passim.

antidemocratic consequences that would inevitably follow.[23] Years later, Mussolini's intellectuals confirmed Kautsky's fears. They had no difficulty whatsoever tracing the "metamorphosis of Bolshevism" into something that looked remarkably like Fascism.[24]

What all this suggests is that the left/right distinction as it has been insisted upon by political and social scientists is quite irrelevant to any serious cognitive purpose when applied to the study of fascism and neofascism. "Neofascism" simply cannot be identified with the right. As history amply demonstrates, generic fascist elements are to be found as frequently among movements and regimes on the putative left as on the presumptive right. In fact, most right-wing conservative and libertarian movements share nothing with paradigmatic Fascism.

To search out an eccentric like Julius Evola in order to make a case for a right-wing occult and antimodern contemporary fascism is evidence of the failure of enterprise. Fascism was no more "traditional" or conservative than were the Futurists or the radical leftists of Italy's syndicalist movement who supplied much of its initial leadership. No matter how many individuals or groupuscules become enamoured of Evola's fancies, they will not represent the "rise of neofascism." Sharing nothing with the Fascism of Mussolini, they would be more a curiosity than a threat to democracy.

In reflecting on the political movements and regimes we have considered, their identification as "neofascisms," except in the rare instance, has served very little purpose. While the black protest movements of the twentieth century shared some features with Mussolini's Fascism, their intransigent racism rather suggested kinship with Hitler's National Socialism. Recognizing that, it really would serve little cognitive purpose to identify them either as "neofascist" or "neonazi." As with communities that have suffered protracted abuse at the hands of others, their racism constitutes one form of predictable, if lamentable, response. In and of itself, that may make them morally objectionable, but it does not make them either fascists or neonazis.

One of the many things absent that might qualify them as fascist or nazi is their general indisposition to employ violence in the service of their cause. Central to the Fascist conviction in their moral right to rule was their submission that they were under a moral obligation to employ violence to ensure compliance.[25] Conversely, in the two cases here considered, that of Garvey's Universal Negro Improvement Association and Elijah Muhammad's

---

[23] See Karl Kautsky, *Gegen die Diktatur* (Berlin: Litfass, n.d.), *Terrorismus und Kommunismus* (Berlin: Verlag Neues Vaterland, 1919).

[24] See Tommaso Napolitano, *Le metamorfosi del Bolscevismo* (Milan: Fratelli Bocca, Editori, 1940).

[25] One of the great moral scandals that shook Fascist Italy during its first years in power was Giovanni Gentile's affirmation that the truncheon carried by Fascists constituted a "moral force." See Giovanni Gentile, *Origins and Doctrine of Fascism (with Selections from Other Works)* (New Brunswick, NJ: Transaction, 2002), p. 64.

Lost-Found Nation of Islam, neither was disposed to wholesale political violence, either because it was evident that any such violence would be counterproductive in the long term or that it would be met by such counterforce in the short term as to be suicidal. That probably means that black protest in North America will find it extremely difficult to act out whatever racism it may be incubating. However hateful its ideology, there is small likelihood that it will ever find expression in the murderous racism we identify with Adolf Hitler. Black protest movements give little evidence of being truly revolutionary.

Whatever racism rankles in the bosom of members of black protest movements in the United States will probably find nonviolent forms of expression. The most revolutionary forms of contemporary black protest in North America are clearly content to leave anti-white violence to Allah.

Identifying black protest as "neofascist" or "neonazi" does absolutely nothing to assist in resolving the differences between blacks and whites in the United States. Like white racism, black racism offers nothing that might pass as a goal culture. There is no program to be found among the major exponents of radical black protest that serves any rational purpose. The developmentalism of Garvey's Universal Negro Improvement Association was assigned to a future African empire. The better world of Elijah Muhammad was in an "afterlife" that no one in our time would live to see. Whatever elements of fascism or nazism found in such groups are sterile of any serious consequence.

In the United States, the resolution of racial problems has proven to be very difficult, heartbreaking, and time-consuming, but progress has been made and the life conditions of black Americans have significantly improved over the past half-century. Unless black political movements make the mistake of identifying themselves with external enemies – such as Islamic *jihadists* – there is promise that all Americans can anticipate a future innocent of the scourge of racism. In the interim, the energy that sustains black pseudorevolutionary movements will, in all probability, flag, leaving us to deal with the standard, if complex, problems of interracial relations. To identify the black protest movements in the United States as fascist or neofascist does nothing either to inform or assist in dealing with any of our problems.

For even more reasons, Hindu nationalists do not qualify as neofascists. Only post-Maoist China seems to share enough traits with the Fascism of Mussolini to qualify. Its identification as neofascist suggests real research possibilities as well as implications for political behavior in real life.

Most of the remaining candidates that fill the recent publications devoted to the postfascist study of neofascism rarely deal with anything resembling Fascism. Some of the talk of a fascism found among those of the "radical right" turns on the notion that one or another group indulged itself in "prejudice" and "intolerance" – as though the Marxism-Leninism of Stalinism and Maoism dealt exclusively with right reason and tolerance.

We are told that the radical right, of which fascism serves as a subset, taps into "uninhibited forms of aggression and unreflective modes of self-delusion" – once again as though such behaviorial traits are found nowhere else.[26]

These kinds of discussion, whatever other purposes they may serve, certainly tell us little if anything about Fascism, fascism, or neofascism. For historians and social scientists, understanding Fascism has proven less difficult than trying to comprehend something called generic fascism. Trying to fathom something identified as neofascism has shown itself to be more problematic still.

Mussolini's Italy was a kind of laboratory in which a recently reunited, economically laggard nation sought to close the distance between itself and those nations of Europe that had achieved preeminence in the eighteenth and nineteenth centuries. While Marxism spoke of revolutions in advanced industrial environments – and made revolutions in economically backward countries – Fascism transformed the Marxism it had inherited and formulated the first coherent national socialism. Since then, the nondemocratic, developmental revolutions of the twentieth century have almost all shared selective ideological and/or institutional features with paradigmatic Fascism. That was the case not because revolutionary leaders had immersed themselves in Fascist doctrine, but because they faced the same critical issues that had prompted Fascist intellectuals to Marxist heresy.

Through the remainder of the century, doctrinaire Marxists proceeded to some of the same "reforms" of traditional Marxism undertaken by Fascists in their time. Much of the elaborate theoretical work of Karl Marx and Friedrich Engels dissolved into the opportunistic renderings of Joseph Stalin and the uninformed pretenses of Mao Zedong.[27] What emerged was something very much akin to Fascism. For most of the twentieth century, because of the insistence on a left/right distinction, and the propaganda imperatives generated by the "war against Fascism," few chose to recognize what had transpired. They sought, instead, to find a generic fascism that might serve as the repository of evil in the world. Even imperial Japan was conceived an implausible Asian embodiment of fascism.

With the passing of the Second World War, historians and social scientists acknowledged the shared features of Fascism and Marxism-Leninism, but so involved in the cold war were most academics that the employment of the concept "totalitarianism" brought little real enlightenment. The debate

---

[26] See the discussions in Sabrina P. Ramet (ed.), *The Radical Right in Central and Eastern Europe Since 1989* (University Park, PA: Pennsylvania State University Press, 1999), pp. 3–4.

[27] See the discussion concerning the decay of Marxism in Mao's China in A. James Gregor, *Marxism, China, and Development: Reflections on Theory and Reality* (New Brunswick, NJ: Transaction, 1995).

continued, unresolved, until the disappearance of the Soviet Union and the passing of Mao Zedong.

Only in our own time has it become possible to trace the political, ideological, and economic development of the former Soviet Union and the one-time Maoist China. Soviet Marxists have long since given themselves over to a form of nationalism and etatism that, if not subject to too close an inspection, might pass as neofascism.[28]

Post-Maoist China provides an instance in which knowledge about Fascism might actually be important for any analysis of what the People's Republic has become. Yet, the academic search for neofascism rarely deals with China – a nation that gives every evidence of being a determinant factor in the history of the twenty-first century.[29]

Attendant upon all that, there remain a number of scholars and journalists preoccupied with what they perceive as an emerging phenomenon: the rise of "neofascism" in Europe and North America. The resultant product, by and large, contains unconvincing accounts of small groups of marginal persons, animated by impulses having very little to do with historic Fascism. Where actual neofascists were identified, they were, more often than not, mischaracterized – a consideration that has become evident in the continued insistence that the contemporary Italian Alleanza nazionale is "neofascist."

The academic and lay search for neofascism has not been a notable success. It has provided some interesting stories about Fascist nostalgics and about some clinically disturbed individuals who, in other times and in other climes, would be simply dismissed as members of that minority of eccentrics and criminals who will always be with us. The academic study of what is an important topic deserves better.

---

[28] See the detailed discussion and supporting documentation in Gregor, *Faces of Janus*, and *Phoenix*, chap. 7.

[29] See the extended discussion and documentation in A. James Gregor, *A Place in the Sun: Marxism and Fascism in China's Long Revolution* (Boulder, CO: Westview Press, 2000).

Index